WILLIAM CAMROSE: GIANT OF FLEET STREET

WILLIAM CAMROSE

Giant of Fleet Street

by his son
LORD HARTWELL

WEIDENFELD AND NICOLSON
LONDON

First published in Great Britain in 1992 by
George Weidenfeld & Nicolson Limited
The Orion Publishing Group, Orion House,
5 Upper St Martin's Lane, London WC2H 9EA

A catalogue reference is available from the
British Library

ISBN 0 297 81281 5

Filmset by Selwood Systems
Midsomer Norton
Printed in Great Britain by
Butler & Tanner Ltd, Frome and London

Contents

CONTENTS

Illustrations

The fiftieth anniversary dinner of the birth of the *Daily Mail*, 1946.
(Illustrated London News)
Playing croquet.
On his yacht.
With Sir Ralph Gore, Commodore of the Royal Yacht Squadron.
(Illustrated London News)
With Molly ready to receive guests at the first *Telegraph* General
Election results party, 1950.
Receiving an honorary degree from Churchill, Bristol University, 1951.
At Chartwell, Churchill's house near Westerham, Kent.
Churchill speaking, after unveiling a plaque to William, in the crypt of
St Paul's Cathedral, 1956.
William's widow arriving for the St Paul's ceremony.

At a luncheon Mr Frank Harris [a member of the Oscar Wilde set and a journalist] wishing to shine, blurted out, 'All the evil in the world is due to Christianity and Journalism.' Arthur Balfour, contemplating the proposition for a moment, replied, 'Christianity of course, but why Journalism?'

Winston Churchill, *Great Contemporaries*

Preface

When my parents were getting on – my father was seventy and my mother four years younger – once an England hockey player but now crippled with arthritis in both knees – I suggested to each of them, as offspring will, how they should achieve something fresh. To my mother I suggested that, as she had been an accomplished amateur painter before marriage, she should take up painting again.

'Molly,' said my father, 'that is an excellent idea'; to which she replied: 'I shall do nothing of the sort.'

I turned to my father. I suggested to him that, in view of his extraordinary powers of observation and total recall, his great achievements and his knowledge of the leading men of half a century in journalism, business and politics, he should write his autobiography. 'William,' said my mother, 'that is an excellent idea'; to which he replied: 'I shall do nothing of the sort.'

I still think my mother would have got pleasure from painting but I soon understood why my father would have none of my suggestion to him. He liked to be recognised for what he had done in a life of struggle, but he did not want to talk about it to the world. He hated 'self-advertisers'. Anyone meeting him for the first time would have recognised him for a considerable man, but if they had been perceptive would have recognised, too, his innate shyness and reserve. Not that he was an introvert. He never 'rowed back' nor mused over 'might-have-beens'. The past was behind him and he was not interested in reconstructing history. Anyway, as I said, he was against it.

It is permissible, however, for his family, who without exception had a fervent admiration for him and retain a great fondness for his memory, to take a different view.

The first biographer was to be his grandson, Robin, third Earl of Birkenhead, a professional historian, who began the task in 1976, more than twenty years after my father's death. Unfortunately he found that my father's habit of tearing up so much of his correspondence left him woefully short of raw material (or 'papers', as historians like to call them), particularly in relation to his career up to the buying of the *Sunday Times* in 1915. Birkenhead was only nineteen when my father died and so did not have the advantage I have of much personal recollection. Accordingly, he dropped the project after a year, but not before filling a notebook with the observations of some of my father's younger contemporaries, which I have used, with quotation, in the following narrative.

I myself took over the biography when I retired from Fleet Street in the autumn of 1987. It was too late then, of course, for further interviews, though a few early papers have turned up since Birkenhead, who died in 1985, abandoned the enterprise. I have, however, had the benefit of my own memories and those of my family, and extensive access to books and private diaries, as well as to old newspapers and periodicals in the British Museum Newspaper Library.

It is a filial but not, I think, a sycophantic book. Like everyone else, my father often made mistakes. Where I think he was wrong I have said so. In short, I hope it will seem the sort of book an independent author would have written, had he had access to all my sources.

The book is different from most I have read about press proprietors. Newspapers are as competitive as any other fields of endeavour. People run newspapers with the object of being more successful than others 'in the same market', as the jargon goes. And even the boundaries of 'markets' are blurred. It is idle, therefore, to discuss controllers of newspapers without describing what the competition is doing. Some books have been published about leading proprietors with hardly a mention of other newspapers. The late A.J.P. Taylor, for instance, managed to publish the official Life of Lord Beaverbrook, controller of the *Daily* and *Sunday Express* and the London *Evening Standard*, without once mentioning my father, Beaverbrook's exact contemporary, with whom he had many dealings and even a precarious friendship. There is therefore much treatment here of newspapers other than those controlled by my father, and of their proprietors – but no moralising.

Similarly, it is idle to discuss politics without discussing politicians and their reactions to each other. Thus, for instance, I make no apology for rather long passages which deal mostly with Stanley Baldwin, Neville Chamberlain and Winston Churchill, with only glancing reference to my father. For those who have no personal memory of the state of the world before 1939, I have provided fairly long summaries of the great issues of the day – the subject matter of the newspapers – this time with hindsight.

Introduction

William Ewert Berry was born in 73 Thomas Street, Merthyr Tydfil, Glamorgan, South Wales on 23 June 1879. What sort of place was it to be born into?

Wales is two-thirds mountainous. The Cambrian mountains, a hundred-mile range of grit and slate, runs from Snowdonia in the north to the Brecon Beacons, with small rivers from its sides. At the southern end, thirty miles from the sea, a smaller range runs at right angles. In Pembrokeshire, in the west, the land is rolling. In the east rise the high mountains of Glamorgan and Monmouthshire. They thrust their bony fingers southward into a narrow strip of fertile soil, the Vale of Glamorgan. The clefts between the fingers are what are known everywhere as the Welsh Valleys, the site of what, in the half-century to 1914, was the most prolific coalfield in the world.

The end of the Ice Age came late for Wales. Colonisation even of the coastal areas had to wait for the melting of a vast ice sheet stretching down the west coast from Scotland, which finally discharged itself into Cardigan Bay in mid-Wales. Among the earliest settlers were metal workers or traders from northwest Spain, who settled in northwest Pembrokeshire, home of my father's immediate ancestors. (This may explain why I myself was once identified in a San Sebastian newspaper as an Asturian peasant.)

This tribe is credited with having shaped the 'blue' stones for the inner circle of Stonehenge around 4000 BC. Its members are described as of a 'type with broad heads, strong jaws, very dark hair and tall build'. They were distinct from the now much more numerous Brytons – 'little dark people with dark hair and eyes, rather long heads and slender build' – who filtered from the east into Wales with their Brythonic Celtic speech (the forerunner of Welsh) in the last centuries BC.

After the Romans had left came the Goedels from Ireland, Scandinavians, Moorish pirates and, most importantly, the Normans. Henry I brought sheep-farming Flemings[1] into Pembrokeshire, while Henry II augmented them with King Stephen's demobilised mercenaries. There-

---

[1] Two centuries later Edward III introduced Flemings into the West Riding of Yorkshire to teach the locals 'what to do with their wool'.

after South Wales was quickly anglicised from the top and most of the fertile land was parcelled out to feudal landlords, increasingly absentee, whose nominal descendants retained their hold into Trollopian times. Except in the western promontory, the language remained Welsh. Though the principality of Wales was never a unity there remained through the Middle Ages a legend that the Saxons had tricked the Welsh out of their English territory. The bards sang of a new Arthur who would reconquer their lost land. Surprising as it sounds to the modern ear, the accession of the half-Welsh Henry VII stilled their song and, until Lloyd George, nothing more was heard of Welsh political nationalism. And Henry VIII, by his Act of Union, was able to despoil the Welsh monasteries as well as the English.

Until the beginning of the eighteenth century, South Wales was a poor, agricultural backwater of the British Isles. There was not a town of more than 1,000 souls and even a hundred years later Cardiff, the largest port in the world in 1900, could only manage 2,000. Since Roman times there had been mining of copper and of gold, silver and lead. When the Kentish iron smelters had burnt down much of the weald for charcoal, they had moved to the Welsh valleys, whose steep sides they similarly denuded.

Even in 1760 South Wales was still a largely agricultural province. Merthyr was still a village and the valleys to the west, below the Black Mountains, slumbered.

Owing to the Cambrian range, commerce ran east and west, so that South Wales looked almost exclusively to Bristol and London. Drovers regularly ran 300 and 400 head of cattle to Smithfield. Some of them grew fat enough on the trade to set up as bankers. Exports were channelled through Bristol, which even by 1600 boasted a population of 12,000, the third largest in the kingdom.

All the while lay a great, thirty-mile-wide oval of coal and, along the top edge, of iron ore and limestone (which removes phosphorus). It was not until the mid-eighteenth century that the technique was developed of smelting iron with coke rather than charcoal. Demand for cannon, through the Seven Years' War, the American War and the Napoleonic Wars, and for iron rails at the beginning of the railway age, stimulated ingenuity. There began an enormous ingress of labour into the iron area, which became a Welsh Klondyke; but, as there, only a few quickly became rich.

Thus, rather late, the Industrial Revolution came to South Wales. It did not develop there: it was brought from England. Nor was it locally foreseen. The great landowners, under whose feet the riches lay, saw nothing out of the way in the use of their agricultural land for mining. They demanded no royalties. The first great ironfield, Cyfarthfa, on the outskirts of Merthyr, was formed out of fourteen farms in an area twelve miles by four and was let on a 99-year lease at £100 p. a. in 1765.

The pioneers, their capital, and their skilled labour were all English. Nor were the pioneers chancing their arm in the American way. They were already wealthy men who had heard of the natural riches. They were multi-trade merchants whose head offices were in London, and in some cases whose wealth had been made in trade with the American colonies and the Caribbean.

Behind them came the unskilled – agricultural labourers from Pembrokeshire and the mountains; Irish fleeing from worse poverty; Midlanders; Scots and later, when superior foreign ore began to replace native ore, Spaniards. When trade slackened from time to time, the local people would say: 'There's no one on the Brecon Road.'

Soon after the mid-century, ironworking, and now steel production, reached its peak, supplying the world with rails. But it was not to last. First, production began to retreat from the valleys as superior foreign ore flooded in; secondly Europe, and America after the Civil War, assisted by tariffs, woke up.

As ironworking, and now steel, declined, the population still rose. Coal, which had hardly been exploited as a commodity before 1850, was revitalised by the new technique of deep mining. The field was found to be immensely rich in steam coal, which beat any in England for heat-by-weight and lack of clinker and smoke.

Merthyr's reign as the queen of South Wales now began to decline. Soon it yielded to Cardiff as the largest town and as coal mining multiplied tenfold, some of the population moved west to the rich valleys of the Rhondda, where wages were higher than in iron. The mines were fragmented, the wages low, strikes frequent. Productivity in the last half of the century actually fell. The great days, though they only lasted until 1913, were yet to come. Thereafter, first steel and then coal production steadily fell until now there are no mines in the valleys, which are beginning to look as they once looked so long ago before the Kentish charcoal men came. Merthyr itself, now prosperous with light industry, stretches a dozen miles down the valley.

In a hundred years Merthyr achieved many 'firsts' – first in the world for cannon, for rails, for coal, and for largest town in Wales. It might even have had a 'first' for the steam train, twenty years before Stephenson's Rocket, had it not foundered on ill will between the inventor and the iron-making canal owners.

The human price was horrific. By 1850 it had achieved another 'first' – the worst record of health standards in England and Wales (except Liverpool). This was before the second industrial revolution, of coal for sale, got underway.

The population had jumped from 1801's 7,000 to 22,000 in 1831, to 35,000 in 1841 and 46,000 in 1850. Of the 46,000 in the town, 18,000 were 'hands' at the four great ironworks, all in easy walking distance.

As a spectacle, it was described as:

This narrow valley is blocked to a great extent by the enormous black banks of cinders etc ... constantly [enlarged] ... The tips in progress are formed of hot cinders ... they are on fire from nearly top to bottom, glow like lava. Rivulets of hot water wash the bases of these gloomy banks ... At night [the scene] is wild beyond conception ... The wind adds reality ... gives vastness and sublimity to a picture lit up by a thousand fires. The vivid glow and roaring of the blast furnaces near at hand – the lurid light of distant works – the burning headlands ... the coke hearths [now] bursting into sheets of flame, now wrapped in impenetrable clouds of smoke ... the wild figures of the workmen, the actors in this ... infernal scene.

But in the near-hovels, conditions were the opposite of sublime. There Vulcan (and his children) became Caliban.

As the population poured in there was no infrastructure to meet it. A few company-owned shanties were put up round the works for the skilled men and conditions there were always a little better than in the town.

There were few independent shops in Merthyr – or, indeed, anywhere outside the old market towns. Wages were paid fortnightly or monthly or even, at the great Dowlais works, quarterly. The truck system (said by owners to keep down drunkenness) and company shops, where the currency was company money, flourished.

Merthyr itself was described as 'a rude and shapeless cluster of dwelling houses', of 'vicious construction' and populated to an abnormal extent by 'single men, far from home ... where drunkenness, violence and prostitution flourished'. They were huddled in close courts and narrow alleys and mud-floored cellars.

It was almost destitute of drainage, with 'few or no water closets. Those existent were filthy, full to overflowing'. Nightsoil was thrown into the streets or river. The streets themselves were unpaved and many of them impassable for carts in the winter.

One account goes on:

In the face of the wall on the roadside (on the top of which a kind of parapet was built in front of the houses) were several openings. In these [were] mounds of human ordure, and the disgusting aspect of the whole made me marvel in the neighbourhood of the largest works in the country, perhaps in the world – in the broad open day, offensive to the sight and the smell ... such as is rarely seen in any town, village or city in the kingdom.

Water could only be fetched from the springs, themselves contaminated by cesspools, and their neighbourhood, as the wait was so long, became a kind of squalid Lover's Lane. There was no street lighting. In the town there were thirty-one burial grounds surrounded by houses.

Death rates were high. The first (temporary) officer of health, appointed in 1853, reported the average life expectancy of tradespeople was thirty-two for miners and seventeen for ironworkers. Accidents at work, and violence away from it, took a steady toll.

It was cholera which at last brought the ironmasters to their senses. Cholera had been endemic since 1832. In 1849 it killed 1,524 people or one death in every twenty-eight of the entire population, and in 1854 another 424. At last the Merthyr Board of Health set about demolishing the worst tenements, streets were macadamised, pavements laid and pure water from filter beds supplied by standpipes to 1,000 houses. Cholera struck again in 1866 but two years later ninety miles of sewers had been constructed and the disease was finally banished. The mortality of children under five fell – to 434 per 1,000.[2]

Much remained to be done and it was done only slowly. As late as 1897 (the year before my father left for London) the death rate at around 27 per 1,000 was a good ten percentage points worse than the average of sixty-seven large towns in England and Wales. Even in 1902, my grandfather put 'Merthyr death rate is the highest in the Kingdom ! !' as a heading to his election address for councillor.

Diptheria, measles and scarlet fever were rampant. Average age of death, which in 1850 had been seventeen and a half, had only risen to forty-four. Even in 1905, Board of Trade inspectors could write a sizzling report on Merthyr's shortcomings – scores of houses unfit for human habitation ; unhealthy tips ; no sanitary records.

These appalling figures were not surprising. Apart from a couple of 'fever wards' converted by the Poor Law Guardians and a single, wooden, fever hospital set up by the local Board of Health (precursor of the District Council) there was in the whole area but a single general hospital and that founded and maintained in Dowlais by voluntary effort.

It closed down in 1882 and for six years no operations or treatment could be performed except in the home. At last, in 1888, a permanent, voluntary, twenty-four-bed general hospital was built (a twelve-bed children's hospital closing at the same time) and this was to be the nucleus

---

[2] Higher than the 304 per 1,000 in Kabul in 1988 during the Soviet occupation – *Daily Telegraph*, 15 May 1989.

of the major Merthyr hospital,[3] which still flourishes. Visiting nurses and midwives came still later. At a meeting of the hospital governors in February 1894, it was announced with satisfaction that the nursing institute was nearing completion and that nurses then 'would be sent out without having to send to Cardiff, Swansea, Bristol and other places'.

Local opinion put the slow progress down to the refusal of the Privy Council to grant 'incorporation' (into a borough) at a time when Wales, not just South Wales, had become the first country in the world in which the urban population outnumbered the rural.

Incorporation finally came in 1907, after which Merthyr quickly moved into the twentieth century, but only by means of high rates, which kept out new industry at a time of high unemployment. The tardiness – incorporation had been refused ten years earlier – was blamed by William Hadley, an ex-editor of the *Merthyr Times*, on, 'great landowners, coal and iron owners, house owners, shop owners and men owners. Their influence chokes every proposal of local reform'.

*　　*　　*

Chroniclers tend to concentrate on what is wrong rather than what is less exceptionable. Certainly my informants, whose family memories go back to the turn of the century, would violently disagree with my diagnosis so far. The chroniclers have, it seems, failed to distinguish between the two Merthyrs, upper and lower Merthyr, not to be found on any map. The whole town is shaped like the letter 'Y' : the main section, lower Merthyr, is built round the small village of the early nineteenth century, while the arms, collectively upper Merthyr, are the spin-off of the two great iron/coal complexes from which the prosperity of the whole town derived. It was in upper Merthyr that the slum conditions, with their attendant poverty, drunkenness and violence, prevailed so long.

Even so, lower Merthyr must long have lagged behind most towns in all the ordinary amenities. At 600 feet it was exceptionally wet, windy and grimy. There was but a single park, at the neck of the 'Y'.

Lower Merthyr was a narrow strip sloping sharply to the southward and tilted east to west – no more than 1200 yards by 700. It was in the bottleneck of the weir-stuffed Taff river to the west, and to the east, confining rough ground rising to 1200 feet. It was here that the middle class were concentrated and here that a strong civic sense developed. It was no dormitory town. There was quite a deal of decorous social life. Everybody

---

[3] My eldest uncle, Lord Buckland, who, after uncounted local benefactions, was made a Freeman of Merthyr, twice proclaimed that the hospital was best left to total voluntary support. And so it was, until 1948. Meanwhile, after his death in 1928, it was estimated that his two younger brothers had given it the best part of £250,000.

knew everybody else. If a man had not been born in Merthyr then, however long he had lived there, he was still 'not a Merthyr man'. That was said of my grandfather, a resident of thirty-seven years, in the 'welcome' at his induction as Mayor in 1911.

It was, however, in both senses a 'small town'. I cannot forbear to quote an anecdote of 1896. The Merthyr Chamber of Commerce spent a whole morning deciding to send a delegation to the Town Council complaining about the chronic state of the roads in Merthyr and its neighbourhood. To which the strange answer came back that the Council had lately exchanged a large steam roller for a smaller one. It does not seem to have done much good, nor on the other hand to have led to municipal depression. Twenty years later, at my grandfather's funeral, the minister of the Market Square Congregational Chapel, where he had always worshipped, was able to say:

> Our architecture may not be particularly beautiful or inspiring; our streets may not be particularly clean or city-like in their breadth and general appearance but Mr Berry loved them all.

Meanwhile, what of the temper of the people? The great landlords, whose fiefs had grown by marriage over the centuries, were completely anglicised. On the whole they were not bad landlords (provided their tenants voted for them), nor was there the antipathy between them and the rural community, as in pre-Revolutionary France. But they and the gentry, whose tenants, outside Pembrokeshire, spoke only Welsh, were much more class-separate than in England. In the 'Age of Enlightenment' it had become unfashionable to converse or write in Welsh (the same attitude of mind as in Russia or Hungary at the time). They ran local government. Their younger sons, who had been educated in England, filled many of the livings of the Anglican Church. Before 1870 no Welsh Bishop had been appointed since the accession of George I.

Before the ironmasters, there were few middle class. As the method of production became more complicated a bureaucracy emerged, spilling off lawyers, bankers, coal entrepreneurs, local Welshmen, who ventured capital for a deep mine or two. They, too, cultivated the English language 'for English had become the language of promotion'.[4]

Methodism had made inroads in the early eighteenth century but as the Welsh population began to stir, Nonconformism generally gained ground. The Anglican Church remained organised for a thin rural population on a scheme conceived before the Industrial Revolution. Parishes, which were

---

[4] The phrase was coined by English educational commissioners in 1847. It was resented by nationalists but accepted by the majority.

also the local administration unit, were designed for a thinly spread population and, despite its rapid concentration, not a single new one (unlike in England) was created throughout the nineteenth century. Tithes were farmed out, church schools, in any case now too few, were closed to the children of Nonconformists, even burial in Anglican churchyards denied them, while no new churches were built for the incoming population.

South Wales had for long been more religious than southern England. Evangelism, with its emphasis on the next world, and its emotional preachers, had an obvious appeal to the poor. As roots were torn up and great shifts in population gathered force, the Anglican Church in its complacency was seen to have nothing to offer. It became a focus for national resentment.

In its horrible heyday, Merthyr was not only the most populous town in Wales, but it had the most public houses and chapels per capita of any area in the principality, and probably in Britain as a whole. The people who had any aspiration to raise themselves out of the squalor – either in a practical way or even just in their dreams – needed spirituality through religion and music. There was much chapel-going and much singing to try to mitigate, and even temporarily eliminate, the mental and physical anguish.

The new population built its own chapels around which community life revolved. Before 1870 there was no state education – even then rate aid was principally directed to Anglican schools – while in Glamorgan in 1850 nearly half could not write their names. In the chapels, Sunday schools were set up where adults as well as children were given a basic education based on Bible reading. Eventually the investment in education in Merthyr was one of the highest in the country, with no less than three grammar schools when the population stabilised at 50,000.[5]

Initiative came from below as well as from above. The minister, as well as the deacons, was elected and formed the cell of democratic government, secularly unknown until 1884. The chapel was almost a community club. Apart from education it provided a respectable kind of entertainment : hymn-singing, discussion groups, outings for the children. It had its own social conscience, eschewing swearing and promoting personal responsibility and temperance. Years later, when my father was rich and famous and living in England, he still yearned for the hundred-fold ringing of the bells, church and chapel, all over Merthyr on New Year's Eve.

In so far as Nonconformism tended to radicalism – it was anti-Anglican

---

[5] Some of the ironmasters set up 'works' schools and night schools but these were not available to outsiders.

establishment, anti-tithe, anti-squire and anti-landlord – it was gradualist and in no sense revolutionary. Hence Nonconformism was a natural ally of Liberalism. Gladstone called Nonconformism 'the backbone of the Liberal Party', particularly as he needed its votes to secure Irish Home Rule. From the 1884 Third Reform Act onwards, almost all of the thirty-four Welsh MPs were Nonconformist Liberals. In 1887 Gladstone made Welsh Disestablishment a part of official Liberal policy (not achieved until 1920). The case was well put by the pastor of Market Square chapel :

Those who have never been in the English agricultural districts can form no conception at all of the prestige enjoyed by the clergy in those places where the Church is dominant and when people have been accustomed to see the clergy taking the first position socially, and with respect to hospitality and educational matters and all kinds of public functions. No one who has been living in England for some time can form any idea of how completely things are reversed in Wales and how universally Wales is Nonconformist. No greater nonsense has ever been spoken than those expressions contained in the address of the Archbishop of Canterbury and other bishops with respect to the Church of England being the Church of the poor in Wales. Nothing but ignorance of the state of affairs could ever have dictated such a letter ... Everybody knows I am on good terms with the Church of England and as a Dissenter have no wish that the ancient legacies which rightly belong to the Church of England should be confiscated.

Welsh nationalism, however, was never a serious movement until after the Second World War. The now famous entry in an English-edited Encyclopaedia Britannica: 'Wales – see England', caused no stir at the time and Bishop Basil Jones of St David's could write blandly in 1886 that, 'Wales is little more than a geographic expression.' Even the 'triple Welsh Harp', thought to be the staple of Welsh identity, was found to be a nineteenth-century Italian baroque artefact. Lloyd George, a Northerner and only four years an MP, briefly espoused it in 1894–6[6] but his campaign was soon seen for what it was – a chance for the North to dominate the commercial South, a parliamentary power base for Lloyd George himself, perhaps a counterpart to Joe Chamberlain's Birmingham caucus.

Nevertheless, there was a feeling of 'Welshness' rather like, in England, the feeling of being a Yorkshireman. This was shared by the English-speaking southern Pembrokeshire and southwest Glamorgan, as well as by the general body of Welsh speakers. My grandfather, who came from

[6] 'Several members [MPs] congratulated Wales ... I talked Home Rule for Wales and all the nationalist stuff.'

Pembrokeshire, did call that county 'little England beyond Wales'. (North Pembroke, which was not English-speaking, was referred to rudely as 'Up the Welsh'.) But that did not prevent him from describing himself as Welsh (nor would it have deterred him to have known that Bloomsbury was to refer to every man jack of them as 'the unspeakable Celt'). He spoke only a little Welsh and his sons hardly any. My father, writing in London only three years out of Wales, could describe an industrialist in flattering terms but add, though teasingly, that he had an 'appalling Welsh accent'.

*　　*　　*

This was the society in which my grandfather, then aged twenty-seven, settled when he brought his wife of four years, and a daughter of three, to Merthyr in 1874.

CHAPTER ONE

Merthyr

MY GRANDFATHER, JOHN Mathias Berry, came of a family of tenantry first recorded in 1750. Their farm lay in the hamlet of Wolfsdale in the 8,000-acre parish of Camrose, two miles north of Haverfordwest, part of the English-speaking part of Pembrokeshire. The farm was part of the estate of Golden Grove, seat of the Welsh Vaughans and, after 1804, of the Scottish Lords Cawdor; an estate so large that Cawdors could be Lord Lieutenants of Carmarthenshire or Pembrokeshire.

JMB, born in 1847, was the only son of a third son, himself only fourteen when his father left the farm, with quite a substantial dwelling (Upper House), to his two much older brothers. That third son was described in parish records as a 'farm labourer', a term then applied to any farm worker not a land tenant. A typical Welsh farm was a family unit. He was well enough off to be able to carry, free of charge, all the materials for the first Congregational Chapel in Camrose (the family had originally been 'Church'), and give the young JMB a pony. His principles were not as sound as his generosity. JMB used to recount that his father regularly got drunk at Haverfordwest market, so drunk that his friends used to load him on his horse, itself so well drilled that it carried him home unguided and even knocked on the door with a hoof.

JMB was sixteen when his father died and soon went to work on the Great Western Railway, which had not long penetrated the area. He is next heard of on his marriage at the age of twenty-three, when he described himself on the marriage certificate as 'station-master', probably meaning section manager. His bride was Mary Ann Rowe, daughter of a 'writer' (administrator) in Pembroke Dock, known in the district as 'the proud Miss Rowe', and to her husband as Polly. JMB had probably got to know her through a cousin whom he often visited.

By the time of his marriage, the GWR had transferred him 100 miles north to the end of a branch railway at Welshpool, just on the Welsh side of Offa's Dyke. Three years later he was moved again, to the Taff Vale Railway, the narrow-gauge railway which linked Merthyr and burgeoning valley lands to the great port of Cardiff, forty miles away.

At Merthyr the couple set up house in Thomas Street on the eastern

1

edge of the town: the brickworks to the south, the workhouse to the north, 'gloomy Dowlais', the great smoke-palled tips of the 'iron town', looming 500 feet above them on the near horizon, only the new synagogue intervening. Here, in Thomas Street, all their three sons were born.

JMB at this time was a straight-backed, clean-shaven six foot one – later he grew an Edward VII-style spade beard – full of the sternest Victorian principles. Withal he was greatly interested in people, in the community at large, and longed to play a constructive part. Probably because of this he soon threw up the railway job and became a travelling salesman, dealing principally in tea, then an expensive luxury and sold by the ounce.[1] It was not a matter of money, though he had to watch his pennies, but of freedom from the routine of an office job. He joined in most local activities: he became a Mason,[2] and later Grand Master, of the Merthyr Lodge; joined the weekly debating society; was proud of his two stripes in the local volunteers; played cricket and quoits, and taught at one of the three Sunday schools. He started a 'ragged school' (for waifs and strays); was the first Secretary of the Merthyr Liberal Association and election agent for the senior Merthyr MP, D.A. Thomas, later Lord Rhondda; and organised relief for the many industrial disasters which struck the neighbourhood. He was also an amateur boxer. One day a man tried to squeeze past Polly as she walked down the street on his arm. JMB felled him with a single blow. They walked on.

He was bonhomous but also formidable. During his year of mayoralty he had two memorable victories: the first when he slapped down the stipendiary magistrate who, without his authority, had sought to requisition troops, a year after Tonypandy, to police a strike; the second when he outfaced Lord Stamfordham, George V's Private Secretary, who had repeatedly changed the itinerary for the new King's first visit to Wales, eventually cutting out Merthyr. JMB's telegram read:

Lord Stamfordham, Windsor Castle, London [sic]
Telegraph received note that their majesties go direct to Dowlais [i.e., cut out Merthyr]. What other alterations as address approved by home secretary and illuminated stop 10,000 children invited stop choir 1,000 voices rehearsing stop police arrangements made also territorials

[1] The business had been started by Scotsmen who, when tea became cheaper, switched to Scotch wool blankets and later formed the Merthyr and Aberdare Credit Drapers Association.
[2] Masonic aid had been sought by the 'Independents' (mostly Scotsmen) to build the Market Square Congregational Chapel.

2

engaged to line streets stop contract for decorations let. mayor, merthyr tydfil.

The King came.

Towards the end of his mayoralty none thought it at all extraordinary when he closed a heated discussion almost conversationally: 'I am afraid of no man.'

There were four children of the marriage: Beatrice (Beta), six years the eldest, Seymour (born 1877), William (born 1879) and Gomer (born 1883). The elder brothers were inseparable (though Seymour put corks in his shoes to compensate for William's increasing height); the much younger Gomer too often left out. Out of school, on 1d. a week pocket money, they loved roaming. There were no cars then and away from the high street the land was too steep for gearless bicycles, even if their father could have afforded them. (A local newspaper advertised them at '12 guineas, monthly payments'.) Sometimes they boarded a horse tram which plied the mile-long road between Cyfarthfa and Merthyr station. A favourite joke played on little Gomer was to walk behind a (horse) tram as it speeded up and then make a rush for it, leaving him toddling behind.

A few years later, when William had gone to London, Seymour could write: 'I miss you very much now. If it was not for the business I do not know what I'd do. There's not a single chap in M.T. I can make a friend of ... Jack Davies is as big an idiot as ever.'

They made a fearsome couple at marbles, one tossing and the other scooping the pool, while their opponents were still calculating. For both were mercury-quick in mental arithmetic which, throughout their lives, they used to outsmart slower minds. I don't think William ever progressed to algebra and certainly not trigonometry. All his business life he had a horror of graphs – fortunately logarithmic graphs were unknown to him. I heard him say to the newly joined Advertisement Director of his newspaper chain, Allied Newspapers: 'Never bring a graph into this boardroom again.'

Both were educated at St David's Primary school at 2d. a week and then at the Higher Grade school, the first in South Wales to give free education to those passing an examination. William was the more bookish of the two – it was said of him: 'You can always keep him quiet if you give him a book.' He may also have had the run of the 5,000-book subscription library (there was no free library in Merthyr at that time) of which his mother was the librarian. (She was described, in a reader's letter to the *Merthyr Times*, as 'kindness and courtesy personified'.) Seymour was the 'high-spirited rip'.

3

At the Higher Grade school William was taught by a graduate of Edinburgh University who befriended him, lent him books and even, for a time, interested him in moths and butterflies. Later he advised him to seek opportunity in London. The advice was deprecated by JMB, who regarded London as a haunt of vice in the same way as William deprecated his four sons' membership of White's Club.

A slightly unlikely story has it that Willie, as he was known throughout his Merthyr days (or Tombstones to his schoolfriends because of his large front teeth), followed this advice and confided in a woman friend of the family that he wanted to go to London but only had 15 shillings in the world, upon which she gave him a sovereign.

When William was thirteen and a half he had a stroke of luck. His school class was entered for a précis competition to summarise a lecture on 'Pessimism'. The judge, the Editor of the *Merthyr Times*, awarded him first prize and wrote on his paper, 'This boy should take up journalism as a career.' The judge, William Hadley, found that he knew the winner's father and arranged that when he was fourteen he should become an apprentice reporter. Later in life, William said that up to that point a journalistic aptitude had never occurred to him, though he had been seeing a weekly magazine for boys since the age of eight.

(Meanwhile Hadley moved away and their paths did not cross again until William made him Assistant Editor, and a year later, when the long-time Editor of the *Sunday Times* died in 1932, appointed him to the chair.)

Just at this time JMB decided to settle down. His constant travelling must have made him familiar with the Merthyr district and was an ideal background for starting his own firm as an auctioneer, estate agent and accountant. This was no easy road to affluence: the *Merthyr Times* carried advertisements around that time for four other such firms. Four years later, in 1898, his eldest son, Seymour, joined him and quickly stimulated the business to such an extent that when he sold it in 1916 for £7,714, it was the largest such firm in North Glamorgan, working closely with other market leaders in the larger towns of Cardiff, Swansea, Newport and Carmarthen. Seymour by then had gone far enough in that field and was just beginning as one of Lord Rhondda's bright young men in the coal and steel business. His role, which was to become Rhondda's successor, was then not quite established, for in the probate of JMB's will in March 1917 he described himself, aged thirty-nine, as 'retired auctioneer'.

Seymour's move into the firm was involuntary. He had stayed on at school, become a pupil-teacher and finally an assistant master. Eighteen months after that graduation, always an impatient man, he was prosecuted for striking a child. He was acquitted but after the case the chairman of the bench took him aside and told him that, though he had been rightly acquitted, teaching was quite the wrong profession for him.

JMB's methods were typical of the senior Deacon of the Market Square Congregational Chapel. He permitted himself the occasional small advertisement but otherwise waited for business to come to him. Seymour never turned a client away. If there was nothing suitable on the books he would tell the customer to come back next day, when he was sure he would have just what was wanted – and, with a bit of salesmanship, there was. JMB was shocked but could not deny that the business of J.M. Berry was looking up.

Though Seymour was an inspired auctioneer and supercharged with vitality, he naturally took a few years to get into his stride. His inborn impetuosity did not always impress his father, who recorded at the outset:

> Seymour has just come in full of excitement. Phillips the Grocer wants £2,000 [some £60,000 now] at 4 per cent can you oblige him – must have it now. Make £40 – looks well on paper doesn't it?

One gets the impression from this sort of comment and his own asides in his letters that Seymour was less a man of the world at this time than his younger brother, whose press cuttings show surprising maturity in a nineteen year old. After all, Seymour had no experience outside schoolmastering before he was twenty-one, whereas William was mixing with businessmen from the age of fifteen. Even after the development of his formidable powers he retained a certain naïvety. In one civil-court appearance he was reluctant to leave the witness box after being cross-examined, convulsing the court when he said, 'Aren't you going to ask me any more questions?'

As time went on, Seymour began in-and-out speculation on the firm's own account and on one occasion got stuck with a few broken-down cottages and a worked-out drift mine – to the delight of some of his contemporaries. Such lapses were increasingly rare. It was not many years before he was building houses for sale or rent and, for a time, collecting the rent himself. His method was to use a clerk from his office to 'knock up' the tenants, so that when he came up each was waiting with the rent book. This not only added a personal touch to the landlord/tenant relationship, but also saved the wages of two rent collectors.

His greatest single coup was, in 1909, negotiating the sale to the town corporation of Cyfarthfa Castle, the 1835 'Scottish baronial' seat of the

5

late Crawshay iron dynasty, and 400 acres. After this JMB was able to retire and move to a large Georgian house[3] and three acres next to Cyfarthfa Park (which had been the Crawshay home before they built the castle).

In 1911, Seymour wished to expand. All three local banks refused to lend him money. Instead, he went to London and proposed a deal to the National Provincial Bank. In addition to a large loan[4] they would buy the lease of a fine building belonging to his father-in-law, themselves occupy the ground floor and sub-lease the other three floors to him at £100 p. a. In this way he got his loan, provided a £6,000 return to his father-in-law, secured a prestigious new address, Bank Chambers, and cemented a lifelong association with one of the great London clearing banks, the first into Merthyr.

The loan enabled him to enter a wider scale of business. Merthyr itself was depressed but the whole coal business of South Wales was booming, spinning off prosperity to small partnerships and individuals. Seymour saw the opportunity both to them and to himself of forming them into limited companies. He was mainly responsible for setting up building companies, which erected terraced houses in many towns, and for building clubs for owner-occupiers. Additionally, he managed a large number of houses and other properties for private clients. Many of these tied colliery cottages were sold off at £150 to £200 each, paid for by colliers in £10–£20 instalments.

Housing was not his only preoccupation. He financed companies which built and ran cinemas in at least four towns. In Merthyr he floated two stationery and printing firms, one of which published a weekly periodical in the Welsh language, now owned by the Welsh Congregational Union. In 1916 there were some fifty or sixty company registration plates at Bank Chambers.

During the early part of this period, JMB's life style did not change overmuch. Up at 6.30, a cup of precious tea placed on his neighbour's party wall, a substantial family breakfast with prayers (and perhaps a side of bacon from Camrose cousins), lunch at midday with meat and wine (but no alcohol for the children), high tea at 6 with cold meat and salad, then reading, a cigar, and in bed by 10. On Sundays, two visits to the Chapel to hear the great preachers, with hymn-singing before the second, and strictly no play. He liked to tell stories himself but he also encouraged the children to go their own way – he often lectured at Sunday schools on the need to 'get on' and once dissuaded his neighbour

---

[3] Gwaelodygarth, still known as 'the Berry House'.
[4] I don't know how large. The branch records were destroyed by fire in the Second World War.

from fetching back from the army his son who had rebelled at following his father into teaching.

At first JMB walked everywhere, except when his wife went with him, in a gig. Merthyr was no place for long skirts. Later he bought the first motor car in Merthyr (and one of the first telephones). Thereafter, in the summer, he took what family was still left at home (including his mother-in-law, who had come to live with them) to Tenby, in Pembrokeshire. At Swansea the boys had season tickets for the swimming bath and watched cricket through the railings.

*   *   *

The *Merthyr Times*, very much the second paper in the town (circulation 2,250), to which William went on Tuesday, 2 May 1894, aged thirteen years ten months, was a weekly founded in 1891 by a consortium of small businessmen. According to Hadley, its (third) editor for six months at the end of 1893, it had been started on a shoestring in 'some local political feud'. According to a later editor, it was not only Liberal but Liberal 'with pronounced Liberal propaganda'. By Hadley's time the proprietors had melted into the background as he makes no mention of them and evidently never discussed policy with any of them. He was a strong Liberal himself but also a professional journalist of sixteen years' standing in Northampton and Rochdale, with a phobia of biased reporting. Just as evidently, he was disappointed at what he found. 'The office was small and meanly equipped, the staff inadequate.' Indeed, throughout its eight-year existence, its reporting staff were described as 'the editor and the reporter' (singular). There would also have been a sub-editor, part-time correspondents paid on space, in the areas around Merthyr, and one staff reporter further afield. In addition, there were apprentice reporters who normally, if they stayed, would become fully fledged after six years. As for the printing staff, there was only one when the paper started, though later, when jobbing (general) printing was begun in 1895, the 'hands' grew to twenty-five.

The Merthyr area was still prosperous in Hadley's time. Steel-making had not yet fully started its swift decline, but the prosperity had not filtered through to the paper: it had never made a profit and it is unlikely that it ever did.

William was the younger by a year of two apprentice reporters, both on 5/- a week. The tone of the paper, under a new editor,[5] 'could have caused no qualms to JMB, advertising itself as:

---

[5] The editor lasted only nine months. William's next meeting with him was nearly half a century later when, on buying the 3,000-acre Hackwood Park in Hampshire, he found him to be vicar of

It is essentially a
FAMILY PAPER
And every care is taken to exclude
ALL IMPROPER MATTER
From its Columns

Advertisers will know how to Evaluate the
Value of this Feature

William's first job was as a police court reporter – in knickerbockers, the equivalent of shorts a generation later. He had some coaching in shorthand outside the office, encouraged by the editor, 'the best short-hand writer in South Wales', but I doubt if he ever mastered it. Years later he used his own special form of speed-writing, and a shorthand bible I found in his library did not look well thumbed.

His reporting was, as it should have been, purely factual. The only lightness was provided by the sub-editor, who recorded the procession of drink fines under such headings as 'The Drink', 'The Alcohol Brigade', 'The Alcohol List', 'Beery Cases', 'The Unsteady Ones', 'Devotees of Bacchus'. There were, too, all the odd 'crimes' of parochial life – sleeping in a haystack (ten days), playing cards on the pavement (2/6d.), leaving horse unattended (5/-).

As for the prose, the straight reporting was sound enough but the descriptive writing often appalling. The editor who followed Hadley wrote a weekly column of astonishingly pretentious and sycophantic verbosity, while a reporter – or perhaps it was an apprentice – could begin a comment on the weather: 'The controller of the meteorological department in Dame Nature's workshop seems to have gone to work this season by contraries.'

William and his fellow apprentice, Willie Cole,[6] did not quickly lose their schoolboy exuberance. There was much larking about when they were waiting to be sent on jobs. On one occasion they jointly broke a plate-glass window and were charged 5/- (a week's wages) by an angry shopkeeper. William couldn't pay his share and for years afterwards this was a joke between them in a fairly regular correspondence. He never did pay, but when Cole was struggling in the ruinous conditions of South Wales in the late 1920s, William offered to guarantee his sons jobs when the time came.

After about a year, Willie Cole having departed to help set up his

---

the parish. William came to his aid by buying the vicarage, thus preventing the amalgamation with a neighbouring parish during the incumbent's time.

[6] One of Willie's sons, Mr David Cole, became Editor of South Wales's foremost paper, the *Western Mail*, and was later Chairman and Chief Executive of Thomson Regional Newspapers.

own family business, William, standing in briefly as 'the reporter' without serving his apprenticeship, was transferred to be assistant to the manager of the commercial department. The transfer, I think, was a result of a little exercise in private enterprise. He conceived the idea – Willie Cole's son says it was his father's originally – of selling off unused newsprint (known in the trade as white waste) to shopkeepers, a few sheets at a time. The return was meagre, but to a boy on 5/- a week it was something. The manager must have thought him a lively lad. Under him, William would have been in and out of the case room when the advertisements were set and would have got a grounding in the display of type. (He said afterwards that he had done everything that can be done on a weekly paper except 'stick' type.) They were a professional lot there, boasting that they were the first trade union (Typographical Association) team in South Wales, a boast promoted by the management, who published it in the paper.

When William was sixteen, he had another stroke of luck, although of a less agreeable kind. The manager went off with the petty cash. William went after him, brought him and the cash back, and was installed in his place.[7]

A year later, in January 1897, the paper was bought, in mysterious circumstances, by one Edwin Davies of Brecon. Davies, who also became Editor for a spell, was a model for all newspaper proprietors (a model rather out of fashion nowadays).

At his first staff dinner in March he thanked the staff 'for welcoming him to their midst', while the managing director, who, as the most important staff member had been put down to propose his health, remarked on his 'degree of dignity and geniality which makes him an ideal employer'.

Davies had started as an apprentice printer in Brecon, becoming foreman printer (combined with freelance feature writing) and then Editor of the *Brecon County Times*. In the same year, at the age of thirty-seven, he and his wife had bought both the Brecon paper and the *Merthyr Times*. He had evidently given some assistance on the printing side in the birth of the *Merthyr Times*, but the meaning of another section of the managing director's dinner speech I have not been able to fathom: 'To some extent the *Merthyr Times* owed its birth to him but he did not then anticipate his present association with it. Circumstances due rather to the treachery of others, than to his own

---

[7] I have searched the files of the *Merthyr Times* – and the *Merthyr Express* – for details of this episode, but have found nothing. As my father never romanced I can only conclude that the matter was hushed up as it would not have done the precarious reputation of the paper any good. His terse account of an exciting personal episode was typical of him.

inclination, had directed his footsteps to the direction of the *Merthyr Times*.'

Certainly, the trio of original proprietors had never been respected. Only one of them ever attended the annual dinner and at one, when none of them was present, the slow progress of the paper was put down to their 'inexperience'. But 'treachery' I cannot explain. What does seem very possible is that William, as Commercial Manager, played some part in the negotiation for the change of ownership. The price cannot have been much, as the paper folded twenty months later. At the dinner from which I have already quoted, Davies went out of his way to single William out. He said he was 'especially grateful to Mr Berry, Mr Stewart-Smith [Managing Director] and Mr Phillips' (overseer, news department). As William was only a stripling of seventeen and a half and just recently promoted, the naming of him ahead of the managing director suggests a more than ordinary service.

William was not without self-confidence at the dinner. He had been put down to propose the toast of the trade unionists in his own department but, owing to an absence, also found himself landed with toasting the editorial department as well. In the latter he was reported as giving 'a speech characterised by that species of brevity which is the soul of wit', but added rather cheekily that 'he had been associated with six editors and about a score of reporters'. (Actually, three of the editors had been before his time.)

Work did not prevent him from playing some part in the social life of the town. In the New Year of 1898 the *Merthyr Times* recorded his having attended three balls with Seymour. Their sister Beta, now married, who most likely would have taught him to waltz – in a rather agricultural style – never went with them and they were never reported as being in a party.

While both Seymour and William lived in Merthyr, they still roamed. They got caught up in the riots of 1898, when looting and stone-throwing strike demonstrators penetrated the centre of Merthyr. They were standing in a doorway watching the proceedings when police patience broke and a baton charge began. Their pates were only saved by Seymour's ready greeting to a charging policeman, 'Good evening, Sergeant'.

William became a competent billiard player, probably at local billiard halls, though there were several billiard 'leagues' in the area. He is unlikely to have played at the Merthyr Liberal Club, firstly because of the subscription and secondly because their billiard room was directly above the editorial room of the *Merthyr Times*. When the politics of the paper changed to Tory in January 1897, the new owner/editor often complained of the noise and stamping from above. He would have known that the club had been founded at the instigation of JMB six months earlier.

William must have played other ball games for, though he had no particular style, I remember his good eye when playing cricket with him in 1919 or 1920. He liked kicking footballs about with his sons when they were old enough. Later he was a passable game shot, of the snap-shooting variety as suited his temperament.

In July 1898 William answered an advertisement in the *Daily News* from the London financial weekly, the *Investors Guardian*, and received a reply on 6 July in a telegram as economical with words as ever William achieved in later life:

Berry auctioneer Merthyr[8]
Depends on applicant 35 [illegible: some variant of 'shillings'] offered.
[No signature]

Notice given was short. On Saturday 22 July he was off. The *Merthyr Times* noted his departure under the compendium heading 'Local News':

It is the custom of young Merthyrians to go to the Metropolis nowadays. The latest departure is Mr W.E. Berry, who has been associated with the commercial department of the *Merthyr Times* for the last five years. He has obtained a position on the *Investors Guardian*, a position which we feel sure he will fill with credit. He left Merthyr on Saturday, many of his friends accompanying him to the station to see him off. On Friday he was the recipient of a walking-stick as a parting gift from the members of the *Merthyr Times* Chapel. Mr W. Jones, in making the presentation, spoke of the good feeling which had always existed between Mr Berry and his co-workers and he wished him all success. Several members of the Chapel followed in a similar strain.

Those few commentators who, during his lifetime, wrote speculatively about William's departure, saw it as some kind of Dick Whittington act; the first conscious step on the ladder towards being a great newspaper proprietor. I do not think he saw it in that way at all. He had already some realisation of the small-time nature of South Wales and undoubtedly he saw London as the place for an enterprising young man with a feeling for business. But he did not see his way at all clearly. As he told me once, his immediate desire was to make quite a lot of money. (His brother Seymour jokingly addressed William as, 'Bill Berry,

[8] JMB's telegraphic address.

MP, Merchant, The World'). As Aristotle put it: 'First acquire an independent income and then practise virtue.'

His chance in London aroused some hesitation in JMB, not because William was unready but because he thought London a city of low morality. A granddaughter (Beta's daughter) later quoted JMB to Birkenhead as having said: 'Here are ten sovereigns [£300 today]. There is no more to come.' This, as proved by letters quoted in the next chapter, is a gross exaggeration. What I conclude he meant was: 'This should be enough to be going on with until I see what fist you make of it.' He was evidently not among those who saw William off, but I am quite sure there was no resentment on his son's part. All his life, all three sons had the greatest affection and respect for their father.

CHAPTER TWO

London – Pre-*Advertising World*

WILLIAM, NOW SIX foot and half an inch, broad, wavy black hair parted in the middle (he used both brushes at once), clean-shaven as he always remained, desperately thin, arrived at Paddington station on a Saturday night with £10 in his pocket and, I daresay, some small savings, and next to no clothes. Evidently he had no lodging arranged but perhaps a letter to the pastor of a Congregational Chapel from the pastor of Market Square. He would not have wanted the expense of dawdling around with a cab carrying his trunk while looking for lodgings. Seymour was to write four days later that their parents 'say that if there is another Congreg. Chapel you would prefer, you can go there', while JMB mentioned, 'Your mother will see about all your clothes and send them on in a day or two.'

Though he did not stay there for much more than a month, he was first taken in at Forest Gate (some four miles from the *Investors Guardian* office), from where he would walk to work. Once there he was allowed to charge horse buses up to expenses, though he usually ran between stops and pocketed the cash. Since weekly magazines keep regular hours he would have had his evening meal at home while he lunched on a twopenny bun – probably the equivalent of today's hamburger. At this period he neither drank nor smoked, so 35/- would have gone a long way.

Apart from having next to no clothes, he seems to have had only one pair of boots, so that his father could write: 'We are sorry to hear that your feet are so bad you must look after them and bathe them in salt and water you must not think so much of the cost as comfort the streets of London are very trying.' This to a man who, all his life, was a compulsive walker. The Merthyr leaving present was only the first of many dozen sticks he accumulated throughout his life.

JMB went on:

No doubt you see it strange and a little lonely to be moving about London without knowing anyone however I hope it will wear off by degrees it is something for you to know that we are all anxious about you and ready to assist you in every way possible – there are a great many enquiries about you and all say that you are sure to do well.

On reporting to the office, William found that reporters on the *Investors Guardian* were expected to contribute also to its sister paper, the *Country Gentleman*. This latter was a forty-year-old weekly (selling at 6d.) which had picked up three others on the way – the *Sports Gazette*, the *Man about Town* and the *Agricultural Journal*. The amalgam was not unhappy. The first part of the magazine was a solid four pages of society gossip, quite racy and not particularly sycophantic, upwards of 100 items in a single issue. The second half catered entirely for upper-class sports – racing, polo, cricket, shooting and the like – with a little agriculture thrown in. What William contributed to the *Country Gentleman*, for which his background and experience would have been little suited, I do not know. It must have been something: in later years he said that he had been employed by both papers. But it could not have been very much since there is no cutting from it in the cuttings' book (bought round the corner in Cannon Street), which he pasted up uncharacteristically neatly. At first, cuttings were identified as 'Investors Guardian', 'Investors', or 'I.G.', but after August there is no attribution, just the date.

His first entry is for 3 August 1898 in respect of a company meeting held on the first Wednesday after his arrival in London. It is, as far as I can see, a totally competent piece of work of some 600 words – factual, workmanlike, without a trace of Merthyr journalese, and only one long word where a shorter one would do.

An I.G. reporter was expected not only to report and comment on a meeting but also to persuade the company secretary to put the formal report of the proceedings as an advertisement in the paper. He told his father of this requirement in a letter on his second day of work, which prompted Seymour to write back: 'Did you succeed in getting any Coy Secys to let you put their report in the paper? How are you getting on with the Editor, does he talk to you or confide in you at all?'

Actually, William does not seem to have been very successful as a canvasser. He did secure a one and three-quarter column advertisement from his very first meeting, but in the next three months, only two more. It has to be remembered, however, that of the twenty-nine items he contributed during that time, more than half were on general financial subjects and his total non-score was ten.

His confidence soon grew. Only a week after his first meeting he was wittily rebuking Sir Arthur Guinness, Chairman of Arthur Guinness, Son and Co., the still-famous brewers, for a mean dividend.

William at first wrote home favourably about his lodgings. Seymour wrote to him on 27 July: 'Pa and Ma were pleased to find that you attended Chapel on Sunday ... they are also pleased that you are so comfortable in your lodgings with so many classy companions but hope you will not place too much confidence in them.'

A month later he had changed his address to the opposite end of London, to Kensington High Street, still a tidy step from Cannon Street. There, his landlady was a penniless widow, Mrs Norman, with a small son, Roland. Roland, eventually a good-looking and dashing young man, became attached to him and always called him Uncle William. William befriended him throughout his life, though he found his business methods too unorthodox for his taste. When William had a house of his own he used often to ask Mrs Norman and Roland down.

He was already installed in Kensington when his father, mother and fifteen-year-old Gomer came to visit him at the beginning of September, and afterwards his mother referred to the 'dear Mrs Norman'. Preparatory to the visit, JMB was still fussing about his son's soul:

> We are very pleased ... to find you are getting on so well. You must have had a busy week by the paper ... You do not say anything about how you spend Sunday and I do not want to moralise with you but I am exceedingly anxious about how you spend Sunday. I know there are many pitfalls in which a young man is liable to fall and now is your hardest time. I have implicit confidence in you but I hope you are not trusting in your own strength alone but you are asking God to help you ... how are you getting on financially and if you want any help you know where to send ...

Whatever good that homily did, the effect was not long-lived. My knowledge on this only goes back to the time of his married life. Neither of my parents went to church or chapel until he became a 'squire' in 1921. Morally, however, he remained a Nonconformist. He detested the Roman Catholic Church, eschewed promiscuity, swearing, and even slang, and was censorious of heavy drinking, particularly of spirits.

Back at the office, William scored quite a coup at the company meeting of Harmsworth Brothers, the collection of magazines built up by Alfred Harmsworth, later Lord Northcliffe. Harmsworth and the company's solicitor had some difficulty in persuading the holders of preference shares that an alteration in their rights would actually benefit them. The argument seemed to have reached an impasse when William whispered the answer to a newspaper colleague, who passed it on to Harmsworth. In his report, William explained it to his readers: 'We understand that ...'. What was at stake was the market value of the preference shares.

By the company's proposal, the shares would rise in price – as they did – whereas the holders would only lose if the company came a cropper, which seemed, and was, most unlikely. The argument had been conducted at cross purposes. It is ironic that, a quarter of a century later, William and Gomer should find themselves the largest shareholders in what now became the Amalgamated Press (later still IPC) and should themselves be Chairman and Deputy Chairman respectively.

After the meeting, Harmsworth stopped William and offered him a job. Why he refused I never could quite make out. If the job had been on the *Daily Mail*, which Harmsworth had just launched with staggering success, I daresay his answer might have been different; but the atmosphere of the meeting was nothing but magazines. I do not know whether Harmsworth had yet developed the habit, for which he became well known, of taking people up and then forgetting their existence. Anyway, William sometimes mused in later life whether he would have made a good subordinate, but I loyally told him his masterful temperament would not have kept him in such a job for five minutes.

In point of fact, he stayed the course on the *Investors Guardian* for three months. Then, in the middle of October 1898, he was summarily fired.

One thing I am pretty sure of is that the row, whatever it was, was with the manager, not the editor. One story was that the manager had been drunk and that, in his absence, William had altered the wage book to increase his own salary. This seems most unlikely. He was always an impatient man in small things but most patient in the long view. Such a ridiculous stratagem, which would have been certain to rebound sooner rather than later, can be dismissed out of hand.

The other explanations were given by William himself. In an interview in 1934 he said that his dismissal was 'over a difference of opinion'. In another in 1949, now more mellow, he said it was 'because of incompetence'.

I am inclined to favour the 1934 version. After all, the manager was doing the same job on a larger scale as William had done for two years in Merthyr and it is difficult to imagine his not proffering suggestions. I have no idea what they might have been, but his eye might have lighted on the fact that in some issues the amount of editorial was down to two and a half pages out of sixteen. The magazine had started an unscheduled, midweek twelve pages from time to time, but maybe the manager was slow on his feet. William was described a little later by a subordinate as 'like a tornado in action'. Perhaps the manager did not like the blast.

He said later that 'he did not try very hard' to get another job, and on another that his hardest time was to get one. I am quite sure that, even though he did not go back to Alfred Harmsworth, the latter is the correct version.

Meanwhile he continued to send back marked copies of the I.G. to his parents hoping not to arouse their fears, though no more cuttings were pasted in. He also did some freelancing, which was easier then than now (newspapers had smaller staffs), though I am sure he would not have made Harmsworth's grand remark that 'I could take a penny bus-ride and return with a story that any newspaper would be glad to print.' He also did a lot of reading, trying to catch up on an education which, all his life, he felt had formally ended woefully early.

At Christmas, with time on his hands and little money in his pocket, he returned to Merthyr by tramp steamer – with a coffin as his fellow passenger and a captain who revelled in greasy food which, for the only time in his life, he found he could not face at sea.

Back at Merthyr, he was still officially 'in work', but he suspected his parents knew the truth. I think he underrated himself as a white liar. It was not until mid-January that JMB wrote anxiously:

> We had your letter this morning but we have not received the paper for the last 2 weeks how is this is everything alright if any thing happens you must let me know if you didn't we should be very much vexed and grieved. Drop a line by return.

and three days later:

> We had your note this morning and it was just as we expected, never mind it cannot be helped keep up a good heart any help you want you shall have, shall I send you money mind let me know in the next how you are off. DAT[1] is expected out end of this week when I will go for him – Do you think an introduction to Lloyd George any good or Tom Ellis. Our Minister is very friendly with both. Is there anything you think I can do – it will be a good chance to get hold of them when the House meets – your Mother is in a way about it she fears you will get low but I tell her you are not such a coward as that. You need not trouble if you are out for six months as it is no fault of your own you have struck Well goodbye I got a sale in the Bush today Seymour will write tomorrow We all join in best love,
> Your affec. Father,
> J.M.Berry.

---

[1] D.A.Thomas, MP (later Lord Rhondda). JMB was his constituency agent.

Seymour wrote on the back:

> You keep your eyes open and we can keep you until you get another job. I will take care that our profits go up proportionately now that you are awaiting events ... I think Smith ought to put little things in your way. You have done so much for him.

His mother followed this in pencil a day later with:

> Pembroke House,
> Merthyr Tydfil,
> January 18/99

> My dear Willie,
>   I said on Sunday I would give you a good scolding for picking my last letter to pieces as you did but I will forgive you under all the present circumstances.

William had evidently been amusing himself by criticising his mother's grammar. *En famille*, he was always inclined to tease when slightly bored. I remember particularly one occasion when a close friend, who had a maddening habit of saying 'you see' every second sentence, was telling rather a long story at dinner among three or four of his children. William made no attempt to interrupt except to chant 'one, two, three', etc. He got up to sixteen.

His mother's letter went on:

> Now my dear boy be sure don't be depressed because you are idle but keep up your spirits there is a silver lining to every dark cloud and yours will be bright again soon be sure you don't want for anything and don't hesitate letting us know and you shall have it by return of post, you are the chief topic of conversation in the house all day. I wish Mr D.A. Thomas were better then your Father would see him. We are so glad you are in a comfortable home. What work are you doing at home. When you wrote let us have all particularly. Gomer is come home with a bilious attack has gone to bed is better now but the rest will do him a lot of good he has it very hard now sale time[2] but he intends writing you tomorrow when you will have all the news in spiffs etc. Now my dear I will conclude with love from all and your loving Mother

> PS my love to Mrs Norman

---

[2] Gomer, now aged fifteen, had already gone to work in Manchester House, the leading drapers in Merthyr.

(An angry comment is written by William in much stronger pencil across one corner of the letter:

'No ink in this
house you know
can't afford it'.)

Gomer did not write next day, but finally got round to it on 8 February:

Dear Bill,

I suppose Mother has told you about my coming home bilious well I am now recovered. I suppose you wish you had something to do. Well anyhow it was a nasty thing to do getting you up there for 5 months [sic]. I think I had better write to them and tell them who I am. Well it is a good job you are in comfortable lodgings with parents who are willing to do anything for you so cheer up. Our sale commenced last Friday, the following is a list of spiffs I made up to date.

Mine

Friday	Saturday	Monday	Tuesday
3/-	2/5	1/10	1/8

Apprentice 5 weeks after me

2/6	2/-	1/4	2/-

——

Seymour has just gone to Nom Coms Ball he did not seem to want to go much the attraction was Florence Daniel. The weather is awfully wet here. I do not know what to tell you as you have such a string of correspondence this week. Bill can't you do something on a similar line as Waste Paper[3] or get advertisements for Edwin Davies. Mr Benjamin often asks after you. That baby[4] is getting a fair nipper. You ask her 'Where is Uncle Willie' and she will look at once at the door. The Miss Pegg are going to open a school. We have had a servant today from Tredegar We have let our house to that Mr Hall of William Street.

This is all news I have so with fond love,
I remain,
Your loving brother,
Gomer

[3] See Chapter 1, p. 9.
[4] Beta's daughter, Doris.

Cheer up Bill there is a good time coming.

In later life William said he was out of work for four months. The end of February would have been the end of that period and, if the new job he then got was not yet the 'good time' Gomer predicted, it was a great deal better than nothing. He became a sub-editor on the Mercantile Press Agency, a financial newsagency, at the reduced salary of 18/- a week.

Sub-editing on a newspaper is, of course, a highly responsible and, in its higher reaches, exciting job. Many a distinguished editor has got his start in that role. But the status of a sub-editor on a newsagency is more lowly. He has, of course, to be meticulously accurate but the finished product is only someone else's raw material. In William's case his job would have consisted mainly of making digests of documents, company reports and accounts coming into the office. Eighteen shillings, against his previous thirty-five, represented pretty accurately market value.

William certainly did not boast of the job's importance to his father, who wrote on 26 June:

Your Mother and myself heartily congratulate you on your attaining your twentieth birthday you are just on the threshold of manhood and at an age where it is easy to make a false step but there is one great comfort your mother myself have and that is we feel confident that you are strong enough to resist any temptation from whatever quarter it may come, of course we shall always be delighted with any progress you may make in the work but we would both rather you to be poor than you should in any way go wrong but we rest satisfied by God's help that wont happen. I do not know what is best to send you so if you will accept the enclosed pound and buy what you like – goodbye post going.
With best love,

Your aff. Father,
JMB.

Sometime round the turn of the century, William answered an advertisement for the post of manager for the Kennel Publishing Company at £3.10s. a week.

First a word about that company. It was owned by a Mrs Weightman, a vivacious and frequently rich Anglo-Australian. As a teenage girl she had emigrated to Australia with her mother and married a state senator much older than herself. Bearing him a son, she had soon left her husband and made a mini-fortune from personally exploiting a gold drift which the professionals said was already worked out. Thereafter the drift was called the Midas mine, and she herself, Princess Midas. The son, as soon as he was old enough, also worked in the mine and discovered in himself a dramatic talent for reciting the more exciting parts of Shakespeare to the off-duty miners in the outback. He came to London about 1896, played some minor stage roles, and was later followed by the Princess.

At first she backed him but then discovered a passion for dogs. She was the first Secretary of the Ladies Kennel Club, of which Queen Alexandra was persuaded to become Patron. It was a short step to buy a prosperous magazine called *Our Dogs*.

But dogs were not enough. Contrariwise, she started a magazine called *Our Cats* and put in her son, now called by his stage name, Sydney Carroll, as Editor-in-Chief (he couldn't have been Editor as the latter was always addressed in print as 'Dear Madam').

Carroll was an imaginative journalist and an ingenious publicist. He launched the magazine with a dinner, serenaded by music-hall celebrities, for cat's meat retailers who thereafter sold it together with the meat down the basement steps in the smart part of town. But the Princess quickly discovered he was no good with figures – he never was – and advertised for a manager.

As William left no recollections about his entire time in that role, I must tell the story in Carroll's own words, written forty years later, while cautioning that Carroll's heart was always in the stage and that he lived in a world of the impresario's exaggeration:

We received between 300 and 400 applications.

I went though every one for my mother, and boiled it down to a choice of 20. I interviewed this last lot personally. And among them came a young man of obvious character with a plausible tongue, a dynamic drive, a handsome face, and a faint, very attractive Welsh accent. He got the job. His name was William Ewart Berry.

It is easy to praise oneself for picking out a winner *after* he has won. But I have always been proud of picking Bill Berry before he had even become a starter.

We were intimate friends although I was nominally his boss and was making comparatively a lot of money while he was making a little. I used to chaff him about his good looks.

'You ought to understudy George Alexander,' I used to say. 'You'd make a fortune on the stage!' But I knew it was in business that Bill Berry's future lay. Never a thing went wrong that he could not explain away and not only explain away but convince the complainer that the complaint was either unreasonable or that he was really grateful it had been brought to his notice and that it could never possibly occur again.

I used to watch him going through the accounts. I could more easily understand how Maskelyne did his tricks than how Bill could add up a pageful of figures at a glance. It was, to me, magic.

In another passage, Carroll showed that William was still a teetotaller, as he mentions him being fooled by Princess Midas' sherry trifle.

I cannot name an exact day when William took up the post of Manager at the Kennel Publishing Company – that was the strange name of the company which published *Our Cats* and the *Journal* of the Ladies Kennel Club but which had nothing to do with *Our Dogs*, published independently. But I should guess the date was the end of January 1900. On 31 January the three months' subscription rate advertised over the masthead on page three at last came into line with that on page one. Hitherto the first had signalled 3/3d. and the second 2/6d. William, a master of detail, would not have failed to notice the nonsense for a single week.

In June 1900 William celebrated, or rather attained, his twenty-first birthday. His father wrote:

My dear Willie,

Just a line of hearty congratulations on your attaining your 21st birthday. You are now in every sense a man and I feel confident that you have sufficient common sense to keep yourself as far as it is possible for a man to do unsupported and that you will never do anything that will give you cause for regret in the future. I earnestly pray that God will spare you for many years to live a good and useful life and whatever position you may attain high or low you will not forget your duty to him – a good name is better than riches – your Mother heartily joins me in congratulations. We do not know what to send you so have sent you a cheque for three pounds to buy what you like. Seymour is writing same post so he will give you all the news. Please remember us kindly to Mrs N – and accept our very best love and our hearty good wishes for your future welfare.

Your affec. Father
J.M.Berry

And Seymour added, with another cheque of consecutive number:

Friday 8 pm

Dear Willie,

Just a few lines in order to wish you many happy returns on your 21st birthday. You have now reached the eve of manhood and are no longer a boy (in the eyes of the law). The advantages of being over twenty-one are too numerous for me to enumerate. I am enclosing in JMB's cheque 20/- as a small memento and will leave the spending of it, to your discretion. Mind do not squander such a large sum on riotous living. I would send more only you know I cannot at present afford it altho I hope to be a millionair (bothered if I can even spell it) some day.

Well I sincerely trust that you will be spared to see your lofty ambitions realised, and that your career which now looks so prosperous will continue to climb to loftier heights.

Your affec. Bro.
Seymour.

As with the *Investors Guardian*, disaster struck without warning. Princess Midas sold *Our Cats* – a pretty slim production – to another cat lover, and both William and Carroll were out of a job. Carroll got a year's salary from the new owner, but I doubt whether William got more than a month's.

The strange thing is that William never cashed the two cheques he had for his twenty-first birthday a year earlier. I still have them, in their envelope, immaculate, as they were ninety years ago.

CHAPTER THREE

Advertising World, Marriage

WILLIAM KEPT NO letters from home for eighteen months after his twenty-first birthday in June 1900, but I judge the date of his dismissal from the Kennel Publishing Company to be about August or September 1901. At twenty-two, however, he was much more mature and experienced in the ways of London than he had been at nineteen, when he suffered near-despair. Three years on, after his periodic visits home, he was able to write:

> The inhabitants of Wales rank with the best businessmen of the day when they come across the border ... But at home they seem different. The ignorance and prejudice still prevailing, even amongst the middle classes is astounding, and there is no more backward section of the British Isles in the adoption of new ideas. Gradually with more full intercourse with 'people from other countries', as a native would say, up-to-date methods are creeping in ...[1]

In all his time in London he had been doing his reading in a public library – almost certainly at St Bride's Institute, next to the Wren church (built on the foundations of a Mithras temple) of the same name and almost opposite *The Daily Telegraph*, where he was to be based for the last twenty-five years of his life. The library, whose foundation stone had been laid by the Prince of Wales in 1893, was almost a club, free to all those working in the Fleet Street/East Strand area[2]. Aside from newspaper and magazine reading areas there were facilities for 'Bagatelle, Chess, Draughts, etc.'. For the affluent, the hall was licensed for 'Music and Dancing, Entertainments, Balls, Meetings, Exhibitions, etc.', plus there was a seventy-five-foot swimming bath. There were 7,500 general books in the library. Attached was a printing school with 1,300 volumes on printing and allied trades and, most importantly, 'nearly 3,000 works relating to the Art of Printing, Specimens of Typography etc.'.

[1] First issue of *Advertising World*, 1901

[2] That it was so used is shown by an entry in Wareham Smith's (first Advertising Manager of the *Daily Mail*) *Spilt Ink*: 'Went to St Bride's for a bath' (1896).

Looking round, William would have seen that there was a continual flood of small magazines on all sorts of topics, obviously run on a shoestring. There were American, as well as English, trade magazines. In particular, he would have noticed ten American advertising magazines and but a solitary English one. It was here, I am pretty sure, William got the idea that there was a 'gap in the market'.

Advertising, anyway, was much in the news. Few practised it but many talked about it. For the most part the man in the street regarded it as an aberration of those over-smart, bragging Americans, while Gladstone was still quoted as having said, 'When I want mental relaxation and amusement I never fail to find it in the advertising columns of the American press.'[3] One advertisement which he liked was for *The Solid Muldoon*, a Colorado paper: 'The only fearless, wide awake and red hot newspaper in San Juan. Democratic in politics, independent in development: and no religion to speak of. She's a daisy.'

The very idea of publicity had had a bad name since a hoax was forced on Queen Victoria by Phineas T. Barnum, who intrigued with the American ambassador to get his midget, Tom Thumb, presented at Court. For decades afterwards something had only to be dubbed 'Barnumesque' to be deplored. Even so, it was catching. Thomas Lipton (who, in the 1920s, was to straddle the avenues of top-snob Newport, Rhode Island, with streamers saying, 'Buy Lipton's tea', while challenging for the America's Cup – still a gentleman's sport) had young, tartan-covered pigs driven through the streets of Glasgow under a banner proclaiming, 'Lipton's orphans', and delivered monster cheeses, pulled by elephants or steam engines, to his shops.[4] But he failed where Barnum had succeeded.

Queen Victoria refused to accept a five-ton cheese for her Golden Jubilee. October 1901 (the Queen had died earlier in the year) saw the end of a nationwide row over a vast hoarding advertising Quaker Oats (American, of course) on the cliffs of Dover, the English gateway from the Continent. The town council had to get a special Act of Parliament to bring it down.

In terms of British taste, posters, on the other hand, were 'in'. Poster advertising had for many years been a thriving and well-conducted business: its standards were vetted by a national committee whose veto was absolute. The use of well-known artists was common, so much so that their works were sometimes known as 'the poor man's art gallery'.

---

[3] Of business he said, 'Nothing but the mint can make money without advertising.'
[4] In 1933 Lipton, now in his dotage, was at last elected to the top-snob Royal Yacht Squadron, but died a few months later.

The idea of any other sort of advertising was only just becoming respectable and no longer universally regarded as American brashness. But it was still suspect. 'Truth in advertising in those days was less of an inspiration than an irony. People were not expected to believe an advertisement.' The consequence was that the serious London papers were reluctant to accept any display advertising at all. (Even the popular *Daily Mail* did not carry display advertising on its front page before November 1901.) If they did, they would allow only capital letters and no copy, whereas the Americans 'tried everything from a plain unvarnished statement ... to a lengthy dissertation including quotations from the most up-to-date modern poets'. The advertisers for their part kept the same message for a twelve-month and, if sales fell off, assumed, in modern marketing jargon, that the public had sampled the product and rejected it – so there was nothing to be done. In any case, they did not know where their advertising was to be placed. It was handled by placing-agents, known as 'farmers', who obtained discounts for large spaces and farmed them out piecemeal at full rates.

Before 1900 'there was nothing which could be called an advertising profession'. Advertising agents, after all, are the middlemen of commerce. They don't make anything and they don't sell anything. Therefore they tended to be regarded as parasites, socially as well as professionally, who collected a commission for a service that could be performed without them. The idea that marketing required expertise and was different from producing something at a price penetrated only slowly and much of the early advances were made by American agents or those who had served an apprenticeship in America. Businessmen laughed with Mr Gladstone at American hyperbole and were astonished and mystified that Wanamaker, the great Philadelphia store owner, employed an 'expert' at a liberal salary whose occupation was to 'turn out naive productions by the yard – and never repeated'.

In 1901 there were already 'house [advertising] magazines'. While some of these were good productions, they did not pretend to embrace any commodities outside their own firms. One of the best was *Medical Reprints*, with a subscription list of 4,000 doctors, edited by Thomas Russell, advertising manager of a firm of importing chemists. Russell, later Advertising Manager of *The Times*, the first independent advertising consultant and founder of the Incorporated Society of Advertising Agents, was not only a successful businessman and fine writer, but also widely travelled in America, Canada, India and Australia, and a friend of the editor of *Printers' Ink*, the leading American advertising magazine.

William later recorded that he had 'received much information and advice' from Russell, but only after he had taken the plunge and decided to start his own monthly advertising magazine, the *Advertising World*. He took the first step by printing a 'recording' copy to establish the title, producing probably only the half-dozen copies necessary. It was not even a dummy: it did have 'The Advertising World October 1901' on the top of its two pages but all the matter was a straight reprint from the *Lady Exhibitor* of 'Stable, Farm and Dairy', type probably still standing after the *Lady Exhibitor* had gone to press so that the expense would have been minimal.

The only competition at that time was the *Advertisers' Review* which, despite a large format, was a thin eight-pager, full of lifted American copy and knowing little features headed 'Printers' Ink Nuggets', 'Bits from Brains', 'Advisor Aphorisms', and suchlike. William was not to know that E.S. Day, the Editor of that organ, whose resignation was announced in the 30 September issue, was himself to start a rival, *Progressive Advertising*, on 25 October. He did not know and he was not to care. Day had not got the point of the world of advertising at all, just about to take off in this country. I am indebted to the sometime archivist of The History of Advertising Trust, David Linton, for an independent opinion:

> The strength of [the *Advertising World*] over both its 'independent' contemporaries lay in its all-round coverage: agencies as well as advertising, news of personalities as well as businesses – hence a focus for the burgeoning social side, and prestige of advertising. The interchange of original material with the USA [the 'American Letter' probably procured by Russell, printed anonymously like every other article in the early issues] was a regular feature from the first issue and was clearly a bonus.

When the first number of the *Advertising World* came out on 1 December 1901, its welcome from its rivals was various. Day, who in the opening number of *Progressive Advertising* had damned his previous stable, claiming first that he had tried to buy the *Advertisers' Review* from its proprietors and secondly that their (the proprietors') 'interests had frequently clashed with the interests of [the *Advertisers' Review*]' of which he was then Editor, sneered at the *Advertising World*:

> If there were any question of competition ... which there is not ... I would say that one month of my paper contained as much reading matter as three months of the *Advertising World* and draw other conclusions which would be odious to that paper: but I do not believe in that kind of thing and it is always best to credit one's readers with

sufficient intelligence to see these things for themselves ... My best wishes for its success.

The *Advertisers' Review*, on the other hand, no doubt nettled by Day's strictures on itself, commented: 'We are very pleased to welcome it to our midst and hope it will long occupy the *vacant niche* [my italics] it has come to fill.'

In any case, Day repeated in *Progressive Advertising* many of the mistakes he had made in his previous editorship and packed the paper with trite maxims such as one used to find in Christmas crackers. One column-and-a-half article betrayed his amateurism. It was entitled 'Enthusiasms' and extolled the manufacturer's belief in his own product and the extension of enthusiasm to his salesmen, with never a mention of the advertising agent.

*   *   *

The first thing to do was to find a cheap printer with a slot. Carroll, his old 'boss' but now firm friend, had the same problem. Having shown himself he could create an asset – he had established *Our Cats*, only to find that his mother thought it something to sell off – he now lighted on the idea of starting *Caged Birds*,[5] a market only catered for as a minor section of the more general *Feathered World*.

They were both uneasily aware that for every three magazines starting there were two failing for the simple reason that canny printers, lacking entrepreneurial enthusiasm, gave no more than a week's credit. The result for all too many would-be Napoleons of publishing was that, without working capital, any revenue from advertising passed straight to the printer who, in many cases, needed the cover price as well. I think William must have been first with the idea – Carroll's publication was a month behind – of going to Birmingham. There, with less experience of fly-by-night publishers, three months' credit could be secured. The disadvantage was that J.G. Hammond, whom they found, was a cantankerous fellow who peppered his clients with pettifogging complaints. Carroll took much longer than William to amass enough cash reserve to return to London.

The printer found, they took two rooms at 10/- a week on the first floor of 72 Fleet Street (it is now occupied by Willerby & Co., Tailors), the building owned by Robert Blatchford, Editor of the radical *Clarion*, then a power in the land, just up the street from *Progressive Advertising*. They shared an office boy to whom they paid 7/6d. a week.

[5] In the late 1920s Carroll sold it to William, by now Chairman of Harmsworth's old magazine conglomerate, the Amalgamated Press, for £80,000.

There was not much time – only eight weeks before publication day. William now began the most testing time of his whole life to date. He had told Merthyr what he was up to and his father, through Seymour, had promised him £100, to be placed in a new company, based on their joint names, Ewart, Seymour & Co. Ltd. They kept this company in being for twenty years.

When William went to draw on the account, he told me, he was met by the fatherly manager of the Temple Bar Branch, Westminster Bank, 'with a long white beard', who asked him what he wanted the money for. 'To start a magazine', he replied. 'Do you think there is really room for yet another magazine?' 'Just one.'[6]

William had not only to write the whole magazine except for the American letter:[7] he had to get all the advertising, send out invoices, put the paper to bed (forty-eight hours in Birmingham) and arrange for distribution. His method was to canvass all day, when he was not collecting editorial information, and write most of the night, supported by endless cups of black coffee which he made himself. I expect it was at this time he took to smoking cigarettes – cigars had to wait quite a time. At the end of one interview he did record that the subject had given him a cigar 'which proved to be excellent', but I am sure he could not have afforded a regular supply.[8]

He was an ingenious but not a natural canvasser. He was inclined to flare up if spoken to contemptuously. He put up with the editor of the *Daily News* telling him that he couldn't take advertising in an advertising paper because his usual clients would think he was short of it. But he had a shouting row with Kennedy Jones, the rough-spoken Editor of the *Evening News* and Alfred Harmsworth's right-hand man. Gomer, when he later joined his brother, found it worthwhile to turn the other cheek, but he usually came back with something in his hand in the end.

When canvassing at that time, the advertiser had usually not only to be sold the idea but also the copy. For most of his potential victims, certainly for many of the smaller ones, William would have proofs of advertisements set in advance. To save money, he would probably have used St Bride's printing school, and his experience of using type there,

---

[6] It seems to have been well into the twentieth century before bank managers regarded publishing with enthusiasm. When Alfred Harmsworth went to Coutts Bank in 1894 to raise £25,000, backed by securities, to buy the London *Evening News* (founder member of his newspaper empire), the manager said that, in his banking experience, 'there were several ways by which a man might be certain of losing his money and none of them more certain than running a newspaper'.

[7] Russell had agreed to write a regular column, 'Confessions of an Advertising Agent', at 25/- a time (the highest article fee for several years); but owing to some muddle, it did not appear until issue number two.

[8] Common cigars at that time cost 3d. each (five for 1/-).

as well as at the *Merthyr Times,* would have helped. At that time office telephones were by no means universal and those who had lately installed them were proud of their new 'working tool'. One of William's tricks was purposely to print a man's telephone number slightly wrong. He several times landed an order about to be refused when the victim, cursorily scanning the proof, suddenly exclaimed, 'Look, you've got my number wrong'. I forgot to ask him whether he had found it an advantage to come clean.

In all, he won twenty-eight separate advertisements, occupying fourteen of the thirty-two pages plus four-page cover, netting £91 (about £3,000 today). In addition there were two and a quarter pages of contra-advertising[9] to cut down his costs – one advertisement for his blockmaker, another for his printer and a third for his landlord. Allowing for his editorial calls and his many failures, that is pretty good going for a lone canvasser who is editor, publisher and accountant as well. No one was to know. In the first issue readers were told firmly that editorial enquiries must be addressed to the Editorial *Department* (my italics), while advertising queries should be sent to the 'Advertisement Manager', yet another of his hats. No wonder that in the first number (though never again) he signed the four pages of news and comment (called 'Gossip',[10] a word he later abhorred) with the single word 'Atlas'.

William had evidently persuaded his father beforehand that the first issue was going to be a success and that Gomer, at seventeen and a half, should give up the coveted position of window dresser[11] at Manchester House (the largest store in Merthyr) to join him in London.

> 21 Victoria Street,
> Merthyr Tydfil,
> Dec. 6, 1901

My dear Willie,

We had your book [a term for any multi-page publication but now only used in the printing trade] this morning and are very pleased with it you must have had a big job to put all that matter together. I sincerely hope it will take on and then it will be all right but you must not expect success at once perseverance generally works out its own reward. Gomer has been vaccinated and is not very well he is

---

[9] Free advertisement in return for a service.

[10] In the second issue, the feature changed its name to 'Notelets' (though only at the last moment, as 'Gossip' still appeared in the contents index) and finally, in June 1902, to the smoother 'En Passant'.

[11] Fifty years later, at his magnificent regency house, Dropmore (near Taplow), a guest threw down his tie in the heat. Gomer picked it up, saying, 'That's no way to treat a tie,' and deftly coiled it as if to be put on display.

home today he is looking forward to coming to London but I think as the time is drawing nearer he is not quite so anxious it will be all right as he is going to you. Don't you think you could make some better arrangements as to Lodgings. I should like if you had the use of a sitting Room and get more Meals in the House. We will have a chat when you come down. What day are we to expect you? We have sent you two *Expresses* today Seymour sent one and so did I. You will see by it that we are still progressing. How is Mrs Norman is the will out. Have you sent a copy of your Book to the *Express* [the *Merthyr Times* was long gone] and do you expect any of the Papers to review it if anything appears we should like to see it – we shall expect letter on Sunday [Dec. 6 was a Friday] we all join in best love.

Your affec. Father

JMB.[12]

The January issue was, of course, already in course of preparation and there were less than three weeks before press time. Gomer, if he came at all, could not have arrived in time to help much: he started canvassing (he was already a salesman, though one to whom the customer came) for the third issue of 1 February. There is a story, too, that another of his jobs was to drop the unsold copies over Blackfriars Bridge.

*   *   *

In the paper, William wrote: 'No less than fifteen well-known advertising agents have posted us their congratulations and the number of advertisers who have written ... and enclosing subscriptions have exceeded our most sanguine expectations.'

He even went on to commend a reader's suggestion that the depth of the magazine should be dropped from eleven inches to the more popular nine inches, even though, with extra paging, it would considerably increase costs. He drew back in the February issue and finally 'revamped' in June.

The tribute, though it came much later, that he most valued (and printed on the first editorial page) was from the Editor of the Boston *Fowler's Publicity*, a book of over 1,000 pages 'recognised as the greatest work on the subject ever published':

MY DEAR SIR – Specimen copy to hand. THE ADVERTISING WORLD

---

[12] It is only now, reading these letters for the first time, I realise that William's invariable 'signing off' to his children, small or large: 'Yours affec. WEB' or, after he became a peer, 'Yours affec. WEC', was not his own idiosyncrasy.

interests me. It is business through and through. It is not filled with theoretical bubbles, or talks about nothing against time. It is a genuine trade paper of the greatest of all trade stimulants, advertising. Accept my congratulations.

Sincerely yours,

NATHANIEL C. FOWLER, JNR.

It was a vindication of William's stated aims:

The main idea ... is to make the paper useful. Whether a man is spending £50 per annum or £50,000 we shall aim to be of service ... he would direct special attention to the Illustrated Review of the month's advertisements. The article deals critically with [those] that have appeared in the newspapers, the magazines and on the hoardings ... The interviews with Successful Advertisers and with Advertising Agents ... there is no part of an advertising appropriation unattended to ... the news of the month completely recorded ... thorough impartiality and the independence ... assist in relations with patrons.

I have searched the issues of *Progressive Advertising* and can find no mention of Mr E.S. Day being similarly honoured. That gentleman must have been singularly miffed at the Annual Bohemian Concert of the Fleet Street Club in the King's Hall at the Holborn Restaurant, which William recorded in a full-page report of Pickwickian amiability:

Half-way through the concert the Chairman rose and said that the proprietors of the ADVERTISING WORLD had sent a photographer to take a flash-light photo of the audience. It was, he said, quite a departure in the advertising line and reflected credit upon the enterprise of that advertising trade paper. The photo was successfully taken ... and is printed in full supplement [double-page spread] to this number.

Though only a quarter of the 250-strong audience were named, William was careful to record the presence of 'Mr E.S. Day', *tout court* without the addition of 'and party', which most others enjoyed. It took Mr Day two years to come again.

* * *

Advertisements for the January issue were not such a hard slog. William had secured repeat orders from fifteen of the original clients (though he, who insisted that they should 'change their copy as often as desired', would have had to write many of them himself). Additionally he secured a half-page of classified, and, on the editorial side, a column of answers to correspondents, submitting points of criticism as invited in the first issue.

Two months after Gomer's arrival the office was moved to Granville House, Arundel Street (off the Strand and nearly opposite St Clement Danes, now the RAF Church) where, on the top floor, there were three small rooms instead of one at the *Clarion*. The AW had been six months at the latter and the lease was doubtless breakable, though contra-advertising continued into the May issue.

William moved out of Mrs Norman's and the brothers took bachelor rooms in Butler Street, St John's Wood. According to Gomer, looking back in 1967, they lived excessively frugally. They cooked bangers on a gas ring in their rooms at night and took it in turns to have lunch 'at the ABC for 9½d., pudding 2d. extra'. I find the alternating lunch hard to believe. Surely the unlucky one could have afforded a 2d. bun, which had been William's sustenance at the *Investors Guardian*, or at least revictualled himself on the other's pudding. Perhaps, however, Gomer did not bring home much 'bacon' to start with, a little at sea in a strange city. Anyway, his boast was that the very first advertisement order he landed (for 5/- in respect of Kenyon's Undertaking Establishment) was not for the AW but for the Paddington Chapel *Journal*, supporting a Congregational Chapel, the daughter of whose chairman he was to marry.

Professionally, in order to seem an established firm, they were called Mr Berry and Mr Gomer respectively (this stuck for fifteen years). When 'Mr Gomer' was told he looked remarkably like Mr Berry, he replied easily, 'Oh, all Welshmen look alike.'

After a short interval they moved to Baker Street, making the walk to the office easier.

In June the change, ruminated on in the January issue, took place. The page area was cut down to make a much more professional-looking job, the size increased to sixty and then sixty-four pages, and a coloured cover added. This latter was a three-colour work (eventually eleven) which, I'm afraid, would have been sneered at by modern designers. It was of a very serious lady, apparently dressed in a curtain, with her forefinger on a globe, pointing at London. At least it was a great improvement on the simple black globe-circle with the title picked out on it in white. It evoked enormous enthusiasm in Merthyr.

Seymour wrote:

Dear Boys,
   Your [indecipherable] to hand we have only had time just to glance at it but it has simply stunned me. It is magnificent I can

hardly realise such a thing possible. It is the most beautiful pubn I have ever looked at. The Printing is grand and the designs of some of the adverts are wonderful. I need not tell you that we are more than proud of you and the go ahead propns. You have done better than we ever could have dreamt of and too much credit cannot be given you. The show of ads will frighten people. It is amazing. I have enjoyed reading the 1st 'En Passant'. Father and Mother are struck. Once more Hurrah.

In haste,

Yours affectionately,

S

Am glad to tell you am only £10 off my desired total. Things have turned up all right. S.

Seymour's enthusiasm was soon justified. In the anniversary, ninety-two-page issue of December 1902, William wrote in the paper that it was 'prosperous' and from May 1903 comes the first eyewitness accounts of the workings of Ewart, Seymour & Co. It is from Edward Hart, eighteen-year-old nephew of John Hart, the printer whose poster artists also designed the coloured covers:

It was Bill Berry who engaged me. We had dined overnight with my uncle [John Hart]. In his office the next morning Bill took me by the arm and said: 'Now we'll go along and see my young [now twenty] brother Gomer. You'll be working mostly with him'.

Bill, by the way, was shamelessly Bohemian in dress. A double-breasted blue serge suit hung from him like a sack. But Gomer, the 'outside' man, was a stickler for appearances.

My first impression of him is that he had his brother's blue-black hair, strong white teeth and the pallid complexion and lilting accent of the Rhondda Valley mining town they had so recently left to seek their fortunes in Fleet Street.

Gomer, to appear older, had begun to cultivate a moustache. He was faultlessly attired in the mode of AD 1903; black frock-coat, narrow white vest-slip, high stand-up collar, immaculate cuffs (detachable), neat tie-pin. His buttoned patent-leather boots, I learned later, cost 10s. 6d. He got them from an American chain store which polished them free at any of its branches. That was the price too, of his glossy topper – ironed free at any of the Cuthbertson branches. Gloves and umbrella, of course, and a blue melton overcoat with black velvet collar. Face values were more important then even than today.

I recall that as we entered his little sparsely furnished office he rose from behind the cheap table that served as desk, shook hands and offered his brand-new silver cigarette case. Both brothers were chain smokers. They favoured Gold Flake at 5d. for twenty.

My enrolment as the first advertising, circulation and editorial assistant to their first venture was marked by a little ceremony. Gomer ordered morning tea – brewed in the caretaker's attic at 3d. a pot. We shared it.

Then he introduced me to the staff – both of them. Arthur Brialt, a pimply adolescent from Clerkenwell, was book-keeper, invoice clerk and 'publisher'. He worked at a trestle table. On publication day he checked subscribers' lists, verified addresses on wrappers and stamped them. His colleague was a very junior, romantically-minded, frizzy-haired stenographer, Doris Tweedle. She came, by horse-drawn bus, from Cricklewood and pounded a green-ribboned Yost[13] typewriter till 6 pm. Our assistant was a nondescript office boy. At 25s. a week I was the staff's highest paid member. I had a room in West Kensington, handy for the old Earls Court Exhibition where a 10s. 6d. season ticket solved the nightly amusement problem. Bed and breakfast cost me 15s. a week. I lunched daily with my employers at an ABC shop.

Our duties were clearly defined. Bill used to sit at a small deal-topped table dashing off copy in tall sloping longhand on yellow flimsies, bought by the ream. He wrote at high speed and had a liking for crisp monosyllables and short 'pioneer punch' phrases: 'Much must still be done. This is why.'

Here, Hart was not as perceptive as in the rest of his account. William, in his early days, prided himself on the ability to write in different styles for different circumstances. Once, he told me, he submitted a job application in three different styles – or it may be he rang the changes as each application failed. On the AW I can detect four styles. It is the last of these that Hart is poking fun at. In the early issues, copy was sometimes short and there was an occasional 'end-column' signed EMESCO – I suspect a variation on the AW's telegraphic address EWESMO – an obviously hasty collection of small ideas and written in the style Hart takes off.

Then came the interview style. Though William announced in the preamble to an interview that he would 'submit him [the interviewee] to the rigours of an interview', his style was entirely to lead the subject

---

[13] There was frequent Yost advertising in the AW, no doubt 'contra'.

in the most general terms so that he could talk at length, rather than to be the cross-examiner. For instance: 'Do you agree, Mr Beville that, taken as a whole, British advertisers need to wake up?' or: 'What do you think, Mr Beville, about the alleged supineness of current business methods in the general management of a business?'

The 'En Passant' notes – anything between 200 and 600 words and occasionally much longer – were written in a measured but unponderous leader-writer's style.

Style, of course, emerges not only in the manner of writing but also in the attitude to the subject. Running through early issues of the AW one can detect at least three what would now be called campaigns, except that there is no reiteration nor even clear variations on a theme. Instead, a subject is only taken up a second and a third time when something new occurs to justify returning to it. The tone is firm but calm, and unrancorous.[14]

One such was a campaign for audited circulations – then quite rare – as instanced by Russell when he became the only man allowed to interview Moberley Bell, the Manager of *The Times*. 'The circulation of *The Times*, Mr Russell, is Mr Walter's [the proprietor] private business.'

During the Boer War, the circulation of Harmsworth's *Daily Mail* had advanced to the million mark and in 1902, just at the war's end, had increased its advertising rate by 50 per cent, from 30/- to 45/- a single column inch. All London newspaper circulations naturally dropped after the war but the *Mail*, which had led the way with published certificates, issued no more. In June 1903, William wrote a mild 'En Passant' calling attention to the lapse. There was no comment next month but an (advertising) agent was allowed a prominent letter, which must have been damaging. The agent alleged the circulation had dropped to 650,000 and added: 'The old verve, audacity, energy and brilliant word-pictures and other effects in picturesque journalism ... have disappeared.'

In August there was a second 'En Passant' calling attention to two more agents' letters and saying that the *Mail* had been asked to reply but had not. Only at the end of a further 'En Passant' in September was William able to announce a 'stop-press' *Mail* Certificate of 836,231 for seven months with the paper's lame addition 'in spite of the dearth of news calculated to arouse popular excitement'.

---

[14] Though he admired Barnes, the first great Editor of *The Times*, he deplored his contemptuous feelings for his readers, which earned *The Times* the nickname 'The Thunderer': 'John Bull, whose understanding is rather sluggish ... requires a strong stimulus ... he dozes composedly over his prejudices which his conceit calls opinions; and you must fire ten-pounders at his densely impacted intellect before you can make it comprehend your meaning ...'.

William concluded:

With all modesty we think we can safely say that the management of the *Daily Mail* in issuing this certificate have been influenced in no small degree by the correspondence and comments which have appeared in the *Advertising World* as the organ of British advertisers.

The campaign almost came to a stop in October as yet another advertising agent commented that the published figure was better than expected but that the advertising rate was still high after a '130,000 drop in circulation'. William seemed to close it with a nice note commending the *Mail* for 'an eminently straightforward statement: an example to other newspapers'.

But he hadn't quite finished with Harmsworth. In November he called attention to 'the certificated circulation of the *Daily Express*' (started by C. Arthur Pearson in 1900) showing a rapid rise to 342,497 (up 100,000 in a year), exploding the *Mail* claim to be five times any competition. He added:

We ventured to predict a year ago that the *Daily Express* would soon, at the rate of progress it was making, be an exceedingly formidable opponent to the *Daily Mail*, and it looks very much as if that prediction is about to be realised.

Harmsworth himself attempted to ignore the criticism. At the annual meeting of the Amalgamated Press (his magazines, the first of which had been *Answers to Correspondents*) in January, he made a self-righteous speech attacking other people's unpublished circulations: 'We know what might have been a very valuable medium in 1903 may be of very little value in 1904' (a not too distant parallel with the condition of the *Mail*). He went on to explain that his own specialist director was a much better judge of the worth of papers to advertise in than the agents who only went where they got the highest commissions and were fit only to arrange the design work.

William's reply to all this was surprisingly mild. He made no mention of the *Mail* controversy and only rapped Harmsworth's knuckles for his attack on the agents. He ended:

Mr Harmsworth's encomiums on publicity should certainly be widely circulated, for they may do much to encourage the young advertiser to persevere, and the old advertiser to rigorously overhaul his organisation and arrangement.

The fourth style is shown in his monthly critiques of individual advertisements. I give an example on pp. 40–1. But after letting himself go, he concluded one with:

> So endeth our monthly essay. We do not hope in these articles to create any very different opinions, and give our ideas in all humility. The subject of advertising is one which the more it is considered makes one say, as Newton did about knowledge in general, that we feel like children picking up pebbles on the beach.

*　　*　　*

Back at the office, Hart continues his account:

> Gomer and I went out after ads. at £6 a page [unchanged since the 1901 launch] pro rata, and annual subs (6s. post-free) [also unchanged] usually pre-paid out of petty cash. We presented engraved cards and carried specimen copies of the current issue, artfully concealed. The Gomer overcoat had an inner pocket to hide the magazine. He advised me to have my coat similarly modified, 'It keeps the specimen clean and flat,' he explained, 'and doesn't give us away as canvassers when we go into an office.'
>
> Gomer and I took turns at canvassing the provinces. My tours were extended because Bill did not hold with unnecessary return journeys to London: a waste of time. Between attempts to sell space and chase subs I wrote about posters which graced and disgraced the hoardings and reported on the inner workings and mail-order systems of national advertisers, who usually ordered a few hundred copies.
>
> All this meant dull weekends in cheap commercial hotels of industrial towns, with a nightly report to be posted to both brothers – 'even if it means late-fees'. My expense accounts were closely scrutinised. Never could I have got away with an unvouchable halfpenny. Once I took a four-wheeled cab. That was on a foul day in Manchester. 'Sheer profligacy!' Bill called it. Then he threw back his head and roared with laughter, in which Gomer joined.
>
> As finances improved we forsook the ABC for a new restaurant near the East Strand Post Office – the Colonade – which was becoming a rendezvous for advertising agents and national newspaper advertisement managers.
>
> Among its habitués, I recall Jack Akerman, Murray Allison and Sir George Newnes' young nephew Ashby Goodall – all of the Spottiswoode Agency; advertisement managers Wareham Smith (*Daily Mail*), George Whetton (*Daily Express*), Harold Durant (*Daily Mirror*), George Hussey (*Daily Chronicle*), Harry Simonis (*Morning*

Leader), Jack Salt, (*T.P.'s Weekly*), S.H. Benson; Buckie Taylor of Lyons' and many other 'useful' contacts.

After a 1s.6d. lunch Bill and Gomer would play 100-up in the billiard room of the Howard Hotel, Norfolk Street, giving me a cup of black coffee and the odd cigarette as marker's fee. Sometimes they challenged Goodall and me to a foursome which they always won. They loved billiards second to rugger and third to hard work.

It was, I now realised, an unusually happy and intensely human little office, with brotherly affection and mutual goodwill as the mainspring. I know of no men more devoted to each other or better loved by their staff than were these two young bachelors.

In the second half of 1904 it was evident that the AW was taking off. In September the size had been increased to eighty pages and had been maintained at that figure until the Christmas issue, which was 128 pages. The future of the paper was clearly set fair as 1905 was to prove. Just at that time a family crisis arose.

Seymour, who had been poorly for some months, was diagnosed as suffering from tuberculosis. His doctor declared that there was nothing for it but a Swiss sanatorium from which, so local legend ran, few returned. When William heard the news, he descended on Merthyr and persuaded his parents that he would do the doctoring. Fresh air, good food, exercise and regular habits were the secret of long life. He would himself take Seymour to a bracing climate and impose his own health regime on him, whether he liked it or not. And that is what he did.

Engaging an acting editor for the AW (J.R. Charter,[15] who stayed until its sale in 1909) he took a large double room at the Tregenna Castle Hotel at St Ives, on the northern tip of Cornwall. His first step was to have all the windows taken out and, to keep the cold night air at bay – it was a cold winter – bought a paraffin stove. Because of Seymour's condition they had meals before the other residents, who remained unmollified since the public rooms were made almost uninhabitable by the bitter draughts and the smell of the stove. By day Seymour was made to play golf on the local nine-hole course, rain or shine. At meal times, William, according to a friend's account, fed him 'cream and porridge and meat and cream and soup and fish and cream and pudding and cheese and cream and cream and cream and cream'. Long after, when someone harked back to 'that time when William saved your life', Seymour retorted it was the time 'when Bill took me down to Cornwall and fed me so much cream he ruined my liver'.

---

[15] Charter, a year older than William, had trained on Newnes' magazines and had been London Editor of the *Belfast Newsletter*.

Advertisements under the Searchlight.

Article No. 2.

It seems to me that in these monthly dissertations on the merits and demerits of particular advertisements, a scale of point would prove useful, for while it is impossible to gauge the value of an appeal to the public by any rule of thumb and personal predilection must play the strongest part in any criticism or attempted analysis of an advertiser's efforts, there are certain simple and definite questions which the critic or judge may ask himself, and to each of which he can attach a certain relative value. The first consideration in an advertisement is—will it advertise ? It is superfluous to remark in this connection that the majority of public announcements merely fill space. This power of attracting attention let us call Noticeability. Out of a possible 100 points it deserves a full 35. Secondly, will the advertisement create a demand for the article advertised, and establish sympathetic relations between the advertiser and advertisee. This power I shall labour Persuasiveness, and allot another 35 points for, as I am of opinion it is of equal importance that an advertisement should influence (*vide* the derivations of the word : *ad-vertere*), as that it should excite notice. Lastly, has to be considered whether it achieves its purpose in the most effective way, which quality we may label Workmanship, and award 30 points for. There are, of course, many features to be found in advertisements, but all of them, I think, are either supplementary to or comprised in one or other of the above headings. It is also true that at various stages of an article's career different styles of advertising are necessary, but in considering any advertisement, no matter what other points it may have there, questions cannot be disregarded :—

1. Does it attract attention ?
2. Is it profitable ?
3. Is it well turned out ?

The second question hinges very much on the first, whilst the first and third are independent, for an advertisement to be profitable generally has to be both noticeable and workmanlike, whilst we may have an artistic advertisement which does not attract attention, and which is therefore unprofitable, or we may have an advertisement which attracts attention but to an irritating degree, or with a repellant design, and is therefore unprofitable.

Now to the subject of our study. This advertisement of Calvert's Carbolic Ointment is well worth analysis, despite certain flagrant violations of the fundamental principles of good advertising, for many reasons. It shows how a business man may wander blindfolded in the fields of publicity with only vague instinct as his director ; it shows how he may be groping in the right direction, stumbling feebly on in the right path, but still stumbling, with many splashes into puddles and falls into ditches, ultimately arriving at his journey's end ; true, but with what difficulty, how painfully tortuous his progress !

This advertisement of Calvert's Carbolic Ointment shows to a singular degree how the mind of the advertiser can, when composing a " call," become subordinate to his feelings ; how like a man unaccustomed to public speaking, and brought upon his legs before an audience, he can flounder and wobble from one good argument to another, while taking the fullest advantage of none. This advertisement attracts attention. So does a drunken man, and both are equally forcible and equally feeble. This advertisement is a profitable advertisement. " Then," says the advertiser, " it is a good advertisement, for I only advertise to make money." But it is only comparatively profitable. It is not a good advertisement, for not a single point could be given to it on the score of workmanship, and it is only comparatively profitable, for greater chances, I venture to say, lie hidden somewhere near that young woman, the boy, and the hoarding, than the advertiser seems to be aware of. Will someone tell me why do advertisers content themselves with fourth-rate designs, whilst insisting on first-class and therefore most expensive media. Is it with some asinine idea of saving on the former the cost of the latter? Whatever the reason, I fear the practice will continue

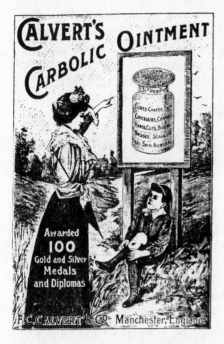

despite what may be said against it, and that it will remain one of the mysteries of our business life and human weaknesses. Not that the design under consideration deserves better treatment than it has received. Let us *look* at it. It does not call for examination. Why is this melo-dramatic young lady pointing to this ridiculous signboard, and cuddling her parasol, instead of thoughtfully bending down, tenderly applying some of that marvellous ointment to the bruise on the poor boy's leg, and binding it up with her pocket-handkerchief?

In the name of kindness and common-sense does she woodenly and uselessly point to the virtues of Calvert's Carbolic

without demonstrating them? Since she thinks so well of it, how comes it she does not carry a small tin of it about with her for possible emergencies? Of what avail is it? What satisfaction is to the boy to have something pointed out to him when his shin is tingling with pain, so acute that he is obliged to sit and pull down his stocking to see the extent of his injuries. Let us overlook the obvious defect in the draughtsmanship in making one of the young lady's arms just as long when fully extended as the other is from shoulder-blade to elbow joint. Let us disregard the distracting notice on the young lady's dress which for the moment makes us think that either she or her costume has been awarded 100 gold and silver medals and diplomas, and let us listen to the conversation, evidently, *i.e.,* according to the design before us, going on between these two. Put the following words underneath the design, and see if in any one particular the dialogue does not fit it?

Young Woman: Go home to thy mother and tell her to apply Calvert's Carbolic ointment to that bruise.

Boy: It's a ten mile walk from here.

Young Woman: See, it is advertised on yonder hoarding just behind thee.

Boy: It's rude to point, besides that won't heal my cut.

Now, how did the boy get that cut? Did the other boy, who perhaps kicked him on the shin, run away as soon as the young woman came in sight, and why is such a senseless young woman out without her keeper? How is that hoarding going to stand up without supports? Why are there no creases in the poster, presumably pasted upon it and over its joints? How long really are the young woman's legs? Will the swallows ever come back again? These are things this advertisement makes you think about. But it is a question if thinking about them helps the purpose of the advertisement. Much more could be said about this most uncommon creation, but enough is as good as a gorge.

A New Calendar.

Our readers will have noticed in our advertising columns that Messrs. Hart and Co. are sending a unique calendar to any who care to send for it. It is quite up to the usual class of work done by this firm, and we would recommend those who have not already sent to do so.

After their first, natural unpopularity, William became friendly with a man of about sixty, born in Dublin, of independent means, Thomas Corns, his much younger wife Agnes, and their nineteen-year-old daughter Phyllis. They were wintering there, but Corns was rather bored without male company. He liked talking to the brothers about business and, when Seymour had been consigned to an early bed, playing billiards after dinner.

After about six weeks, Seymour was pronounced cured and the rest of what had now become a party returned to London. There, William was asked to dinner at the Corns' house at 2 Bolton Street, Piccadilly, where he saw a photograph of the elder daughter, Molly, on the piano which, he was told, she was the only one of the family who could play.

Molly was at this time twenty-one and had for long been fretting for want of an education. She had had a governess, had been taught drawing (she drew rather well), music, spoke French after a year with an Orléans family, read voraciously, but was denied all her pleas for something more solid. She had whiled away some of her time by taking up hockey seriously. At seventeen she was Honorary Secretary of the Worthing Ladies Hockey Club, with thirty members, and on one occasion played for England.[16]

Suddenly, a year earlier, her mother's great-aunt had died and left her a £500 legacy. Ignoring her parents' opposition, she joined another girl, an American, and together with the girl's mother as chaperone, took ship for a year at Radcliffe Women's College, now part of Harvard University, where she lived in lodgings at Cambridge, a suburb of Boston.

Soon after William's first visit to Bolton Street, Molly – or the Duchess as her father always called her – returned. William and Molly took an immediate fancy to each other and in quite a short time they were engaged. Taking her out to lunch at the Savoy, seeking to impress her as a man-about-town, he was taken down a peg when she sent the wine back, saying it was corked. If she had sent a second back, he was afraid he couldn't have paid.

The style of the wedding presented a problem to my mother. Her reading had included Theosophy; she had attended lectures at the

---

[16] This was a claim she made late in life when suffering from arthritis in both knees. She revealed her achievement for the first time then, saying to a friend as she sank into a wheelchair: 'Who, seeing me now, would think I had played hockey for England?' There is no record in the *Hockey Field* of her playing other than scoring goals for Worthing but Miss T. Morris, Secretary of the All England Women's Hockey Association, wrote to me: 'In those days teams may well have played although not on the official list for the year.' In the *Hockey Field* there are only eleven players shown for the whole of each year.

Queen's Hall by Mrs Annie Besant, the President of the Theosophical Society, and, though never, so far as I can establish, a member, came under her influence.

The objectives of Theosophy were conventional enough by modern standards: 'A nucleus of the universal brotherhood of humanity, without any distinction of race, creed, sex or colour, to encourage the study of comparative religion, philosophy and science, and to investigate the unexplained laws of nature and the powers latent in man.' It was Mrs Besant's interpretation of them which caused schisms.

Mrs Besant had been, by turns, married at seventeen to a dour Anglican clergyman, a collaborator with Charles Bradlaugh of the atheist Secular Society, a Malthusian, a Fabian Socialist, under the influence of Bernard Shaw, and finally 'mesmerised by the throbbing voice and compelling eyes' of the Russian Mme Blavatsky, founder of the Society. Reading her 'lectures' and studying photographs of her meetings, one can understand a little the effect on unsophisticated audiences of her stunning evangelical oratory, obviously extemporary and drawing increasing strength from the enthusiasm of her listeners.

The trouble with her creed was that it was hierarchical. All wisdom, she announced, had come to this planet from 'the Lords of Venus', whence it had been disseminated to Priests/Kings who, in time, devolved it to authoritarian churches and governments. But devolution could go no further, since 'mankind' (materialistically, the masses) 'does not change much'. Hence, among Christian churches, Greek Orthodox and Roman Catholic were in the direct line but most Protestant sects and democratic governments were not.

I do not know how literally my mother took Mrs Besant's teaching, but certainly it had an effect on her. All her days she was interested in the idea of life on another plane, half believed in transubstantiation and was sure she was psychic. She was a good deal of a rebel,[17] out of tune with the ceremonial trappings of organised religion, possibly heretical or at best hypocritical. When it came to the form of the wedding she insisted on a registry office, where priestly intermediaries did not come between the man, the woman and the deity.

Family reaction to a registry office wedding was hostile. My mother was hurt that her rich father,[18] whose favourite daughter she was, only gave her £5 as a wedding present and did not attend. Nor did William's

[17] When I was a teenager, my father used sometimes to call out 'Up the Rebels' in a jocular manner, usually when playing family bridge. At the time I thought it was some obscure Irish allusion. Now I think he may have been teasing my mother and that it was a private joke between them.

[18] When he died in 1915 he left £60,000 (some £1,400,000 today). By a will of 1896 he left everything to his widow.

parents. The only witnesses were my mother's mother and her sister. This did not prevent cordial relations. Agnes Corns had a dog called Spot. William was soon able to cry 'Spot barred' (a billiards term, which amused Corns) whenever his mother-in-law began one of her interminable anecdotes about the animal.

But it was not until eighteen months later that a full Anglican wedding took place at Christ Church, Down Street. Both families turned out in force, Seymour was best man, and the church register was signed as if the first ceremony had never taken place.

My mother never deviated from the tenets of Christianity, but for some years neither she nor William 'went to church'. It was not until 1921, when they moved to a house near Chertsey where she had long conversations with the parish priest, the 'saintly and cultured Canon Tringham', that she returned to the fold of the Church of England. Thereafter both of them went to village services regularly for the rest of their lives, and, as Winston Churchill said of his own marriage at about the same time, lived happily ever after.

CHAPTER FOUR

Friends, *Health & Strength, Tribune*

I CAN FIND no evidence that William ever relaxed in mixed company before his marriage, just as he and Seymour never took any girls to the Merthyr balls. All his friends were from the advertising, printing or publishing trade, though his favourite evening was to tour the billiard halls with an amateur champion, named Roberts, who played with a walking stick – to which a tip had been added. He would have met a wider circle at the Sphinx Club, of which he was a founder member in 1904 (there were thirteen of them). This, a model of the New York Sphinx Club (1896), was a 'society or club to assist in the evolution of the advertising profession and to constitute a medium for the personal exchange of ideas and experience' (advocated in the AW two years earlier). This met monthly, in white tie and tails, at the Hotel Cecil (now the site of Shell-Mex on the Embankment). Its membership, at first fifty, then a hundred, was of much more than advertising agents. It included big advertisers (like W.H. Lever – later Lord Leverhulme of Unilever – and A.W. Gamage); proprietors (like C. Arthur Pearson and Sir Alfred Harmsworth – now a baronet – and his MP brother, Leicester); editors (like Robert Donald (*Daily Chronicle*) and Kennedy Jones, but not the 'quality' editors); hoarding owners, block-makers, and half a dozen members of the Royal Academy, though Burne-Jones and Alma-Tadema asked to be excused on the grounds of age and only Tenniel refused. Guests included Marshall Hall and Max Beerbohm.

Each month a special topic was chosen for debate and reported verbatim in the AW. The speeches still read well. I like very much the ready answer given by an American, Ralston Balch (of Scott & Bowne, owners of Scott's Emulsion), later one of the most requested after-dinner speakers in London, to the difference between publicity and advertising:

Publicity is the Art, or Accident, by which the attention of people is focused on any Person or Thing to good or no advantage.

Advertising is the Art, or Purpose, by which we focus the attention of people with such force as to impel them to part with money.

Each speech, however short, was reported in full, except that of Mr

W.E. Berry, which was 'subbed down' by him to the maddening, 'After Mr W.E. Berry had spoken ...'.

At the founding meeting, William sat next to Herbert Morgan. I expect that he already knew him but his friendship with him was to last the whole of his life. Morgan, a year younger than William, the son of a Welsh clergyman, had spent his teens in America and came back bubbling with ideas. He went on bubbling until he died at the age of seventy-one. At his death in 1951 he was described in the *Sunday Times* as:

> that rare spirit, the business man whose love of artistry was never a veneer, but a sincere and ardent passion. He was equally at home conferring with statesmen and leading lights of commerce as he was with theatrical and music hall celebrities. He loved parties and was an ideal host, prodigal almost in his hospitality.
>
> Business and official connections and hobbies were alike incongruously extensive. They ranged from printing, publicity and photography to potato crisps and coffee; from the War Office and the Ministry of Munitions to Malvern College and the Three Arts Club; from industrial design to hospital management; from exceptional skill in punting to golf.[1]

He was also something of a snob. He once said that the way to get on was to have one's name connected with a 'good charity'. His enemies said that he had made an early start by insinuating himself into a group standing with royalty and then using the photograph to advertise his connections.

Morgan first made his mark in advertising in Spottiswoode's Advertising Agency, where he set up a five-man team of designers and copywriters. In February 1905 his whole team was headhunted by Charles Hornby, grandfather of Sir Simon Hornby and present Chairman, and the man who diversified W.H. Smith from their original business of London newspaper wholesaling and railway station retailers. There he set up a 'studio', showing original designs and examples with the slogan, 'Not only advice but ideas while you wait.' This was first advertised under his name for Spottiswoode's in the AW and then repeated almost word for word on behalf of W.H. Smith. He was given the then high salary of £1,000, plus $2\frac{1}{2}$ per cent commission on turnover over £10,000, as Controller of Printing. One of his first contracts was

---

[1] According to the AW, Morgan's golf handicap was six in 1905, William's eighteen, Gomer and Allison (see below) twenty.

for the AW (Hart having retired). The new sophistication of the covers was immediately obvious.

As the W.H. Smith house magazine remarked of him a few years later: 'Morgan ... took [the opportunity] with such purpose that his influence was felt in every printing shop in England ... his ingenuity lay in linking up the renaissance ... in decorative art with the needs of commerce ... His personality was stamped on the whole of constructive printing. His was logical idealism.' Even the historian of W.H. Smith, Professor Charles Wilson, who did not approve of him, admitted, 'Morgan powerfully shaped an industry – advertising – still devoid of tradition, still in plastic condition.'

All his life, Morgan, too, was the author of phrases that stuck. Some of them survive. He was the inventor of the phrase, 'Business as Usual' in 1914 when the war was expected to be won by Christmas. He put the 'Mac' in Macfisheries when Lord Leverhulme bought the 700-square-mile island of Lewis in the Outer Hebrides. He organised for Leverhulme his 400 shops, including one in Bond Street where: 'a luxury shop ... resembled more an aquarium than a fish-shop; the fish were displayed in tiers of artificially cooled glass containers, behind an entrance-front as splendidly embellished as the baths of Caracalla'.

On leaving the board of Lever Brothers after Leverhulme's death, Morgan coined the word 'crisps' for Smith's Potato Crisps, a company of which he became Chairman. He inspired the Selfridge's Information Bureau and, when it failed to re-open after the Second World War, persuaded William to start one at *The Daily Telegraph*. He organised the first antiques fair (though the idea originally came from Sydney Carroll) and was the first to suggest the Festival of Britain, 100 years after Prince Albert's Crystal Palace Exhibition.

Albeit, though he was the first President of the Society of Industrial Artists and Designers, to the artist he was basically a businessman and to the businessman basically an artist. He liked spending money socially and he never kept much of it. Sometimes his refrain was plaintive: 'I *am* a businessman, aren't I?' But he could not keep up the maintenance of his wife, with whom he split soon after marriage and she, like so many of William's acquaintances, kept writing to him of her troubles.

Underneath, Morgan was a lonely man who would often do something he disliked for the sake of company. He was an appalling sailor but often went on William's yacht. On one occasion, when William and Molly were setting off on a mad weekend to find the last of their favourite Perriet Jouet 1911 at the Tregenna Castle Hotel, St Ives, Cornwall – there were four half-bottles, all flat – Morgan enquired of the weather forecast on Friday night and, hearing the worst, said to the steward, 'Barker, I'm going to bed now. Call me with a peach on Monday morning.'

But he was always a stimulating companion, immensely observant and with a fresh viewpoint on everything.

Eileen Hunter, the daughter of Edward Hunter, another long-standing friend, sums up his attitude perfectly:

> Herbert Morgan [was one] whose financial resources were something of a mystery most of all to himself, but whose gregarious geniality won him a permanent place in the group surrounding the Berry brothers. He was dark, rubicund, hospitable, and loved to gather a genial company around him – in fact could not bear to be alone. He was chairman of numerous concerns and besides was well-read and entertaining. We got on agreeably from the start and he never made me feel as a child that my precocious sorties into adult conversation were misplaced or pert, and I expanded in the warm climate of his temperament like a plant in a well-heated greenhouse.
>
> His craving for perpetual company did not, however, lead him to be undiscriminating – he much preferred the right people; and once when I was grown-up and dining at the Berkeley with him, he sent first, not for the menu, but for the list of those who had booked tables, and running his eyes rapidly down the list, a long one, exclaimed indignantly to the head waiter, 'But there's no one coming here tonight – no one at all!' After which he hurried me through an excellent dinner, calling on me to help him despatch the bottle of champagne so rapidly that I felt blown up to twice my size, and bustled me to another restaurant where an Austrian in *Lederhosen* with enormous knees and chubby buttocks scraped away on a schmalzy violin. Here again however the assembled faces lacked significance and it was not until the early summer dawn that we started up in the dusky coverts of the old Four Hundred a score or so of the elite, the eminent and indisputably well known.

Another friendship which was to last all their joint lives was Edward Hunter, five years older than William. Alone of his friends in the early years, Hunter came of an affluent, middle-class background and had been to Rugby. After being apprenticed to a firm of printers, at the age of twenty-four he set up his own firm of process engravers in 1898 on £500 borrowed from his father, with whom he still lived in a stylish house at Westbourne Terrace, Bayswater. From this acorn grew the oak of Sun Printers. While throughout their whole careers he was intimate with William and participated in some of his deals, he had odd streaks of secretiveness. William was much miffed, not so much commercially as personally, when Hunter decided to retire and, without a word, sold the *Sun* to another firm when it would have fitted very well into William's Amalgamated Press.

His character is described by his daughter, who felt for him as she titled her biography of him – *Profound Attachment*:

My father's attitude towards his own success was curious, for although he was proud of his achievements, he had a nervous fear of ostentation: I was implored not to reveal at my day school that we had three cars. He would become plunged in gloom at a restaurant when faced with a bill he could well afford, and would dilate on the pleasures of life of frugal toil, or gloomily opine in the midst of a rich repast that we should all feel better had we dined on bread and water. On more than one social occasion he pointed out his four daughters with a flourish and exclaimed, not as the mother of the Gracchi did 'These are my jewels!', but 'Why I am poor!'

I think this ambivalent attitude towards the fortune he so brilliantly and energetically accumulated was a positive dislike of being considered wealthy and a fundamental timidity that made him averse to mixing with the kind of people whose company he could afford, but whose way of life intimidated him. Even with the man who was his great friend, William Berry, with whom he embarked on many business ventures, he kept the place he had assigned himself, that of the man in the background who sailed in the big yachts but did not own one, who was in on the big deals, but never drew attention to the fact and who sedulously avoided most of the trappings of the rich ...

Apart from mutual benefits of their many common business interests, William had the most bracing and tonic effect on my father, chaffing him out of his pessimism, establishing as a permanent joke between them my father's Puritan strictures, and exposing good-naturedly the inaccuracy of his pose as a humble creature of small significance – a pose which, I think, he found useful at times as a screen and cover for not at all small or insignificant activities.

Gomer Berry ... was entirely different in appearance and character from him, being, I judged, of a more retiring nature but capable of sudden outbursts of gaiety and *bonhomie* which were startling by contrast with his habitual air of nervous diffidence. He lacked his brother's easy confidence, and when they split up their newspaper interests ... I thought the difference in their personalities became more marked. William always seemed to know exactly who he was and where he was whereas Gomer appeared, sometimes, to be groping for a true identity and to be confused by the welter of alternatives with which his wealth and power presented him ...

[My father's] puritanical attitude towards wealth and high living, his not always quite sincere stressing of his own unimportance, and his elaborate pessimism beneath which, I felt, lay a life-long craving for reassurance.

As he grew older, he more than once, when discussing over dinner with William the plans for a delectable cruise, would refuse to go on account of his great age, stating glumly that should he expire during the voyage a burial at sea would be inconvenient and disconcerting for everyone on board. These points being readily conceded, he would sit back convinced the matter was settled, and beneath the continuing flow of cheerful chatter would brood on the sadness of being a 'back number' ashore, while his friends sailed the seas having a far better time without him. But although William had nodded understandingly over the hock and claret there would come a brisk change of tone with the brandy and cigars, when my father would find he had been manoeuvred with much good-humoured laughter into agreeing that if a coffin were taken along – just in case – and a Union Jack for, as William would add slyly, 'We must send you off in style', he would do what at heart he really wanted and accompany them as usual.

A third friend of this time was an Australian, Jim (Murray) Allison. His father was the Manager of His Majesty's Theatre in Sydney. After sheep shearing, he was studying to be an artist, when Thomas Russell came visiting. At Russell's suggestion Allison came to London, but was at first unable to find any post. In his own account of it, he earned a precarious living by drawing the menus for a feeding house in the Euston Road. Once, he claimed, he did himself out of a meal 'by doing a menu so good that it lasted for two days'.

Morgan's departure from Spottiswoode's was Allison's opportunity. (Whether this was at William's suggestion I do not know; Allison later recorded that one of his early calls was on him). His rise was meteoric. At first he was paid £3 a week plus commission, but so much of the business was his that the commission was commuted for shares. The second time this happened Allison found himself the second-largest shareholder and, as Spottiswoode himself did little, he as good as became, with Goodall, head of the firm.

He was soon writing regularly for the AW. Round about this time he was also publicity agent for Sandow, the 'strong man'. With humorous, pale blue eyes, he was a man of the greatest vitality. His advertising maxim was, like himself, 'bright and breezy'. When Thomas Russell resigned from *The Times* as Advertising Manager following Harmsworth's takeover in 1908, Allison succeeded him. There he suggested the *Daily Mail* Ideal Home Exhibition to his opposite number – it has been a money-spinner to this day.

In 1924, when Allied Newspapers was formed, he became Advertising Director for the whole group, though in later years he was often the worse for drink and, Gomer told me, had to be kept out of sight from William. By this time, Gomer thought, the fire had gone out of him and the only major contribution he made was to 'find' George Simon in Cardiff to be Advertisement Manager of the *Daily Telegraph*, later Managing Director.

After joining *The Times* Allison married an extremely pretty girl who had briefly been an actress. They bought a period house at Runnymede.

Eileen Hunter puts the flesh on the bones again:

He was the pet and *infant terrible* of everyone. He possessed an adorable wife called Elsie whose dark sweet voice flowed like soothing honey over his escapades and misdemeanours. 'Yes, Jimmie dear – no, Jimmie darling ...' I do not remember him so well, but I shall never forget Elsie, so pretty with her infectious laugh and readiness to love the whole world if it would allow her. She and Jim once rented our house in Cresswell Gardens for a couple of months and after our return I heard my father, half laughing, half shocked, relating to Herbert Morgan that the bathroom floor had been left covered with violet talcum powder, and that his modest supply of port had vanished, Jim having explained engagingly that he had thought the contents of the cellar were included in the rent.

I am convinced that had it been anyone other than Jim who had treated him in this way, a grave view indeed would have been taken, but Jim's vagaries and assumptions of generosity in my father and his friends were seldom disappointed, for they generally gladly traded their usual conceptions of correct behaviour for the indulgent pleasure of pardoning his gay effrontery.

These were three of those who attended William's bachelor party. One of them must have drawn the portrait *Goodbye Bill Berry Bachelor* (see illustrations). Others were Wareham Smith, Cockney Advertising Manager of the *Daily Mail*; William Wallace, owner of Carlton Studio Advertising Agents; Joe Thorp, Morgan's copywriter and, according to

Smith, a 'cultured man' of great volubility; H. Powell Rees,[2] lately London Manager of an American house who had just set up his own agency; Goodall,[3] Carroll,[4] and, of course, Gomer.

*   *   *

Following his marriage and the confirmation of the acting editor as editor of the AW, I get the feeling that the head of steam in the AW became a little lower. Advertising grew so that editorial grew accordingly. But the paper no longer seems to have quite the originality and freshness of the early numbers. There are fewer provocative 'En Passants' and the paper seems to be conducted more according to a formula. I deduce that marriage was a spur to ambition and William realised, with the AW spinning on, he must now seek further publishing opportunities.

Meanwhile, early in 1906, he made his first visit to America, accompanied by Molly, now heavily pregnant. There he put Molly in a New York hotel and started on a tour which was to include, besides New York, Montreal, Philadelphia, Chicago and San Francisco.

No sooner had he set off than he was recalled to New York, where Molly had given birth to a daughter, Mary, one month premature, on 4 March. The birth was so sudden that the baby had to be delivered by hotel staff before the gynaecologist Molly had engaged could arrive. I do not know whether William took Molly and the baby on his resumed trip; but in any case he was due in San Francisco on 18 April.

Let Hart take up the tale again from the Ewart Seymour office:

We had his itinerary. He was to be in San Francisco on the day of the devastating earthquake. Ignorant of his last-minute change of plans we feared the worst. No work was even attempted that morning as the early evening editions splashed further grim details. Twice Gomer sent out for more cigarettes and feverishly smoked mine while the boy dawdled. We exchanged desultory conversation. Lunch-time came and went. None of us left the office. We were all in this – even the office boy. Then the cable arrived. The Tweedle, white and trembling, brought it first to me.

'Hadn't you better open it and break it gently to Mr Gomer?' she suggested. 'Take it straight in to him', I told her. 'Whatever it is he had better read it alone. Just hand it to him and nip out.'

---

[2] Rees's partner, McLeod Moore, was killed in the First World War. William and friends paid his debts and endowed his wife and daughter. After the Second World War, William took Rees's son on as his confidential secretary.

[3] Five years later Goodall was killed in a motorcycle accident.

[4] William had lately become godfather to Carroll's son.

As she hurried back from his room, diplomatically closing the door behind her, we heard a strange sound – half sob, half excited yell. A moment later Gomer rushed out to me – shaking, incoherent and waving the message.

'Bill's safe!' he kept repeating. 'He's safe, Hart: he's safe! He didn't go! Look: read this!' The cable was typically laconic: four words: 'Ewesmo London Safe Bill'. I forget where it was handed in.

Gomer, in those days devoutly religious, almost dragged me back to his room. With tears streaming down his cheeks he dropped to his knees on the threadbare carpet, raised his arms and offered a prayer of thanksgiving, breaking occasionally into his native Welsh. I joined him ... Then, after making a few reassuring phone calls, he took me out to lunch.

* * *

The new venture which William had had his eye on for some time was a monthly magazine *Health & Strength*, a periodical for physical culture, then a newish idea, following the Admiralty's appointment of a PT adviser in 1900. As early as September 1902, the American letter in the AW had noted the great success of such US magazines – one for men and one for women. 'We gather from an advertisement in the *Advertising World* that physical culture has also caught on pretty extensively in Britain.' Certainly, *Health & Strength* advertised regularly in the AW and William wrote a number of approving notes. In 1902 it had boasted a circulation of 60,000 with a sixty-four-page paper. By August 1904 it had had sunk to 43,000 and was sold to a new owner, whose first step was to remove the ban on advertisements for patent medicines, drink and tobacco.

Hereabouts was the borderline between austere uplift on one side and 'the body beautiful', with its 'page three' posters and ambiguous personal advertisements, on the other. (It was a borderline which Sydney Carroll did overstep when he bought the paper in 1920.)

William must have been negotiating to buy *Health & Strength* for some time before he left for America, but control did not pass until a fortnight or so later – 12 March 1906 – when the bank account for the new *Health & Strength* company was registered in the names of Gomer and Sydney Carroll.

In the chair William found another Welshman, E. Stewart Smith, who had been his Managing Director on the *Merthyr Times* and was a fellow member, with Seymour, of the Merthyr Excelsior Debating Society. William did not take over the editorship himself (he still based himself in the AW office), but his hand is immediately evident in the editorials expounding the paper's general attitude and in the numerous 'stunts' conducted.

The magazine was defined as 'The National Organ of Physical Fitness, devoted to subjects appertaining to Health, Strength, Vitality, Muscular Development, Food, Clothing and the General Care of the Body'. A famous example was chosen to illustrate the message:

> Eighty per cent of the ailments people suffer from are the direct outcome of rank stupidity ... The case of Mr Chamberlain is a striking example. For years Mr Chamberlain was cited as an instance of what a man could do without exercise of any kind. During all the stress and strain of the Boer War Mr Chamberlain's only exercise was the absolutely necessary walk within the walls of Government Buildings. His pitiful and absolute physical collapse is a matter of history ... Mr Gladstone was hale and vigorous to the end of his days ... *Health & Strength* is for everyone who believes in being 'fit' as opposed to an ailing whining liverish state. There is nothing cranky or 'strong mannish' about it ... for men and women generally and not only for the athletic.

Later, the message was truncated to 'A journal of Hope and Courage for the Unhealthy and of Instruction for the Strong'.

To the modern 'keep-fitter', whose imagination has, until very recently, been boundaried by jogging and the ordinary sports, the wide choice of article subjects to illustrate the general maxims will surprise:

Why are Foreigners Stronger than Britons?
How music affects the health.
Are women growing taller?
Training for a long distance walk by a Famous vegetarian Pedestrian.
Dancing as an Exercise.
Physical Culture among the Ancients [fully clothed, of course].
The Physique of a Tent Dweller.

Sex also had to be treated, but as a soporific. A series of articles, which would have seemed dull to Marie Stopes, was printed on 'The Bodily Desires' by the Revd Conrad Noel, honorary organiser of the Church Socialist League.

When William, who at some expense had just reintroduced the alcohol/patent medicine/tobacco ban, appealed to Beerbohm Tree to support Mr Gladstone rather than Mr Chamberlain, he had a set-down. Even so, he saw the joke and printed his message in a box on a main page: 'A good way to preserve one's health is not to think about it. The main thing is to be careful in the selection of one's ancestry ... if my digestion shows signs of rebellion I take lobster and stout in order to assert the dominion of mind over matter.'

Besides brightening up the editorial, William showed his professionalism in insisting that the magazine always appeared on the first of the month and not, as the previous management declared, always 'trying to get to it'. Instead of charging 1/- for 'Answers to Correspondents' and allowing the answers to run up to 750 words in some cases, he merely stipulated that each question should be accompanied by a coupon from the previous issue. He cut down the amiable volubility of the 'Answers Editor' and managed over 100 items to the page, each of two to ten lines. A year after taking control, he called for '100,000 readers' but, not getting them, went weekly and reduced the price from 2d. to 1d. in September 1907. Just how far he had hitherto failed was shown by his announcement that the first weekly print of 70,000 copies had sold out. 'At one bound the high extra number ... attained by the monthly was nearly doubled ... when you have read it, pass on your copy to a friend'.

The most memorable feature of *Health & Strength* was the 'acquisition' of a young Danish physical training expert, Lieutenant Jorgen Muller, late of the Royal Danish Engineers. As inspector of the Veglefroid Sanatorium for Consumption, he had written a book, *My System*, which had sold 200,000 copies in Germany. The system consisted of an hour's exercise, with no apparatus, for women as well as men, which could be performed in the home. William repeated that Mullerism was not 'strong man' doctrine. Indeed Muller himself, though marvellously fit and strong, was not a muscle man and by no means marvellous to look at. William introduced him to his readers, with his tongue surely jammed in his cheek: 'At the age of seventeen he entered the University of Copenhagen to study Theology. His "call" however came, not from the Church but from Mankind ... he was destined to serve as an Apostle of physical regeneration'.

Immediately, William announced a lecture tour of the industrial North and Midlands. In the month of October he took halls in nine towns, starting with Newcastle. There, in the town hall, the first lecture was a flop since whoever had made the booking had failed to discover that the famous singer, Melba, was appearing there on the same day.

Reading the reports in the local papers, I get the impression that though very large halls had been booked – the Manchester Free Trade Hall held 4,000 – the turnout was disappointing, and conclude that there was too little advance publicity. Anyway, those who did not attend missed a stunning performance.

The routine was to get the mayor, or some local bigwig, to take the chair, and then for William to take Muller through his system. Before launching on this there were the spectaculars. The *pièce de résistance* was called 'The Suspended Anvil':

> He lies with the back of his head resting on a chair and his feet on the other, while a couple of smiths with great sledge hammers hammer away on a 200lb anvil, placed directly on his stomach . . . I have stood by with mingled wonder and admiration.

Another trick was for William at some point to seat himself on a chest of drawers and continue his remarks from there. Meanwhile, Muller would lie down on the floor, hook his feet under the chest and lift it up, William and all. After that came the demonstration of exercises for ordinary people.

After *My System* had been translated, Muller wrote a second book, *The Fresh Air Book*, and others, all published by *Health & Strength* and producing a steady source of income until the magazine and its ancilliaries were sold in 1920 to Sydney Carroll for £4,866 (now about £90,000).

Well before that, Muller had ceased his visits to our house, where my mother took little trouble to make him welcome since he frequently spat, explaining that not to was bad for health.

*   *   *

Before the success of the weekly issue *Health & Strength*, which now began to earn decent money, had probably been making a hole in their pockets and they had had to subsist on the AW. Hart, on leaving late in 1906, recorded:

> After three very happy years with the Berry brothers I too had bought an engagement ring and despite their countless acts of kindness I felt that my future lay in more promising fields. The possibilities with Bill and Gomer were, I thought, already exhausted. Their early struggle was still on and they were paying me all the paper's resources could stand – £2.10s. a week and commission.
>
> A newly launched paper offered me £3 a week and a higher rate of commission as advertisement manager. Said the brothers; 'We must not stand in your light. But remember, your job will always be open if you want to come back to us.'
>
> With their joint blessing they gave me a cigarette case (which I lost on Gallipoli), a 100-tin of gold-tipped Egyptians and a leather wallet on the flap of which I later read a gilt-blocked inscription – with the compliments of a widely advertised soothing syrup!

A letter to my new boss, signed W.E. Berry and countersigned J. Gomer Berry, testified to past services on a 'difficult' proposition and added, 'A paper such as yours will give far wider scope than ours to Mr Hart's undoubted energy and ability.'

On that happy note we parted. Within six months my 'wider scope' paper had lost its wealthy backer and I was on my way to Australia.

William's reference to a 'difficult proposition' probably applied more to his joint interests rather than to the AW alone. With both papers 'in the black' he seems to have been struck with a mood of euphoria – at least that is how it seems with hindsight. At the end of 1907 a new morning paper, the *Tribune*, was visibly failing and William sought to take a hand in reviving it.

The *Tribune* had been started some seventeen months earlier by Franklin Thomasson, son of a Bolton industrialist. He had been left £1 million by his father, who was said to have stipulated in his will that the son, who had no newspaper experience and who acquired no reputable advisers, should start a new paper. The paper was aimed at *The Daily Telegraph*, then with 300,000 circulation, the strongest of the 'heavies'. Thomasson was bitter that the Liberal Party (in particular Augustine Birrell), just returned to power at the 1906 landslide, encouraged the paper throughout its short life but never came up with any money.

Together, the editor who had never edited (he had been an evening news editor which means 'director of reporters'), and the manager who had never managed a publication (he was Ralston Balch, who did not give up his proper job as Advertisement Manager of Scott & Bowne) tried a succession of 'bright ideas' having little relation to the bread-and-butter job of producing an all-round newspaper.

The Editor, one William Hill, 'caused to be set up in type and paid for several thousand columns of editorial matter, most of which were never used'. He was finally got rid of by what became the popular Fleet Street device of sending him on holiday, in Switzerland (latterly a long cruise has been conventional), before informing him of his successor. The latter made some effort to popularise the news but kept great slabs of Liberal punditry. The manager, for his part, having announced that the daily net sale would be printed from the first issue, contributed a direct delivery scheme, avoiding commission to the retailer.

These brief facts I have obtained from William's 1939 pamphlet, *London Newspapers: Their Owners and Controllers*, and 1947 book, *British Newspapers and Their Controllers*. He went on to say that he had had 'several interviews' with Thomasson even after being told that the *Tribune* was losing £1,600 a *week* (£60,000 today). He made 'a proposition to him of going half-shares in an attempt to win success on different lines'. Instead, Thomasson shut the paper down 'quite abruptly'.

I know what the 'different lines' would have been because William employed them in his two great life-saving feats of the first half of the twentieth century – the *Sunday Times* (with few talented staff) from 1915 and *The Daily Telegraph* (with many) from 1928 – but how he could have financed them I cannot guess.

Weekly magazines could be run on a shoestring. Sunday papers in those days could lean very largely on contributors. But daily papers demand and demanded large, full-time staffs. Costs could not have been materially cut down and it would have taken months, at the very least, before advertisers could be coaxed into what had seemed a forlorn enterprise. The paper occupied no 'niche' position: the competition was intense. William had no capital and, as far as I can tell, no prospect of borrowing big money. Nor can he have proposed to Thomasson that the latter should continue to finance the losses in the short term; otherwise he would surely have been less laconic. I can only conclude that if Thomasson had accepted his offer, William would have gone bankrupt and his hard road to riches and fame would have been yet stonier. I say this in spite of the fact that William first gave the above account thirty-two years later, in 1939, when he was fully mature and ranked already with the great self-made newspaper men of his era. I ought to defer to his superior status and enormous wisdom and experience, but I don't. Perhaps the explanation is that, by 1939, he had proved to the world that he was a master of 'different' lines and he had, in the course of implementing them, jumped many perilous financial hurdles. And the enormous hurdle of 1907 seemed not all that greater through the haze of hindsight.

Over the years, many articles were written about the Berry brothers, mostly by those who did not know them well. In these William was often represented as the dashing ideas-man while Gomer appears as the wise, restraining hand. In general, I think the latter picture is grossly exaggerated though Gomer, just married, would no doubt have had a fit to find himself personally committed to a quarter of the *Tribune*'s losses.

CHAPTER FIVE

Boxing, Penny Illustrated Paper, Outbreak of War

IN LATE 1909, William decided to sell the *Advertising World*. After some negotiation, the sale took place to a syndicate formed by J.A. Akerman,[1] the eldest of three brothers all in the publishing trade, whose paths crossed again several times in later years. The price was £11,000 (now about £400,000), which enabled both William and Gomer to move out of lodgings into houses in the country. William's was two miles from Weybridge, Surrey, and a mile's walk to the nearest station. He renamed the house St Michael's, after his father-in-law's house at Worthing. It stood in two acres with a tennis court, having three reception rooms, four double bedrooms, a dressing room, a bathroom and a separate lavatory. On the top floor there were day and night nurseries and a double bedroom for two maids. A cook had a room beyond the kitchen.

In December, his Sphinx friends got up a splendid dinner 'to the Founders of the *Advertising World*' at the Hotel Cecil. One hundred and two guests attended, in addition to JMB, who came to London specially. The chair was taken by the recently knighted Sir George Riddell, a wealthy solicitor, self-made in small-business property dealing, who had become Chairman of the *News of the World* in 1903.[2]

There were messages from Alfred Harmsworth, now Lord Northcliffe, and C. Arthur Pearson; three supporting speeches – one each from advertisers, advertising agents and advertising managers – and a concert

---

[1] Akerman was later Advertising Manager of *The Times* and its Associate General Manager. After that he was Vice-Chairman of Provincial Newspapers, which owned the Argus Press. In 1937 Argus suffered the double blow of losing the *Morning Post* printing contract when the paper was absorbed by the *Telegraph*, and of paying £20,000 in libel damages to William and the *Telegraph* for an article printed in Oswald Mosley's scurrilous magazine, *Action*.

[2] In the First World War he was the liaison officer between the national newspapers and Lloyd George, though he used much of the information so obtained for his unsigned weekly political column. He caused the *News of the World* to buy Walton Heath golf club (not sold until the advent of Rupert Murdoch), where he often played with the Prime Minister, to whom he gave a house overlooking the course. He was also press liaison officer at the Paris Peace Conference in 1919 and the Washington Naval Conference in 1921. He was the first Chairman of the Newspaper Proprietors' Association, becoming Lord Riddell.

to follow. Oddly, by modern standards, wives of the founders were not invited.

Ralston Balch, introduced by Riddell rather sniffily as 'our professional orator', referred to William's 'quiet, somewhat cool and pleasant smile which indicates, as it always does, that that man is not out merely for the money part of it, but he is there to play the game, because he loves the game'. He concluded felicitously:

Here amongst us tonight who crowd round the chariot wheels of the car of their success is their father and I do not hesitate to say, admiring William and Gomer Berry as I do, that they owe something to that father who, I am sure, is the proudest man in the room tonight.

JMB was called on unexpectedly and, though he said he was accustomed to speak after dinner, felt unable to express himself as he would like to have done.

William drew the loudest laugh of the evening when, in replying to the flattering remarks about the *Advertising World*, he said:

Listening to the speeches I have one regret and that is, the new proprietors could have had the opinion of representative gentlemen who have spoken before the purchase price was settled.

My aunt Phyllis, my mother's younger sister, who had helped him in a minor way at the *Advertising World*, told me years later that once he had finished with something he never gave it another thought and found that he never seemed interested in talking about the *Advertising World* after moving on. This was borne out in that Gomer kept the fifteen bound volumes of the paper until his death, while William retained only the first.

There was one last fling at the Sphinx Club in March 1910 when Mostyn Piggott, as Chairman, took the mickey out of William (now thirty), one of five 'young men' – the others included Morgan (twenty-nine), Ashby Goodall (thirty), and Wareham Smith (thirty-five) – who had conducted a debate on 'What is Wrong with Advertising':

They appeared before me as youths but although the make-up was excellent you could hear the creak of their aged joints. Every crisp little impromptu that fell from them betrayed the old Adam ... the evening has shown that the chief trouble with advertising is the five young men.

* * *

Among the many subjects covered in *Health & Strength* was amateur boxing, treated as a science rather than as a bloody contest – something akin to fencing with the foil. In Regency days boxing had been a gentleman's sport. Three rounds in his Bond Street training rooms with 'Gentleman Jim' Jackson was quite the thing for the young man about town. Prize-fighting had only got a bad name in the middle of the nineteenth century, when 'patronage passed from the hands of gentlemen into those of ambitious promoters and swindlers ... whose only idea was to fleece the public ... the audiences consisted less of interested spectators and more of thieves and pickpockets'. Driven from this country by the police, the last prize-fights took place on the Continent. 'Ruffianly crowds crossed the channel,' like football fans of the 1980s, 'for the purpose of anything from loot to murder.'

Boxing regained some of its respectability, but not a lot, with the adoption of the Queensberry Rules in 1860. Thereby, hitting below the belt, gouging and kicking were outlawed and, above all, gloves were compulsory. Gloves were not to spare the struck but the striker, whose knuckles would never stand up to in-fighting. Boxing then became more a test of skill than of endurance. That is not to say that boxing became elegant at a stroke. One Joe Ward, whose training recipe was the 'four three's' – 'three doses of salts, three sweats, three vomits, three times weekly with victuals three parts dressed' – was far removed from the style of Gene Tunney debating with Bernard Shaw.

With the rise of the popular press in the 1880s and 1890s, boxing matches were often promoted by newspapers and editors, refereed by sporting journalists, thus drawing back the crowds of respectable working class. It was a slow process. One old-timer was heard to exclaim: 'You will scarcely believe me when I tell you I would rather go to a fight than to Church.' Another, now in 1906 a 'second', recalled 'the bad old days' when they did their fighting anywhere: once he had fought in a chapel near King's Cross.

The final return of 'Regency status' came with the establishment of the National Sporting Club around 1900, with its own rooms at Covent Garden, supported by the immensely rich (175,000 acres) Lord Lonsdale – 'the Sporting Earl', Master of four of the smartest hunts, and eventually a Knight of the Garter. There, Lonsdale established much stricter rules: minimum weight gloves, maximum length bandages, fifteen rounds only except for championship fights, exact weight classes, and annual Lonsdale belts. Evening dress was *de rigeuer* and door keepers were choosy about admittance.

The new set-up was described as:

A Bohemian world of good-fellowship and tough fibre which nursed the sport of boxing through its infant years and sent it, adolescent, to school at the Pelican Club [in Paris] and the Blue Anchor [Shoreditch] and finally graduated it to the university of the National Sporting Club ... The graduate of the NSC became the grown man of Holland Park and the Albert Hall [championship international fights].

The new popularity of boxing led to round-by-round reporting in local papers and large ephemeral sales. What the local papers did not provide was news of fights elsewhere and of the rise of champions who might soon fight in their area. It was with this realisation that William, on 11 September 1909 (at the time when he had decided to sell the *Advertising World*), published the first issue of *Boxing*. A title of the *Health & Strength* Company, he claimed it to be 'the only paper in the world solely devoted to Boxing'. He announced its intention in an editorial which sought to assure the public that boxing was not, as so often assumed, a degrading exercise:

For a long time boxing journalism was regarded as little removed from gutter journalism and it was with recognition of this fact that we ventured to issue the paper ... Gt Britain needs MEN, will always need MEN, and we *know* that the best nursery in which men can be cultivated is the boxing ring. A boxer *has* to be sober, *he has* to be steady, he must be courageous, cool and self-controlled. He is taught to respect himself and if he is to achieve any measure of success he has to cultivate his brain. No boxer of any prominence ever existed yet who has not improved by his practice of the sport. He may have been a blackguard, but if so he would have been one anyway, a greater blackguard than he would have been had he not become a boxer, for the very simple reason that any and every blackguard tendency is a direct handicap to success in the ring ... simple isn't it?

I think it was a coincidence that the advent of *Boxing* was almost simultaneous with a tremendous clerical hullaballoo against the sport. The second issue recorded:

The parson is up in arms all over the country, but especially down in South Wales ... he is distressed, and therefore thundering out his disapproval of boxing, contests of every description ... they are brutal and degrading spectacles and his wonder is great that members of his congregation can attend these and yet venture to his official presence on the Sabbath following.

In South Wales, what provoked the din was a series of matches at the only large hall in the Merthyr area, the Pavilion at Mountain Ash in the Aberdare valley. It turned out that two tradesman directors of the Pavilion were also members of the Free Church Council, who preached on Sundays. They were made to resign. A protest meeting of delegates of all the Free Churches (Congregational, Sion Congregational, C.M. Baptist, Primitive Methodist, Sion Wesleyan, Unitarian) was called and a resolution passed calling for the intervention of the National Federation of Free Churchmen. The meeting was convened by the superintendent of the Prudential Assurance Company (no doubt fearful that his weekly doorstep contributions would be pre-spent on betting) and a magistrate took the chair. For several Sundays, preachers thundered.

The language of protest is similar, though more extreme, to present-day discussion, except that no mention was made of brain damage. Anathemas hurled were 'insane exhibitions ... drive the nation back to brute force ... brutal as physical exercise ... foster the lowest animal instincts of human nature ... young people are being contaminated ... bad company ... language in the train ... demoralising in the extreme ... wholly antagonistic to morality and religion'.

William waited for some weeks and then replied with arguments reminiscent of his claim to call Lieutenant Muller, lapsed theological student, the 'Apostle of physical regeneration':

We have already pointed out that boxing, whatever else it is, is the surest method of cultivating self-control and even temper, qualities which are not always conspicuous in the make-up of the most eloquent divines ... even the churches, the schools are always urging their disciples to 'Fight the good fight'. Don't they want them to go into training for it then, that they abuse boxing so strenuously? True that they recommend that the enemy should be smitten 'hip and thigh'. So that it is just possible that boxing practice may discourage their followers from adopting their specially recommended trick of hitting below the belt.

The riposte did not convince William's mother, who asked whether he could not give *Boxing* away.

Meanwhile, the clerical campaign failed. There were no more fights at Mountain Ash but boxing mania moved to the more 'enlightened' areas of Cardiff and Swansea. Crowds flocked there right up to the outbreak of war in 1914.

What happened was the direct result of the decline of Nonconformism following its great revival at the end of the century. I am indebted to

Mr Ray Boston, former Director of the Centre for Journalism Studies, University College, Cardiff, for the explanation:

> This was a last desperate attempt on the part of local Nonconformist ministers to regain their former absolute control over local communities.
>
> For most Welshmen ... the 'two nations' of Church and Chapel were as important as the two nations of Disraeli. Membership in one or the other was essential and led to almost continual class conflict.
>
> There was an increase in the intensity of this conflict following an unexpected Liberal victory in the General Election of 1906. When working-class voters, hoping for an increase in the ILP [Independent Labour Party] representation at Westminster, saw that over 200 Nonconformists had been returned on a Liberal Party ticket, they immediately lost all interest in both Liberalism and Nonconformity. They let it be known that they were much more interested in 'bread and cheese' issues, in the worsening relationship between capital and labour. They were no longer moved, they said, by the old Dissenters' arguments against pubs, music halls and 'politicians cited in divorce cases'.

Thus it was that 'pulpit politics' was born – and why the Independents and Baptists lost 20,000 members between 1907 and 1909, the pulpits becoming more and more like Radical and Socialist platforms.

It must have been at this time that William picked up one of his favourite stories:

> *Friend* (meeting Congregationalist pastor in a train): 'How are your attendances?'
> *Pastor*: 'Terrible! terrible! [then brightening] But, thank the good Lord, the Baptists are doing no better.'

*　　*　　*

At *Boxing*, William was a fulltime editor again, maintaining only a supervisory role at *Health & Strength*. His first step was to take to the road. By the third issue, that is to say within a fortnight, he was able to say that 'our travelling boxers ... have visited every suburb in London, after having traversed all the principal streets, and have also paid visits to Birmingham, Bedford, Northampton, Luton, etc., creating intense interest and winning generous applause all along the various routes'. The boxers were assembled in the back of an open lorry (see illustrations), whose sides let down to reveal the ropes of a miniature boxing ring and the words 'Boxing, every Thursday, one penny'. The seconds have their pails and towels: the referee is William. Unfortunately, local papers refused to give free publicity; I can find no account of the 'road show' in any of them.

The clientele of boxing enabled him to be much more gregarious than on previous publications. More time was spent outside the office than in it. The boxing writer, for that is what he had now become, had to have the same wide range of contacts as the racing writer, with the difference that there was no Jockey Club, Tattersall's, or buttoned-up owners, to dampen enthusiasm. There was no British Board of Boxing Control until after the First World War. Without the boxing writer, the sport would have been localised and the crowds and stakes minimal.

He was sought out by everyone remotely connected with the principals: the boxers themselves, trainers, managers, promotors, old 'seconds', touts and hangers-on of every degree of honesty or lack of it. A great deal of time was spent watching boxers in training and talking to their trainers. At a time when newspapers had hardly emerged from their eight-page format, it was nothing special for *Boxing* to cover the training of a single contender and his previous fights over three pages. William travelled to Paris for big fights, but America by boat was too far afield. He told me that, on one occasion, knowing the boxers' styles intimately, he was able to write up a terse cable to five times its length and find that, when American cuttings came, little had been wrong.

Boxing thrives on personalities. William was fortunate in his timing in so far as three of the colourful professionals were Welshmen, each with a Lonsdale belt at their weight. Later came the incomparable flyweight, Jimmy Wilde, also a Welshman, who was 6 stone 12 pounds fully dressed. He loved to describe how Wilde, arms dangling at his side, would advance slowly and then launch himself, as if from a catapult, to destroy many a Goliath a stone or so heavier.

A particular favourite was Georges Carpentier, as handsome as a film star, and his wily trainer Descamps, who spoke good English. One of Descamps' tricks was to let a nervous opponent sit in the ring alone for sixty seconds while the crowd became impatient and then to shine a triumphant spotlight on Carpentier emerging from high up in the building. Just after the First World War, William took my brother and myself to see Carpentier in training. He showed us the two punches with which he was going to knock out, I think, George Cooke. We went to the fight. It was over in fifteen seconds. As Descamps said: 'I make the bullets: Georges fires the gun and that is why we are rich.'

After the fights were over, all mixed convivially at the National

Sporting Club. As a one-time attender wrote in one of William's house magazines in 1926:

There was a big steak supper about 1.30 am ... William Berry seemed on happiest terms with Seymour Hicks [actor], Lord Tweedsmouth, Jimmy Wilde, Eugene Corri [referee], Sir Walter de Frece and with that literary and artistic coterie which finds pleasure in the brisk sport of the backers and dandies of older days.

Boxing was a twenty-four-page, small, half-sheet paper on cheap newsprint with no cover and poorly printed photographs – a great difference from the calendered *Advertising World*. There was next to no advertising, except for 'contras' from *Health & Strength*, but the cover price was raised from 1d. to 2d. for thirty-two-page special issues (usually for particularly interesting fights). The first print order was 100,000, raised to 250,000 by 1914. During the First World War, and well into the demobilisation period, the circulation must have been very much less.

William said later that *Boxing* never made a profit but, in retrospect, I daresay that he mixed in the obviously bad war years to some extent with the better pre-war period. Along with *Health & Strength*, he sold it to Sidney Carroll in February 1920. It is impossible to say for how much as both titles were in the same company. A few years later Carroll sold it on to a boxing promoter for £1,000, though it has to be remembered that the paging of national papers had greatly increased and their circulations were now in the millions.

*   *   *

I don't know how long William retained the editorship of *Boxing*, but it was certainly well into the time when he became Editor also of his next acquisition. In June 1910 he bought the *Penny Illustrated Paper* from the *Illustrated London News & Sketch* for, I imagine, a small sum. It had been going for fifty years but at that time looked an unlikely horse to come from that august stable.

The *Penny Illustrated Paper* (or PIP as it was always called) was a thirty-two-page weekly on newsprint with no discernible target audience. At some time it had absorbed the *Garden & Poultry Fancier* and still carried a page for smallholders. There were two pages for children, one for women, one for hobbies, two pages of *Punch*-type funny cartoons, a page of theatre notes and a four-page story. For the vaguely political-minded there were the 'Editor's Notes' (very bland), a page of political cartoons, and a double-page drawing of events relating to politics. In short, it was a rather dull mish-mash of low comprehension.

William took on the new task of a general paper, without the restriction of a specialised readership, with enthusiasm. In the first issue under his control he announced pithily: 'PIP is going to lead penny journalism. Wait and see.'

What he meant by that claim I do not understand. Penny illustrated weeklies had been successful twenty years before but all others, as far as I have been able to discover, had died by this time. The *Daily Mirror* had already prospered, but that had far more illustrations than PIP ever attempted. The *Daily Mail* was nearing a million sale but one of its slogans was 'a penny paper for a half-penny'. The *Daily News* and *Daily Chronicle* had followed after the Boer War. Perhaps William was thinking of 'a twopenny paper for one penny'. Anyway, that is what he seemed to have attempted. He transformed PIP into a species of middle-brow review, a cross between the modern *Spectator* and the dentist's waiting-room *Punch*; but crisper, more lively, interspersed with general, topical articles which seem out of place and humdrum by modern standards. The spirit was conveyed by Tim Healy, QC, when he had to define it in court as 'a half-humorous journal, shooting folly as it flies'.

Mostyn Piggott, one of the star speakers of the Sphinx Club, was brought in as a satirical writer, together with the provocative essayists G.K. Chesterton and W.R. Titterton: there was a Book of the Week, and much more sophisticated political notes. There were extracts from US Sunday papers about British 'notabilities'; Answers to Correspondents (both general and financial); a summary of racing tips; a half-page of jokes; little competitions; large, *Punch*-like political cartoons and a one-page short story.

The star 'folly shooter' was Titterton who, years later, was still writing for William's *Daily Telegraph*, though in a more restrained way. His was the pen which landed PIP in a celebrated libel action. His article was titled 'Is the *Daily Express* a German Spy?' Even then, when personal attacks were easily condoned, the language must have seemed fairly extravagant, for William wrote under the heading in prominent italics: '*The Editor takes no responsibility for this little journalistic frolic on the part of Mr Titterton, who is well-known as a bold and original writer.*'

Part of the 'frolic' had been to name three individuals, alleged to be conducting the *Express*, whose pragmatism was said to be opposed to their principles, particularly in their relation to the newly formed Territorial Army. Titterton dealt directly with their foreign origin and observed that they were all Jews, though this latter reflection was not out of tune with the feeling of the time, filtering down from the unpopularity of Edward VII's friends. Some play was made with their names: Blumenfeld,[3] the Editor, American-born son of German immigrants, had married a Miss Blumfeld. Ellis Barker, a naturalised German, had changed it from Elzbacher.

Nothing serious happened at first. Blumenfeld refused to write a letter (he was 'too old a bird for that') and insisted on William making an apology, which they worked out together in three-quarters of an hour at the *Express* office. It was a friendly meeting because at the end of it Blumenfeld showed him 'his method of making up the *Express*' – the first time William had had a glimpse of the working of a national paper.

Three months after the appearance of the apology, one of the minor characters took action and forced Blumenfeld to follow, on the grounds that the apology had been altered to include his name, whereas he had intended to exclude it.

PIP went down for £800 with costs, which together must have amounted to well over £1,000 (£35,000 today), a heavy blow to a small private company. There was no appeal from the jury's verdict for no disputed matter of law had arisen. Nowadays there might have been an appeal that the judge had misdirected himself. His cross-examination was remarkable in its length and hostility. William held his own well enough in defining the impossible – humour – but his sub-editor was inexcusably mauled for a civil case: 'I've met your sort before.'

The case had been expensive but it had its compensations. William had arrived. In a full-page, signed article, he was able to record:

I have to acknowledge with many grateful thanks the scores of messages I have received in connection with this case from all parts of the country and particularly Fleet Street. They come from people I know, people I know of, and people whose names are entirely unknown. They include, I am proud to say, many men at the top of the tree in the newspaper and publishing business and in the sphere of journalism. Severe though the financial loss may be, everything else connected with the case is clear again.

It had been a *succès d'estime*. No longer had William to describe himself diffidently, as he had done in the Sphinx debate of the previous year, as a 'nondescript publisher'. There is no doubt that the favourable publicity he had earned enabled him to command the credit for his first entry into national proprietorship three years later.

[3] R.D. Blumenfeld, ex-News Editor of the *Daily Mail*, had taken over the editorship from its founder C. Arthur Pearson, who owned in addition the morning *Standard* and the *Evening Standard* (incorporating the *St James's Gazette*).

As far as PIP itself was concerned, the satirical formula does not seem to have worked in the long run. I suspect the old readers were turned off and there were not enough of the new. After eighteen months yet another formula came up and the paper came to be described as 'Stories, Pictures, Competitions, Fun and Fancy'. Out went Piggott and in came pages of jokes by Harry Lauder or Arthur Bouchier, the actor/manager. There were no more articles by 'names'.

The front-cover political cartoon was dropped in favour of a drawing of Britannia with whimsical ditties on her shield, like 'Balfour has gone/who cares a straw/we've got PIP/and Bonar Law'; or 'Said Winston Churchill/to FE/"The Best of us/read PIP"'. Perhaps they may be explained as the spirit of the age or, alternatively, too much adrenalin. Northcliffe, who was fourteen years older, loved rhyming slogans like 'Daily Mail/Never Stale', or 'Weekly Dispatch/Best of the Batch'. Churchill, five years older, permitted himself a top-secret message to Roosevelt: 'No more let us alter or falter or palter/From Malta to Yalta, and Yalta to Malta.'

Banal or not, circulations must have improved again, for in January 1913 it was claimed that 'the demand for PIP last week broke all records', whatever they may have been. Evidently the recovery was not enough, for two months later the masthead read 'PIP' (very large) 'with which is incorporated *London Life*' (much smaller), the sequence only to be reversed, for good, the following week.

Through its short, new life, PIP can hardly have paid (there was never much advertising) and I suspect William lost interest in it towards the end. Certainly that is the impression one must get from the casual reference to a political note of July 1912: 'We are opposed to women's suffrage.' William knew very well of his wife's quite active part in Mrs Fawcett's 'orderly militant' suffragist (not suffragette) movement – Molly had even carried a banner in the 13,000-strong march from the Victoria Embankment, past all the clubs in Pall Mall, St James's Street and Piccadilly, to the Albert Hall in June 1908. If he had really wanted to argue a matter on which he knew my mother felt strongly, he would surely have insisted on a serious case being put.

From the time of his marriage and throughout their joint lives he always talked over his big decisions with her even if she did not always fully understand the details and it would have seemed to her a slap in the face to have her convictions so airily dismissed.[4]

---

[4] Years later, after William's death, she chided Churchill when he came to lunch on her yacht: 'I was marching but you were against us.' She did not remind him of one of his least telling retorts to a heckler of the time: 'I am not going to be henpecked on a matter of such grave importance.'

As their son-in-law, the second Lord Birkenhead, wrote on her death in 1962:

[He] never took an important decision in his professional career without seeking her advice on the shrewdness of which he placed implicit reliance ... Her integrity was so clear and so simple that people meeting her for the first time realised that this was an altogether exceptional woman, and when they came to know her better realised how much their lives had been enriched by her friendship.

*   *   *

There is evidence that, by 1911 at least, William was doing a little speculation on the Stock Exchange. There is a letter of 8 January 1912 from his father-in-law, wintering as usual, now, in Cannes, discussing various stocks on a man-to-man basis. On the back of the envelope of another letter in January 1913 are pencilled notes which can be deciphered to show that he had invested £1,170 on his own account and £163 in his children's names (there were three now). One of the stocks named is also on Thomas Corns' list. By 1914 Corns was feeling his age and, before his death in October 1915, he leaned more and more on William for the conduct of his affairs. Meanwhile, the Stock Exchange had been shut down until January 1915.

August 1914 found William, a married man of thirty-five, overage for army service. When the age restriction was lifted he joined up (voluntarily attested, it was called) on 11 December 1915 and was given a postal order for 2/9d., a day's pay and rations. (Like his father's cheque for his twenty-first birthday, he kept it: I still have it.) Much to my mother's relief, for by this time he had a large debt and five children, the call at that time was more for munitions than for men. It was not until the 1916 bloodbaths of attrition that he would have been called up, by which time he had been struck down by peritonitis and nearly died. I remember visiting him in his nursing home, to be entertained with white-icing chocolate biscuits and be shown the two pipes sticking out of his stomach. Not being allowed a telephone, he entertained himself by teasing the nurse and once managed to get her to wash the same leg twice in his blanket bath.

He came out 'Category C' – suitable only for a desk job in England – and thereafter was exempted as a newspaper editor.

CHAPTER SIX

Purchase of *Sunday Times* and White Saga

AT THE TIME of his marriage, William had given his address as the National Liberal Club, Whitehall Place.[1] Afterwards he continued to frequent it. It was but a short walk from the Strand. There in the bar room one met people of many kinds. Gossip, otherwise known as 'information', is the raw material of journalism and in his quest for it William was no different from anyone else in the business, though in later life he liked to put on the appearance of disapproval. Once, when quizzing my wife on some scandal of which, as usual, she seemed to know everything, he managed only a twinkle when he finished the exchange: 'Are you sure that is all? Well, I think it's perfectly disgraceful for you to concern yourself with such things.' His exact contemporary, Max Aitken, made Lord Beaverbrook in 1916 when he refused a minor job in Lloyd George's new Government, and thereafter controller of the *Daily Express*, *Sunday Express* and London *Evening Standard* until he died in 1964, who tended to use gossip raw, was franker: 'I'm really just an old concierge: I like to know what's going on.'

In the lunch room at the National Liberal one day in April 1915, William made a contact which was to launch him into national newspapers. He was lunching with one Jimmy White. As White was instrumental in that launch, and as William's name was sometimes linked suspiciously with his until his spectacular suicide twelve years later, his career is worth mention.

James White, two years older than William, was the son of a Rochdale bricklayer. After working as a ten-year-old in a cotton factory, a stint as foreman in a local building firm, a navvy on a South African railway, and, back home, a brickwork contractor, he built houses for sale and soon was buying and selling existing real estate. He once went bankrupt but repaid all his creditors with interest. At nineteen he owned a circus and ran it for two years.

Bald with a black moustache, like many Lancastrians, he was of medium height and rather squarely built ... He gave the impression

---

[1] He had joined in 1903, proposed by Horace Holmes, Chairman of the Paddington Congregational Chapel and Gomer's future father-in-law, and a Smith of W.H. Smith's Advertising Agency.

of considerable vitality and physical strength, but what stood out were his eyes: cold, deep blue and very penetrating. These not surprisingly mesmerised the more impressionable, but he knew precisely when to radiate charm and turn on a very frank and engaging smile which gave his face boyishness and sparkle. He never lost his Lancashire accent.

William had first met him in 1911 when he burst on the London scene as a boxing promoter. Jack Johnson, the black, heavyweight champion of the world, was coming to London on a vaudeville tour and announced beforehand that, on arrival, he would fight anyone willing to challenge. White privately met the young British champion, 'Bombardier' Billy Wells, promised him a £2,000 fee and thereupon, under the cloak of a 'Manchester Syndicate', offered a total purse of £8,000 (£230,000 now), the highest ever in England, for the contest. At first the whole sporting press, except the Manchester *Sporting Chronicle*, opposed the fight on the grounds that the eighteen-stone Johnson, master of the American 'in-fighting' school, would massacre the classical, English-style, twelve-stone Wells, who had only just reached the top ranks. William was soon converted and, after White had revealed himself, told his readers that he had seen the contract but could not immediately tell them what was in it. It transpired that Johnson was ten years the elder, had not fought for three years and was flabby by two stone, while Wells was 13 stone 10 pounds and the champion whom William claimed he had first named as the 'White Hope'. But he still categorised the challenge as 'a match', 'a contest', 'a crime', 'a folly', or 'a huge joke': and argued for and against in long leading articles.

The fight was to take place in the new Empress Hall, Earls Court, with seating capacity of 18,000 to 25,000. Full-page advertisements appeared in *Boxing* for tickets from 5 guineas (£150 now) to 10/6d., bookable at 'all libraries and leading hotels and at the offices of [*Boxing*]'. White sold the cinema rights for £5,000 and exclusive interviews after the fight, from both contestants, to *Boxing*.

A fortnight before the day, two enormous spanners were thrown in the works by the Revd F.B. Meyer, a Wesleyan Methodist, who rehearsed all the old arguments of South Wales two years earlier, and by *The Times* (now owned by Lord Northcliffe, but not, I imagine, motivated by him). The latter pronounced, notwithstanding that black had fought white many times, if Johnson won, 'disturbances could well erupt in every part of the Empire'.

Meyer first worked on Edward White (no relation), Chairman of the

London County Council, who threatened to withdraw the Earls Court Exhibition licence and caused William to explode:

> Sportsmen should ensure ... our next body of governors ... should consist of human beings with red blood in their veins, and not curiosities from a museum or freaks from a fair ... The only argument [Edward White] has advanced for the consideration of the Earls Court licensees is [that it] will vex the souls of the Synod of the Second London District of the Wesleyan Methodist Church. A sad thing admittedly.
>
> The proprietors of Earls Court and the promoter ... seem to be absolutely unmoved. And we think with reason.

But that was not enough for Meyer. He threatened to travel to Balmoral to petition the Home Secretary, Winston Churchill, then in waiting on the King, to stop the fight on moral grounds. Whether he went or not, Churchill announced that, after legal advice, he had decided there was a case for the Director of Public Prosecutions to contend there was danger of an affray.

Meyer had timed his campaign well, though on the last Sunday but one before the day he infuriated the *Church Times* by praying in his sermon for the 'conversion' of the two boxers. The *Church Times* replied tartly that the one matter not germane to the controversy was religion, inferring that Meyer had no standing.

The fight, two and a half months in the making, was to be on Monday 2 October. Writs, two of them, were not served until the previous Tuesday and came to court the following day. That at Bow Street attracted the larger crowd. Sir John Simon, the Solicitor-General, appeared for the Director of Public Prosecutions and F.E. Smith was to defend. Even those hitherto uninterested looked forward to a contest between two of the most formidable advocates of the decade.

Sporting Life, the foremost sporting paper and in whose office contracts for the big fights were usually signed, took up the cudgels for Jimmy White. The question at issue, it said, was whether boxing for a purse was illegal – prize-fights definitely were. The difference was that boxing for a purse was 'intended to terminate before serious injury – not until one or the other is incapable of going on'. The renowned referee, Eugene Corri, had been engaged, and Lord Lonsdale's rules were to be enforced. Lonsdale himself, like *Sporting Life*, thought the boxers ill matched, but wrote in that paper:

> White is a most excellent organiser and takes great interest in boxing

and is perfectly capable ... his name is almost a guarantee that there will be no breach of the peace or undue force.

It was not to be. Simultaneously in the High Court a judge granted an injunction on the use of Earls Court. The proceedings were brief and the Bow Street action was abandoned almost as soon as it had got under way.

Accounts long after the event allege that White pocketed all the entrance money, but the opposite seems to have been the case. He announced that all was returnable but ticket holders were entitled to bring two guests for the Monday event which, instead of Johnson/Wells, offered six contests including Carpentier, the nineteen-year-old French welterweight champion. Alternatively, they could exchange them for a fight at the Palladium, where Wells was hurriedly matched against 'Gunner' Moir. At Earls Court, 'Mr James White had a rousing and sympathetic reception.' Ten days later White announced he was putting on three contests at weekly intervals at Camden Town Theatre. But Meyer[2] was implacable. He pursued White from hall to hall and terrorised the leaseholders into withdrawing permission. The only place he could find where there were no leaseholders was a hall at the Elephant and Castle which, holding only 2,000, was no place for a big purse.

> Mr White is one of the most unfortunate promoters. Switched from one place to another, almost of necessity there was grumbling at the inadequacy of the arrangements.

Sporting Life concluded:

> Mr James White will in all probability be mulcted of a large fortune: the only bright spot has been the courage and determination that [he] has displayed consistently.

He was, indeed, mulcted. But it took some time before he admitted defeat. Seven weeks after the injunction, *Boxing* recorded that White 'had paid Johnson £1,500 but wants £500 back'.

He must have been very nearly cleaned out for, according to Carroll, he borrowed £500 from William, who had a whip-round among his friends. He did, however, repay it, and later recounted in his bluff way that 'the smartest thing he had ever done in his early days was to

---

[2] It transpired that the Revd F.B. Meyer was much more than a Victorian spoilsport. At this time he was writing regularly for 'improving' magazines intended for Sunday schools. Sir John Hammerton, long-time Editor of the Amalgamated Press's Educational Book Club, had a great 'respect for his sincerity and quality of his mind'. Four years after this episode, William was using his name, together with Baden Powell, Conan Doyle and other public men, as endorsers of the value of the Muller 'system'.

William's parents at the time of their marriage in 1870. He, John Mathias Berry (he called himself JMB to his children) from a family of tenantry, was a Station Master on the Great Western Railway. Some of the family's detractors later alleged that he was a porter. Who ever saw a railway porter in a frock coat? She, Mary Ann Rowe, was the daughter of a 'writer', an administrator in Pembroke Dock. She was known locally as 'the proud Miss Rowe'. JMB always called her 'Polly'.

JMB as Grandmaster of the Merthyr Masonic Lodge. He was 'introduced' at the same time as D. A. Thomas (later Lord Rhondda) Liberal M.P. for Merthyr, whose Agent he became.

Left JMB and my grandmother, taken at the time of his Mayoralty of Merthyr.

Polling day, April 7th

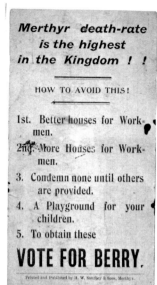

**Merthyr death-rate
is the highest
in the Kingdom ! !**

HOW TO AVOID THIS!

1st. Better houses for Workmen.

2nd. More Houses for Workmen.

3. Condemn none until others
are provided.

4. A Playground for your
children.

5. To obtain these

VOTE FOR BERRY.

Printed and Published by H. W. Southey & Sons, Merthyr.

JMB's Election Address when he first stood for Councillor of the new Borough of Merthyr in 1902. The slogan 'Merthyr death-rate is the highest in the Kingdom!!' bears out my description of the insanitary conditions in Merthyr described in the Introduction. These conditions, in some part, were still persisting, four years after William had gone to London.

Below William aged seventeen. By this time he was Manager of the *Merthyr Times*, having chased after his predecessor who had gone off with the petty cash.

The office of the *Merthyr Times* (weekly) where William went to work in 1893 as a cub-reporter at the age of thirteen and ten months. The upper floor on the left was occupied by the Merthyr Liberal Club, started by JMB, as the Liberal Agent for the constituency. The noise from the Club annoyed the editor, when the paper's politics changed from Radical to Tory.

William's favourite photograph of his elder brother, Seymour, at about the same age. William who had had the closest relationship with Seymour always kept this photograph in a silver frame on his mantelpiece after Seymour's death.

Part of a letter written to William by his mother in pencil on January 18, 1899. The occasion was when William, alone in London, confessed to his family that he had been out of a job for three months. The letter reads: '... there is a silver lining to every dark cloud and you will be bright again soon be sure you don't want for anything and don't hesitate letting us know [at] once you shall have it by return of Post, you are the chief topic of conversation in this house all day. I wish Mr. D. A. Thomas [M.P. for Merthyr] were better your Father would ...' William has written in much thicker pencil across the top: 'No ink in this house you know can't afford it'. He seems to have written the comment in frustration. He kept the letter.

JMB towers over his three sons. Taken at Christmas 1901 when William had just published the first number of the *Advertising World*. Between him and his father is the youngest brother, Gomer, eighteen, who was to join him in London on the advertisement side of the *Advertising World*. Gomer, who had been a window dresser in the largest Merthyr store, was a little apprehensive of London. Two years later he had grown a moustache to make himself look older. On the left is Seymour, now twenty-four, who was already nagging his father to depart from his conservative ways as an estate agent.

become associated with boxing, for it was there that you meet the boys with money to burn' – 'moogs' he called them, in his Lancastrian argot.

White's forte was as a judge of real estate as others were of horseflesh. (He tried the latter but, apart from Irish Elegance, a poorly bred stallion which won a number of important races including the Royal Hunt Cup at Ascot in 1919, made a poor fist of it: at one time he had 200 horses without much success).[3] If he had stuck to real estate he would have ended up seriously rich and, though ill educated, would have been remembered as an immensely stimulating card who knew everybody and everything and had showered his native Rochdale with benefactions. He is now remembered principally as a company promoter, which means a man whose schemes too often benefit himself and impoverish others. He stayed closer to his companies than today's asset strippers but he was often unlucky, or reckless, in his timing. He engaged in grandiose industrial expansion, principally in Dunlop Rubber and in Lancashire cotton, but both collapsed in the post-war slump of 1921.

At the time of his lunch with William of which I wrote at the start of this chapter, White was financial adviser to Sir Joseph Beecham, of Beecham's Pills, to whom he had suggested the largest ever property deal – to buy the Covent Garden estate from the Duke of Bedford for £2 million and 'unbundle' it. The deal had been signed just before the outbreak of war in 1914 but Beecham/White could not complete since the Bank of England banned public issues for 'inessential purposes'.

At about this time, Sir Joseph's son, Sir Thomas Beecham, the famous conductor and musical impresario, said perceptively of White:

> He was dashing and effective in the opening stages of a financial adventure, but later on, and if there were occasions to make a wise retreat, he was apt to become apprehensive, sometimes to the point of panic ... he had considerable charm of manner: an easy capacity for making money, and still easier for spending it. He once confessed to me that life without £100,000 [£1.5 million now] was not worth living ...

In 1915 the Covent Garden deal was still hanging fire. A new scheme was ready for signature in December 1916, but fell down on Sir Joseph's sudden death. Meanwhile, White's own vehicle for obtaining information – his capacious office in the Strand – continued on its way. Sir Thomas described it:

> ... a rendezvous for all sorts of and conditions of Londoners,

---

[3] Gordon Richards, the future champion jockey and then a stable boy, recounted in *My Story* how immensely popular and generous White was.

politicians, newspaper proprietors, actors, jockeys and prize-fighters, and through this variety of acquisition he sometimes acquired information on current events of importance before the outside world had any inkling of them.[4]

*   *   *

To return to the lunch at the National Liberal. Towards its end, West de Wend Fenton, Oxford-educated turf gambler (once warned off) and new owner of the *Sporting Times* (the 'Pink Un') two years younger than William, came over to their table. He asked White whether Sir Joseph Beecham would be interested in buying control of the *Sunday Times*. White knew that Beecham was worried enough with the Covent Garden situation and in any case neither of them had the aptitude nor knowledge for what must be a long slog. Though it was not losing money, its circulation trailed far behind the *Observer*, the other quality Sunday. There was no quick turn to be made.

These considerations could not have taken more than a moment to pass through White's quick mind. He told Fenton he should address himself to his companion, Bill Berry. Fenton remembered the PIP case and knew he was speaking to a professional.

Fenton did not own the shares: he had an option on them. They were owned, 57 per cent of them, by a naturalised German, Herman Schmidt. The *Sunday Times* official history speaks of him having to sell as he was in internment. I think this unlikely. He had started the *Sunday Special* in 1898 and in 1904 had, on payment of £5,000, amalgamated it with the *Sunday Times*, which had an older title but a minimal prosperity. It is hardly possible that the authorities would have waited nine months after war's outbreak to put inside a man who had held an honorable and prominent position in this country for twenty years. When it was wanted, his signature was readily available. His London address, at which he was listed as holding a few preference shares, was the same in 1918 as it had been at the time of the sale. The fact of the matter was that, however long he had been naturalised, ordinary people now regarded him with suspicion, just as dog owners were now putting down their dachshunds. Anyway, he was hard up.

It turned out, however, that Schmidt might not be free to sell. One of the directors, Esmond Caillard, was a younger brother of Sir Vincent Caillard, Finance Director of Vickers the arms manufacturer, one of

---

[4] In the late autumn of 1916, White told Beecham of the plot to oust Asquith. After getting a put-down from a cabinet minister, Beecham reported it to Margot Asquith in December, a week before it happened. She replied, 'Nothing but death can remove Henry.'

whose two principal salesmen was Basil Zaharoff. Zaharoff, possibly at the prompting of Vincent Caillard, who on several other occasions partnered Zaharoff in deals unconnected with Vickers, was owed £10,000 by Schmidt (who had been receiving no dividends) and had filed a petition in bankruptcy. This at first he refused to withdraw, 'having no wish to see a stranger walk off with the *Sunday Times*'.[5]

Others interested, either as directors or shareholders, were Dr Jameson,[6] colleague of Cecil Rhodes and late Prime Minister of Cape Colony and Sir Arthur Steel-Maitland, representing Conservative Central Office[7] and afterwards Minister of Transport in Baldwin's 1924–29 Government. They agreed to a sale provided that William submitted to a clause in his contract stipulating that 'the political policy' of the paper would 'not be changed without the consent of the directors'. On this Zaharoff was persuaded to take his money and run.

William said many years later that the price was about £75,000 (about £1.8 million today). Looking at the accounts now, and bearing in mind that the worst trading conditions of wartime were becoming clearer week by week, this seems a pretty stiff price.

Indeed, in an examination of all William's deals in the years to come, one never comes across a bargain, let alone a niggle. Anyway, the one firm figure I have is £50,000; an overdraft of 1 per cent over bank rate (then 5 per cent), minimum 6 per cent, at Temple Bar Branch of Westminster Bank guaranteed by Sir Joseph Beecham and supported by the deposit of 38,281 shares[8] (57 per cent). This was presumably the payment to Schmidt, who included in the package 6,000 6 per cent preference shares. These were given to Beecham and White as their commission but, according to Gomer's recollection, bought back 'within a week or two' by the two brothers. The agreement, but not of course the guarantee, also provided for free advertising of Beecham's Pills in

[5] Bernard Falk, *Five Years Dead*. Falk, Editor of Northcliffe's *Sunday Dispatch* at about this time, is my only reference for the debt. Mr Antony Allfrey, author of the recent Zaharoff biography, *Man of Arms*, tells me he has found no record of Zaharoff's involvement, adding that his documentation of this period is meagre. Zaharoff's only other known interest in a British newspaper concerns *The Times*. According to Campbell Stuart, its then Manager, Zaharoff tried to buy it in 1922 on Northcliffe's death.

[6] Jameson and Rhodes had briefly owned the *Sunday Times* before the *Sunday Special* amalgamation and had tried to sell the former for £5,000 to Sir Arthur Pearson.

[7] According to A.J.P. Taylor, *Beaverbrook*, it was customary for Central Office to subsidise newspapers by taking a share interest. He writes that others newspapers so supported, though he makes no reference to the *Sunday Times*, were the *Observer*, the *Standard* (Daily) the *Globe* (Evening) and the *Pall Mall Gazette* (Evening). According to Blumenfeld (Beaverbrook Papers), Central Office bought a controlling interest in the *Daily Express* from Sir Arthur Pearson (who had gone blind) and only later shed it when more money was required.

[8] Issued capital was 67,257 £1 ordinary shares and 30,000 £1 6 per cent preference shares, participating after a certain ordinary dividend.

the *Sunday Times* and *Health & Strength*. During the first year of the guarantee there was a column advertisement in nearly every issue of the former. This stratagem would never have occurred to wheeler-dealer White. William must have harked back to the first issues of the *Advertising World*, when he paid his suppliers by contra-advertising.

Esmond Caillard remained on the board, whereas Jameson retired from the scene and may have sold his shares which, together with Fenton's option[9] and Zaharoff's debt, would account for the extra £25,000. I have no information about Steel-Maitland, or what share-holding, if any, Central Office retained. William, in any case, had no opinion of him. Fifteen years later he complained to the editor of *The Daily Telegraph*:

> Why oh why the half column of Steel-Maitland's book? ... Steel-Maitland is one of the worthy duds on the Front Opposition Bench ... to give him this space for a pamphlet on a problem which he does not attempt to solve is calculated to make us supremely ridiculous in the eyes of the political public.

I suspect that he may have relied on Caillard to keep the paper Conservative, since the brothers' contract contained such a clause, dependent on 'the directors'; but it was not signed until September 1916 (by Caillard and White), retroactive to June 1915. I can find no record of it being deleted and conclude it was soon regarded as a dead letter.

Where the brothers found the £25,000 from I do not know. Nor do I know how they so quickly found another £6,000 to buy back the preference shares. There is a shorthand note in the file, taken down by William's secretary at the time of the Mrs White affair (see below) saying, 'Mr Hu [presumably Edward Hunter] was in on the deal at the time and knew all about it.' I daresay that Seymour, too, may have helped, though he was still only in the estate agency business. But at the end of it they must have been pretty stretched. They still had the profits from *Health & Strength* and their contracts gave them £1,250 for William, plus 10 per cent of the gross profits, as joint managing director and managing editor; for Gomer, £750 plus 5 per cent on gross advertising revenue, as joint managing director and advertisement controller. They also received £100 each as directors. How much they drew I will discuss in a later chapter. Against that they had £3,000 a year to pay in bank interest. Meanwhile, I record that my mother told an informant after the Second World War that 1915 had been William's

---

[9] Fenton had originally paid £500 for an option on the *Sporting Times*. Perhaps £5,000 would have been a suitable sum for the *Sunday Times*.

toughest year and that he had sometimes worried whether he could carry on. This is borne out in a letter his mother wrote him on his thirty-seventh birthday:

> Gwaelodygarth House,
> Merthyr Tydfil,
> June 22/16

My dear Will,

I am thinking of you, and remembering that it is your birthday tomorrow, accept my fondest wishes, for every happiness, and much love, it seems such a short time that you were a little one running about and now you are a tall man, brimming full of energy, and life, and grasping so many things that you are beyond all my expectations. I trust that you will succeed in them all above all that you may have your health, but I fear you are taxing it very much just now remember the candle wont burn both ends the same time, take a little rest between and give it to your children so helping your dear wife at the same time ... now I must close with fondest love and remain,

> Your affectionate,
> Mother

Beta's handwriting follows:

My dear Bill,

I endorse all Mother has said and hope all will turn up trumps. S saw DA [Lord Rhondda] today and he was very pleased about Paragraph in S.T.[10]

*   *   *

In 1938 the £50,000 overdraft came back to haunt him for a spell. It concerned White's widow: so I will here briefly finish the White saga.

After 1915 William continued to go, off and on, to the White *salon* and for some years they kept in touch. After all, William had saved White from a second bankruptcy in 1911, and without White, William would not have been able to buy the *Sunday Times*. It is possible that there may have been some association with the three brothers' speculation in a Lancashire cotton firm, Joshua Hoyle, in 1919, for White at that time formed a cotton 'trust', to which he added greatly increased manufacturing capacity. It came on-stream just as the market collapsed.

Thereafter, White's schemes grew grander and grander. No sober-sided man would have given him *carte blanche* to deal with their money.

---

[10] A reference to dealings 'at steadily rising prices' in Consolidated Cambrian, Rhondda's expanding coal combine, now being quoted in London as well as on the provincial stock exchange.

For a long time he remained on top of the wave, though some of his greedy associates floundered in its trough. Finally he met his doom 'taking on some of the toughest operators in the business world, the oil speculators'. In 1927 he clashed with one Edward Mackay Edgar, a man as hot as himself, forced him off the board of British Controlled Oilfields and tried to corner the shares. He found himself short of nearly £1 million and was already committed to paying £300,000 for Wembley Stadium, just being completed.

He gave up. He died alone in his grand country house, Foxhill, in Surrey. He left a rather touching note for his butler: 'Go easy with me, old man: I am dead of prussic acid.' He also left a number of not so touching letters accusing his friends of letting him down, which did not turn up until many years later – it may be they were inventions of Mrs White.

His funeral was of flagrant vulgarity. There was a farm wagon procession, groaning under elaborate wreaths, complete with pipers: 'a veritable who's who of celebrities from the sporting, theatrical and financial worlds who either turned up in person or sent their limousines or floral tributes, and thousands of ordinary people came by charabanc or motor car ... the little church had seldom seen a costlier funeral'.

The widow did not attend. William did. Afterwards, some people pointed the finger at him, suggesting that he was somehow involved in White's machinations, that he had let him down at the critical moment. Others, more sapiently, commented that it was a brave act, laying himself open to just such imputation.

William recalled that he had not seen White for eighteen months and that White had died owing him £25,000 (£325,000 now). There were many others too. At the suggestion of Lord Beaverbrook (though he had gone abroad when the time came and never did contribute) William organised a fund aimed to yield £10,000 for the benefit of the widow. Many, however, refused, claiming they had repeatedly lost money in White's schemes. The twenty-four that did raised £7,400 (£125,000 now). William and Gomer both put up 1,000 guineas, as did Gordon Selfridge and Sir James Dunn, a bond-selling colleague of Beaverbrook in their earliest days. Others, with smaller gifts, included Sir Harry McGowan (Chairman of ICI), the Barnato brothers, Sir Abe Bailey, W.M. Singer (sewing machines), Lord Dewar, Lord Dalziel, Sir Herbert Austin (motor cars) and F.A. Szarvasy (financier, who had saved Dunlop after White had overexpanded it).

Barclays Bank and a Huddersfield stockbroker were made co-trustees and all should have been well enough. It wasn't. The White friends knew nothing of Mrs White's habits, which were as bad as could be.

Besides the trust fund she had some money of her own, a house by the sea and the lease of a house in Park Street, Mayfair. She splashed money about, entertained in restaurants, drank freely, and as soon as they were old enough, did not get on with the three children.

A year after the setting up of the fund, William and Gomer gave £100 a year to a children's fund and only Lord Dalziel gave anything more – £25. William could never bear to see anyone else mal-administering and inevitably got drawn into correspondence. Soon he was paying for all the children's private education, with Mrs White pleading for money for their holidays, which at first she sometimes got. Equally inevitably, Mrs White battened on him and, up to the time of his death, was continually asking for 'loans' of £20, £10, £5, or £3,000 to 'start a business'. Her best trick was to ask for £20, get £5 and then, after a week or so, seek 'the balance'. As late as 1951, by which time she had remarried, he gave her a covenant for £100 a year towards her rent, which went straight to the landlord and could not be used for any other purpose. The only time she got a flat rebuff was when she asked for a second 'whip-round'.

Very few of Mrs White's letters (I have three files of them) were appreciative. Often she would call at the office to try to see him, and always failing him, his confidential secretary, who had been manager of the *Sunday Times* in 1915. She never got upstairs, but this did not prevent her leaving rude messages through the switchboard. Usually she complained of her trustees or of her heartless treatment by 'Jimmy's old friends'. She put it about to doctors and schoolmasters that William was her son's legal guardian. To one of them she provided a letter, alleged to be signed by Jimmy White, claiming debts by William which he dismissed angrily as 'the work of a demented mind and false almost in every word'. One correspondent, sending William a copy of the letter, began his letter offensively: 'The mills of God in turning have put in my hands the enclosed letter.' It took William six months, in 1931, to get the writer to be 'man enough to apologise'.

Once, in 1937, ten years after her husband's suicide, she remembered 'when my husband bought the *Sunday Times* for you'. This might have alerted him. He got a more definite warning when one of Mrs White's daughters wrote to him that, through her godmother, she had heard of a book that was being written. Mrs White had purported to find an old bank letter, showing White advancing £50,000 to William instead of procuring Beecham to guarantee a loan. It was said she was to have a ghosted life of White written, in which this tarradiddle would be published, claiming that, as the £50,000 had never been repaid, his estate was the legal owner of the *Sunday Times*. Erstwhile 'friends' were to be approached to 'make a few people sit up'. Hannen Swaffer, the notorious gossip-writer of the *Sunday Referee*, was to write a preface.

For a time William was disturbed. He asked the Temple Bar Branch of the Westminster Bank to turn up its records for 1915, only to find that they had been destroyed. Determined not to be muck-raked by this outrageous sponger, William, through his solicitors, Slaughter & May, and after taking senior counsel's opinion, hired a pair of private detectives, whose exploits read like those of Inspector Clouseau. The detectives, whose bill came to £78.12s., did, however, establish that the only notes compiled were in a few exercise books and the 'printer' dealt only in stationery and Christmas cards. William decided there was nothing more to do for the time being. A little later the son wrote to say he had got 'the book' from his mother, but William did not want to see it. Still she went on begging until the time of his death, when she sent a birthday card to the new Lord Camrose. She disappears from the file in 1957, when, although remarried to a 'civil servant', she tried her old ploy – a loan in advance of income from the fund.

It was an unnecessary diversion. Temple Bar Branch should have known that, in 1915, £50,000 was far too large a sum to authorise on its own. Head Office would have had to make the decision.

There it is, in their records, as large as life:

London County & Westminster Bank Directors' Committee Minutes

Friday 4 May 1915

The following advances were sanctioned:

Temple Bar   Berry & Berry
£50,000 for six months at 1% above Bank Rate, minimum 6%. Against guarantee of Sir Joseph Beecham and shares in the *Sunday Times*.

White had not even been a co-guarantor.

*   *   *

The next entry in the bank's records (2 June 1916) shows the loan reduced to £48,500, subject to £3,500 reduction the same month and £5,000 at the end of the year. A year later, even though Sir Joseph Beecham was dead, the rate was reduced to half per cent over bank rate and the total owing to £35,000. On Christmas Eve 1917, the last entry, the original sum had been almost halved at £28,400.

CHAPTER SEVEN

Sunday Times 1915–1923

IN 1915 THE Sunday quality[1] press was barely ten years old. In the first half of the nineteenth century the *Observer* had had some influence, while in the 1880s the *Sunday Times* achieved sales of 35,000. It was, however, limited by the larger readership of the literary reviews like the *Cornhill*, the *Fortnightly* and the *Pall Mall Gazette*, which cornered the best young writers. Ownership changed hands too often for continuity. Finally, a new owner threw out culture and, though much of it was later restored, the paper entered the new century with nothing left but a distant reputation.

The outbreak of the Boer War led Sir Edward Lawson, principal owner of *The Daily Telegraph*, to announce he was going to start a *Sunday Telegraph*, whereupon Alfred Harmsworth, whose immensely successful *Daily Mail* was just coming up to its third birthday, followed suit. The date coincided with the great Nonconformist revival. The uproar was immense – much greater than the Nonconformist uproar against boxing ten years later. Votes of censure were passed by the Presbyterian, Congregationalist and Baptist Boards of Ministers. The president of the Newspaper Society (representing provincial newspapers) wrote slyly that the idea had emanated from 'one who belongs to a race that does not recognise our Sunday'; articles appeared in the *British Weekly* and the *Methodist Times*. Lord Rosebery, ex-Prime Minister and popular racehorse owner, forgetful of his Rothschild wife, lent his name to the clamour.

What had prompted Lawson and Harmsworth to enter the Sunday field, apart from the extreme weakness of the opposition, was the excellence of their distribution systems, where inefficiency had for long been the bugbear of the small circulation papers. The advantage was short-lived. All three main wholesalers, including W.H. Smith, who had a monopoly of railway bookstalls, refused to handle. After seven and six weeks respectively, the *Sunday Telegraph* and *Sunday Daily Mail* closed down, leaving the tiny *Sunday Times*, *Observer* and the two-year-

---

[1] I use the term in its present-day sense: 'news' to inform, 'views' to persuade, and 'arts' for those with some interest in books, drama, music or painting.

old *Sunday Special* in possession. Perhaps their sales were so small that the changed attitude of the wholesalers did not matter and the inspiration of the first two papers (whose proprietors were husband and wife) was personal rather than commercial.

Whatever the explanation, it soon ceased to be relevant. Six years later, in 1905, Harmsworth, who had withdrawn the *Sunday Daily Mail*, paid £5,000 for the *Observer*. As a price, it was high for the property: sales were '2,000 in winter and 4,000 in summer'; but low for a man whose personal income[2] after tax was £115,000 (about £4.5 million today). Beyond offering the editorship to J.L. Garvin, literary critic in the *Fortnightly Review* and leader and special writer on the *Telegraph*, he seems to have confined his interest to using the *Mail*'s distribution system with some small effect.

In 1908 Garvin did accept, in return for a fifth-share interest in the paper. He quickly collected 'a very fine team' of arts writers and himself became known for thundering leader-page articles of enormous length on such highly topical subjects as naval building, airplanes, the Territorial Army, tariffs and House of Lords reform.

In three years he had raised the circulation to 39,000 and the paper showed 'a small uncertain profit'. Meanwhile, Admiral 'Jackie' Fisher and Lord Roberts used Garvin for their leaks on comparable Anglo-German strengths – in the same style as to Churchill before the Second World War. The *Observer* soon became compulsory reading for all those interested in the arts and the great issues of the day. The circulation soared to an unheard-of level for a Sunday paper – 200,000 – and the profits were such that Garvin had untouchable editorial independence.

The link with Lord Northcliffe, as Harmsworth had now become, had ended in 1911 when Garvin's policies continually clashed with those of the *Daily Mail*. Northcliffe was arbitrarily offensive to those who could not answer back, but all reason and charm to those in a position to stand up for themselves, like his 'dear Garvino'. Friendly bickering had been frequent between the two but the break became inevitable when Northcliffe woke in a Brighton hotel on a Sunday morning and read the *Observer* contents bill outside: 'Tariff Reform: Answer to *Daily Mail*'s "Unanswerable Question" '.[3] Northcliffe gave Garvin three weeks to find someone to buy him out. The new owner, who also bought Garvin's share, was W.W. (later Viscount) Astor MP, who had no inclination, nor experience, to interfere.

[2] Mostly from Harmsworth Brothers (later the Amalgamated Press) with its magazines, which included *Answers, Comic Cuts, Home Chat, Marvel.*

[3] I may not have got the wording absolutely correct, but that was the gist of Garvin's humorous tale at lunch in 1946. It is borne out by his article of 12 February 1911.

This was the opposition when William took control of the *Sunday Times*, incorporating the *Sunday Special*, on 6 June 1915. The change came in a single-column announcement towards the bottom of the second news page, between two small items, one headed 'Wrongful Dismissal' and the other 'Strike Settled', reproduced here in exact size:

THE "SUNDAY TIMES."

The controlling interest in THE SUNDAY TIMES has been acquired by W. E. and J. Gomer Berry, of the firm of Ewart, Seymour, and Co., Limited, Windsor House, Kingsway, W.C., publishers.

June 6, 1915

If over-modest, the announcement was a repudiation of the long-established custom of an unctuous preamble to a purchase. When Northcliffe made his first assay into newspapers with the purchase of the London *Evening News* in 1894 (for £25,000 or, after inflation, about half the sum William had paid for the *Sunday Times* twenty years later) he wrote a main page panel: 'free from fad or prejudice ... gospel of loyalty to the Empire ... unfalteringly Conservative ... advanced democratic platform ... sympathetic towards Labour ... friendly to every phase of communal advancement ...', and a good deal more.

The *Sunday Times* circulation, static at under 20,000 since 1910, had been rising with the war and was now around 30,000. Advertising revenue for 1915, despite the talk in the *Sunday Times* official history, *The Pearl of Days*, of lucrative government advertising, was the lowest since 1909. Profits, after the preference dividend, between £5,000 and £7,000 in the earlier years, had been badly hit. The turnout for the whole of 1915 was a trading loss of over £2,000.

Now, ten years later, William had the chance to run a newspaper on the 'different lines' he had urged on Thomasson, when the latter was letting the *Tribune* run down. 'Different lines' involved first of all getting the balance right – the balance of news, sport, features, the arts, leading articles, one with another – for which a single guiding hand is required. That evaluated, the presentation of each can be considered in detail. It was not so much a question of who does what but, at first, how *he* should do it. The *Sunday Times* of June 1915 had some good things in it, but looked at as a whole it was plain chaos.

In an obituary in 1954, W.W. Hadley (Editor of the *Sunday Times* from 1932 to 1950) repeated the tale of a contemporary that William, normally calmly decisive, in those days was 'like a tornado – working swiftly, moving vehemently from one task to another and impatient with slower-paced colleagues'. Looking at the last issue of the *Sunday Times* before he took over, I am not surprised. The tiny staff – Leonard Rees the Editor, who had started with the *Sunday Special* in 1897 and who died in the *Sunday Times*' chair in 1931; the news editor; the sub-editor; and sundry 'Saturdays only', needed to be told of the error of their vast omissions. If a good deal of exaggeration was needed, then so be it. William did admit to raising his voice to the printer betimes but, to his family later, denied rather unconvincingly that he ever swore. The tornado quietened down in later years, though just occasionally there were alarming gusts. In the early 1930s, he reduced his nephew, Business Manager of the *Newcastle Evening Chronicle*, to sobs on the telephone, reporting the incident with astonishing lack of self-revelation: 'I wouldn't have minded if he'd thrown the telephone out of the window'. After the Second World War, when he had handed over to me the day-to-day running of the *Telegraph*, he once leaned across his desk to me and said: 'You should slap the news-editor's face.' Hadley himself wrote that, in his 'five happy years' as editor, William 'only once said something that hurt. He gripped both my hands and said, "Forget it! Forget it!"'

Looking back so long afterwards, I think he never understood how terrifying his momentary exasperation could be to the recipient. Most terrifying men mean to terrify. They are bullies. William's lightning flashes were only destructive if they met a non-conducting surface, like his nephew. On the single occasion that I, with the privileged impertinence of a son, lost my temper: 'If that's the way you want it, you had better get someone else to do the job': he seemed genuinely puzzled. 'Oh, I didn't mean it like that,' he replied.

William, more than any other editor I have heard of, always insisted that, in so far as a newspaper consists of so many parts, and as no one reader wants to read everything, the parts must be arranged cóherently and, as far as possible, in the same place every week. The reader must be able to find his way about. Moreover, the reader does not like being jostled. In the days of his maturity he would say that readers would not notice much change in format from issue to issue, but that if they were to look back for a month they might be astonished by what quiet change had taken place.

I am perhaps anticipating. The news presentation of that last pre-William issue was so awful that any change would have been for the better. Evidently in the editor's eye, if he used his eye at all, the paper began on the leader page and then was continued on to the facing page, the main news page. The leaders went on till they stopped, perhaps leaving a void into which was put a poem, or, on the want of it, three police court items. Then began the usual weighty war situation report/article by a retired colonel. The last column was soon reached and the article overflowed on to the top of the first column of the main news page (hardly any newspaper carried editorial on the front page at that time). The main story of the day headed the second column. If it, too, overflowed, the turn occupied the top of column three. Other stories, long, short and middling, waited their turn. Where they fell was dependent on the order, indiscernible, in which they were put in. In army terms, the raggletaggle dressed by the left.

The heading sizes were indiscriminate and sometimes there were white spaces left in the middle of the page which the sub-editor had not found time to fill. The rest of the paper, though, had a mass of fillers, which were put on a particular page not because of relevance but because of their relative length.

In the early years William, though he had titled himself Managing Editor, acted as chief sub-editor himself on Saturdays.[4] All his life he saw sub-editing as the key role on a newspaper – the task of evaluating (copy-tasting), checking, arrangement, allocation of stories to particular pages; the power to see the possibilities in the seemingly dull, to develop them or have them developed; to downgrade and condense as more important items come in; to discard the woolly; to tell a story in arresting sequence; to signpost in cunningly worded headings in pleasantly contrasting types.

The tricks of the trade, an outsider might say, but the key to the sustained attention of the reader. A prime example of their flowering in a popular paper was the *Daily Express*, edited by Arthur Christiansen in the late 1930s, 40s and 50s, described honorifically as 'a sub-editor's paper'. I seldom saw William angrier than when, enquiring of a nephew (another one) after six weeks' sub-editing as to how he liked it, was given the reply, 'Oh, I think I have pretty well mastered it.'

The managing editor, or chief sub-editor on a small paper, has the preliminary task of preparing the dummy – the sequence of blank pages marked out only in columns (seven in the case of the *Sunday Times*)

---

[4] He rarely got home before 4 am on Sunday morning. It was a Sunday treat for my brother and myself, aged about eight and six, to pull his bedclothes off to get him up for lunch.

and the position of advertising indicated.[5] On these, features or news, or a mixture of both, would be catch-lined, together with the estimate of their length. In that last pre-William issue, the chaos on those 'away' pages was almost as great. Features written on Friday night found their predestined place, but anything relating to them but written on Saturday might be anywhere. In that issue, 'music' was printed on pages four, five, twelve and seventeen, with twelve lines on page six.

While many newspapermen who have written memoirs tip their hats to William as a 'great journalist', almost all of them have been puzzled by his refusal to appoint great writers as editors, wondering how his papers prospered exceedingly notwithstanding. His two great successes – the creation of the *Sunday Times* as the leading Sunday quality paper and the phoenix-like revival of *The Daily Telegraph* from 1928 – were edited by the same two men almost throughout their lives. Both had been inherited from a previous regime. Leonard Rees had become Editor of the *Sunday Special* in 1897. He was a good but not outstanding writer. Arthur Watson, appointed in 1926, retired as Editor of *The Daily Telegraph* in 1950 at the age of seventy, but wrote only rarely. Why, those newspapermen asked, did William not appoint some giant of opinion who would set his stamp on the paper and get it talked about and listened to throughout the land? Where was his C.P. Scott,[6] the 'founder' of the world-famous *Manchester Guardian*; his J.A. Spender of the *Westminster Gazette*, 'read by people of all shades of opinion'; his J.L. Garvin of the *Observer*, even his W.T. Stead, who invented 'stunt journalism' in the *Pall Mall Gazette*? Perhaps it was, as Leonard Russell observed, 'not a good idea to have two lions in one cage'.

The answer was supplied in 1947 by William himself: 'More than one newspaper has been ruined by the brilliant writer placed in the editor's chair.' The fact is that brilliant writers are born with the potential of brilliance, but so are sub-editors.[7] They are seldom born of the same mother. Each of them needs time and experience to develop. Few journalists have the aptitude to be equally good at both.

The chief executive on the news side, whatever his title, not only has to have the experience and aptitude to do every job himself when necessary but, equally important, to direct other people. He is the

---

[5] As business then still worked a five and a half-day week, the make-up was often thrown out by late advertising.

[6] Scott's career confounds those who argue which of youth or experience is the more important in journalism. He took the editor's chair at twenty-six and left it at eighty-three.

[7] I am here using 'sub-editors' as a compendium term for those with a nose for news and an intuition of how to present it. Christiansen used to say that he had always in mind a yuppy in Norfolk with a wife and two small children.

conductor, while 'the brilliant writer' is the chief violin. He need not go to the length to which Harold Evans went in his brief tenure of the editor's chair at *The Times*, of moving the arts writers around as they seemed to be getting stale in their specialities. On the contrary, as Christiansen wrote: 'An editor must know the kind of work the members of his staff do best and the courage and wit to let them do it.'

Scott, who as often as not was incommunicado for two hours in the afternoon writing 'the long' (leading article) and was regularly in London picking up and forming views, coined the immortal phrase: 'Facts are sacred, but comment is free', but his subordinates were sadly mortal in interpreting the first half. Spender, who was so eagerly read, ruined his paper by giving no importance to late news. Garvin, at any rate in his later days, never came into the office before Saturday, and sometimes was still adding to his article in the second edition.

'Brilliant writers' tend always to be crusading in political or social fields and it is their views on such topics that lead political observers to classify their papers. But it is not, or should not be, a proper classification of the whole. Even Leonard Russell, with his very long experience, could write of those early days: 'Mr William Berry ... and Leonard Rees were in touch throughout the week about Sunday's paper. It would not be true to say that a political line was being evolved because the war had confused all that.'

It would not have been true to say that at any time, war or no war. Of course they would have been conferring on the subjects of articles and their authors. But their minds were not dominated by search for a policy as if the *raison d'être* of a newspaper was to constitute a political 'opposition' or ginger group. When William was building up a paper he always knew what the gist of leading articles was going to be – though he never went to the length that Gomer went, when he eventually had control of the *Sunday Times*, of having them sent by despatch rider to his Buckinghamshire home to be passed before printing – and William always, if necessary, took responsibility for the line later.

Indeed, when he was later not so much in touch day to day, he was sometimes irritated to hear people say the editor acted independently. He was not greatly concerned in the manoeuvres of politics, or politicians, but he was always deeply interested in their relative strengths of character, just as Beaverbrook, a bit like a woman, was interested in their weaknesses. I think Russell was only half right in saying that, 'Berry was a natural Conservative and upholder of authority, even if he imagined at this time that he was Liberal in his political outlook.' His stance on character in politics, even though with hindsight he can be seen to have been mistaken on this occasion, was vividly illustrated

at the time of the break-up of the Coalition in 1922. He was in America
for three weeks before that event and so can be excused for not picking
up the gossip, so long bottled up, about Lloyd George and his equally
venal Chief Whip, Captain 'Freddie' Guest. His stance was also con-
ditioned by his previous support of Lloyd George over the Chanak
Crisis when it was proposed, without the agreement of the French or
the Dominions, 'to chase the Turk out of Europe' (though on 8 October
in his absence the *Sunday Times* switched tack following a sour letter
from Bonar Law in *The Times*). The ostensible flash point was exasperation at the monopoly of power in the hands of Lloyd George,
Austen Chamberlain and Birkenhead. On 20 October, the actual day of
the famous Carlton Club meeting,[8] he gave an interview to the *Christian
Science Monitor*:

> There is only a real difference of policy on one outstanding issue ...
> protection ... I should respect the choice of the nation if it fell on so
> thoroughly honest a man as Andrew Bonar Law but ... he is not in
> the same flight with Mr Lloyd George, with the latter's personal
> charm, his unparalleled political sagacity and his compelling moral
> fervour.

A strong proof that William at thirty-nine, twenty-five years at work
and not yet at all affluent,[9] regarded himself more as a businessman
than a former of opinion, was the murky affair of the *Daily Chronicle*
in 1918.

Lloyd George, assisted by Bonar Law, had manoeuvred Asquith out
of the Prime Ministership in December 1916, but almost all of the other
Liberal leaders, and a large section of their backbenchers, had gone too.
Lloyd George had no political fund – that was soon put right – and no
guaranteed press. The powerful, Liberal *Daily Chronicle* had turned
against Asquith but its proprietor, Frank Lloyd, was not in good health.

Only a month after taking office, the new Prime Minister dropped
hints to Robert Donald, the remarkable editor who seems nowadays to
be largely forgotten, in the presence of Neil Primrose, Lord Rosebery's
elder MP son, that he would like to secure control. Through various
intermediaries abortive efforts were made to persuade Lloyd to sell at
half his price and to bamboozle canny old Lord Leverhulme (he had
bought a peerage in the meantime) into putting up the money.

A second phase began in 1918, when Lord Beaverbrook attempted

---

[8] The Conservative Party decided to leave the Lloyd George Coalition, precipitating a General
Election.
[9] Both he and Gomer now each had six children.

to put together a syndicate which would give him control and £20,000 in commission. In return he would guarantee *Daily Chronicle* support of Lloyd George for five years. There was some suggestion – though Beaverbrook later denied it, laughing boisterously: 'My God, no!' – that the *Daily Express* would be committed as well by the guarantee. After a while, Frank Lloyd would have nothing more to do with a gossip-generating Tory nor Donald with a 'Canadian financial buccaneer' (which was one up from his earliest soubriquet on his arrival in England: 'the little Canadian adventurer'[10].

Then Lloyd George lost confidence in Donald in May 1918 when the *Chronicle* seemed to side with Asquith in the Maurice debate[11] and a third phase began.

I cannot be sure of the exact details of that third phase, since they are recorded only in letters[12] from Guest to Lloyd George or his secretary. It seems from one of those letters that Beaverbrook, though he could not be a front man as Frank Lloyd would have nothing more to do with him, was still interested financially ('I have our Max in the office with all the details'). Somehow Sir Henry Dalziel, MP, proprietor through his wife's money of *Reynold's News* (later sold to the Co-Op) and buyer/seller of several small newspapers, secured an option on the *Chronicle* and attempted to form his own syndicate. Guest added a larger syndicate of his own, the biggest subscriber being the immensely rich fourth Marquess of Bute, owner of half Cardiff, who would certainly have known Lord Rhondda and now, after the latter's death, Seymour, chairman of most of the Rhondda companies.[13] Meanwhile William, probably through Beaverbrook, had found out what was going on and, stipulated by Bute and supported as a professional by Guest, had put in for 'complete commercial control'.

Guest's letter adds:

One last matter ... the Berry's have an opportunity of selling the *Sunday Times* – to Max Beaverbrook [for £200,000] I have agreed with them that they shall *not* do this until our deal is through. This

---

[10] The phrase was coined by Balfour's secretary.

[11] General Maurice, sacked Director of Military Operations at the War Office, had accused Lloyd George in a letter to *The Times* of lying over the numbers of combatant soldiers.

[12] August and September 1918. After his death, the Lloyd George papers, like others intended for biography, were bought by Beaverbrook from Frances, Countess Lloyd George. They are now in the House of Lords Record Office.

[13] Bute was not a politician but when he expressed himself at all he was a Free Trader and a strong supporter of Lloyd George. He had had an interest in coal but later sold his last coal mine to Seymour's partner, David Llewellyn.

leverage is very important as Max can help or hinder us greatly, though indirectly.

The deal did not go through (a different one, with the Lloyd George fund putting up most of the money, was concluded by the end of the year), nor did the sale of the *Sunday Times*. Nothing whatever was written about it until 1972, when Beaverbrook's biographer, A.J.P. Taylor, and the *Sunday Times* official history, both came upon the papers. William did write laconically in 1947: 'The *Sunday Express* saw the light of day in 1918 after abortive negotiations between Lord Beaverbrook and myself, whereby the *Sunday Times* might have passed into his ownership ...', but that is all. Both the other authors conclude that the Berry brothers submitted to a Guest veto on the sale on the supposition that they were Lloyd George supporters through thick and thin. But a press list of political affiliations drawn up by the Coalition Whips Office in 1920 casts doubt on this. The *Observer*, still out ahead at 150,000 circulation, is described as 'very friendly', while the *Sunday Times*, now at 80,000, is 'semi-friendly'. (As one would expect, the *Sunday Express* is 'erratic'.) My own conclusion is that Guest was too clever by half. He destroyed Beaverbrook's leverage, whatever that was, and Beaverbrook pulled the plug, leaving the Berrys with no contract. It can hardly have been Lloyd George's doing because, though the final deal cost his fund £1 million (on which he made a 200 per cent profit in 1926), Dalziel remained as Chairman and got his peerage, free, in 1920. The Berry brothers missed a lucrative long-term contract and the manoeuvring power of money in the bank, but they might otherwise have been prevented from their extraordinary flurry of activity in the next three years.

*   *   *

William's first chance to show how a great political event should be treated journalistically came with the shattering incident of the Lansdowne letter. The Marquess of Lansdowne, lately Governor-General of Canada, Viceroy of India and Foreign Secretary, wrote a letter to *The Times* after Russia had ceased to fight in November 1917, espousing a compromise peace. It got all the more publicity because *The Times* refused to publish it and it appeared in *The Daily Telegraph* instead. Let Russell describe impartially the *Sunday Times* reaction:

> It was the *Sunday Times*' first real test under its new owners, for more conventional denunciation was not enough, and it came out of it with distinction ... [There were] two representatives' views ... on the leader page side by side, one a decent straightforward attack by Lord

Sydenham [lately Governor of Victoria, Australia and Bombay, and Secretary of the Committee of Imperial Defence] the other a rollicking bitter savaging by G.K. Chesterton. The leading article ... was in that tone of exasperated charity culminating in a crushing finale which marks the outstanding operator.

*   *   *

So precarious was the financial condition of the paper in 1915 that there was no question of adding to the editorial staff. Indeed, even when it was making considerable money in later years it was always William's policy to pay well for contributors but to keep the permanent staff at a level which would now be unbelievable. When *The Daily Telegraph* spawned the *Sunday Telegraph* in 1961 its initial staff was around fifty, soon rising to seventy, not counting those 'Saturdays only'. When the *Sunday Times* moved its printing, and its staff, to the *Telegraph* in 1932, it was said jokingly that they arrived in a taxi.

Soon the presentation of the news became more dashing. Much more white space was used and a seven-column 'streamer' headline often strengthened the main news page. By the end of the First World War the layout was more modern than *The Times* or the *Telegraph* and, except for the later addition of pictures, lasted well into the 1930s. Occasionally there were lapses in the attempt to print the latest news. In one early issue, the lead story in column one was of the German capture of a key Verdun fort. In the right-hand column, under the heading 'Late War News', the fort has been retaken. On 30 January came the first Zeppelin raid on London. William was walking homewards after putting the paper to bed when he saw a Zeppelin picked up by searchlights. He returned to the office and got out the only Zeppelin edition of the London press.[14]

On the leader page, as I have already recorded, Lord Sydenham and G.K. Chesterton (of *Penny Illustrated Paper* days) were imported as regular contributors. Certainly the latter was engaged by William. He told me that, so taut was Chesterton's writing (and a lesson to latter-day prima donnas) he once took an hour to cut his column-length article by five lines. For economy's sake, contributors never got proofs (author's corrections cost extra) until the arrival of Edmund Gosse who, needing the money, had lowered himself to write literary journalism and then been unaccountably turned away by the *Daily Chronicle* in 1919

---

[14] Unfortunately the issue is missing from the British Museum Newspaper Library.

after Donald's dismissal.[15] He never came into the office and his copy could never be touched.

There were at first few regular 'arts' writers of distinction, who count so much in establishing the reputation of a quality Sunday. There was a dramatic critic, an art correspondent (who lasted until 1937) and music notes by the editor himself.

Books were the weakest feature. In June 1915, coverage consisted mostly of short summaries, probably taken from the publisher's blurb, and few what would now be called reviews. Not till after the end of the war did Rees secure the two Titans of books and music – Edmund Gosse, friend of all the late nineteenth-century 'Olympians', and Ernest Newman. When Gosse died in 1927 his successor, Desmond MacCarthy,[16] was suggested by my mother.

Rees and Murray (the latter with a little of the slam-bang style of the popular journalist, which led to friction with Rees) wrote most of the leading articles, though William lent a hand when he had a subject. After he had himself 'attested' in December 1915, he wrote several times on the Derby scheme (a modified form of conscription), which was known to have been worked out but which the Government, so like all governments, was holding back from publication. One can detect William's 'En Passant' style in his obvious reference to Northcliffe's *Daily Mail* (all his life he regarded Northcliffe, particularly in his early days, as the greatest journalist of the age, but he was often wary of his methods): 'the paper which gets things done – an ambiguous and perhaps doubtful diploma by the way – was engaged in a remarkable warfare ...'

When, after a time, William gave up being chief sub-editor himself, he was still the 'working journalist' on Saturdays. Russell relates:

> The new chief sub-editor had been entirely unimpressed when Mr William in his shirt-sleeves had stalked into the room with page proofs in his hand and said, 'There's a lot of corrections here.' The chief sub had barely looked up. 'Right-o,' he said, 'shove 'em in that tray and I'll see to 'em when I get time.' It had become known that Mr William ... had approved this attitude as that of a keen man; he often had a word of praise for diligent servants of the firm.

He had little opportunity of getting outside London to report the war effort but in 1916, and again in 1917 to Verdun (when he re-met

---

[15] Gosse, at one time Librarian of the House of Lords Library, had been Co-Editor of the unsuccessful *Daily Mail Literary Supplement* in Northcliffe's early days.

[16] Stephen Koss, in *The Rise and Fall of the Political Press in Britain*, claims that the *Sunday Times* had rejected a book review by Desmond McCarthy in 1922 'making sport' of Lloyd George.

Carpentier), he volunteered for conducted tours of the front for editors. The Somme tour, in 1916, on the hundredth day of that bloody and almost fruitless campaign, presented the obvious dilemma of pointing the finger or overdoing the anodyne. He attempted no purple passages but instead wrote three columns of close type (about 4,500 words) obviously meant to boost home morale with the high spirits and efficiency of all arms, both at the front and in rear areas. He even had a good word to say for the War Office. He refuted Churchill, who had made a speech in the House of Commons complaining that too many fit young soldiers were being kept on jobs behind the line. On the contrary, he wrote, these men were recuperating after extended service forward and were doing a splendid job refurbishing anything that could be refurbished – British and German hand grenades (!) bombs, dud shells, rifles, old boots, uniforms, debris of any kind – reminding him of 'the claim of the Chicago stockyards that they use all the hog except his squeak'.

Newsprint rationing was quickly relaxed after the First World War – unlike its ten-year continuance after the second – and the *Sunday Times* was able to expand its paging. Moreover, the exclusion of most other subjects in favour of war topics was no longer necessary. In particular, expansion took the form of a steady stream of memoirs by leaders from both sides. The *Sunday Times* in 1919 ran the stories of Admiral Tirpitz and of Bethman Holweg, the German Chancellor in 1914. The greatest coup was the Diary of Margot Asquith, wife of the deposed Prime Minister, in two volumes. Like so many good serials, they were not good books, but instead had enormous vitality and offensive anecdotes in every second paragraph.

The first volume cost only £1,000 as against the estimate of its worth by the editor of Northcliffe's *Sunday Dispatch* (who had not heard of it in advance[17]) of £2,500. But William kicked himself after the event when he refused to buy Lytton Strachey's icon-busting Life of Queen Victoria, an enormous success as a book. I am not sure that his self-recrimination was justified. It was the sort of book from which it would have been difficult to get the same impact with disjointed excerpts at weekly intervals.

His 'blockbuster' would have been the *War Memoirs* of Lloyd George. This was announced in August 1922, when Lloyd George was still in office. William led a syndicate which contracted to buy world rights for

---

[17] The editor was surprised not to have been rebuked by Northcliffe. He did not know that Northcliffe himself had miffed it. Northcliffe had received a letter from Mrs Asquith asking him to be kind to it. Without replying he arranged that the editor of *The Times* should see her 'in a day or two'. Thereafter, as he had done several times in the past, he refused *Sunday Times* advertisements.

£90,000, of which £15,000 was the *Sunday Times* share; minus, probably, £5,000, which he would have been able to earn back for other Empire serial rights.

Uproar was immediate, not only from all leaders of opinion but also from all the French press, that money derived from war leadership should be the property of the nation rather than of a single individual, however distinguished. It was the same argument as that used of 'the war of the soldiers'. The war had not been won by the generals but by Tommy Atkins. The *Daily Mail* (Northcliffe was dead now) observed that it was easy to see why Mr Lloyd George, expecting the early collapse of his Government as the result of his failure to get any money for reparations from Germany, should be writing his £90,000-book for Sir William Berry (as he had now become). 'As he has not made Germany pay he is going to make Sir William Berry pay.'

At first Lloyd George seemed to capitulate and said that all proceeds would be given to charity. But Lloyd George was never a man to go quietly. Three months later the United Press Agency announced that, while the *War Memoirs* would naturally be several years in preparation, the author had contracted to write weekly or fortnightly articles on topics to be chosen. This time it was the turn of the world publishers to explode. They threatened to bring a High Court action to compel cancellation of the contracts, to which he yielded with reluctance and did not return their £5,000 deposit until 1925. Finally, in 1933–6, William again bought the *War Memoirs*, for *The Daily Telegraph*, and though by this time public interest had largely evaporated, some 20,000 copies a day were added by the serialisation.

Another ingredient of the paper marked out for expansion was the realm of 'gossip', or topical notes, as he visualised them. This was made up of three separate 'columns' of differing emphasis. Most important was a feature by T.P. O'Connor, the Irish nationalist MP, father of the House of Commons and veteran journalist. After a stint on the younger Bennett's *New York Herald*, he had made his name as a brilliant parliamentary sketch writer of the 1880s, had started an evening paper and for many years was Editor of *T.P.'s Weekly* and other weeklies in the same style. His feature was called 'Men, Women and Memories', written in a style, as he described it himself, 'previously regarded as impertinent, if not indecent'. People in the public eye 'shall be presented as they are – living, breathing, in blushes or tears – and not merely by the words that they utter'. A second, anonymous column, beneath O'Connor, was entitled 'Talk of the Town' by 'Atticus', a non-political version with less use of reminiscence. Yet a third, on a different page, was a social gossip column by 'Mayfair' in the same style as the *Country*

Gentleman to which William had been supposed to contribute as part of his first job on the *Investors Guardian*.

As a result of these activities and the improvement of the arts pages, the circulation of the *Sunday Times* continued to increase at war's end when most papers suffered a natural contraction. The 30,000 circulation of 1915 had risen to 55,000 in 1919, jumped to 80,000 in 1920 and was 110,000 by 1923. Three years later, it was described in the *American Editor and Publisher* as 'probably one of the most brilliantly edited newspapers in the country'. The paper was now in the same league as the *Observer*, but it took ten years' slog to get by. Similarly, following the loss in 1915 and hardly break-even results for the two years following, profit in 1918 had risen to the 1913 level, nearly doubled in 1919 and 1920, halved in the slump of 1921 and finally surged ahead thereafter.

CHAPTER EIGHT

1918–1923

AT THE END of the war, William was still spending most of his time on the *Sunday Times*. However, he now left after the first edition, around 6 pm on Saturdays, and had changed his editorial title from Managing Editor to Editor-in-Chief.

Meanwhile, Seymour had prospered mightily by association with Lord Rhondda, first as his principal lieutenant, then as his 'stand-in' when Rhondda entered the Government in December 1916, and finally as a partner with his daughter, Lady Rhondda, on her father's death two years later. By 1919 he had become a director of 'over forty companies'. His biggest coup was the purchase, on deferred terms, of John Lysaght, a large private steel company owned by an old Irish family who thought it was time to sell. He bought it for £5 million and sold it three months later to another steel company of about the same size, Guest, Keen & Nettlefold,[1] which had already bought the Dowlais, Merthyr, steelworks from the Guests, for £6 million. Seymour took his two brothers to a board meeting of the latter company and convinced them of the benefit of the amalgamation. 'It's a bargain,' he concluded in his auctioneer's patter. Seymour became Vice-Chairman and William went on the new board. Before this Seymour had cut his brothers in on several of his smaller deals and he, in turn, had become a director of the *Sunday Times*, holding a small number of preference shares.

William, for his part, had formed his own small London coterie which used to meet for lunch on Saturdays, at which time most of them had finished their working week. At the suggestion of Joe Thorp, they called themselves 'The Moderately Successful Merchant Adventurers'. The team, which was probably never complete at any one time, consisted of those who had been at William's bachelor party: Herbert Morgan, Jim (Murray) Allison, Wareham Smith, William Wallace, H. Powell Rees, Edward Hunter, Sydney Carroll and Gomer, with the addition of Major Count Vanden Heuval, always known as Van. He was a naturalised

---

[1] When Seymour became Vice-Chairman he discovered that the land on which the Dowlais works had been built was only an annual lease, inhibiting development. He succeeded to the chairmanship when the old chairman died. The brothers took a large part of the purchase price in shares, leaving Seymour as the largest individual shareholder in Guest, Keen.

Dutchman of an Italian opera-singer mother ('an impressive old lady, all in black with a black lace scarf over her white hair, an ebony cane and a most authoritative manner',[2] who lived in Paris). Van was ten years younger than the rest of them, though he was already in advertising in 1909 when he attended the dinner for the founders of the *Advertising World*. During the First World War he had been in MI6 in Switzerland, where his many languages could be exploited, and he was to repeat the exercise in the Second World War, when he partnered Allen Dulles (brother of John Foster Dulles) in the closing stages. By now he was Commercial Manager of Eno's Fruit Salts, but already looked, with his toothbrush moustache and delicate hands, more like a diplomat than a salesman. Eileen Hunter describes him as 'grey-haired, grey-eyed, small featured with a caressing speaking voice, a slight foreign accent and elegant figure – in fact a charmer'.

What the Merchants adventured into I have rarely been able to discover although, for William's part, I think they were given underwriting in many of the large ventures in which he now was about to invest. This was a time when a lot of small business ideas were being exploited and the Adventurers between them had many contacts. They seem to have found their meetings fruitful and their camaraderie stimulating. According to Edward Hunter, 'Deals however important were often concluded on the nod – a mere handshake sealing an inviolable and trusted bargain. Once a bargain was gone back on, the backslider became an outcast from the group.' It may have been a 'backslider' who was the subject of a mysterious caper by William and Colonel Fred Cripps[3] (elder brother of Sir Stafford Cripps, Attlee's Chancellor of the Exchequer and his exact opposite). Dressed in cloaks, they were supposed to have cornered their victim in his office. There they uncovered soda water syphons and, standing on either side, soaked him.

*   *   *

In 1919 there were three financial morning papers. Early in the year, William bought the smallest of them, the *Financier and Bullionist*, so small that the purchase did not earn a mention in the trade press.

In November he bought the *Financial Times*, the market leader, which

---

[2] The 'old lady' once 'auditioned' my eldest sister but 'was sadly disappointed'. Like William, my sister had no ear for music.

[3] Cripps was ruined by the Russian Revolution. Before the war he had owned an export-import business in St Petersburg.

had been controlled since 1904 by Sir John Ellerman,[4] a self-made accountant who had amassed the largest fortune in Britain, in shipping and investment trusts. No one ever pulled off a bargain with Ellerman but the deal made sense to William as the *Financial Times* owned the St Clement's Press, printers also of the *Sunday Times* as well as of the majority of prospectuses, then burgeoning after the long sleep of war. The evening *Star*, stable companion to the Cadbury-owned *Daily News*, commented:

> Messrs Berry who own the *Sunday Times*, have just purchased the *Financial Times* and thus another important newspaper deal ... the transaction is a rather natural development of the business enterprises of Mr W.E. Berry, a man of wide financial and commercial outlook and I fancy is an admirable type of the 'ten thousand a year man' for whom Sir Albert Stanley is searching [Stanley, later Lord Ashfield and unifier of the London Underground, was President of the Board of Trade].

How it was financed I have found no record, except that part of the bill was set off by the £150,000 sale back to the old shareholders of their periodicals, headed by the prestigious *Drapers' Record*. The deal was said to have involved about £300,000.[5]

The *Financial Times* purchase was followed a week later by that of H.R. Baines, publishers of the oldest daily picture paper, the *Daily Graphic*, the weekly *Graphic* (a rival to the *Illustrated London News*) and the *Bystander* (a rival to the *Tatler*). The *Daily Graphic*, at a circulation of 80,000, was, however, way behind the *Daily Mirror* (Lord Rothermere, over 1 million) and the *Daily Sketch* (Sir Edward Hulton, 840,000).

The deal was announced baldly in *The Times*, with a curious rider, on the main news page: 'The scheme will meet with opposition from those who are aware that these shares formerly changed hands at more than £40 each.' (The offer, recommended by the directors, was £32.) Northcliffe turned out to own forty-seven shares. It may have been his practice, like William later, to hold small parcels of shares in newspaper companies in order to get their balance sheets. But the phrase 'formerly',

---

[4] Ellerman had for long held an interest in newspapers, though he took no part in their editorial direction. He admired Northcliffe and, in its early days, bought a share in the *Daily Mail* from one of the brothers, St John, who needed money for investment in Perrier water. He became a shareholder in *The Times* when Northcliffe bought control in 1908. Later he owned the *Illustrated London News*, the *Tatler* and the *Sphere*.

[5] *Daily Mail* estimate. The brothers acquired 'over £140,000 of the £172,000 nominal ordinary capital and 28,000 of 100,000 preference'.

without specifying how long before, or in what circumstances, seems unprofessional. Northcliffe commented to Howard Corbett, later Manager of *The Times*: 'I feel sure I could have got much more for them.' The next day he added: 'I enquired about these Berrys. They are quite respectable.' To Wareham Smith he said a little later: 'I hope these Berry people are all right. I admire them but they have not the experience of running a group of newspapers. It is a fearful strain.'

By this time William had begun to be noticed in the political world. In recognition of the rising reputation of the *Sunday Times* he had already been invited several times to Lloyd George's 'breakfasts' (since they did not start till 9.30 they were really brunches). Now that the 'Berry interests' included the new purchases, he began to be worked on by the Prime Minister's press secretary, a buccaneering civil servant brought from the Ministry of Munitions, William (Bronco Bill) Sutherland.

Sutherland, a notorious manipulator, reported to his master:

[The Berry brothers are] in the habit of talking a bit about the need of new men in the Government, the desirability of dropping Walter Long, Austen Chamberlain,[6] etc. ... [but that was to be tolerated as they had] considerable ambitions and intend, if they can, to rival Northcliffe [Northcliffe did not die until August 1922].

They are spending a lot of money on the *Sunday Times* and intend to make a big thing of the *Graphic* etc., newspapers which they have recently acquired ... they are men to be taken seriously ... Their public ambitions at the moment are to become JPs[7] [which Sutherland said he had already requested the Lord Chancellor (Birkenhead) to arrange] ... with a little effort I am sure we can keep them substantially in hand.

In the following year the pace – and the size – of expansion quickened, which may have been made possible by the profit on the Lysaght deal. In September 1920, William was approached by Sir Clarence Smith, Chairman of Cassell's, the book and literary magazine publishers established in 1848. Cassell were short of working capital but already had a debenture outstanding. The deal involved 'over £500,000' (around £7

---

[6] This was the same opinion as expressed by Cecil Harmsworth, Northcliffe's brother, to Lloyd George, before the 1918 General Election. After that election the Conservatives were in the majority in the Coalition Government. Long and Chamberlain had been the two contendants for the Conservative leadership in 1911, with Bonar Law slipping in as *tertius gaudens*.

[7] The reference to JPs is not quite so dismissive as might appear. JMB was a JP for a long period while Seymour, as a 'Merthyr boy' as he always called himself, was already one. William never had such an ambition but Gomer, who had the greater aspiration to be a country gentleman, became not only a JP but high sheriff as well.

million currently). Cassell, who published under the imprint of La Belle Sauvage, had a prestigious backlist, had had a bad patch in the first decade of the century, but had now been brought round. It is possible that William thought the purchase meshed with an interest of the *Sunday Times*, giving it special opportunities for the serialisation of important books. Certainly, he asked Cassell[8] to make a joint book/serial offer for Lloyd George's *War Memoirs* in 1922 and there may have been others. Perhaps it was a precedent for Roy Thomson, when Gomer sold the *Sunday Times* to him in 1959, followed by the purchase of no less than six book publishers.

Two more deals followed quickly in 1920. The first, the purchase of Weldon's, publishers of fashion magazines, was small by the brothers' previous standards but illustrative of their financial methods – the financing of 'equity' by heavy gearing.

May I here interpose a short lecture for the benefit of those not financially literate.

The ownership (equity) of any limited company commands the disposal of the profits after paying the interest on loans. If the proportion of fixed interest capital (debentures or preference shares) is high in proportion to ordinary capital, the company is said to be highly geared. This is nowadays frowned upon. If, say, total profits are £1,000 and fixed interest is £750, then a 25 per cent fall in profits means no surplus for the ordinary shares: a 50 per cent fall means that there is not enough money to pay the fixed charges. That means either that the preference shares acquire votes and so may now control the company or, worse, that if the debenture interest cannot be fully paid, the debenture holders may force a liquidation and leave little or nothing to the other classes of share.

If, on the other hand, the company prospers and earns 50 per cent more, £1,500, the ordinary shareholders are entitled to £750 or three times more than before. This is the 'gearing'.

Such a set-up is, of course, risky. Moreover, unless the preference shares are made redeemable at a premium, at some fixed date, purchasers require very high interest rates to compensate for what is now regarded as certain inflation. In the 1920s and 1930s there was no inflation – in

---

[8] The Literary Editor of Cassell's was Newman Flower. According to Simon Nowell-Smith (*The House of Cassell*), Flower 'sensed the value of getting first-hand accounts of the events and policies of the war from those who had been responsible for its conduct'. The newspaper/book publisher relationship is not always happy. The author is keen to have his book published in full. The newspaper is prepared to pay more than the book publisher but fears that the two or three years' wait necessary for the book's completion will reduce its impact.

fact the value of money steadily increased from its low point in 1920 until 1933.

The Weldon deal was an extreme, almost bizarre, example of heavy gearing. I suspect it may have had its origin at a meeting of the Merchant Adventurers, since it concerned at least four members – William, Gomer, Edward Hunter and Wareham Smith. Weldon's consisted of a number of women's fashion magazines, with an emphasis on patterns for home dressmaking. There seems to have been no connection with any business the brothers had so far conducted. Nor were women's fashions any part of their, or their associates', expertise.

Their interest may have been roused by the observation of the current 'boom and bust' of the post-war business cycle. Women's fashions had changed radically since the war and the competition of smart 'ready-to-wear' in the shops was still in its infancy. Hunter's Sun Engraving was already doing some block-making (illustrations) for Weldon's and he would have known best about Weldon's fortunes. On examination, it was found that the directors, members of the Weldon family and no business people, were making very large profits and building up very large reserves for which there was no obvious need.

William, it must be supposed, then went to the directors and put to them a most ingenious proposition. William and Gomer, he proposed, would take over the control of the business for a token payment of £5,000 in a new class of deferred shares, the equity. All the existing shares would become fixed interest, but with a higher rate of return than they had been receiving. This interest would, of course, be a first charge on the profits of the company but, to guard against the business cycle turning down, the brothers would guarantee the payments from their own resources for seven years. The effect of these arrangements was to increase the reward of the existing shareholders by 30 per cent (£7,000) and to leave the remainder of the profits (the 'equity') to William and Gomer. It was a classical case of 'gearing'. The fortunes of the existing shareholders were secure but the prospective profit (a gamble) of the brothers was unlimited. Sun Engraving got a larger share at the block-making while Wareham Smith, who had retired from the *Daily Mail* after a heart attack, was made Advertising Manager at £1,000 a year and £1,000 expenses.

The arrangement worked very well for all parties for several years until the ready-to-wear competition became stiffer, when profits were affected. The brothers had already drawn £85,000 on their £5,000 investment by 1928 when the guarantee ran out. For them 'the party was over', but they still kept faith with the original shareholders. They surrendered their equity share and their control to Edward Hunter, who reorganised the company, but gave a further guarantee, not so big this time, but for a higher figure than had been the original entitlement. Finally, the whole business was bought by William's Amalgamated Press in 1941, when home dressmaking was thriving once more.

Reading between the lines of a 1928 letter from Edward Hunter to William, suggesting the reorganisation, his view is clear that the company had suffered a lack of management and direction. He could not have taken very seriously the explanation of the brothers' resignation from the board: 'Your directors have left no stone unturned to ... maintain the Company's earning capacity ... [They] have during the last seven years devoted much of their time ... now have so many other duties ...'. Bluntly, though the original shareholders had got a more than fair deal, the company had been 'milked': more money had been paid out in dividends to all recipients than had been earned. It was the least admirable of their publishing investments. Even so, it is fair to observe that it was never treated as the poor relation of their rapidly expanding group. When, in 1924, a dinner was given to the Berry brothers by the directors of their many concerns, Weldon's was included as part of the family, though it is perhaps indicative that the man (not a director) to speak for Weldon's was Wareham Smith. (All the same, I don't expect the dressmaking directors were dab-hands at public speaking.)

The other contemporary deal in 1920, was with Kelly's Directories, a 120-year-old firm with 115 directories and its own printing works. This deal was said at the time to have come about by chance.[9] The Berrys had their eyes on Strand House, the headquarters of W.H. Smith, which was just being vacated and would provide ample office space for their entire group.[10] They were beaten to it by Kelly's and riposted by buying Kelly's themselves, financed as to 20 per cent by Cassell's. Of the remaining 80 per cent, all three brothers contributed, Seymour, now the best off of the three, taking one third, all by bank loan.

This latter purchase led to an important milestone in their career – the acquisition of a third partner, Sir Edward Iliffe. Iliffe was joint owner, with his elder brother, of the Associated Iliffe Press, publishers of a number of specialist magazines like the *Autocar*, the *Electrical Review* and the *Farmer and Stockbreeder*. William thought Iliffe's would fit very well with Kelly's and asked Iliffe, whom he did not know, to come and see him. At first Iliffe refused to sell, but on reflection thought

---

[9] There is evidence, however, that the head of the Kelly family was anxious to sell out.

[10] To encourage the group spirit they started the Berry United Sports Club. Judging by the times of the principal events at the first meeting, this seems to have filled what used to be called 'a long-felt want'. The mile was won in 5 minutes 4.35 seconds and the quarter mile in 56 seconds.

it would be interesting to see what price William might offer. He therefore sent him his last two balance sheets and was astonished to get a letter back by return offering him £1 million in cash, which was exactly double what the two Iliffe brothers, who had spent much of their lives in it, had estimated the business was worth for the purpose of one brother buying out the other. The offer was typical of the way deals were done in those days – no accountants and no lawyers. Iliffe was asked to stay on as Chairman for three months but later bought back 30 per cent of the shares. Over the next twelve years he became a partner with the Berrys in the much bigger deals yet to be made.

Edward Iliffe, two years older than William, was the son of William Iliffe, printer and property investor, of Coventry. He had played a large part in building up the business. As a young man he had been a pioneer motorist in the days of the red flag and was a county-class tennis player. At the end of the First World War he had been knighted for his work as Controller of Machine Tools under Churchill, as Minister of Munitions. After his father's death he had moved the business to London, where, as an offshoot of the *Autocar*, he had started his own insurance company. He had many industrial contacts and a high reputation in the City. Two years later he was to be offered a safe Conservative seat in Parliament.

As a small boy he had been befriended by the twenty-one-year-old Alfred Harmsworth, the Editor of William Iliffe's bicycling magazine. (William Iliffe was the first printer of *Answers to Correspondents*, though he refused to launch the magazine himself. Iliffe abandoned the printing when the unpaid bill had mounted to £1,000 after three or four months – compare William's original capital of £100 for the *Advertising World* fourteen years later. Years later, Edward Iliffe had the embarrassing duty of presenting to Northcliffe the original dummy of *Answers to Correspondents*, which turned out to have been a paste-up on a copy of Sir George Newnes' *Tit-Bits*, its precursor in the same field.

Though he lacked William's dash, Edward Iliffe was a good judge of men, of great shrewdness, with a Midas touch.

* * *

Whether or not Northcliffe had inspired the sour *Times* note on the *Graphic* deal, he made handsome amends a year later. In December 1920, he published, under his own known pseudonym 'Z', a flattering article on the leader page of the *Daily Mail*, entitled 'A New Power in Fleet Street':

There has arisen, almost during the past twelve months a new power in Fleet Street ... There are three brothers in the Berry family, and they are called the busy Bees ... the financial genius of Mr Seymour Berry was utilised by the late Lord Rhondda but Mr Seymour, like his brothers, has long been entirely 'on his own'. He is a director of more public companies than any man living. He thinks in millions.

The other brothers, Mr William E. Berry and Mr J. Gomer Berry, buy newspapers and printing businesses ... that wonderfully successful periodical, the *Advertising World* ... What they have made [of the *Sunday Times*] everybody knows ... In their hands the *Daily Graphic* has been remodelled on thoroughly up-to-date lines ...

Quite recently the Berry's have astonished the publishing world by taking over the famous House of Cassell ...

It is often asked, 'Who is behind them?' The answer is: Nobody. They are operating with their own money and nobody else's. They are an ideal combination. Mr William assumes editorial combination of all the publications; Mr Gomer exercises the business control. In all important matters, however, they act together ... Both have the saving grace of humour. They have never courted publicity, and they are content to work in modest offices. [On another occasion Northcliffe, who had a very grand office at the *Daily Mail*, pronounced 'Big rooms, big minds'] ... They enjoy to the full the amenities of success.

There is no record of how often William had met Northcliffe, after that very first meeting at Harmsworth Brothers (see Chapter 2). Northcliffe had probably become aware of him for his continual criticism of the non-publication of *Daily Mail* circulation figures 1902–3 and certainly when he accepted to join the Sphinx Club in 1905. Perhaps they met again through the good offices of Lord Riddell, when the latter was first Chairman of the Newspaper Proprietors' Association, but certainly not through Lloyd George. Northcliffe, after all, regarded himself as *sui generis* and would heartily have agreed with Beaverbrook's toadying note to him not long before his death: 'You are the premier figure in journalism in the whole history of the profession.'

It is obvious, however, from the personal tone of Northcliffe's *Daily Mail* article that their paths had crossed. The one certain meeting is recorded in a Northcliffe letter to Beaverbrook in December 1920, when the former, having left the Newspaper Proprietors' Association because he would not restrict printers' wages in the slump of 1921, was having second thoughts. He now invited Beaverbrook to lunch for a meeting of the 'sacred caste of Newspaper Proprietors for a simple repast and pow-wow'. He similarly asked Rothermere (*Mirror*), Burnham

My mother, Molly Corns, aged about twenty, before her marriage. In those days it was considered 'fast' for young girls to put their hair up. This was the photograph which stood on the piano of the Corns house at 2 Bolton Street, Piccadilly. William saw it when he dined with the Corns family while my mother was away in America giving herself an education, denied to her by her parents, at Radcliffe Women's College. From the strong character evident in her face one can see why her father called her The Duchess.

Above left My mother after marriage in 1905. She was twenty two: he twenty six.

Above The cartoon presented to William at his bachelor party.

Thomas Corns, my mother's father. A man of independent means, he had some success on the Turf, where he was highly respected. Died 1915.

Above The first cover of the *Advertising World*, designed, if it can be so described, by the printer.

Right A later cover of the *Advertising World*, designed by Herbert Morgan. At first it was printed in full colour but later, for economy, converted to black and white.

William's truck advertising *Boxing*, which toured many towns. At each stop the sides were let down revealing a boxing ring, complete with boxers and seconds with their pails of water. William stands at left as the impresario.

A publicity 'fight' picture set up to advertise *Boxing*. William is shown as referee. The 'boxers' were Eugene Corri, a famous referee, and Jim Driscoll, a champion featherweight.

Drawings made for the dinner given to William and Gomer after their sale of the *Advertising World* in 1909. Left – William, Centre – JMB, Right – Gomer.

'Here amongst us tonight' said the proposer of his health, 'who crowd the chariot wheels of the car of their success is their father and, I do not hesitate to say, admiring William and Gomer Berry as I do, that they owe something to that father who, I am sure, is the proudest man in the room tonight'.

JMB, called on unexpectedly, said he was 'accustomed to speak after dinner but felt unable to express himself as he would like to have done'.

(*Telegraph*), Riddell (*News of the World*), Dalziel (*Chronicle*) and Berry – but not, it should be noted, those whom he thought 'were only in newspapers for money': Lord Astor (*Observer*), the Cadbury's (*Daily News* and (evening) *Star*), and Cowdray (*Westminster Gazette*).

Northcliffe had finished his December 1920 article on the Berry Brothers with the sentence, 'They enjoy to the full the fruits of success.' This was not yet quite true, but in the two years since the end of the war their life styles had changed considerably. In December 1918 William had indeed moved house, but only up the road. The new house was a little bigger than the old one, to accommodate the growing family – there were now six children. There were now three acres instead of two, two grass tennis courts instead of one and, what must have been a selling point, a billiard room masquerading as a study (there was sometimes an enforced hush round it while he wrote leaders for the *Sunday Times*). Whereas he had walked to the station before the war, he now had a chauffeur who drove him to Walton station for Waterloo. He sometimes had the car fetch him back, and when my brother and I would bicycle out to meet him for a car-ride home, our bicycles thrown in the back.

At weekends he would drive himself. He could not have afforded to be a 'pioneer', but had been taught by my mother towards the end of the war. On the inaugural lesson my mother knocked down one of the gateposts while he, on the return journey, smashed the other. Not for nothing was the car, an open Chevrolet, called 'the iron'. He was a normally competent driver except for two idiosyncrasies – he had a phobia of motor-bicyclists and no clear idea of how to reverse. He once turned round and chased a motor-bicyclist who had caused him to brake while I, as a schoolboy, recorded in an essay on a family trip (which he unaccountably kept): 'We had a race with an OHV Sunbeam motorbike which we failed to pass as there were no long stretches of road'. On a much later occasion he almost flattened my brother's following car when, having missed a turning, he suddenly reversed into us without turning his head.

For recreation he liked tennis, played golf occasionally at St George's Hill, and, in the summer, no doubt initiated by Herbert Morgan, took to punting.[11] All his life he loved walking – as witness the parting gift

[11] He used to recount how he had been rebuked by Lord Desborough, the hero of all things aquatic, whom he did not know, in a Thames lock: 'Take your hook off my punt, Sir!' This was as nothing to the 'insult' offered Lord Desborough by William's future son-in-law, the second Lord Birkenhead, who, being punted by Desborough, dived in to 'save' him when the latter had already suffered the humiliation of falling in – this to a man who had swum Niagara, not once, but twice: the second time because his friends would not believe the first.

of a walking stick from the *Merthyr Times* printing chapel when he left in 1898. For a bet he once walked the nineteen miles from London to Weybridge in evening clothes, arriving at two o'clock in the morning, with ruined shoes, to a very sour welcome.

He had played whist at home in Merthyr and after the war was taught bridge by a schoolboy friend of my brother. He had a good card sense but no idea of, nor interest in, calling. He once made Sir John Reith, who had never played, make a four against Herbert Morgan and Campbell Stuart, the Managing Director of *The Times*. They won the first two rubbers as William always called 'Three No Trumps', and were only worsted on the third.

Three months before Northcliffe's article – and it was to this, probably, that he was referring – William moved out of the suburbs into real country near Chobham Common. His purchase was of a large neo-Elizabethan house, Barrow Hills, Long Cross, in 200 acres. The house, big enough to have house guests as well as a growing family, had been built by Sir John Mullins, senior partner in the renowned stockbrokers, Mullins Marshall. It had a fine Japanese garden, laid out by Japanese; a home farm; a park (also used as the village cricket ground); a magnificent show of rhododendrons in front of the house, and a bank of horse stalls (Mullins' daughters had been horse mad). William, though he had not ridden before, now always rode before breakfast, usually with my eldest sister Mary, prior to catching the 9.10 am for London. He joined the Garth hunt and always wore its pink coat at Christmas.

Before this time he had begun to worry about his children's education, particularly that of his sons – my mother had very definite ideas about her daughters. Though he did not regret his early start in newspapers, so missing proper schooling, he was always conscious of his lack of academic background, particularly in the Classics and in languages. I can see him now, propped up in bed after dinner, studying a French primer. In those days, as now, boys were supposed to be registered at birth for the best public schools. Not having been able to do so, he now put my brother and myself down for four. In the end he got all his four sons into Eton. In my case he had to work very hard on the housemaster (my brother was already there) to take me a year early as the latter was about to retire and his list was not transferable to his successor. He gained his point by calling on the housemaster every Sunday and fascinating him with a serial story about the skulduggery of the Lloyd George Fund.

*   *   *

In the Birthday Honours of 1921, William was made a baronet. It is customary nowadays to assume that all 'Lloyd George honours' were paid for. I am pretty sure that, in this case, it was not so. Indeed, most of the newspaper honours at this time are documented and I have come across no evidence that any of them was bought. Even Northcliffe's account of his peerage in 1905 (from Balfour, though there is some evidence that it was instigated by Edward VII), was a joke: 'I bought my peerage like an honest man.' Lloyd George, more than any other political leader of modern times, was hypersensitive to the Press, there being no other media. He timed his big speeches outside parliament for Saturday afternoons so that he would get maximum coverage in the evenings, the Sundays and, as they still behaved as if the Sundays did not exist, in Monday's dailies.

Besides, as newspapermen were politically non-competitive,[12] Lloyd George preferred them as boon companions. They did not have to 'buy'. He 'bought' them, with his charm: his honours were consolidation. Only the King kept the numbers of their honours down. There are several extant letters from Lord Stamfordham, the King's Secretary, to 'Freddie' Guest, the Coalition Chief Whip. In 1919, for instance, Stamfordham objected to a peerage for Sir Edward Russell (*Liverpool Post*) on the grounds that he was eighty-six and that press honours in the list already amounted to six.[13] I think William had first been offered a knighthood but, as a strong family man, had turned it down.

As his publishing interests extended, William increasingly 'identified himself with all the benevolent institutions associated with the printing and publishing business'. He also became President, in turn, of the publicity clubs the Aldwych and the Thirty Clubs. As President it was his responsibility to invite distinguished guests. On his list were Lloyd George, Churchill, Birkenhead, Curzon and Leo Amery. Churchill and Birkenhead later became his friends. He must also have had special regard for Curzon. When the latter was dying and reduced to reading only the *Daily Graphic*, William had an edition specially printed for him, reporting his good progress.

Time and Tide[14] wrote of him:

---

[12] The exception was Beaverbrook, whom he shopped in 1916 when he formed his first cabinet. Beaverbrook, then Sir Max Aitken MP, was expecting the Board of Trade but felt rebuffed when he was only offered an under-secretaryship. He took a peerage in consolation and, so he said, ever after regretted it.

[13] One of them was Hulton, who had been put down for a peerage but was downgraded to a baronetcy. Rothermere's viscountcy, though the King thought his conduct as Air Minister with Sir Hugh Trenchard, Chief of the Air Staff, had been reprehensible, was allowed through.

[14] 28 February 1924. In assessing this extract it has to be remembered that *Time and Tide* had been founded (against William's advice) and was edited by Lady Rhondda, as a child more friendly with William than with Gomer.

'The controlling brain in the House of Berry is that of Sir William Berry, the Editor-in-Chief of the *Sunday Times*. He is forty-four, tall, distinguished, well-groomed always, popular, shrewd, very tactful, a first-rate after-dinner speaker, a man of marked social gifts, extremely likeable, genial, smiling, kindly, enjoying life very much ... he is singularly mellow, unhurried in manner, calm-minded, pleasant. His face bears no expression of self-conscious power or arrogance ...'

Sir William's brother, Mr J. Gomer Berry is less expansive, more self-contained, quieter, less communicative than Sir William. He is also less keen on social and public life and if there are any speeches to be made or any functions to be attended, it is Sir William one sees there. [Sir William] has an exceedingly pleasant voice and a fund of good stories ...

This is a little unfair to Gomer. Already he had taken on the chairmanship of the Management Committee of the Infants' Hospital, Vincent Square. Over the years he raised a great deal of money, including his own, on its behalf. He was, however, feeling the strain now and about this time expressed a desire to 'consolidate', by which I believe he meant building up the properties the brothers had acquired and reducing their bank borrowings.

They had made money out of the Lysaght deal, but their investments in Seymour's coal enterprises were beginning to look doubtful. Gomer was perhaps more aware of the phenomenal run of prosperity in the publishing business ever since 1917, with the exception of a short-lived slump in 1921. His wife, too, was not well. In the event, she died in 1928.

William would have none of it. When, in March 1923, the biggest deal so far presented itself he had no hesitation – only to be baulked by Lord Beaverbrook for a second time.

CHAPTER NINE

The Hulton Deal

IT IS NOW mid-1923. Sir Edward Hulton, owner of a giant group of publications[1] based on Manchester (or Cottonopolis, as it was then still nicknamed) is ailing and wanting to sell – for cash. An obvious purchaser would be Lord Rothermere, now the owner of the *Daily Mail* after his brother Northcliffe's death. Rothermere is already working hard on his ambition to become the richest man in England, though he is still bested by Sir John Ellerman and Lord Derby. Hulton, however, does not like Rothermere. Himself 'unpredictable, uncouth, dour and suspicious', he perhaps sees in Rothermere a mirror image. Anyway, he has never forgotten a dirty trick played on him in 1915. At that time, Hulton planned to start a Sunday edition of his picture paper, the *Daily Sketch*, but he had first to apply through trade associations for a newsprint ration. Much of UK newsprint was supplied by companies controlled by Rothermere, who thereby came into possession of confidential information and decided to pre-empt Hulton with a Sunday edition of the *Daily Mirror*, in the inside of a week. Hulton was, and still is, very bitter. He does not go along with the view of Rothermere, now becoming accepted, of a hitherto open-handed charmer, embittered by the desertion of his wife and the death on the Western Front of his two elder sons.

* * *

There is no evidence to prove that Hulton and Beaverbrook talked the matter over (except a solitary reference in their correspondence in which Hulton mentioned provincial papers he had been offered 'at four times their price'), but it would be surprising if they did not. Both had country homes at Leatherhead, Surrey, and indeed Beaverbrook had helped his neighbour to get a private telephone line. Beaverbrook, who did not then own horses, with his wife joined Hulton's party at the Derby. Long after Hulton had ceased to be of any use to him, Beaverbrook took pains on his behalf. He instructed the *Daily Express* correspondent to send 'new' medicines from New York and had them delivered to the

---

[1] The *Financial Times* described the group of two dailies, three Sundays, and one evening as 'embracing two thirds of the population and wealth of industrial Britain'.

South of France by special messenger. He oversaw the investment of the Mary Hulton Trust. Hulton, for his part, signed his letters 'love from us all'. After Hulton's death in 1925 his widow wrote: 'My old darling *loved* you.' Beaverbrook befriended their adolescent son, Teddy,[2] and gave him unfruitful lessons in public speaking. Then, as throughout his life, Teddy spoke like a machine gun short of ammunition.

In short, they were friends.

Beaverbrook being the gossip he was, it is inconceivable that he was not one of the first to know what was in Hulton's mind. In any case, there was plenty of time to talk about it. There had been a leak in the summer that William was in discussion with Hulton.

It was Hulton who had made the first move. About April, William called on him 'by request' at his home in Great Cumberland Place. A number of conversations and interviews took place, extending over a period of three months. The period was longer than might have been expected because William's legal adviser, Cowan, senior partner of Slaughter & May, went down with acute appendicitis. In August, Hulton's solicitors, Linklater's, wrote to William in Scotland, giving Hulton's final terms. These were accepted and a formal agreement was drawn up for signature in October.

*　　*　　*

At this time Beaverbrook, who had been obsessed with politics until nearly the end of the war, was becoming increasingly concerned by the running losses at the *Daily Express*. It was not that he could not afford them. He had come to England in 1910 worth £5 million and added to that sum by judicious speculation. But he realised that a paper not supported by its readers, and needing subsidy, can have little influence. As he wrote to D.J. Robertson, his long-time Managing Director, in 1948: 'All I want to see is a great newspaper and so absolutely set up in finances that no other newspaper can ever challenge us.'

In 1923 this happy position was far from achieved. The *Daily Express* had begun to make money in the last year of the war but the *Sunday Express*, started as a seventh-day edition of the Daily in December 1918, was still a problem child. Though a popular paper, its circulation, now at 150,000, was little more than William's prestigious *Sunday Times* and, some said, had already cost £2 million from Beaverbrook's own pocket.

Beaverbrook's position had already been improved by his curious friendship with Rothermere. Two men more opposite could hardly be

[2] Later, founder of *Picture Post*.

imagined. But, as Northcliffe, who regarded Beaverbrook 'with a mixture of condescension and mistrust',[3] had written: 'Max A [Aitken] has always fascinated Harold.' His friendship with Harold Harmsworth, Lord Rothermere, was the best investment he ever made.

Beaverbrook had first met Harold Harmsworth in 1912 when the latter consulted him on Canadian investments. A year later Harmsworth declined a joint deal in the control of the *Daily Express* as it would involve him in opposition to his brother, Northcliffe's *Daily Mail*. In 1914 Beaverbrook was buying Canadian ordinary shares on joint account. When Beaverbrook was made a peer in 1916 Harmsworth, now Lord Rothermere,[4] was one of his sponsors at the introduction. Early in 1917 he was instrumental in getting Rothermere made the first Minister of Air ('I am more indebted than I can say'[5]). At the same time, Beaverbrook wrote to Rothermere about a Canadian bank deal: 'I have received so many favours from you that I feel myself pledged to do everything in my power to carry out your wishes.' He is also on record as instructing Blumenfelt, Editor of the *Daily Express*: 'It is not good business to attack Lord Rothermere even by implication. We are in the middle of complex paper deals with him, and he has always been most generous in these matters.' A further deal was completed in 1919.

There was no competitive angle to their friendship until Northcliffe died in August 1922 and Rothermere bought majority control in Associated Newspapers (*Daily Mail*, *Sunday Despatch* and London *Evening News*) from the estate in September.

Beaverbrook was immediately aware of the changed situation and recorded later: 'I [was] confronted by the colossal form of Lord Rothermere standing astride the path, as in the past I was confronted with the more meteoric personality of his brother.'

Rothermere, on the other hand, seemed to have no inkling of Beaverbrook's enormous ambition. He was even seemingly unaware of the stealthy encroachment of the *Daily Express* on *Daily Mail* supremacy, under Northcliffe's less certain control. At Northcliffe's death the *Express* had already advanced to almost 800,000 against the *Mail's* million and three quarters.

He seems to have thought his new possessions entitled him to unexampled authority, at the same time bolstered by an alliance with

---

[3] Beaverbrook returned the compliment: 'His promise once given was inviolable – but it was hard to know the exact point at which he intended you to believe that the promise had been given.'

[4] Peerage recommended by Asquith, in return for playing down publicity of the Marconi scandal involving Lloyd George, Lord Murray and Rufus Isaacs.

[5] At the end of the war Rothermere, who had been a Liberal, wrote to Lloyd George complaining of Conservative attacks on press lords, adding, 'I accepted the Air Ministry with great reluctance.'

his principal competitor. He revealed his extraordinary arrogance to Beaverbrook in private correspondence. A few examples suffice:

12 Apr. 1923
    If I disapprove of the new leader I intend after the turn of the year to start a campaign to give the Liberals a chance, increasing drum fire ... as the election approaches.

26 Apr. 1923
    If Bonar [Law] places himself in my hands I will hand him down to posterity at the end of three years as one of the most successful PM's in history ... I know exactly how it can be done.

20 June 1925
    Winston has treated me with great incivility. To me more than anyone else he owes his return to the political scene. Yet he brings in a budget taxing artificial silk without consulting me ...

Two months after taking over the *Daily Mail*, Rothermere made an approach to Beaverbrook in the most casual way imaginable. At the end of a typewritten letter in payment of a bet, he added in his own handwriting: 'How would you like me to purchase an interest in your newspapers? I am off to Cap Martin [his house in the South of France].'

Beaverbrook jumped at it: 'Replying to your postscript – of course I would like you to purchase an interest ...' and, after giving him an account of the *Express* finances, spelt out the mutual advantages – assured newsprint supplies and a virtual cornering of the drapery advertising in the penny morning papers. As a result, the newly formed *Daily Mail* Trust brought a 49 per cent interest in the *Express* in return for 4 per cent of the trust and £200,000 in cash.

Though Beaverbrook said later that he had warned of his own financial policy, it took a long time for the penny to drop. Only five years later, when the *Express* circulation was much closer to that of the *Mail*, did Rothermere begin to complain of the unequal results. The *Express* paid no dividends but used its profits to build up its business while being subsidised by rising income from the *Daily Mail* Trust. He wrote despairingly, but not yet with full awareness of his past naïvety, to a senior executive:

The fact is <u>I must have Beaverbrook's interests</u> [Rothermere's own underlining] so that the 49 per cent minority interest can at any early date be in receipt of an adequate return ... moreover the *Daily Mail* newspapers *may sooner or later* [my italics] be seriously affected by the competition of Lord B's newspapers.

He offered Beaverbrook £2.5 million to sell up, but only if the latter guaranteed not to have any further newspaper interest 'within 100 miles of London'. A few months later Beaverbrook told J.C.C. Davidson, Chairman of the Conservative Party: 'I shall go back to New Brunswick and retire a failure if I don't succeed in killing the *Daily Mail*.'

In public, in return for being backed by Rothermere as the rightful leader of the Conservative Party, in preference to Baldwin, he acclaimed Rothermere as 'the greatest trustee of public opinion ... in the history of journalism'. Only when the *Express* had passed the *Mail* in 1933 did Beaverbrook agree to unlock their interlocking share interests.

*   *   *

In 1923, most of this was to come. I have recorded it in order to explain Beaverbrook's first thought when he heard that Hulton wanted to sell. In addition to his Manchester papers Hulton had, in 1916, picked up the London *Evening Standard*, now making a decent profit in the quality field. This would complete Beaverbrook's trio: a daily, an evening and a Sunday, without whose complement, he grandly told Roy Thomson when he came raw to Fleet Street later, there was 'no future' for any proprietor.

Hulton, of course, was in no mood to sell piecemeal and Beaverbrook had no ambition for a provincial empire. A joint bid with Rothermere would be the solution. There is no evidence whether or not he put this to Hulton, but certain evidence that the two peers had discussed it. It would have taken no time at all for Beaverbrook to find Hulton unwilling to do business with Rothermere but enough for the latter to lose his temper and, in his elephantine way, try to frighten Hulton with an announcement in the *Daily Mail* on 20 September that he was to launch a new evening and a new Sunday paper in Manchester, a manifestly stupid enterprise.

Beaverbrook seems to have had an outside source for the progress of the Hulton/William deal, which he heard was to be signed on Monday, 1 October 1923. The price was to be £6 million with an immediate down payment of 5 per cent, or £300,000. The total was an enormous price, more than £100 million in today's money, and something far bigger than William had attempted before. Beaverbrook said that at first he was 'doubtful that Berry could complete the deal', but 'on 28 September, three days before the sale [date] he was convinced Berry meant business'. The sequel was given to the bureau chief of the *New York Times* ten days later and, from its wording, could only have come direct from Beaverbrook: 'He [Beaverbrook] dropped round to see Hulton late at night [Friday 28 September]. There he was shown all the documents necessary for the sale of the Hulton Press.'

There, Beaverbrook persuaded Hulton to have his own name substituted by presenting a 'cheque', written on a sheet of Hulton's notepaper. It was the size of the cheque which prompted Hulton to go back on his word. But what was the size and what was its form? Charles Wintour, twenty-five years a Beaverbrook editor, quotes 'private information' for the following:

> ... an immediate deposit of £1 million. He left the cheque by the bedside and with Hulton's written acceptance of the deal in his pocket hurried back home. Hulton's family were furious when they discovered what had happened and rang the bank to see if Beaverbrook had the money. The bank said he had no account with them. Within twenty minutes there was another phone call to say the cheque would be honoured. Beaverbrook had telephoned his friend Reginald McKenna, Chairman of the Midland Bank, who agreed to honour the cheque.

Mr Wintour's 'private' source overlooks Beaverbrook's extreme sophistication as a financier and Hulton's as a money-maker (even though the latter knew nothing about the Stock Exchange). Is it conceivable that Beaverbrook would draw a cheque on a bank where he had no account or Hulton accept such a huge sum (about £20 million now) as a bond, without guarantee? How could the family have checked with the bank, late on a Friday night? Why, in any case, were they 'furious' since, according to the *New York Times*, the position of Rothermere had not yet been mentioned. William's own information at the time was that the cheque, indeed for £1 million, was a 'certified' cheque: one which has already been presented to the bank and endorsed 'certified funds available'. It would have to have been sought at least twenty-four hours before Beaverbrook 'dropped round'.

The *New York Times* goes on, explaining that it was now Beaverbrook's intention to sell the papers on, having extracted the *Evening Standard* for himself. Back at his own telephone:

> Of course there was Berry and it was just worth trying him, so *information was conveyed to him* [my italics] that he could if he liked have the rest of the publications, but Berry did not seem to grasp the idea and said nothing.
>
> Lord Beaverbrook *then thought* of Rothermere [my italics]. It was common gossip that he was not satisfied with the position of his newspapers in Manchester, and it had even been rumoured that he was about to start a northern daily. Lord Beaverbrook called him up

on the telephone and told him in his own offhand manner the proposition he had to offer and Rothermere equally nonchalantly accepted without ringing off.

That is the inside story of the biggest newspaper deal that Fleet Street has ever known.

Beaverbrook's motives are clear enough. He wanted the *Evening Standard* and he wanted to cement his 'partnership' with Rothermere. He tied the latter yet closer to him by selling him a 49 per cent non-dividend-paying interest in the *Evening Standard* and accepting a further parcel of dividend-paying *Daily Mail* Trust shares. Otherwise he got control of the *Evening Standard*, whose offices and printing works happened to be next door to those of the *Daily Express*, for nothing.

But what of Rothermere's motives? The talk of his 'dissatisfaction with the position of his newspapers in Manchester' is rubbish. He had only one paper in Manchester and that was the northern edition of the *Daily Mail*, already in competition with Hulton's *Manchester Daily Despatch*. He said later:

There were no subtle implications about the transaction. It was solely a business decision, based upon ordinary commercial considerations. My whole and sole object was to obtain for the shareholders of the *Daily Mirror* and the *Sunday Pictorial* the control of the two news-papers from which they had most to fear, the *Daily Sketch* and the *Sunday Herald*. I foresaw that unless I did this my newspapers might possibly have to fall under the skilful direction of Sir William Berry continually increasing competition from their Hulton rivals ...

Actually, as we shall see, Rothermere sold these papers to William two years later, and it turned out that the *Daily Sketch* did pass the *Daily Mirror*, before the latter went 'sensational' in 1935 under another control. I think his motive was to cut the Berrys, who had come up so fast, down to size, and for himself to be hailed in the American press as 'the Czar of the British Press'. He can hardly have thought then, when their ability to pay Hulton direct had been in doubt, that they would be ready to come back to pay more for much less, which is what happened in the end.

* * *

At the time of the Hulton deal William and Beaverbrook were due to meet at the Aldwych Club on 18 October where William, the outgoing President, was to 'chain' Beaverbrook, the President-elect. The dinner was well attended since, as the *Advertising World* recorded:

In view of recent events in the newspaper world the diners anticipated that a piquant situation might arise ...

There were one or two amusing references from both sides on matters purely personal, but the only 'disclosure' came from Lord Beaverbrook. He admitted [sic] that at one time he thought he had secured the business of the House of Cassell, only to learn on his return from a short holiday in Canada that Sir William had been busy in his absence.

Beaverbrook's 'disclosure' was, of course, a joke. He never had any interest in books or in literary magazines. There is no evidence that after leaving his father's house, he ever read any book, apart from the Bible and a dictionary of quotations, except for a particular purpose. On the advice of Kipling, for instance, he read *Kinglake* to teach himself descriptive writing as Canadian Eye Witness in France in 1915 (which he did, most graphically). On the advice of Churchill, he read Burke on the art of political manipulation.

He and William had known each other from earliest *Sunday Times* days but there was no great cordiality on William's side. There are few letters extant between them, but even allowing for William's ingrained reluctance to wear his heart on his sleeve, it is worth noting how they addressed each other.

In 1921, the first exchange recorded in the Beaverbrook papers, Beaverbrook was already addressing William as 'My dear Bill', signing off as 'Yours ever Max'. William then could only manage 'My dear Beaverbrook' and 'Yrs W.E. Berry'. Not until 1930 was it 'My dear Max' and 'Yours Bill.'

William, as so many, including Churchill, was always fascinated by Beaverbrook. He was fascinated by his gossip, his gaiety and his charm. But he too often found him unreliable, even spiteful, and a bit of a humbug. He was disgusted by his treatment of his wife[6] and, later, his elder son. There is one interesting exchange, of 1930:

William to Beaverbrook:
Your manifesto to the farmers leaves me cold but your boy's achievement [young Max Aitken was playing football for Cambridge in the

---

[6] She died in 1927. It was not until the mid-1930s that he heard from Birkenhead's widow, who had by now become the mother-in-law of two of William's children, the diverting story of how Beaverbrook treated his wife like a servant. The Beaverbrooks and the Birkenheads were travelling together by train. As they reached the carriage, Beaverbrook said over his shoulder, 'Gla—dis [pronounced Glaedis], get the tick—uts.' Lady Birkenhead earned a venomous look from him when she took Gladys by the arm and said, 'You'll do no such thing. Let the men get the tickets.'

annual match against Oxford] is one of which you must be more than proud.

Beaverbrook to William:

I went to see him play. Next day I was ill on account of nervous tension. Neither politics, nor business, ever had such a demoralising effect on my nervous system.

William commented: Was there ever such rubbish!

My mother, who though reserved outside the family circle, was an excellent judge of character, always distrusted Beaverbrook and thought that William saw too much of him. Her enduring suspicion was justified when, during the Second World War, Beaverbrook gypped William a third time, now purely out of malice.

Beaverbrook, for his part, respected William and his achievement but was jealous of him – jealous of his sudden rise, his happy home life,[7] and of the general acceptance of his personal integrity. As an example of the latter I quote Sir Roderick Jones, General Manager of Reuters news agency, in 1925: 'William Berry, with the big way of looking at things which has brought him deservedly to such eminence ...'. A further example comes from Lord (Eddie) Winterton,[8] who went to consult William, in 1930: 'Lord Camrose whose shrewd and balanced judgment in crisis I have always found invaluable'. Beaverbrook himself commented on the home life when William brought a new country house:

Here Lord Camrose will set up his home with his family about him.

He has many advantages. One of them is a good family devoted to their father. Another is a wide personal popularity, such as few men in his position have known. For the power of the newspaper owner has usually proved an insuperable obstacle to personal popularity. [He] has, too, the gift of zest and natural high spirits.

Such advantages make the path of life easy for a man.

*   *   *

There was no bond at all between Rothermere and William but this did not prevent Rothermere, eleven years his senior, from saying, when they met accidentally at the Savoy Hotel early in 1924: 'Are you still on for a deal?'

[7] Another story of Lady Birkenhead's was set in Beaverbrook's London home, Stornoway House, when he showed her round the house and said, 'This is the ballroom [pronounced with a short "a"]: has Camrose got a ballroom?'

[8] MP 1904–51, a Minister in four governments.

CHAPTER TEN

Allied Newspapers

IT WAS WELL into the New Year of 1924 that William met Rothermere at the Savoy. A deal was certainly not in contemplation when all three Berry brothers and David Llewellyn took their families to Madeira for Christmas 1923 and the New Year. A leak must have come from the Rothermere side since a *Times* story on 4 March of the possible resale of the Hulton papers made no mention of the bidder's identity. The next day, the *Yorkshire Post* named the Berrys. By 9 March the *News of the World* (no doubt prompted by Lord Riddell) came up with what turned out to be the exact capitalisation of their new company, at first to be the Empire Press (the *Empire News*,[1] originally the Umpire, was the profit-making jewel in the Hulton crown) and finally Allied Newspapers.

If William had not been so anxious to succeed where he had failed in October, Rothermere's terms could be called outrageous. He had paid £6 million but £1 million of Hulton's own cash reserves had been used for buying Rothermere's already owned Glasgow *Daily Record*[2] and *Sunday Mail* so that his effective price had only been £5 million. These papers he now included but withheld the London-based *Daily Sketch*, *Sunday Herald* and, of course, the *Evening Standard* (which William had dearly wanted). For the rump he now insisted on £5.5 million, and no nonsense about a cash deposit anything less than £1 million. When eventually he sold both these papers to Allied Newspapers he reckoned he had made a profit of £1.8 million.

For all his company financing William always relied on M.S. (Mossy) Myers, a man with an uncanny sense of matching a willing purchaser to a willing seller, who had started his own stockbroking firm[3] at the turn of the century.

He must have had a scheme mapped out in detail in October, but

---

[1] Eventually closed down by Roy Thomson in 1962, though it was still just making money.

[2] Rothermere had put up £7,000 in 1895 to buy the Glasgow *Daily Record*, which was to be Northcliffe's first link in a national chain of halfpenny dailies. Because the *Record* did not at first make enough progress he abandoned the idea of a chain and started the *Daily Mail* instead a year later.

[3] He died during the Second World War but the name of his firm endured until 1989.

this was an altogether tougher assignment. All companies coming to the market at that time had to show a record of profits for the last four years, ideally with a smooth, rising trend, which at this time was difficult for newspaper companies. Most companies had suffered from the recession of 1921 but newspapers, with their dependence on a single raw material, newsprint, whose price had rocketed in 1920, suffered more severely. Nor was conventional thinking on the stock market then 'comfortable' (to use the accountants' phrase) with the fact that 'goodwill' (title or brand name) must necessarily form a principal ingredient of the fixed capital (assets) of a newspaper company. It was prepared to countenance redeemable debentures but tended to frown on irredeemable preference shares at whatever rate of interest.

March 1924 was a very worrying month for Mossy Myers. He counselled William not to sign until 20 March, nor to pay the deposit (borrowed from the Westminster Bank at 5 per cent) before then. Meanwhile, he set to work forming a syndicate of investors prepared to underwrite £4.75 million-worth of 8 per cent preference shares, whose interest would absorb a little more than half the previous year's profits. Their share came after that of a £1.5 million debenture issued to Rothermere. Myers pulled it off by offering unprecedently generous terms. The underwriting fee was to be $7\frac{1}{2}$ per cent (3 per cent is now normal) and a free issue to the underwriters of one ordinary share for every ten preference guaranteed. On top of this, intending preference shareholders were offered a 4 per cent discount for prompt subscription.

To sweeten the pill the *Sunday Times* was purchased by Allied Newspapers for £400,000 (the ordinary shares were by now all owned by William and Gomer), a not unreasonable price, since it had already been worth £200,000 in 1918.

Thus the new company was capitalised for a total of £8.25 million, of which £2 million were £1 ordinary shares (represented only by goodwill) without payment – 545,000 for the 'syndicate', 50,000 to Edward Iliffe, named as a director in the prospectus, and the rest to William and Gomer.

The financial press were by no means delirious – they seemed rather to be stunned – but there was little criticism, except from the *Daily Herald* (deploring the absence of goodwill figures[4]) and *The Times*, shocked by the 'perks' of the syndicate, commenting: 'The vendors rather than the purchasers have had the best of the bargain.' As the financial editor of the *Manchester Guardian* wrote: 'It is plainly without

[4] As the public offer was only for preference shares there was no published balance sheet.

precedent in newspaper history [and] must also rank as one of the most remarkable in the annals of joint-stock enterprise.'

On the evening of the issue, Beaverbrook wrote sourly to Rothermere: 'I hear the Berry issue is not going well.' In fact, the issue was fully subscribed and though the preference shares opened at 6d. discount they quickly recovered. Nowadays the majority of them would have been bought by the big City institutions, but here it was the small investor who came forward. Six months later William announced that there were now 36,000 shareholders in his group, which would have included minority shareholders in the companies outside Allied Newspapers.

As the ordinary shares had not been issued for subscription there was no Stock Exchange quotation and, at first, they changed hands privately at between 10 and 15/-, though the *Observer*[5] noted, 'offers of 15/6 have been freely circulated'.

These last may have been attempts by William and Gomer to increase their holdings cheaply. They did not sell in any volume until two years later, by which time the price had risen above 30/-, peaking at nearly £4 in 1927.

When the first year's results were announced, the pundits, noting that in lieu of an ordinary dividend the whole of the vast expenses of the issue, more than a year's interest on the preference shares, had been 'written off', pronounced them much better than expected. They made no criticism of the cunning 'rider' that though the ordinary shareholders were denied a dividend for 1924, they were allowed a 5 per cent 'interim' dividend for 1925 even before the 1924 results had been considered at the annual general meeting.

*   *   *

Until the Hulton deal, all William's purchases had been based on London. With the exception of Kelly/Iliffe's and possibly Weldon's he took a close journalistic interest in all of them. But the Manchester papers were different. After their emasculation by Rothermere, the group had no London connection, except for finance and the collection of national, as opposed to local, advertising. William's experience in Merthyr had been enough to teach him that provincial centres have their own life and *esprit de corps*. Their values are their own. Their own local squabbles and mishaps are worth far more to them than much greater events elsewhere. Similarly, their political views are necessarily blinkered in so far as their circulation areas are but tiny areas of the

[5] 20 April 1924.

whole country, dominated perhaps by farming interests, fishing, collieries, cotton, shipbuilding or other specialised power blocs. The local paper abhors opinions dictated to it by London or, as one local editor in a nineteenth-century newspaper chain, described it: 'Our politics would come down from London daily, sent by train, packed in a box [a "flong" of a pre-set article in a "mat-box"].'

Perhaps this distinction between Manchester and London was less pronounced in the 1920s, when Manchester was still a thriving metropolis. But if it was not so parochial as other provincial cities, the principle remained valid: local news for local papers.

William's chain was to grow a great deal bigger and his invariable custom was to choose a journalist as a managing director, and though speaking to him often on the telephone, he visited him rarely, letting him get on with it. At the monthly, London-based board meeting, however, though all but the specialist directors were journalists, he would never allow editorial matters to be discussed and once openly rebuked Gomer for trying to do so.

So what were the advantages to the individual papers of forming part of a chain? In his address at a dinner given to William and Gomer by employees of all the companies which they controlled William said:

> They need amalgamation because the economic force of their work today does not permit the small business to exist and pay the wages and salaries required to make the business successful.

At that time, since the Manchester papers had grown up together and the *Sunday Times*, being of a different class, was the odd unmergable man out, that explanation might have seemed a little lame. Perhaps, however, observing the changes that had taken place since the war, he was already thinking of further expansion. The heavy regional political morning paper was on the decline in face of the London press, which was now becoming increasingly national, while the local evening, often without competition, was thriving as never before.

The *Nation and Athenaeum*[6] had already given expression to his thoughts: 'No one supposes his adventures in the newspaper world are over. He is much too young and energetic to cry "Halt!" yet.' The *Nation* went on to suggest that he might 'add the *Daily Mail* to his empire when Rothermere resolves to lay down the too vast orb of his fate'.

This rumour was several times repeated in the 1920s but I do not think there was any substance in it. Yet there was certainly no 'halt'.

[6] 5 April 1924.

In 1925 papers were acquired in Newcastle (an evening, a morning and a Sunday), in Glasgow (an evening from a cousin of Lord Weir) and in Sheffield (a morning and an evening). In 1926 an evening in Middlesbrough was added. And in 1927 Rothermere finally sold to him what he had first claimed to be the dangerous rivals of his *Daily Mirror* and *Sunday Pictorial*, the *Daily Sketch* and *Illustrated Sunday Herald*. The *Daily Graphic*, still so far behind, was amalgamated with the *Daily Sketch* and the *Herald*, so as not to be associated in the public mind with the avowedly socialist *Daily Herald*, had its name changed to the *Sunday Graphic*.

None of these purchases, however, were predatory. Unlike the controllers of some later chains, William claimed that Allied never bought a newspaper which was not offered for sale. All purchases were in cash, financed by debentures on a newly formed Allied subsidiary, Allied Northern Newspapers, with the parent company owning all the ordinary shares and guaranteeing payment of the interest as 'cover' was thin.

At the time of which I am writing there was no Monopolies Commission, nor was there much public criticism of newspaper chains. Specific criticism of William came from the Transport and General Workers Research Department, regularly published in the *Daily Herald* and extreme left-wing periodicals. It was not directed at William, the would-be universal political opinion former, but at William the capitalist, director of some forty industrial companies.

He was alleged to have built up his newspaper empire out of the profits of Seymour's steel and coal deals – particularly coal, as through the late 1920s and 1930s there was much unemployment and poverty in mining areas. He kept silent about these charges at the time and only publicly repudiated them after the Second World War, long after Seymour's death. Then, for the first time, he broke silence in his 1947 book, *British Newspapers and Their Controllers*:

> My position in the newspaper world and that of my younger brother was well-established before I had any connection with [coal and steel companies]. We made a profit – not a very large one – out of an association with steel companies, but as far as coal is concerned we are, on the whole, losers ... [we three brothers] invested a considerable sum to keep going some collieries near Merthyr ... but lost money in the effort ... we would have been richer men today if we had never made an investment in coal companies.

Criticism of chains as such came only from their conduct. During the First World War Northcliffe's newspapers had been pilloried as the 'gramophone press' because they so often played the same tune. Indeed,

Geoffrey Dawson had been forced to resign as Editor of *The Times* because he would not accept Northcliffe's views as relayed to the *Daily Mail* from Paris in 1921. Rothermere, after his brother's death, with the same papers plus his illustrated nationals but minus *The Times*, came in for the same criticism. Their combined national circulation was, of course, enormous and far exceeded the largest provincial chains.

Stanley Baldwin, noting the interlocking shareholdings, attacked Rothermere and Beaverbrook as 'the Trust Press'. 'I care not what they say or think. They are both men I would not have in my house. I do not respect them. Who are they?' The provincial chains, apart from Allied, consisted of a syndicate controlled by Lord Cowdray, Charles Starmer, and the Cadbury/Rowntree families in the Midlands, and William Harrison's Provincial/United newspapers. Harrison's group had no bond except the financial, while the Cowdray Group (which Northcliffe called the Cocoa Press) committed no joint sin worse than the advocacy of temperance. As for Allied, it was, as I have shown, run by locals for locals. It was Gomer, after acquiring control of Allied in 1937, who first aroused public ill-will to the idea of chains. He made them so obvious. He changed the name of Allied to his own, Kemsley Newspapers, and from 1943 published the name 'A Kemsley Newspaper' under the masthead of each publication, even including the *Sunday Times*, William's own creation. Moreover, he caused the chain's London editor-in-chief to exercise a strong local political control and largely centralised the administration. But there had been no charge of restriction of jobs through the existence of chains – except in Newcastle, as recorded in the next chapter.

The only pre-Second World War attempt to brand the big newspapers as combining together against the public interest was made in 1936 by Sir Oswald Mosley in his periodical, *Action*. The 'public interest' he was invoking was the fuller reporting of his own political meetings. He attacked in turn the *Daily Herald*, the *News Chronicle* and the *Daily Express*, seeking to show that each of them had cross-shareholdings in each other. Gaining confidence from their lack of action against obvious falsehood, he next turned on William and *The Daily Telegraph*. This time he had gone too far. What he alleged, as the judge put it, was that William was 'a Jewish international financier with no loyalty to the Crown and no sense of patriotism ... where [his] treasure lies [his] heart will be'.

A feature of the libel case William brought was his courteous 'help', from the witness box, to Gerald Gardiner, a young junior defending the Mosley paper and later Lord Chancellor in Harold Wilson's first Government, in unravelling the capital structures of newspapers, going back to 1910. William was awarded £12,500 in damages and the *Telegraph* £7,500. All of it had to be paid by the printers, the Argus Press, controlled by Jack Akerman (late of the *Advertising World*). Argus had had a bad year as, a fortnight before the case came up, it had lost the contract for the *Morning Post*, amalgamated with the *Telegraph*.

There was, however, evidence that the antics of Rothermere and Beaverbrook had brought the label 'press lord' into disrepute. As Lady Rhondda in *Time and Tide* put the public reaction after the Mosley case: 'Practically speaking, it says: "Oh but *he's* not a Press Lord – he's a decent man."'

* * *

At the end of 1926 the beneficiaries of Northcliffe's will, after lawsuits, finally settled their differences and his controlling interest in the Amalgamated Press, the enduring foundation of his fortune, came up for sale. It was high time. Interest was ticking up on the death duties still owed. The Chairman, Sir George Sutton, was also the executor of the will and he had been criticised by the beneficiaries for selling the *Daily Mail* to Rothermere too cheaply[7] directly after Northcliffe's death in 1922.

Even so, Sutton, who had been Northcliffe's first editorial secretary and had reciprocated the latter's reliance on his 'dear Sutkin' with dog-like devotion, must first have offered the business to Rothermere. Though they had never been close, Sutton was still a Harmsworth man. He later gave up his £30,000-a-year salary, an astronomical figure then, as Managing Director under the new regime and was persuaded to take, at a lesser salary, the vice-chairmanship of Associated Newspapers (the direct holding company of the *Daily Mail*).

Quite why William was interested in the Amalgamated Press is difficult to explain. Certainly he had given the impression that he would buy anything that was offered to him from the publishing world. I think he was fascinated, as were most people in the game, by the Northcliffe name. The Amalgamated Press, originally Harmsworth Brothers, had been the foundation of all the Harmsworth fortunes and to the end

[7] I am not sure this charge was justified. The *Mail*, at Northcliffe's death, needed more money, not less, spent on it to keep the *Daily Express* in check. Instead, Rothermere slashed costs, as he had done in early days whenever his brother's back was turned, and increased the proportion of advertisements to editorial. He eschewed Beaverbrook's sound dictum, 'You can't produce a good newspaper without extravagance'. It was not long before the granite-faced Managing Director, Sir Andrew Caird, and the long-time Editor, Thomas Marlowe, both resigned. The latter was thought to have gone because he resented the interference of Rothermere, a non-journalist, in editorial matters. Specifically, he put it down to Rothermere's insistence that the *Mail* back Lloyd George.

contributed far more than the *Daily Mail*.[8] Their list of publications, seventy weekly, fortnightly and monthly, five serials, eighteen annuals and ten libraries, was not distinguished, apart from the Educational Book Company. (There were also the Imperial Paper Mills at Gravesend, who supplied all the Amalgamated Press publications as well as some newspapers, including the *Sunday Times*.)

Though all of a decent standard, they were described to me by the Managing Director, Harold Snoad,[9] who had been Northcliffe's last confidential secretary, when I succeeded William as Chairman, as 'the Woolworth's of publishing'.

Another reason, though the size of the deal – £8.5 million in cash and debentures – far eclipsed anything William had attempted before, may have been to rationalise his now sprawling empire. The role of the *Financial Times* and of Allied Newspapers was clear, but the scope of Graphic Publications and Cassell's was less defined. As the prospectus put it, 'The amalgamation of the [Cassell] journals with the business of the Amalgamated Press will result in extensive economies.'

The shape of the deal is too complicated to describe in detail here. This time it must have been William, with Gomer and Edward Iliffe, who did the legwork while 'Mossy' Myers' job was relatively simple. The central idea was to buy out the old company, Amalgamated Press (1922) Ltd., refinance it and inject into a new company all the Cassell (eight monthly and four weekly) magazines, plus a radio magazine simultaneously bought from outside. At the same time, Cassell's book publishing side was hived off to Sir Newman Flower, originally trained by Northcliffe, who had played the major part in bringing the firm back from the brink before the First World War.

This time there were no free shares for the 'promoters', Graphic Publications (now wholly owned by William and Gomer), who subscribed £1.2 million for all the ordinary shares while selling the *Daily Graphic* title to the *Daily Sketch* and the weekly *Graphic* and *Bystander* to William Harrison.[10]

---

[8] Northcliffe himself never lost his interest in his magazines. When he went round the world a year before his madness and death, it was not *The Times* nor the *Daily Mail* that he was keen to find on sale. Instead it was *Answers*, his first-born. Late in his career he still went to the Amalgamated Press office once a week to choose articles for their publications.

[9] Snoad accompanied Northcliffe on his 1921 world tour and had the honour (which he did not at all appreciate) of being thrown downstairs. Afterwards he had the job of taking Northcliffe's 'mad' telegrams, sacking most of *The Times* staff, to the post office at Evian-les-Bains. He changed the wording to anodyne, but was careful always to send the same number of words since 'the chief' suspiciously checked the receipts.

[10] Harrison was a financier who had made a fortune out of the forced sale of the German Stinnes estate and had founded Inveresk Paper. He now formed the provincial chain of United Newspapers

The result was the now familiar, highly geared company with £3.5 million debentures and £4.5 preference shares before the £1.2 million of ordinary shares. By comparison, the old company had had a nominal ratio of one preference[11] to five ordinary shares, or, at market prices, one to twelve.

As for the direction of the company, William pursued the same policy as Northcliffe had done before handing over the chairmanship to Sutton. He made no changes among the existing board of directors, which consisted of six editors, each responsible for a group of publications, but added to them Thomas Young, who had been Chairman of Cassell's, and Brian Irvine, the Managing Director of the latter's part-work book company.

The old shareholders were bought out at above market price, representing '17 to 18 year's purchase ... to say the least of it, unusual'.[12] In fact, the total cost was a little less than it seemed as William adopted Rothermere's device in the first Hulton deal of using the acquired company's cash as part payment. As the American magazine, *Advertising and Selling*, commented a little later:

> While the Berry-Iliffe combination controls the A.P., it seldom interferes ... with the management ... and in this way they show their wisdom ... The most popular proprietors in Fleet Street today are Lord Camrose and Sir Gomer Berry. They are fine, straightforward types of newspaper magnates and have the faculty of inspiring love and confidence in their varied staffs.

One further deal must be mentioned. Frank Lloyd, who had been said to be 'ailing' when he sold the *Daily Chronicle* in 1918, was very ill in the spring of 1927. He still controlled the Edward Lloyd Paper Mills, his core business and the largest newsprint manufacturer in the British Isles.[13] He had no heir. Not long before he died in May, 'he had let [William] know that if the business were to be sold ... he would like Sir William and his brother, through Allied Newspapers, to be given the first refusal'. Though there is no record of previous contacts, Lloyd must have formed a good impression of William when he was negotiating for 'full commercial control' of the *Chronicle* at the time of the sale to Lloyd George's syndicate.

and cornered all the illustrated weeklies (*les journaux de snobisme*) by buying the remainder from Sir John Ellerman, in order to obtain 'an assured market for our large output' [of newsprint].

[11] The preference shareholders got their due premium as William had assured them they would when he reported the Harmsworth Brothers meeting in 1898 (see Chapter 2, pp. 15–16).

[12] The financial editor of the *Manchester Guardian*. 'Year's purchase' is the same as what is now called 'Price/Earnings Ratio'; except that it was before tax.

[13] This was a more important consideration than it would be nowadays. British newspapers were largely supplied by British or the cartel-ridden Scandinavian mills. Expanding Canadian manufacture was more interested in the North American market.

William said at the time his reasons for purchase[14] were first, that it was 'a desirable purchase on purely economic grounds', and second that 'this huge paper-making business should be in the hands of the newspaper business itself'. Furthermore, he said, 'If a time of crisis should arise we shall regard other newspaper proprietors ... as partners and entitled to equally proportional rights with ourselves.' (Allied was already taking nearly 30 per cent.) He was as good as his word and later sold a number of Lloyd's shares to other newspapers.

This assurance was not enough for Beaverbrook, whose *Daily Express* had taken all its newsprint from Lloyd's since its launch in 1900. He at once cancelled his contract from a motive, I can only conclude, of jealousy of a 'Johnnie-come-lately'. At any rate, he had no plans. He found himself, he said, at the mercy of 'rings'. 'I may say,' he told Rothermere in September 1927, 'I tried to get newsprint at reasonable prices from every [other] English mill before I turned to the Canadians. I had to use my personal influence in Canada to get the necessary concessions.' The expected co-operation with Rothermere when the latter bought into the *Express* in 1922 seems never to have come to anything. It now began in earnest and Beaverbrook's anguish at finding himself double-crossed by Rothermere makes amusing reading.

Lloyd's was the one large purchase, apart from the *Financial Times* in 1945, that William later resold. One evening in 1936 Ian Bowater,[15] cousin of Eric (Chairman of Bowaters, a rapidly expanding newsprint manufacturer) was dining with his father-in-law, Lord Dawson of Penn.[16] William was there too. After dinner William 'with a wave of the hand said to him, "I can't think what you fellows are doing with that paper mill of yours. Why don't you buy ours? We are not newsprint manufacturers, we are journalists. We don't want a whacking great paper mill ... that is your job"'.

These remarks seemed to be jocular but were followed up, resulting in a decent profit for Allied[17] and the formation of Bowater/Lloyd as producer of 60 per cent of British newsprint.

*   *   *

[14] The terms, for once, were not exorbitant and were financed by Myers' usual debentures at 5 per cent discount, the interest guaranteed by Allied Newspapers.

[15] Afterwards, like several of his family, Lord Mayor of London.

[16] Doctor to George V, who had died in January.

[17] This was hard on Gomer, for whom William had lately obtained a peerage from Baldwin. He had taken his title from the most modern newsprint complex at Kemsley, Kent, where there was a philanthropic connection. Lloyd had planned a garden city, on the parallel of Leverhulme's Port Sunlight. Profit-sharing, he said, could be provided by 'nice houses, comfortable homes and healthy recreation [in place of extra money] in the form of bottles of whisky, bags of sweets, or fat geese for Christmas'.

In spite of his extraordinary range of responsibilities – both his own and through Seymour – William was never a hermit workaholic. By the time of his baronetcy in 1921, only six years, almost to the day, after beginning his struggle with the then little-known *Sunday Times*, Herbert Morgan was able to organise a dinner of over 400 men in his honour at the Savoy Hotel. They included, wrote the *Financial Times*, 'politicians and publicists, commercial and industrial magnates, artists, newspaper men, authors and members of both services'. Morgan assembled the best team of after-dinner speakers in London – at any rate the most sought after – Lords Leverhulme, Dewar, Burnham and Riddell. Northcliffe declined, as he was just setting off on his world tour, and Lloyd George, the Prime Minister, chucked at the last moment.

One of the guests was S.B. (Sollie) Joel, the mining magnate, head of 'Johnnies' (the Johannesburg Consolidated Investment Trust) and a major owner in de Beers diamonds. I mentioned in Chapter 5 William's early attempts to set up a family investment portfolio with his father-in-law. He now took to joining Joel's weekly investment conference, attended by brokers and clients, serving champagne at 11 o'clock in the morning.[18] He struck up a friendship with Joel and was a frequent guest on his steam yacht. There, he teased Joel, who took great trouble with food and wine but tried to economise on cigars by passing a single one under the table. William brought his own cigar case and ostentatiously offered it to the other guests. Joel also had a country house near Ascot where, the day before the 'week' began, he gave a garden party for men only where, as Jennifer would have said in her diary, 'everybody who was anybody was to be seen'.

Another friend acquired at about this time was Birkenhead, seven years his senior, with whom he had had frequent meetings concerning articles for the *Sunday Times* under the general heading 'Contemporary Personalities'. In 1926 Birkenhead got him elected to The Other Club, a dining club started with Winston Churchill in 1911, when they had both been blackballed from The Club, of which Dr Johnson had been a member. I remember William saying of Birkenhead at this time: 'I think he recognises I am somebody'.

William already knew Winston Churchill, but as yet was still suspicious of him. He had attacked him as a 'gambler' in 1917 when he was seeking a political comeback ('it would constitute a grave danger to the Administration and to the Empire as a whole') and would have agreed, if he had known of it, with Churchill's description of himself

[18] Before the first war, 'elevenses' had been common in City pubs, with champagne at sixpence a glass.

to his wife as 'consumed by egotism'; and with Birkenhead, Churchill's most intimate friend, who told the Chairman of the Conservative Party, J.C.C. Davidson: 'Often right, but my God, when he's wrong!' Davidson cited a lunch with William in March 1929 when he recorded, '[William] is very anti-Lloyd George and, I suspect, very anti-Winston ... He feels that Jix [Joynson-Hicks, Home Secretary] ought to go and also Winston from the Exchequer ... Winston is not trusted in the party because he is always out for office and never prepared for opposition ... people suspect he is already in negotiation with Lloyd George to secure a post as second man on the new ship if it is ever launched.'

In retrospect Churchill imagined himself already more a trusting friend than seems to have been William's view. After the collapse of the Coalition in the 1922 General Election, Churchill had found himself, as he put it, 'without an office, without a seat, without a party, and without an appendix'. Though he spent the next six months polishing the first two volumes of his *World Crisis* (serialised in *The Times*, though William would have jumped at them for the *Sunday Times*), he was aware of needing a political platform. William, as President of the Aldwych Publicity Club, invited him to be guest of honour at a lunch in May 1923. There, Churchill seemed to burn yet more boats. According to the *Daily Graphic*, he 'vigorously criticised the Government [Bonar Law's] and attacked Mr Asquith, in his first speech since his defeat at Dundee'. He never forgot that opportunity. After the Second World War he reminded William of that day: 'My dear Bill, who has never wavered nor varied in your fruitful friendship during all those long and baffling and finally tumultous years when you took the Chair for me at that luncheon in 1924.' (He should have written 1923.)

These four, Joel and Birkenhead against Churchill and William, used to make up a strange bridge four.[19] They were playing at William's house in Seamore Place,[20] Curzon Street, after the General Election of 1929 when the *Evening Standard* was brought in, with the heading 'Lord Lloyd sacked'. Lloyd, British High Commissioner in Cairo, had fallen out with Arthur Henderson, the new Labour Foreign Secretary, and had been recalled. Churchill was for treating the issue as a *cause célèbre* and made a fool of himself in the House of Commons. Birkenhead, who remembered that Lloyd, the imperialist, had twice been overruled by Austen Chamberlain in the previous Cabinet, in which both had

[19] Their first recorded game, in 1925, was at Birkenhead's house. Churchill told his wife he had won £50 at sixpence a hundred, though 'the other two were much better than my partner and myself'. This, although Birkenhead's calling was notoriously awful. He once opened with Four No Trumps on the ground that he had four aces.

[20] The 'family flat' in Whitehall Court had become too crowded as there was no room for families.

served, counselled caution and was much quieter in the House of Lords. William told me of the incident and remarked that the episode showed Birkenhead's superior judgment. Politically, William had lost confidence in Lloyd George and had transferred it to Stanley Baldwin and his lieutenant, Neville Chamberlain.

At this time William had begun to take an interest in his domestic surroundings. On buying Barrow Hills he had taken over its undistinguished furnishings more or less intact[21] and had supplemented it only with grandfather and grandmother clocks, for which he conceived an enthusiasm. Now that he had a London house he began to buy pictures and silver, for whose purchase he always relied on advice. For pictures he consulted Frank Rutter, long-time art critic of the *Sunday Times*. It was through him that he made his most spectacular purchase, the now famous Van Dyck of the Abbé Scaglia, at the Christie's Holford sale in 1927. Rutter advised that it was likely to go for around 75,000 guineas.

William arrived late and stood behind the auctioneer's rostrum. For the fun of it he opened the bidding at 30,000 guineas and was a little put out to find there was no other bid. It is such a deep picture that he had nowhere to hang it except on the staircase at Seamore Place.

There were other purchases, though none on such a scale – Maes, Hendrik Pot, Wheatley, Raeburn, Charlotte Nasmyth, Meissonier and a Constable, which turned out after his death to be by a lesser hand[22] – celebrated by a special feature in the *Connoisseur*. He had five paintings by James Pryde, to whom he often lent money, and seven Boudins. He also collected Persian rugs and, advised by his mother-in-law's half-brother, Edgar Asheton Bennett,[23] silver in a modest way.

*   *   *

In May 1928 William suffered a stunning personal blow. Seymour was killed in a riding accident. Impatient and a natural horseman, unlike William, he was accustomed to take a pre-breakfast constitutional, not by 'hacking' but by galloping round and round a field near his superbly placed house in the valley of the Usk. He was indulging this time-saving routine one morning, while talking over his shoulder to his groom.

---

[21] He had also taken over the large indoor and outdoor staff. It was the first time he had had a butler but he was already complacent, as large householders must be, to being robbed on a modest scale. He was much amused by my brother's report of a conversation with the elderly butler: 'Higby, what's claret like?' 'Claret, sir, is a wine I never touch'.

[22] This was not a 'stumer', as were so many of Rothermere's pictures. It had been lent to five international exhibitions before I, who inherited it, tried to present it to the Tate Gallery in remembrance of my wife.

[23] On his death Bennett left his silver collection, valued at £1 million, to Manchester Art Gallery.

There was a line of telegraph poles down one side of the field. Unwittingly he directed his horse towards one of the poles. The horse shied. The rider was catapulted into the pole. His skull was shattered. He was carried back to the house where he had mounted just five minutes earlier. His body was coffined in the billiard room. He was in his fifty-first year.

I was fetched from school to go to his funeral three days later. There was no doubt about his popularity. At every village through which the cortège passed there were knots of people waiting to see it go by. In Merthyr itself they were three and four deep on the pavements. He had only been a rich man for the last eleven years of his life, when the lack of infrastructure I described in the Introduction was having to be made good by private initiative.

The scale of his benefactions was prodigious. He did not operate, as some rich men do today, by setting aside a fixed sum in charitable, tax-free foundations, or by donating a set percentage of his income every year. He gave wherever and whenever the need arose. Anyone with a good cause soon knew where to come. He started in a small way, in 1917, with £1,000 (£14,000 now) to the Memorial College, Brecon, in honour of his father who had died the previous year. Thereafter the list grew apace – hospitals, housing associations, working men's clubs, choirs, universities, museums, Sunday schools, a football club, heated indoor swimming pool, more hospitals. Always his cry was to build and fund hospitals from private sources, to keep them away from the cold bureaucratic hand of the state. In a time of depression, too, he kept open loss-making coal seams and once, in conjunction with others, put up £160,000 to save a group of collieries which had gone into receivership.

Well might Thomas Richards, President of the Mineworkers in Wales, say to a public meeting where Seymour was present:

> Mr Berry is one of the most selfish men I know. (Pause.) The good book says it is more blessed to give than to receive and it is certain that Mr Berry by his munificence is going to grab all the blessings that can be got.

For all this philanthropy, Seymour was made a Freeman of Merthyr in 1923 – only the third. The others, both now dead, had been Lords Merthyr and Rhondda. For it was the town that he most gloried in. Born and bred in Merthyr, he always called himself 'a Merthyr boy'. Though he had no ambition to become a politician he was asked by all three main political parties to be their candidate in the 1922 General Election. Each wanted a popular local man to keep out the Independent

Labour Party (started by Keir Hardie, who had been an MP for Merthyr, but by then degenerated into something like the Militant Tendency today). In the event Liberal and Labour dropped out and he campaigned vigorously for the Conservative candidate. He did not join the party until after he had been made a peer by Stanley Baldwin in 1926 (curiously, though the time of his elevation was in the middle of the coal strike, he never spoke in the House of Lords during his eighteen months' membership).

He was a resourceful businessman with a supreme expertise in finance. He was not a 'nuts-and-bolts' man. In coal, he relied for that on David Llewellyn, a qualified mining engineer, whom he had met by chance in a train in 1916. In steel, he relied, at any rate at first, on W.R. Lysaght, a shop floor manager who had been born into the job.

For all his popularity in the community, Seymour was not universally loved by fellow businessmen. They felt that there was something too good to be true in his undoubted charm, immense self-confidence and enthusiasm, and his lightning calculations. In short, they tended to conclude that he was all too smart and to wonder exactly what was the meaning of his motto, 'The labourer is worthy of his hire, but so is capital.' There were murmurings when he sold his part-owned colliery business, David Davies, to Guest, Keen & Nettlefold, of which he was Vice-Chairman. They said it was a 'sucked out orange'.

In evidence of his unpopularity on the Cardiff Coal Exchange it was rumoured that, when the news of his death was known, the brokers drank a toast to the horse in champagne. I think, however, there is an explanation. When Lord Rhondda was setting up his colliery amalgamations he found that the brokers were playing off each colliery against the next by fixing prices at the pit head and then putting on a large mark-up at the port. Similarly, they had cornered the supply of French pit props and made a fortune out of them. Accordingly, Rhondda formed his own marketing company, Lysberg, which Seymour inherited. All collieries which would co-operate then got the same price, and the pit props were made available with only a small commission.

I wrote above as if Seymour's sudden death was something which affected William above all. Well, so it was. It changed his life. Hitherto, while he had of course seen much more of Gomer, who had been his close partner in everything that they did and with whom he maintained a joint bank account over twenty-five years (he used to lecture us boys on the enormous advantage a team of two brothers had over any single rival), he had always felt a much greater affinity with Seymour. Seymour, with his flashing vitality and zest for life, was William's link with his youth and his family. He could recall so vividly those early years in

Merthyr together; or later, when the two brothers, leaning against the wall of the house, had fallen about laughing over the meanness of the fare after a pre-marriage dinner with Seymour's rich parents-in-law to be; or again, when Seymour and David Llewellyn had organised 'claques' at the far corners of a hall to talk down awkward shareholders at one of William's company meetings. To him, Seymour was a 'man of outstanding quality and ability and with a great human personality – generous, large-hearted, with the courage of a lion and the tenderness of a woman'. Seymour had been the dashing buccaneer; Gomer the quiet, competent pedestrian. Without Seymour, a phase in his life had passed. Though of course he was already forty-eight, he only now recognised himself as middle-aged. The anniversary of Seymour's death was, for some years, a black day for him. He now found, too, that he was the guardian of five young nieces (there was no male heir), the eldest of whom, Eileen, though the most feckless, did cheer him up as, with her vivacious charm, she reminded him so much of her father. He took some grim satisfaction, too, in correcting Seymour's will, which uncharacteristically had been miscalculated.

Seymour had left £10,000 to each of seventeen nephews and neices which, after a £300,000 overdraft and death duties, would have taken more than a third of the disposable estate. William made David Llewellyn, the third executor beside Gomer, resign and cancelled the bequests.

*   *   *

I have brought in Seymour's death a little ahead of the chronology because it was, to William, the end of an era. A new era was already beginning. At the end of 1927 William, with Gomer and Edward Iliffe (and Seymour intended for 10 per cent), had bought *The Daily Telegraph* and thereby aroused the wrath of Lord Rothermere, who saw his position as the 'Czar of British Press' undermined.

CHAPTER ELEVEN

War With Rothermere

THE SALE OF *The Daily Telegraph*, with which I deal in the next chapter, was announced two days before Christmas 1927. Rothermere at this time was travelling in America with his usual circus of an editor, a couple of 'young men', an executive and attendant secretaries. The executive, who I think must have been F.A. Szarvasy,[1] a director of the *Daily Mail* Trust and accomplished financier, later told William that Rothermere had been incensed at the treatment of the *Telegraph* news in the American Press. An Associated Press Agency report, widely printed, said, 'The sale has so much upset every middle-class home in Britain that scores of thousands of upright respectable citizens are now enquiring: "Who are these Berry Brothers?" The simple answer is: "They are the biggest newspaper proprietors in Britain, if not in the world"'. After all, it was only four years since Rothermere himself had been named 'Czar of the British Press' by American newspapers.

The report went on to repeat a rumour, which I believe was entirely baseless, that the Berrys had recently made an offer of $75 million for the *Daily Mail*, 'turned down by Lord Rothermere with some asperity'.

The name of *The Daily Telegraph* was not at that time one to conjure with. It had been a great paper under the first Lord Burnham, but he had retired in 1902. By 1927 its sales had shrunk to 84,000 and its acquisition was much more a challenge than an accolade. It is a puzzle as to why this purchase should have set Rothermere off. After all, it was he himself who had laid the foundation of Allied Newspapers by selling to it the Hulton Manchester papers and his own *Daily Record*, Scotland's only 'National'. Eventually, too, he had also sold Hulton's national picture papers, daily and Sunday, at first withheld for fear that their competition would be too hot for his own.

The truth is Rothermere loved money *and* power. He could not resist a deal which would make him a great deal of money, but having done the deal, he resented the loss of power. He made large profits by starving the *Daily Mail* but felt it somehow unjust that, though it had been his

---

[1] Szarvasy had rescued the Dunlop Rubber Company after Jimmy White had brought it almost to its knees.

own idea, the *Daily Express*, nurtured by *Mail* dividends and its own ploughed-back profits, was steadily catching up. Three years after Rothermere had bought the *Mail*, the *Express* was already outselling it in the London area, though not yet in the country as a whole. He consoled himself too long with the thought that he was Beaverbrook's senior partner and confidant. He thought that he had inherited – or rather bought – Northcliffe's mantle (though he failed to buy *The Times*). But the heady days were over. No longer would prime ministers promise him anything he wanted for the price of his support. Lloyd George had given him a viscountcy (at first resisted by the King) for backing him in the 1918 General Election. He had further enquired whether Rothermere had any relations in the Church – he said he had a couple of deaneries vacant. But Bonar Law, previously friendly, had turned on him when he demanded an earldom for himself and a seat in the Cabinet for his son, Esmond.[2]

Baldwin made no attempt to seek the favour of the press lords, at first treating them 'with silent contempt'. When they began sniping at him, he smote them. He dismissed Beaverbrook, who had used his 'curious friendship' with Bonar Law to 'get hold of much information, which he used in ways in which it was not intended'. His attack on Rothermere must have hurt more:

> The Trust Press is breaking up. The *Daily Mail* is dead: it has no soul. Northcliffe, with all his faults, was a great journalist, with a spark of genius. But this man! I get much correspondence about him. A postcard the other day said: 'If Lord Rothermere wants a halo in Heaven or a Coronet on earth, why don't you get it for him?'

Rothermere, for his part, began to patronise Lloyd George. After the General Strike of 1926, he saw in Lloyd George an authoritarian leader who could become the British Mussolini, his current hero – the anti-Bolshevik who gets things done. His moment of depression after a rebuff had passed. No longer did he think of sublimating his political will to the younger Beaverbrook as he had written in 1923:

> I have cudgelled my brains to devise a scheme by which you could be associated with the political direction of my newspapers ... I am tired of being a galley slave ... my ambition is a life largely of solitude and obscurity. I am now fifty-five, and a poor life at that.

[2] According to J. C. C. Davidson, then Law's Parliamentary Private Secretary, Law was prepared to give Esmond, 'an excellent backbencher', a minor ministerial job, but turned 'pink with anger' when confronted with the full demand.

Hence the news of further Berry expansion infuriated him. He felt that his own prestige, as opinion-former and head of the great Harmsworth family, was under attack. His personal wealth was at its highest. He would smash them. He telegraphed home to prepare a scheme of a great provincial evening paper chain, which would take on all the Berry papers and a good deal more.

By 13 February 1928 an outline plan was ready. It was launched in a 2,000-word article by Rothermere, published simultaneously in the *Daily Mail* and the *Daily Mirror*. He announced the formation of a new company, Northcliffe Newspapers, with a capital of £3 million debentures to be subscribed by the public[3] and up to £2.5 million in ordinary shares to be subscribed jointly by Rothermere himself and by his national newspapers. The object, he said, was to bring to the provinces evening newspapers which would not, as existing evening papers did, 'lag behind' the national press 'in enterprise and development'. Existing papers 'were largely unenterprising and old-fashioned ... bought for the bare-bones of the day's news, especially the football and racing results'. They had 'neither the varied array of entertaining features nor the resources and skill in news presentation' which would ensure the paper be read by an entire household and so be of value to the advertiser. Northcliffe evening papers, to be called *Evening Worlds*, would have a special *Daily Mail* national and foreign affairs news service and a supply of pictures organised by the 'longest established' picture paper, the *Daily Mirror*. They would, however, have an 'independent editorial staff' to deal with local news and pictures. 'Thus the local interest upon which existing provincial evening newspapers rely will be expanded by the aid of a worldwide organisation' hitherto available only in London.

At first this lecture in journalism seemed to be directed principally at lone independent papers, 'isolated economic units' suffering 'in quality from lack of connection with a powerful Press organisation'. But the list of five cities where *Evening Worlds* were to be started – Manchester, Glasgow, Newcastle, Birmingham, Bristol – showed that four of the first targets were in Berry territory. In the secondary list of nine – Edinburgh, Aberdeen, Liverpool, Sheffield, Hull, Nottingham, Wolverhampton, Leicester and Cardiff – only two (Sheffield and Cardiff) were so represented. All the others were independent, and some very strong at that, except Nottingham, which was owned by the Westminster Press (Lord Cowdray, Sir Charles Starmer and the Cadbury and Rowntree families).

---

[3] It was received with enthusiasm and eight times oversubscribed.

MR. CHURCHILL ON THE GOVERNMENT & MR. ASQUITH.

Sir William Berry, chairman.   Mr. Churchill. Lord Wodehouse.   Captain F. E. Guest.

Mr. Churchill vigorously criticised the Government—and attacked Mr. Asquith—in his

The earliest photograph known of William and Winston Churchill together in May 1923. It is of course a dull photograph but nevertheless a memorable one. On extreme right is Capt. 'Freddie' Guest, Churchill's cousin, who had been Lloyd George's Chief Whip in the Coalition Government 1916–1922. The other figure is Lord Wodehouse who had been a Liberal MP but does not figure in Who Was Who.

The occasion was a lunch at the Aldwych (Publicity) Club of which William was President. He had asked Churchill to be the guest speaker, an invitation which Churchill jumped at. Churchill had lost his seat at the 1922 General Election, when he found himself as he put it, 'without an office, without a seat, without a party, and without an appendix'. He jumped at the opportunity for a platform from which to re-enter the political fray. He never forgot it. In December 1945, he wrote to William: 'My dear Bill, who has never varied in your fruitful friendship during all these long and baffling and finally tumultuous years when you took the Chair for me at that luncheon in 1924' (actually 1923).

With Lloyd George in 1923 when he was Guest of Honour at a Charity Dinner of which William was Appeal President. William, like most people, had been taken in by Lloyd George's 'personal charm, his unparalleled political sagacity and his compelling moral fervour'. It was only later that William came to realise that the latter quality concealed an unprincipled mountebank.

William with F. E. Smith (Lord Birkenhead) left, and Sir Thomas Lipton (of Lipton's Tea) at mining magnate Solly Joel's pre-Ascot garden party. The party was given every year at Joel's house, Maiden Erleigh, about 200 men only. As Jennifer would have said in her Diary: 'everybody who was anybody was to be seen'.

'FE' had William elected to the Other Club in 1926 where he made so many new friends from all sides of public life. The Other Club was a dining club founded by FE and Churchill in 1911. William had much more confidence in FE's political integrity than in Churchill's.

Another group at Solly Joel's Garden Party. Left, 'Jimmy' White (the Company Promotor), Gomer (centre) and Herbert Morgan. It had been through White's introduction that William had been able to buy the *Sunday Times* in 1915. I have devoted a large part of Chapter 6 to the 'White Saga'.

A much later picture in 1933 – of the principal speakers at the Derby Dinner, always held the night before the Derby.
Left to right: Sir Abe Bailey (the South African industrialist who was host to William when he spent a fortnight in that country in 1936), Churchill, Lord Derby and William. In the right corner is Sir Simon Marks (of Marks & Spencer).

Below William at the time of the purchase of the *Sunday Times* in 1915 when he made himself Managing Editor. 'Normally calmly decisive, in those days he was like a tornado, working swiftly, moving vehemently from one task to another and impatient with slower-paced colleagues'.

With his two elder sons, about 1921.

Beaverbrook in 1918, when he was Minister of Propaganda. At that time he was negotiating through Lloyd George's Chief Whip to find the money to buy the *Daily Chronicle* in Lloyd George's interest. William and Gomer were to have 'complete commercial control'. In return they would sell the *Sunday Times* to Beaverbrook for £200,000. The deal fell through. The story is told in detail in Chapter 8.

Beaverbrook, more mature, in 1922. The following year he was to diddle William out of buying a large group of newspapers from the ailing Sir Edward Hulton. In a single evening he got his own name substituted in a contract negotiated over months, sold on the papers to Lord Rothermere and kept the London *Evening Standard* for himself at no cost. (Story: Chapter 9).

Evidently, Rothermere had played his cards close to his chest. The day his article appeared, Beaverbrook wrote to him in his usual toadying manner, professing to be taken by surprise:

My dear Harold [all typewritten]

This is really a most splendid and glorious adventure ... I am delighted ... You leave us all behind you in energy, initiative and ability. I can admire but I cannot emulate you. You are now incomparably the biggest figure in current journalism. It is bold enough to start one fresh newspaper – to launch five or seven requires a nerve of iron. You are sure to be successful with your new venture'.

Beaverbrook added (just eight months before he told Davidson[4] that he would go back to Canada if he could not kill the *Mail*):

As for me, I am practically retired. I do not take any interest in my newspapers. I have tried to take an interest in the Cinema but without any success. [Actually, he was to sell a chain of theatres to the Ostrer Brothers at a profit of £2 million this very same year.]

*   *   *

At first there seemed no personal animosity between Rothermere and William. The readers and staffs of provincial newspapers had been insulted but 'Sir William and his brother' were invited to 'welcome experienced and powerful competition to which they have devoted their energies'. Following the announcement of Northcliffe Newspapers, William went to see Rothermere and reminded him that he was bound by the 1924 agreement not to start any new paper in Manchester. In a speech on 17 April 1928[5] William announced publicly that he had his 'personal assurance', though Rothermere did not confirm it in writing until a week later. This did not prevent the latter hinting to Edward Iliffe two years later that the directors of the *Daily Mail* (controlled by him but on whose board he was represented by his son, Esmond) felt in no way bound 'to restrict their activities'.

In the same speech William paraphrased Job: 'He saith among the trumpets Ha! Ha! ... although there has been some thundering of the captains, and a fair amount of shouting, the gates of the citadel have not fallen.'

He went on:

We are promised a perfect deluge of 'bright and up-to-date' evening

---

[4] See Chapter 9.
[5] At a dinner in Manchester celebrating the opening of a new wing to the Allied headquarters, making the works there the largest in Europe.

newspapers. They are to descend on provincial cities like a chain of bargain stores, from John O'Groats to Land's End and from east to west – beautiful buildings, brighter brains, special and unusual features. The buildings are to be architectural possessions of which it is expected you people in the provinces will be properly proud; the brighter brains are yet to be named but a gentleman called Mr McWhirter [McWhirter was the Editor of the *Sunday Pictorial* to whom all job applications were to be made] is sitting in his den waiting to enlist them, presumably from the staffs of those benighted evening papers who are so far behind the times. And the 'special and unusual features' will be hatched in due course.

It took time, of course, to find and build on the sites for these city-central offices, each to be called Northcliffe House. Soon, however, foundation stones were laid in what were to be the major centres – Sheffield, Cardiff, Bristol and, most important of all, Newcastle.

Meanwhile, Rothermere was having second thoughts about the whole new empire. William confided to J.C.C. Davidson, now Chairman of the Conservative Party, on 5 May 1928, that he had seen Robert Donald, late of the *Daily Chronicle* and now a Rothermere confidant, 'four or five times'. Donald had suggested an arrangement to avoid direct competition with Allied and 'to divide up the country'. Allied should sell the *Sheffield Daily Telegraph*, the (Cardiff) *Western Mail* and Bristol. Rothermere, for his part, would cancel the Newcastle venture and 'drop out of Aberdeen'. As a separate manoeuvre, Rothermere was trying to buy the Liverpool papers for £3.5 million.

William had concluded that Rothermere 'now realises that his advisers led him up the garden path much too easily and he had made a fundamental mistake'. However, despite the colossal expense of a nation-wide battle in which Rothermere was so much more heavily armed with money, William had rejected any 'arrangement', thinking Rothermere 'had little to offer'. The battle developed.

Soon Rothermere was busy buying up existing evening papers in lesser centres. He failed in Aberdeen when local directors appealed to William to save them, which he did by buying up shares in the market to make up a majority; but by the turn of the year was established in Gloucester, Lincoln, Cheltenham, Stoke-on-Trent and Swansea. He also failed in Derby, whose leading paper, under threat, sold to Allied. He did, however, secure its weaker rival. The difference in style was shown in Hull. There Allied failed to persuade a numerous family to sell. Rothermere, also failing, finally succeeded by buying a site upon which, he said, a rival evening paper was to be built.

It was Newcastle that Rothermere had chosen as the chief battle-ground. Allied's *Newcastle Evening Chronicle*, a monopoly unlike most other centres in the group, was by far its most profitable publication outside Manchester. A success there, which it was afterwards found Rothermere (who never considered William 'a formidable competitor'), had expected, in three to six months, to bring the whole Allied edifice, with its top-heavy burden of debenture and preference stocks, crashing.

I well remember William's first reaction to the Newcastle threat. Since only the family was his audience, he did not choose his words carefully. He said: 'We shall have to turn round and give them a good paper.' I did not take this as a cynical comment nor did he so intend it. What he meant was that the *Evening Chronicle* was too packed with advertising and that many more pages of editorial would be required.

The *Chronicle* had been running at eight to fourteen pages. By the time the *World* was ready, sixteen pages had become normal and with new machinery installed by the end of 1929, twenty to twenty-four pages were possible, a larger size than any evening paper outside London.

Rothermere seems originally to have cast himself as stoat to the *Chronicle*'s rabbit. His grand new building, designed by a London architect rarely on the site, was quickly seen as too small for the increased competition and had to be revamped. It had been laid out to produce newspapers in tabloid format. When this was realised to have been a mistake, it was found that the machine layout was such as to inhibit the largest broadsheet sizes. There was enough machinery, but it could not all be used at once.

Meanwhile McWhirter, now promoted to Managing Director of Northcliffe Newspapers, together with his editor-in-chief, installed himself in a suite at the Grand Hotel and announced he was ready to recruit. In those days it seems to have been the convention that, while it was in order for staff to seek posts on rival newspapers, it was unethical to entice them – in other words to make extravagant offers not for promotion but for equivalent jobs. At any rate that was the view of the *Chronicle* management. The first to go was the editor, at twice his current salary. The traitor was dubbed double-eyed when it was found he had taken with him a complete list of names and addresses of the *Chronicle*'s local news correspondents (he must already have been under suspicion as William Redpath, acting Editor-in-Chief of all four of the *Chronicle*'s publications, wrote that the list had been deliberately kept a year out-of-date).[6] Redpath's description of the recruiting

---

[6] This may seem unlikely, for it would normally have been the news editor who dealt with the correspondents.

campaign[7] may have been a little exaggerated in the heat of the battle, but the *World*'s campaign was certainly without precedent.

It may not be true that the *Chronicle* buildings was continually picketed to make offers to the staff of whatever department, but a pattern did eventually emerge of engaged staff lying low in their existing jobs and only resigning 'at the last possible moment', when the *World* required them. Apart from the editor, the two biggest catches were the publisher and the circulation manager. The *Chronicle*'s Managing Director, Edward Tebbutt, a fine journalist whom William had made Editor of the *Daily Graphic* in 1920, then Editor-in-Chief of Allied on its formation, and finally transplanted to Newcastle in 1925 when Allied bought in there, was at the *Chronicle*'s Christmas dinner dance at the end of 1928. Tebbutt, himself a lugubrious man whose only recreation was driving fast cars, thought the two curiously elated and became suspicious. He returned to the office at midnight and found that they had both left their resignations at the Lodge. He had their desks forced. Inside was 'information that had been collected without authority about our sales and financial affairs'.

When the *Bristol Evening World* started a few months after the *Newcastle Evening World*, the management there were discovered to have made extravagant offers not just to individuals, but to leaders of sales canvassing teams on behalf of their whole teams. This enabled William to bring an action in the London High Court seeking an injunction. Though an injunction had no chance, the judge allowed Allied's counsel, Sir Patrick Hastings, an ex-attorney general, enormous latitude in introducing irrelevant evidence, including an affidavit by Tebbutt alleging that one hundred of the *Newcastle Chronicle* staff had been taken but not a single one from an independent morning paper in the same town, so seeking to prove that the object had been to cripple the competition. The one success of the action was nationwide publicity for Rothermere's ruthless methods.

William had already rubbed it in in a private correspondence with Rothermere:

> To shelter your behaviour and general assertion that your business is always happy to improve the status and remuneration of journalists is simply begging the question. Mr McWhirter has no idea of this sort in his head when he and his emissaries offer salaries far in advance of what you are paying elsewhere, not only to journalists but to publishing assistants, overseers, telephonists, clerks, typists and even messenger boys ...

[7] William Redpath, '*The War of the Newspaper Giants*'.

Apparently needs must when the devil is on the box and your people do not feel equal to running a newspaper without getting our staff to do it for them, no matter what the cost may be.

*   *   *

The *Newcastle Evening World*'s launch was on 4 May 1929, when the start button was pressed by Lloyd George.[8] It had been planned for, and was, a week before the opening of the great North-East Exhibition (a repeat of the immensely successful National Exhibition at Wembley in 1924). It had been McWhirter's idea to offer every registered reader (who had to place an order for the paper for six weeks) one free admission ticket, a free meal and three free small advertisements in the *World*. In the first three months, almost 200,000 of these packages were distributed and the registrations were consolidated by the usual Rothermere offer of free insurance. Protectively, the *Chronicle* had already begun free insurance in advance.

Northcliffe had said, 'Newspaper warfare is very like trench warfare. Each party sees very little of the other. Both believe in gigantic enemy losses.' So it was in Newcastle, even in personal relationships. Neither side spoke to the other. When Tebbutt wanted to go to Tilley's, the 'best restaurant', he always had his secretary ring first to ensure that if there was to be any party from the *World* there, his table was to be placed as far away as possible. As to the casualties, Rothermere trumpeted in all his papers of the 'Glorious First Hundred Days'. He claimed that the *World* circulation was double that of the *Chronicle* (he was piqued when William dubbed the claim 'amusing') and a little later that the battle was 'more of a recreation than a war'. He owned to having spent £400,000 on the *World* but would not part with it for £1.2 million. In private Rothermere wrote to Beaverbrook in August: 'I am afraid both our multiple newspaper proprietors [William and Harrison, whose Provincial Newspapers were threatened but in fact were never attacked because of the expense of the war with Allied] are going to find themselves in very great difficulties before the end of next year.' Then, significantly, since his original plan had been to start also in Glasgow, but where Allied's was only one of three evening papers: 'What are you doing about an evening paper for Glasgow?'[9]

By October he was a little less optimistic: 'I stand behind the Northcliffe Newspapers Ltd, and I must see this company through

---

[8] Though no doubt he had been 'booked' several months ahead, the General Election was now scheduled for 30 May.

[9] The motive for Beaverbrook would have been to back his newly formed Empire Free Trade movement. Rothermere had previously suggested he start in Manchester as well.

whatever it costs. I have arranged to finance it to the extent of £2 million if necessary.' Meanwhile, Beaverbrook recorded in his file the very next day:

Lord Camrose [William had been made a peer in June] told Mr Blumenfelt Rothermere was losing £10,000 a week in Newcastle. He had 800 [sales] canvassers. Advertising had not been more than £1,000 a week since the start. In Bristol the Berrys were not in the least alarmed because the Rothermere paper is already dead. It is doing very badly and needs a free meal ticket scheme in order to issue figures like the Newcastle net sale.

Rothermere thinks of nothing but money, has gone crazy, is following in his brother's footsteps.

The story got around. At Christmas, *Reynolds News* (a Sunday paper owned by Maurice Ostrer, the film magnate) reported:

... a persistent rumour in City circles that a world-famous peer is privately undergoing treatment for mental trouble and that the specialists do not think his reason will last for more than another year.

The circulation war in Newcastle was as dirty as could be. The *World*'s sales were, of course, artificial in so far as it was largely 'bought' by the free meal offers.

When the exhibition ended, *World* circulation was rebooted by free gifts, aping the current popular national paper war. I have not checked what particular gifts were chosen in Newcastle, but the national menu[10] included, from time to time, fountain pens, cigarette cases, cameras, spoons and sugar tongs, silk stockings, cufflinks, powder puffs, gramophone records, hiking kit, theatre tickets, and circus passes. 'Partial free gifts' – sets of Dickens and encyclopaedias prepared by 75 or 100 editors, as the case might be, were to come later.

The *Chronicle* therefore considered the *World*'s circulation certificates spurious, particularly as they were for short periods during which most of the returned, unsold copies could not have been collected. The *Chronicle* itself published no figures but instead showed them to advertisers in confidence. This worked, as the advertisements, particularly classified, which is the hardest of all advertising to build up, continued to generate the same volume of replies as heretofore. The circulations of both papers were simultaneously increased as their areas were continually

---

[10] The free gifts battle, quickly joined by the *Mail*, *Express* and *News Chronicle*, had been begun by the *Daily Herald*, when it was taken over by Odham's, its printer, and made into a popular paper. By 1931, together with canvassing, it was costing each of these papers £8,000 a week at a time when advertising generally was falling.

being expanded at great expense by selling in villages up to sixty miles outside Newcastle. Paper vans were blocked by each side to delay distribution and each had spies in the other's office. Spurious news stories were planted. Recriminations in each paper abounded and the sins of managements were personalised as if directly committed by Lords Rothermere or Camrose themselves.

So long as Rothermere was prepared to splash his own money about the countrywide struggle might have gone on for many years. But at the end of 1929 came the Wall Street Crash. According to his nephew, Cecil King, Rothermere lost $40 million (then about £9 million, some £200 million today) in one month.[11] At first he seemed to take it almost light-heartedly. He told Beaverbrook he was going to diet at Dr Dengler's sanatorium in Baden-Baden: 'Physically I desire to conform more to the diminished figure of my fortune.' But the decline in trade generally and the fall in price of his newspaper company shares soon produced a more sombre mood. Where he had previously spoken of a 'recreation', he now pronounced: 'In this gigantic struggle victory will go to those who have the longest experience and the longest purse.'

In June 1930, word reached William through some of Rothermere's friends that 'he would welcome some agreement limiting the area of competition'. As neither William nor Gomer were on speaking terms with him after the public exchanges of abuse, Edward Iliffe was chosen as the intermediary, particularly as he, through his father, had been friendly with Northcliffe. Iliffe saw Rothermere in his Paris suite at the Hotel Splendide, where at first he found him 'pretty uncompromising'. The latter said he was still determined to go ahead with his full provincial programme, which would mean 'the ruin of the Berrys'. Iliffe replied that would also mean his own ruin as his financial affairs were 'inseparable'.

Over lunch, Rothermere gradually mellowed and conceded that though he would continue resolutely in Newcastle and Bristol, he would cancel plans in Cardiff, Sheffield and Aberdeen. Birmingham, too, was tacitly abandoned as it would have meant competition with Iliffe's own wholly-owned paper in Coventry. The only concessions Allied had to make were to take over at cost unfinished buildings[12] at the first two centres and not to distribute Cardiff papers in the Swansea area, where Rothermere had just bought an evening paper.

An agreement to cover these arrangements was drawn up, but not signed until July. Perhaps it was for this reason that Rothermere, who

---

[11] Later, though much too late to affect the battle, he lost $36 million in currency speculation, according to his son, forcing him to sell his shares in the *Daily Mirror* and *Sunday Pictorial*, at the same time 'puffing' them in the *Daily Mail*.

[12] These were soon sold without very great loss.

with McWhirter, was 'fronting' the whole provincial operation, did not at once inform Sir George Sutton. Sutton was Managing Director of Associated Newspapers and chaired the annual general meeting on 13 June 1930. At the meeting he announced that the full Northcliffe programme was going ahead for new evenings in eight towns including, specifically, Cardiff and Sheffield. The very next day was the annual general meeting of Allied Newspapers, where William was able to announce the deal. The propaganda victory was the greater since it had been decided not to announce formally the Swansea proviso.

Meanwhile, the battle in Newcastle, Bristol and Derby continued unabated. Allied, too, were feeling the pinch. The three centres were losing £100,000 a year altogether, compared with a profit before the battle in excess of £200,000. Advertising all over the country was down, as were the profits of Edward Lloyd. In 1931 the Allied ordinary dividend had to be cut, thus affecting all three partners, who had also had to find £1.5 million to finance the *Telegraph*. It must have been about this time that William unwittingly impressed a non-newspaper friend with a casual remark: 'If I had to find a million pounds tomorrow I am not sure where I would turn.'

From 1931, Edward Iliffe kept a detailed diary. In it one sees the first sign of a further weakening in Rothermere's morale when he reports, on 13 February, the withdrawal of a £500,000 gift of land for the Foundling Hospital children's playground and his surrender of a £50,000 deposit. At that time Iliffe calculates the depreciation on Rothermere newspaper shares 'has shown an aggregate drop of £38 million from the peak of 1929'.

I tell the story leading up to the climax in note form, culled from the diary:

23 Feb. Gomer sees Sir Pomeroy Burton 'who is in close touch with Rothermere'. PB 'is very anxious to act as go-between' ... R was 'rather worried' over the newspaper situation.

5 Mar. Recorded that Allied's overdraft is at minimum $4\frac{1}{2}$ per cent (Bank Rate 3 per cent). Another company associated with the Partners, but not with Allied, is being charged Bank Rate for £10,000 and $3\frac{1}{2}$ per cent thereafter.

At this point Rothermere seems to have enlisted the aid of Beaverbrook. The latter ran three articles in the *Sunday Express* in April, crabbing Allied shares and debentures. After the second article, William wrote to Beaverbrook:

You and Rothermere have worked so intimately together that when

146

the *Evening Standard* published paragraphs wholly misrepresenting in Rothermere's favour what had happened in the newspaper situation, I did not think it was worth writing.

On the other hand, yesterday's article in the *Sunday Express* on the affairs of my companies is so mischievous that I do feel entitled to ask whether it has your approval.

It would seem hopeless to expect that newspaper proprietors can ever work with anything approaching unity if this sort of example is to be generally followed.

Iliffe notes succeeding letters: 'B was in Munich and hadn't seen *Express*. Later got a copy, but same thing happened next week. B then asks what he is complaining about.'

9 May W replies:

I am of opinion that the matter should be dropped as we seem to be as far apart as the poles in our views of what has happened ... lunch and discuss.

The shaft got home. In 1933, when the battle was over, Beaverbrook sent Gomer a favourable *Sunday Express* notice of an Allied new debenture, 'which represents my view'. Two years later, his secretary wrote: 'The enclosed paragraph from the City Page of tonight's *Evening Standard* was inserted on the direction of Lord Beaverbrook ...'

12 May B to W:

Think it would be a good thing if we talked over the situation. I would like to know so much what was back of the publication in the *Sunday Graphic* of the engagement of my son Max. The editor seemed so certain he was right. I wonder if it was a plant.

The *Sunday Graphic* had published the engagement of Beaverbrook's son Max to a lady who had been living with him for two years and who previously had been briefly a mistress of Beaverbrook. Beaverbrook had threatened the editor wildly. The editor telephoned William, who said he should publish if he were sure of his facts. The story turned out not to be true.

The Iliffe diary extracts continue:

7 May Draft accounts show Allied's profits down £135,000. No further ordinary dividend, beyond $2\frac{10}{2}$% interim.

In all three towns Allied gaining on R. 'His losses three times ours' ('though he can stand it better').

Szarvasy asks W to lunch with R. Very little talk about the battle. R suggested lunch 'next week'. W agrees but stipulates no conditions. 'Last time' R had said he must have Newcastle. (No account of the lunch.)

8 June Oliver Locker-Lampson, MP, lunches with I. Says R 'is genuinely hard up'.

17 July McWhirter (R's 'chief man') sees I. Says *Mail*'s chief pre-occupation is coming fight with *Daily Express*. Said quite openly he would much rather Rothermere were friendly with Lord Camrose than Lord Beaverbrook. They had let the *Express* get to within 40,000 or 50,000 of the *Mail* and it was necessary to put down a considerable amount of money. Now was the time for an agreement to eliminate competition. Says R still had the idea that financial pressure would make us do a deal. McWhirter hints that R 'might offer a very high price for all three centres'.

22 July W and GB think that 'in the interests of shareholders they might be forced to take it'.

24 July R's son, Esmond Harmsworth, is 'evidently very fed up in regard to the *Daily Mail*'. He himself is not allowed to act. The *Mail* organisation is at sixes and sevens. All deplore the losses of Northcliffe Newspapers. [Esmond was also reported to have commented wryly that if were running the *Mail* he would drop all his father's stunts (like praise for Mussolini, the Black shirts and Hats off to Hungary). Instead he would 'make it damned dull and complain about the income tax'.]

1 Dec. R, through Robert Donald [a business associate] suggests Allied should go 40/60 with him in all centres. D says R 'has decided to full steam ahead' in all centres 'eventually bringing us to our knees'.

2 Dec. I saw Whitecroft of the Law Debenture Corporation, who were Trustees for some of the Rothermere debentures. 'Obviously his entire sympathies are with us.'

10 Dec. W lunches with R's brother, Sir Leicester Harmsworth. I didn't think lunch was with R's knowledge. LH says he's going to bring the parties together.

21 Dec. R 'appears to have made a large sum of money' going a bear in the US, 'in the last three months'.

22 Dec. Annual Report of Northcliffe Newspapers. Loss shown as

£62,000 but money advanced by parent company indicates total loss between £400,000 and £500,000. 'Severe references by the auditors'. [The *Investors Review*, which had obtained a copy, though it was not sent to the Press, commented that 'the position looks decidedly uncomfortable'.]

At meeting later R 'bluffed that they were full of money and prepared to go on fighting indefinitely'. [He announced that any provincial newspaper owner wishing to sell should get in touch with the company secretary.]

30 Dec. LH still trying to bring about a deal.

It will be seen that Rothermere had quickly recovered from his mood of pessimism. He thought he had the opportunity of finishing the Berrys off. He had long known that Allied was running a very large overdraft. He now heard that there was not enough money to pay the preference dividend[13] in which case the preference shares would get votes and the Berrys would lose control. On 31 December 1931 he wrote the following letter to Beaverbrook (marked confidential in manuscript):

It is no concern of yours or mine how our competitors raise money for their businesses, but it is a matter of great public concern if the Joint Stock Banks of the country, with much levity, use their depositors money to stimulate competition among newspapers. Frankly, this is what the Westminster Bank has been doing.

A friend of mine, who is a stockbroker, told me that the Westminster Bank's advances are becoming a matter of comment. Anything that is a matter of comment on the Stock Exchange usually percolates eventually to the newspapers.

If the general body of the Westminster Bank's depositors should learn, one day, that large sums of their money have, in the most irresponsible and reckless way, been advanced to newspaper proprietors and newspaper companies, there might be an explosion which would shake the Westminster Bank to its foundations.

I don't in any way wish to press the advantage which Northcliffe Newspapers have secured over the Allied Newspaper Group. I am quite willing to come to terms but the terms would have to be something like the following:

[There follows a complicated scheme which would have given Northcliffe control in all three centres.]

---

[13] The preference dividend had been earned but the overdraft had been run up by newspaper purchases left unfunded because of the weak state of financial markets during the slump.

You may show [struck through] read this letter to your guest if you wish.

My recollection is not precise in this particular. I think, however, that 'the guest' was Brendan Bracken, Chairman of the *Financial News* and founder of the *Banker*, who successively tried to get Rothermere and Beaverbrook to come to the rescue of his newspaper. As a result of this letter, Bracken went to see Sir Charles Lidbury, Chief General Manager of the Westminster Bank, and advised him Allied were being beaten in the newspaper war and that he should call in their overdraft. The story I remember is that Lidbury said briefly: 'Mr Bracken, that's the door.' I suggested to Robin Birkenhead, when he was researching this book, that he should go and see Lidbury who, at the age of ninety-eight, was living in retirement in South Wales. Lidbury, though he received him courteously, said that he was still bound by banker's confidentiality. I have tried to check the story through bank records, which turn out to be silent on the matter. A senior official at the National Westminster tells me, however, that he seemed to remember hearing an account to this effect when he was a very young man.

Lidbury's flat refusal must have been quickly reported to Rothermere, for he now sent a series of proposals through his brother, Leicester, and Cowley, the Chairman of the *Daily Mirror*. By 6 January 1932 the partners had concluded that while 'he will no doubt put up a bluff he does in fact urgently want a settlement'.

The first approach, represented as Leicester's own scheme but identical to that outlined to Beaverbrook, was rejected straight away, Leicester himself admitting it was 'illogical'. Two days later Leicester came back with a second scheme giving a monopoly to Allied in Newcastle but awarding the two smaller centres, Bristol and Derby to Northcliffe. The partners, though they considered they had easily won the battle in Bristol, accepted subject to 'one or two differences'. Their acceptance seemed to have been the smell of blood to Rothermere, who now wrote to William for the first time, proposing a quite different scheme. Finally, or so it seemed, William saw Rothermere and Cowley and persuaded them to revert to Leicester's second scheme.

On 12 January Rothermere tried to alter the scheme in his favour. Two days later (on 14 January) he saw William (at his flat in Stratton Street) and made a brand new offer for all three centres. How his mind was working is revealed in a letter to Beaverbrook of 15 January:

As I have been keeping you informed and taking your advice about our negotiations with the Berrys, I am sending you a copy of the offer (14 Jan) I have made. As you advised I have been most reasonable. [Offer to take all three centres in return for £1 million $6\frac{1}{2}$ per cent debentures. All assets to be kept by respective groups.] From this offer you will see we are making greater sacrifices than they are.

Later in conversation, Rothermere explains to Beaverbrook that if the offer is accepted he will get £230,000 monopoly profits for a debenture charge of £65,000.

At Quaglino's restaurant that night Rothermere tells Randolph Churchill (who is on the *Daily Mail* staff) and Brendan Bracken that 'he was on the point of settling'. Both ring William's son, Seymour, in Manchester, who rings his father.

8 Jan. W sees R again. Says he would accept buyout, but only at impossible price, which he won't name. [Actually, it is £1.75 million debentures.] W says 'to show willing' he'll add to the second Leicester scheme £100,000 6% preference shares in Newcastle. R says he will settle for £200,000. W walks out but they toss in the hall, agreeing £125,000.

The battle was over. Only one *Evening World*, in Bristol, remained. Even that did not stay under Northcliffe control very long. An upsurge of local feeling, prompted by the Bishop of Malmesbury, led to subscription for a new evening paper in Bristol. Within four years the new *Evening Post* had so far thrashed the *World* that a joint company, controlled by the *Post*, was set up to run both papers. The title of the *Evening World* lingered on and finally disappeared in 1962.

As to the financial losses on each side, Allied's profitability was quickly restored. Lidbury came up with cash to pay the preference dividend, the whole overdraft being paid off later in the year by an issue of new preference shares.[14] Rothermere told William his personal loss had been in excess of £1 million, while Edward Iliffe estimated that, when Northcliffe Newspapers went into voluntary liquidation at the end of the year, the total loss of the Rothermere companies had been £4 million.

The real loss was to the people who could not afford it, even though they had briefly enjoyed salaries way above the market rate. In Newcastle, such had been the bitterness for the 'treachery' of *Chronicle* staff staying in place before deserting to the *World* that none of them was ever taken back. A statement to this effect was issued in Newcastle. It led Beaverbrook to write to Rothermere: 'The statement is doing a

[14] This time Mossy Myers' offer of an expensive 'syndicate' was declined and, with Lidbury's agreement, the issue was not underwritten.

great deal of harm in Fleet Street. The whole business is annoying to a degree – at any rate as I see it.'

Of the 'non-traitors', some were taken on by the victorious paper and the remainder, according to Edward Iliffe, were offered twice the normal trade union redundancy terms.

*　　*　　*

The battle had been seen at the start by the *American Editor and Publisher* in publishing terms:

> Lord Rothermere's declaration of war, based apparently upon the principles of modern group industrial methods, group economics and group capacities, ignores every definition of journalism except the industrial.
>
> The Berrys have been chosen, apparently deliberately, as the protagonists of a differing viewpoint – that journalism is primarily a business but not essentially an industry. The provincial editors' only salvation in the face of the industrial and financial resources between which they will be ground, lies in the possibility that newspapering is fundamentally a profession.

On the ground, the outcome of the battle was summed up by William Redpath:[15]

> Camrose put a journalist in control in every centre and gave each local paper autonomy. There was no paper that he touched that did not steadily improve and develop under his inspiration as a result of his great qualities as a journalist.
>
> Lord R believed it was cheaper to create a counter-chain by starting new evening papers – all having the same style and format, using the same features, equipped with interchangeable printing presses, and controlled editorially from London.

---

[15] This was not sycophancy. Redpath's account was written after William's death and long after Redpath himself had gone to other employment.

CHAPTER TWELVE

——

Purchase of the *Telegraph*

I WROTE IN the last chapter that the purchase of *The Daily Telegraph* in December 1927 was 'more of a challenge than an accolade'. The challenge was to restore it to the forefront of journalism without it becoming a 'paper of record', like *The Times*, or a paper of stunts and sensationalism, like the *Mail* and *Express*. Despite his admiration for Northcliffe, William, even in 1947, regarded the nineteenth-century *Telegraph* as having been the 'originator of modern journalism as we know it today'. The old model was not to be re-created. A new niche must be carved out.

Rothermere, on the other hand, who had been so much put out when he heard of the change of ownership, would have remembered it when it was worthy of accolade, before the *Daily Mail* was founded in 1896. It had been the leading daily, the first newspaper catering for a new public wanting all kinds of news, written in a lively way but also with what are now called magazine and feature material, including literature, the theatre, music, science and art. At the time Garvin, whose first London job had been on the nineteenth-century *Telegraph*, described the old *Geist* in the *Observer*:

> It was ordained the paper should take an optimistic view – that it should make the very most of everything vivid and curious, that it should be social as well as political, that as well as informative it should be amusing about life at home and abroad and everywhere. Superior persons might squirm about the 'Corinthian' method but it appealed to the Victorian middle classes; and the thing was done with tremendous zest by a staff riotous with personality – full of comic talent, temperamental eloquence, queer abilities, Bohemian experience. And never lacking amongst these were solid masters of more serious parts of the job.

Matthew Arnold described 'the young lions of Peterborough Court' as blending 'the airy epicurianism of the salons of Augustus with the full-bodied gaiety of our English Cider-cellar'.

The 'riotous personalities' had, however, long gone, and their exuberance faded, as had their progenitor, the first press lord, Edward Lawson,

Lord Burnham. He had been succeeded on retirement in 1903 by his son, Harry Lawson, whose heart was in politics rather than in newspapers. It was not enough for the *Telegraph* that its new principal proprietor was immensely respected and that he had much public service to his credit. There was no board of directors nor general manager and the paper for which he alone was responsible had been, in his nephew's words, 'founded in sensation but nearly dead of respectability'.

The circulation, which had been near 300,000 before the *Mail* era, had sunk to 230,000 thereafter; to 180,000 by 1914; to 130,000 in 1920, and now, still slowly sinking, was barely 84,000. The competition was well ahead. *The Times*, rejuvenated financially by Northcliffe, had retained its political supremacy and, at sales of 130,000, was making good money. The *Morning Post*, more precariously balanced, was at about the same figure.

*   *   *

In 1927 the *Telegraph* was still some way from being a terminal case. Burnham's nephew said that it had never lost money. Edward Iliffe said that it was not making any. Its ownership, however, was complicated. It was a partnership, chiefly of descendants of the first Lord Burnham's father, divided into sixty-fourths. The second Lord Burnham owned or controlled about sixteen shares. With one exception, the rest took no part nor interest in the paper except to receive their share of £124,000, paid out in dividend each year, whether it had been earned or not. Yet the paper needed money spent on it, which Burnham had not got. He had therefore either to make it a public company, seeking outside money, or to persuade his partners to sell. There would be no trouble from them provided they got a good price. He consulted only his thirty-seven-year-old nephew, Colonel 'Fred' Lawson who, though without a formal appointment, was his uncle's deputy.[1] What finally persuaded him to choose a sale was his appointment, at the age of sixty-two, by Birkenhead, Secretary of State for India, to the Simon Commission, which was to spend two years investigating Indian Constitutional reform.

For a sale, Burnham had no one in mind beside William. In July 1927 he wrote to him as Editor-in-Chief of the *Sunday Times*, saying that 'he had noticed' the progress of that paper and enquiring whether William 'would be interested' in trying his hand with a daily newspaper of the same character. There were two meetings, William remembered, the first in the billiard room at the Oxford and Cambridge Club –

[1] In the office he was just called 'the Colonel'. From the figures recorded in his book *Peterborough Court* I calculate he owned one third of a sixty-fourth.

154

Burnham had forgotten to engage a private room. The discussion was in general terms only (most clubs forbid documents) and only at the end of it did Burnham, who, like his father, had never interested himself in their intricacies, promise to send 'the figures'.

William was at first cautious. Having seen the history of the long decline he was not going to rush into it. He put off a second meeting until mid-September, 'because of the holidays'. He might well have been yet more cautious if he had guessed that Rothermere would be provoked into starting a war in the provinces. Then a second meeting took place, at which Lawson was present for part of the time. It was not until 20 December that Burnham proposed his final terms. These were accepted next day by Edward Iliffe since William and Gomer were 'both out of town'.

Lawson had so much impressed William with his knowledge of the business that, at the second meeting, William told Burnham that any deal was off unless a further hitherto unmentioned condition could be granted. Burnham was at first taken aback until he heard that the 'condition' was that Lawson should take the position of General Manager (previously there had been no such appointment, except that the Editor had been called the Managing Editor).[2]

The price was £600,000 in cash and £600,000 on a $5\frac{1}{2}$ per cent mortgage (paid off in 1932). The cash element was quickly reduced to £400,000 when the *Telegraph* paper mill, a ready source of income in wartime conditions, was sold off to William Harrison, still hungry to expand his newsprint conglomerate.[3]

The brothers, however, had no intention of adding the *Telegraph* to Allied Newspapers as they had done with the *Sunday Times*. There was no call to Mossy Myers, no debentures nor preference shares for the public. Not even a limited liability company was formed. It was a straight partnership with all the money for the purchase and development – there must be a complete rebuilding plan – to be found directly from the partners' pockets, the interest being offset against income and surtax. As a first step they raised £1 million from the bank, secured on their respective life insurances.[4]

---

[2] The Editor, Arthur Watson, continued to hold the empty title until retirement in 1950 and, since the anomaly was then overlooked, his successor, Colin Coote, also became 'Managing Editor'.

[3] Three years later, in the great slump, the Midland Bank foreclosed on Harrison. As Blumenfeld wrote, '... the amiable promoter, knew nothing about newspapers and when he came down it was like the stick of a rocket'.

[4] Later they caused the *Telegraph* to borrow £250,000 from the National Provincial Bank, on their personal guarantee and deposit of £400,000 of securities. During 1928, the partners repaid some of their considerable overdrafts by transforming the *Financial Times* into a public company and issuing £1 million preference shares for subscription.

The purchase, on behalf of William, Gomer and Edward Iliffe in equal shares,[5] was announced in the paper two days before Christmas 1927, but the handover was not to be until 9 January 1928. Before the announcement, Burnham told the Editor, Arthur Watson, who 'was careful to tell the staff the news before there was any possibility of their hearing it from outside the office', but who could not allay 'their gloomy apprehension of extensive changes'. Indeed, as Beaverbrook observed in the *Evening Standard*, 'No immediate changes are announced but the Berry brothers do not, as a rule, buy a newspaper and then forget to do anything with it.'

The Times wrote ominously that '*The Daily Telegraph* in future will share a single control with many publications in every part of the country.'[6]

Watson therefore went to see William (whom he had never met) directly after Christmas at the *Sunday Times* office in Arundel Street. There he recounted the staff reaction:

Not a great deal was known about the Berry brothers except that they had bought some important papers, mostly in the North of England, and it was hastily assumed – in the light of some recent experiences – that this was another case of outside interests coming into a business of which they had no inside knowledge ... It was true that the Berry brothers had owned the *Sunday Times* for some dozen years, but it was not generally appreciated how much the improvement in that paper ... was due to their personal and tireless handling, and to the long hours Sir William spent in the office each Saturday ...

I do not suppose Watson put the staff case quite as bluntly as that, but he did report that 'the staff was getting restless'. William, for his part, he found 'completely understanding': 'In the quiet straightforward way with which I later became familiar, he assured me, "There is nobody whom I wish to get on *The Daily Telegraph*[7] and there is nobody on *The Daily Telegraph* of whom I wish to get rid.'

[5] It was quickly arranged that Seymour should put up 10 per cent, reducing the others to 30 per cent each. On Seymour's death six months later his share went to William, who then emerged as the senior partner, with 40 per cent.

[6] *The Times* leader, written by the Editor, Geoffrey Dawson, in a manner proved fatuous by events, deplored the lack of 'a self-denying ordinance [perpetual trustees] by which the Chief Proprietors of *The Times* have placed its controlling shares for ever beyond risk of any similar commercial transaction'.

[7] This had not been strictly true a few days earlier. William had tried to get Garvin, Editor of the *Observer*, as a special writer for the *Sunday Times* in the middle of the year. Now, on Christmas day, he tried to get him for the *Telegraph*. Garvin turned both offers down even though he was warring with his proprietor, Lord Astor. He finally did join the *Telegraph* in 1943, when Astor terminated his contract.

William, indeed, was very conscious that taking on *The Daily Telegraph* was a different thing from taking on the *Sunday Times*. It was true that the average age of the staff was on the old side, with many gaps, but there were many distinguished writers, all steeped in glorious tradition. He had already worked out in his mind how the paper could be repositioned on a rising path without what is nowadays called a 'relaunch' or 'big bang'. But to do that, without ever having worked on a national daily, he must be more than 'chief proprietor'. He would have known the trouble Northcliffe had had with the 'old constitutionalists' on *The Times*, who resisted his 'invasion' of the editorial prerogative. He must have unquestioned authority and, in such company, he must also have a title superior to the editor himself. It was for this reason, so he told me years afterward, that he arrogated to himself the title of Editor-in-Chief,[8] hitherto unknown in Fleet Street, apart from the *Sunday Times*.

As a result of the meeting with Watson, a meeting of the entire staff was arranged for New Year's Eve at the Memorial Hall in Farringdon Street (round the corner from Fleet Street) with Watson in the chair.

William alone of the partners attended the meeting, but he spoke for them:

> We are not approaching the DT as an institution with the idea it had to be torn down to be rebuilt (cheers). Very, very far from it indeed. Some have suggested, an idea which is not in my mind, which had not occurred to me, that the price of *The Daily Telegraph* was going to be reduced to a penny. That is entirely and absolutely untrue (cheers). I am one of those who believe there is still a future for *The Daily Telegraph* at twopence. I have not the smallest doubt of it ...
>
> As I said, we are not contemplating great changes of any sort. There may be things to do, as Lord Burnham has suggested ... But we are hopeful that we shall have very few changes indeed to make. We are very satisfied with the distinction and the policy and the traditions of the DT: what we want to do is to add to them.

It worked. The above is from a shorthand note. William himself recorded years later: 'Lord and Lady Burnham were in tears and a number of the staff were in the same condition.'

*　　*　　*

The decline in the circulation was by no means entirely the fault of the

---

[8] The law still does not recognise the title. In law, the editor is still responsible for the conduct of a newspaper.

editor and his staff. The office building was too small to accommodate the larger staff demanded by post-war national dailies. Consequently there were too few reporters and an over-reliance on news agencies for home news. In any case, a news editor (whose business it is to anticipate the principal stories of the day and to detail reporters to cover them) had only just been appointed, superseding the tradition that the editor himself, among all his other distracting duties, handed out assignments.

To some extent this was due to the parsimony of the old regime, which also kept low the number of pages per issue with the result that the paper seemed 'all advertisements'. The advertisements themselves beside classified 'jobs' announcements (in which the *Telegraph* still excelled) in default of attractive store advertising, had been augmented by pages of features on heavy industry, 'dead' to the ordinary reader.

Though I do not think William ever heard the story, Beaverbrook once recounted how he, before he entered journalism, had received a lesson from Northcliffe:

> Spreading the old *Morning Standard* on the floor, he turned over page after page, paying no attention whatever to the text: he examined and commented on the advertisement columns – he condemned the character of the advertisements. Then he declared, 'This newspaper will die' and it did die.

In appearance, too, the *Telegraph* was unappetising. It had been replanted in 1922, but in order to save money at that time, the new machines had been ordered to the old design so that they could be replaced one by one. Moreover, they retained the column length of the nineteenth century, three inches longer than any other paper, making the page look dull and uninviting.

Worst of all, to William's sub-editor's eye, was the way the news and features were inclined to be crammed into the paper in no set order in the same way as in the 1915 *Sunday Times*, which I described in detail in Chapter 7. Upon this he immediately set to with a will.

Two major decisions had to be made: a new office building, and new machinery. The old building was knocked down and a new one, on an enlarged site, costing £320,000, was supervised by Edward Iliffe. Simultaneously, Lawson took charge of complete replanting at a cost of £250,000.

These, together with the purchase price, totalled £1,570,000, or about £35 million at today's prices. All of this, plus losses now being made through increased paging, and better newsprint, came out of the partners' pockets; soon to be further touched by lower dividends from Allied Newspapers during the Rothermere war. Edward Iliffe recorded in his autobiography: 'I found it very difficult to find my proportion ... without selling securities at a disadvantage. I just managed to get through ... The Banks were very accommodating in those days.' He enjoyed a higher credit-rating than William or Gomer. He was able to negotiate a lower interest rate on his overdraft than he could secure for his partners.

Exactly what sort of paper William foresaw he rarely committed to paper and then in the most general terms, but he was quite clear in his own mind and transmitted his ideas, as we shall see, in the greatest detail. As Watson observed: 'Of the basic character of *The Daily Telegraph* he approved. That was no doubt why he bought it, for he was a man who considered his courses long and carefully. He therefore desired no revolutionary changes.' Indeed, when he had got the paper into the form and shape he wanted he used to say that, though a reader might notice no change from day to day he could be surprised by comparing a current edition with that of the month before. The test of a well-ordered paper, he considered, was that one could 'find one's way about it'. To illustrate the converse, he wrote acidly to Watson one day: 'What an excellent treasure hunt these paragraphs would make in the positions in which they are placed!'

The initial difficulty arose, I think, from one of the least desirable nineteenth-century *Telegraph* traditions. In that far distant time, the boss of the composing room, 'the printer', was boss indeed. It was the job of the editorial to provide the copy, the headlines and page plans on which the major items were to appear, but it was the printer's job to decide what heading types and type sizes were to be used. The result was that everything tended to be jammed up together, with the minimum of differentiation and, in order to get early pages 'away' in sequence, any small paragraphs available were put among unrelated matter. 'Duff Cooper's remarks on Fascism [are] tucked away amongst the theatrical stuff on the Drama page,' William once complained.

The dictatorship of the printer had once been common to all papers. The Printer at the *Telegraph*, Francis Caine, was the doyen of them all. Once, on secondment to the *Daily Mail* in its earliest days, he had ordered Northcliffe out of his own composing room, which explains why at first, though throbbing with new ideas, it looked more like a telephone directory than a modern newspaper.

Breaking Caine's iron rule – though not his heart – was William's first battle. His long experience of composing rooms, first at Merthyr, then at PIP, and above all at the *Sunday Times*,[9] had given him the self-

---

[9] In the 1926 General Strike William himself had 'made-up' feature pages at a non-union printing

confidence to override the 'experts', Caine and Lawson. He knew what he wanted in terms of white space, double-column heads and introductions, heading types and type sizes, cross-heads and use of photographs. In modern jargon he was his own 'designer'. But, as now he never went 'on the stone' himself, it was a hard slog to train the sub-editors to do what, for the first time, became sub-editors' work.

His method of achieving what he wanted was different from that employed at the *Sunday Times*. In the early hours he worked from home. Called at 7 or 7.30, he marked all the newspapers and was ready to dictate memoranda to the editor when his secretary arrived about 9.30.

'The terms,' the editor later wrote, 'were apt to be a little rasping, but it usually happened, when I saw him an hour or two later, that while the criticisms remained the testiness had gone.'[10] His secretary kept copies of the memoranda in loose-leaf folders, covering a period of about four years. Since the folders are listed in his own handwriting, I think they may be among the few of his records he wished to keep. He may perhaps have been inspired by the copies of Northcliffe's unpublished messages to the *Daily Mail*, which he may have obtained from Sir George Sutton, Northcliffe's first and long-term personal assistant, when he was briefly William's Managing Director of the Amalgamated Press.

William's memoranda are fascinating reading to a journalist and I think selections may be of interest to the general reader. They illustrate, as description cannot, the clarity of his mind, his attention to detail, and his extraordinary memory (which ought to be in the armoury of every journalist):

Not given as news at all but is given as a statement by 'an Industrial correspondent'. Should have been given as news with dateline with explanation by Ind. Corr. I do not want the news wrapped up under his cloak, as it were.

Instead of cutting the £29,000,000 Will story, it ought to have been expanded to double its size. Our correspondents send us the news and we seem afraid to make the most of it.

... should use this Will story in some judicial way. This is the case

---

works in Battersea. Typesetters had composed the type but William put them into the page 'formes', 'with the adroitness of a crack stonehand'. From these, cardboard flongs were produced and sent to Newcastle, where the paper was printed.

[10] As routine he would see the editor again about 5 pm, quiz the news editor throughout the afternoon on news items recorded on his own agency tape-machine and talk to the night editor after receiving the first edition at home about 11.30 pm.

of a man who dies with the second largest will on record. He cuts off his son with a gift of his collar studs because of the latter's market operations in Stutz Motor shares ... You will find all this in our files ... it happened within the last four or five years and was the big sensation of New York for several days or weeks. [He had not been to New York for nearly ten years.] The largest will was that of Mr Payne Whitney. Who is Mr Payne Whitney? When did he die: who got his money; how did he make it; and so on and so forth. It jumps to my mind that either Payne Whitney's daughter or sister was Lord Queenborough's first wife. I have an idea that he was interested in polo and was very prominent in American Society. Here is a story which would have given you a splendid interesting and exclusive top, but the man who handled it had as much imagination as a cow. With all due respect, the other people who had to do with it at all in any shape or form seem to merit the same description.

We seem to have nobody on the staff at night capable of taking a decision and of recognising that a decision earlier in the day may be wrong later.

A house is not a mansion nowadays, even when it belongs to the Marquess of Londonderry ...

Our French correspondent states that Madame Doumer died surrounded by her children. The *Express* says that all her children are dead, except for one son, from whom she was estranged and who was not present.

We should be careful in such cases [one of the weddings of Barbara Hutton] not to let the report become too effusive. For instance: 'The blonde bride leaned graciously on her father's shoulder.'

Our sub-editors should now be incapable of things of this sort; [not identifying people in photographs] explain, explain, explain – this cannot be done too often.

In the public mind [Lord] Cadogan is one of the big wealthy landlords of London, and yet he has been bankrupt three times. His family is connected with most of the big houses of London. People want to know why all this should be and, of course, it is easy to get the explanation if we use our wits.

161

A beautiful picture of Finchley's Charter Procession ... half the space of the picture page ... no interesting figures ... we seem to be magnetised [sic] by the look of a picture as a picture ...

Another American message ... How can anybody avoid Income Tax by selling ... shares? At my suggestion it was explained that in America [realised] capital losses or profits rank against Income Tax, a contrary principle to our own. What the Correspondent means in this case is that large blocks of shares are sold when the market is depressed ... to a dummy buyer [and then bought back at that low price].

[William, as a good Anglican, had decreed that the Roman Church should always be described as the Roman Catholic Church.]

The Pope's Encyclical. We start off with ... 'To *Roman* Catholic Socialists' and in the second paragraph put into the mouth of the Pope the words 'Good *Roman* Catholic ...'.

We describe the opening of London's first 'dual' road but we do not say where the road is situated.

A paragraph about Sir William Waterlow and the Blind on p. 15 omits to add that Sir William Waterlow's funeral service takes place today at St Paul's at 11.45 ... people will once again be saying that *The Daily Telegraph* is not to be relied upon.

Is there any reason to continue the old formula 'Lady Cottenham explained what happened to a "Press Representative" last night'? Obviously it could not have been to anyone else ...

I want to have an illustration whenever possible on the main page ...

We had a leaderette on undesirable films a few days ago ... Mr Mills' explanation is ... low down on page 8.

Could we not have picked out the sensational parts of the stories printed yesterday and refuted them? This ... is a thing we should watch for to show the difference between the *Telegraph* and the popular Press.

An excellent little story on the antiquity of mint sauce.

Still a tendency to use photographs of ceremonial openings. We want more pictures of women. The *Mail* has an excellent picture, for example, of Mussolini's daughter and another of the Queen of the Netherlands skating.

Why, oh why, did you lead on the inevitably dull subject of arms conversations when, standing out a mile was the wonderful series of sea and storm stories ... The whole thing is so un-human.

It is a good idea to have every day a human story on the turn [second news] page.

It should always be the rule with any sensational news that we report on at length to have a little bit of the drama of the scene as an introduction.

An excellent story ... of the Fascists at Wortham. I take it we shall be watching this closely and extracting a little more fun from it. This is a capital way of dealing with the Fascists.

There was also some sarcasm, but not very much. He excused his sometimes sharp comments: 'I feel quite at liberty, having expressed my favourable opinion, to express my equally definite opinion of a contrary character ...' In any case, his memoranda were addressed always to the editor or an assistant editor and not, like Northcliffe's, stuck up on the notice board for all to see. Here is a selection:

In the story of the French President's marriage it would have been an excellent thing if the sub-editor had thought of including the President's age ...

It seems to me that some of your sub-editors make a rigid rule of forgetting immediately anything they read in newspapers.

Why feature a hackneyed view of 'Autumn on the South Downs' when we have a splendid picture available on the floods in Venice? ... We must not slip back into the good old days of static pictures.

Hurrah! 'Back to the Plough' on the picture page again today. Why not have the same picture, reversed, again tomorrow?

Is our Crime man still on the staff? The news in other papers would appear to indicate he is not.

Generally speaking, we have a good paper and have not missed too much ... there are one or two Police Court cases [missed] notably the one where a magistrate advised a husband to thrash his wife. I suppose we rejected this because no member of *The Daily Telegraph* staff would ever think of doing such a thing?

On the turn page [second page news] we have a Londonderry House story; on p. 13 we have another and on the Women's Page a third. In each of them Lady Londonderry's dress and jewels are described. Surely there is a story to be got from the fact that she changed from a white gown into an ivory one and also from the fact that she wore two tiaras, one of diamonds and pearls, the other of amethysts and pearls.

I see that according to Marianne Mayfayre [women's page gossip column] Mr Chips Channon, Mrs Somerset Maugham and Mrs Claude Leigh all have black and white rooms. What a bunch of society dames, as Mr Hearst would say!

Frequent complaints of 'gush' on the Women's Page.
Fewer still were threats of sackings:

It only needs one more error of this sort to make decisive changes in the staff essential [leaving out names of Lords' introduction].

The man who handled this story ... is not to handle [any lead story] again in any circumstances.

That *The Daily Telegraph* should be committed to a statement that six machine gun bullets can blow a man to pieces is not to be tolerated and an example must be made.

I have read Throssel [Motoring Correspondent] carefully for the last three weeks he has either gone to sleep or is not capable of supplying an interesting article ... I should be glad if you would give him a month's notice to terminate his engagement. That gives him four weeks in which to make good ...

PS Throssel has written some very interesting stuff. Possibly he is doing other things besides our work. If so, the month's notice will be definite and not probationary at all.

Watson observed: 'It is a remarkable fact – and amongst other things a sidelight on Lord Camrose's character that the resurgence [of the paper] was able to be effected with the old staff, with no more changes than time will always bring.'

William was conscious of this. He told the *World's Press News* in 1934 that he was most proud of the achievement. He doubted whether this had ever happened in the newspaper world before.

In the same interview he assessed the degree of success so far:

My intention is to go on producing a paper with serious subjects, treating politics without 'stunts' and giving all the 'real' news in undistorted form. To some extent we are creating a new public. There has been a big change in public taste since the *Daily Mail* climbed to pre-eminence. Today three other popular newspapers [*Express, Herald, News/Chronicle*] share the *Mail's* field. *The Daily Telegraph* has a field to itself ... If a man or woman [the *Mail* had been started with the slogan 'The Busy Man's Paper'] tries the *Telegraph*, and likes it, they stick to it. They are not tempted away for the reason that there is no other newspaper catering for them in the same way, and they have not been given any inducement to take it in the first place [a reference to free insurance and free gifts, or what William sometimes referred to as the *Telegraph's* policy of No cigars or Nuts].

*   *   *

Unlike most proprietors of the age, William was not a political animal. He was not interested in political philosophy and as war gave over to peace he could see no difference between Conservative and Liberal save their views on tariffs. Consequently he was a 'men not measures' man. As already recorded, until the Coalition broke up, he favoured Lloyd George rather than Bonar Law, because of his charisma. Thereafter, he was shocked at Lloyd George's irresponsible opportunism and, after Law's death, was increasingly impressed by the unifying influence of Stanley Baldwin.

Baldwin claimed himself to be the leader of 'progressive Conservatism' as opposed to the 'die-hard' section of the pre-war party. Baldwin had proclaimed, convincingly, soon after becoming Prime Minister for the second time in 1924:

There is only one thing which I feel is worth giving one's whole strength to, and that is the binding together of all classes of our people in an effort to make life in this country better in every sense of the word. That is the main end and object of my life in politics.

A few months earlier he had declared: 'The Tory party cannot go on on the old lines ... In the past we have been accused, and often rightly, of being too closely identified with vested interests ... if we are to live as a party we must live for the people in the widest sense ... we alone can tackle these social problems.'

How far he succeeded is shown in a quotation of 1925 by *The Times'* lobby correspondent:

Mr Baldwin is doing a remarkable work. He is restoring the whole tone and quality of British politics ... He has brought into public life a pleasant savour, freshness and health that Mr Baldwin has substituted for the overcharged, heavy-laden, decadent atmosphere of post-war days ... in his shrewd and deep simplicity of character, his patience, his passion for the community and its welfare, his refusal to treat his fellow-countrymen as enemies, perhaps, too, in an occasional gauchness and in an essential loneliness of spirit, it is Abraham Lincoln who Mr Baldwin recalls. Like Lincoln, he has that rarest and finest quality of a leader, the power of liberating and calling in aid the deeper, moral motives in the hearts of men ...

Baldwin's reputation today is still sullied by his concealment of the woeful state of Britain's defences in face of the rise of Nazi power. But there is no doubt that he held the country together, in a way which Churchill could never have done, in the crisis of the 1926 General Strike and the Abdication ten years later. He also deserves credit for persuading the Conservative Party, in spite of much backbench feeling, to play a subservient role to Ramsay MacDonald's Socialist rump in 1931. Similarly William was impressed with Neville Chamberlain as an incisive administrator.

In any case, when William took control of the *Telegraph* in 1928, his prime objective was to turn it back into a 'newspaper'. When the purchase was announced in the paper he allowed Burnham to state in a panel on the main news page: 'No change in the political policy is involved.'

Later he was to expand that statement in his own words:

Politically, *The Daily Telegraph* is in close sympathy with the policy of the Conservative Party ... it has no official or financial connection with any Party ... it does not hesitate to express an independent view when circumstances warrant it. Above all *The Daily Telegraph* will be a National Newspaper, serving its readers with candour and enterprise and approaching all political and social problems without personal bias [a dig at Beaverbrook and Rothermere], with a broad outlook, and in an attitude of fair play to all those whose public spirit impels them to take a place in the councils of the nation ...

The principal leading articles on politics, particularly home politics, had been written for some time by J.B. Firth, a classical scholar and historian, with a great gift of style and lucid expression. Firth continued to write the political leaders for some years, though William was soon complaining to Watson that he had no back-up, suggesting a search for 'a young man a year or two down from Oxford or Cambridge with the idea of training him as a leader writer'. He was still watching the pennies, as he added: 'there are rearrangements I intend to suggest which will more than meet the expense.'

I get the impression that Firth[11] was allowed a very free rein, for William is soon complaining that 'the old Conservative devil in him is irrepressible. But the leader was good and quick to the news ...'. For 'the news' was what mainly preoccupied him. In the memoranda one can see what a struggle (how hard a struggle is difficult to be appreciated by anyone who has not run a newspaper with a political attitude) he had to eliminate party bias. He was very conscious of obvious political 'puffs': 'I dislike intensely the fulsome adulation of Mr Baldwin ... no wonder people describe the paper as a "hack party" journal.'

I give a few more examples from the memoranda:

It is a pity we give Mr Baldwin's message such prominence ... not of any great significance ... it will be looked upon as one more piece of evidence that we are a 'Baldwin at any price' journal.

If we use ['Peterborough', the daily Diary he had introduced] to take a definite part in a political controversy the value of his gossip feature must be seriously affected.

It is a pity to say that the Socialist MPs cheered Ll-George last week when he sat down, as I remember we stated at the time that he was vociferously cheered right throughout his remarks.

Our correspondents are still very heavy in hand. They are trying to square up to the strictly party idea ... and are afraid to let themselves go ...

Be particularly careful that we do not overdo the Conservative

---

[11] After the editor, Firth was the most respected member of the staff. At the handover meeting he had sat on Lord Burnham's right.

Association Meeting so as to be described as the Conservative Party organ ...

... political news. [The other papers] get the news – we get the opinions ...

Bailey [parliamentary sketch] seems to be adopting a Government or Party attitude. There is too great readiness to sneer at anything the Opposition does.

The first two lines [of the parliamentary report] impress me as being a sycophantic attempt to make the Government right at any price.

[On parliamentary reports] There is no reason why Churchill should have received half a column and Robert Horne [Chancellor in the last Coalition Government] an inch and a half. Aneurin Bevan and Grenfell both made interesting speeches. Neither is even mentioned.

We have fallen too easily for the trouble in Spain. It is notorious that the Spanish Government is a bad one. It by no means follows that the people rebelling against it are extremists or Bolshevists.[12]

I detest the note of subserviency which characterises the leader on 'cuts'. It is absolutely a Central Office statement. If 'the rest can be left to the Government' what on earth are we writing about the matter for at all? ... What the leader does ... is to say in the most unctuous way that we will agree with whatever the Government may do.

Why is Foss [Political Correspondent] allowed to spoil his note on the Socialists and the Shipping Bill by describing an Opposition amendment as 'carping'?

We are the only paper in London which did not give any part of Mosley's speech ... While I am no believer in the man or his cause we should not entirely ignore his remarks, addressed ... to an audience of 10,000 people.

[12] The *Telegraph's* even-handedness in commenting on Spanish affairs paid off. Just before the Civil War began in 1936 Rowland Winn (later Lord St Oswald), the *Telegraph's* Madrid correspondent, was arrested and sentenced to death by the Republican government. William was about to visit Spain. Thinking an appeal through the Foreign Office too slow he sent a message to Winn at the prison asking him to lunch at the Ritz in Madrid. The governor was so impressed by the apparent importance of his prisoner that he let him out.

Sometimes, his shafts sank too deep. One item in the memoranda observed:

> Foss up to a week ago was fawning and almost grovelling ... In the last few days he has become an *Express* sort of sniper.

In February 1930 the new machinery, giving a modern page size, was ready. The transformation was completed in a single weekend. The paper had already been considerably improved. The circulation slide had stopped. It was slowly moving up, but so slowly. By the end of the year it was nearing 100,000. There now began a discussion as to whether faster progress could not be made if the cover price was reduced to one penny, the price of its heyday. *The Times* was twopence and the populars one penny. The experience of the *Morning Post*, however, had not been a clear pointer.

That paper had reduced to one penny in 1926 and while the circulation had doubled, it had done so from a very low base. It was true that the character of the paper had changed at the same time. Its 'traditional heavy information policy' had given way to news features. The latter were very well done, but bread and butter news was neglected and the leaders continued to be written for what Baldwin called 'the imperialists of the second Jubilee'.

Lawson said afterwards that he had urged that the price of the *Telegraph* be reduced to a penny at his very first meeting with William, who had replied that he must first 'get the paper right', and then, at the handover meeting, had committed himself to 'no change'. (I daresay this commitment was to reassure the staff that the paper was not going to be made 'popular'.) Edward Iliffe, too, wrote that he had made 'persistent efforts' to the same effect, while William had argued that 'to achieve a considerably higher circulation it would be necessary to alter the contents to some extent', but then the danger was that the paper might be classed among the 'populars' and be unable to charge a high enough advertisement rate. Financially, too, a decision was doubtful. The paper was losing at the rate of £150,000 a year, after interest and depreciation, and the forfeit of a penny a copy would immediately add £80,000. In November 1930 the decision was taken, with effect from 1 December, three years after the takeover.

The result was – phenomenal. In a month the circulation jumped to 175,000 and, a fortnight later, to 190,000, whereupon another machine was ordered at a cost of £25,000. But, with the poor trade conditions, a first weekly profit, £457, was not earned until December of 1932, when the sale had gone ahead to 264,000.

The success, in terms of circulation, seems to have induced a sense of euphoria. At the end of February 1931, J.C.C. Davidson, no longer Chairman of the Conservative Party but still a close friend of Baldwin, approached William with the idea of his starting a London evening paper.

The occasion was the continuing campaign by Beaverbrook and Rothermere against Baldwin, with the object of replacing the latter by Beaverbrook as Leader of the Opposition. The object, said Davidson, would be 'to break the "press lords' monopoly"' and to put a more straightforward Conservative point of view, without any attempt at distortion'. The reaction of the partners reminds one of Foch at the Marne. The battle with Rothermere was at its height, trade conditions were terrible, the *Financial Times* was making a loss, even the Amalgamated Press had been affected and they individually still owed vast sums in respect of the *Telegraph*. Anyway, news for an evening paper, particularly for such a far-flung conurbation as London, occurs mostly too late to print. The earliest edition has to be away by 10.00 am and only the central London edition carries anything occurring after 4.30 pm. As for 'straightforward' political news, that emerges mostly in the late afternoon and evening. Nevertheless, the partners accepted the idea with enthusiasm. As recorded in Edward Iliffe's diary, the partners would put up £400,000 in ordinary shares, while Davidson's outsiders would raise another £400,000 in preference shares: 'the scheme would be very attractive'. The only cause for hesitation was that Rothermere would be released from his promise not to start an evening paper in Manchester. Even this does not seem to have dismayed them, for Davidson recorded their view three weeks later that the new paper would 'earn profits rather sooner than the three years which was [William's] official estimate'. I suppose the calculation was that the public had become so alienated from perpetual screaming propaganda that they would jump at a more sober alternative. Fortunately the 'outsiders' could not come up with the money and nothing more was heard of a new evening paper until William was in a far stronger financial position just before the Second World War.

* * *

The partners, at first, do not seem to have appreciated that the amazing jump in the *Telegraph*'s circulation following reduction to one penny was only a first step in a steep progression, which, without any fundamental change in the character of the paper, would carry them to circulation of a million. Seven weeks after the event they were already enquiring 'where now?' Gomer, Edward Iliffe recorded, was 'for a big circulation with [free] insurance' (he did not say so, but Northcliffe had

This section of photographs is devoted to pictures with and of William's elder favourite brother, Seymour (Lord Buckland). Seymour's death in a riding accident in 1928, was a tremendous blow to William, who felt a light in his life had gone out.

With Seymour at William's house, Barrow Hills, not long before Seymour's death. They are laughing about a business deal Seymour had pulled off with Sir Alfred Mond, later Lord Melchett and first chairman of ICI. They neither of them liked Mond, whom they thought a mean-spirited so-and-so. Mond had been haggling over the last £10,000 and Seymour had offered to toss him for it. Mond reluctantly accepted – and lost.

Seymour with two of his biggest salmon catches, 44lb. and 17½lb. He had eight miles of fishing on the Usk which ran through his estate of Buckland, Breconshire. He had never fished before buying Buckland in 1920 but was straight away bitten by the bug, using all daylight hours on the river. He tried vainly to interest his brothers. I once saw all three on the same stretch of river on an ideal fishing day – pouring rain. Seymour was obviously enjoying himself but as for William and Gomer, I never saw a more miserable duo.

MR H. SEYMOUR BERRY AS AUCTIONEER.

An auction sale at Talgarth Mart in aid of the Breconshire War Memorial funds being conducted by Mr H. Seymour Berry, of Buckland, whose enthusiasm was such that he sold and resold stock many times over. — (Photo. P. B. Abery.)

Above Seymour acting as 'guest' auctioneer at a sale in aid of Breconshire war memorial funds. After giving up his first job as a teacher, Seymour had joined his father's estate agency and auctioneers' business. His astonishing vitality and gift of blarney made him an outstanding operator. The local paper recorded that his 'enthusiasm was such that he sold and resold stock many times over'. The regular auctioneer and his staff are on the right.

Seymour demonstrating what might be called 'the St Ives golf swing'. When Seymour fell ill with suspected TB in the winter of 1904 William gave up his job and took his brother to St Ives, Cornwall, and made him play golf (they had neither of them played before) every day, rain or shine. They both of them had good games eyes – they needed them.

All three brothers on William's yacht *Sona*. Seated are my mother (left) and Lillian, first wife of Gomer who stands behind her. Standing on left is Seymour's eldest daughter, Eileen. After Seymour's death, William became her Trustee and, because her charm and vitality reminded him of his dead brother, allowed her to 'get away with murder'.

The scene at Merthyr General Hospital in 1931 when a memorial wing was dedicated by the Bishop of Llandaff, in honour of Seymour. The two brothers are studying the inscription.

INTERESTING PICTURES TAKEN AT THE CEREMONIES.

Right to left: Sir Gomer Berry, Bart., the Bishop of Llandaff (the Right Rev. Timothy Rees), Lord Camrose, Mr. J. James, Mr. W. R. Lysaght, C.B.E., and Sir David R. Llewellyn, Bart.   *Photo: West*

introduced it to *The Times*), and 'matter' on the front page.[13] Edward Iliffe, on the other hand, was for 'a family newspaper with probably 300,000 to 400,000 circulation retaining the small [classified] advertisements' (by not having to make them too expensive). William seems to have kept his own counsel and no new decision was taken, beyond much publicising of the paper in its present form.

And so the steady climb to 520,000 (the highest 'quality' circulation in the world) continued until January 1937 when, to the astonishment of Fleet Street, the partnership of the whole publishing empire was dissolved. How and why that happened I examine in the next chapter.

---

[13] The merit of putting 'matter' on the front page was less obvious than would now seem. Only one of the four leading papers put news there – the *Express*, which had done so since Arthur Pearson started it in 1900. *The Times* was inhibited since it derived much revenue from its personal columns (the 'Agony Column'); the *Mail* normally carried a full-page advertisement there at a premium rate; the *Telegraph*, though it made little money from them, treasured the strong readership-appeal of its births, deaths and marriages announcements. It was not until April 1939 that the *Telegraph* took the plunge; the *Mail* went at the time of minimum wartime paging, while *The Times* waited until 1966.

CHAPTER THIRTEEN

The Split and the *Morning Post*

THE BERRY-ILIFFE EMPIRE, with the Rothermere war won and *The Daily Telegraph* becoming profitable as well as successful, had grown into the most formidable publishing group in the world. Together it printed more newspapers and periodicals, had more employees and more capital employed, than any other. In *The Daily Telegraph* and *Sunday Times*, each the leading paper in the quality market, it had the widest news service at home and abroad, and almost as much influence as *The Times*, while the editors of its provincial papers were respected in their local communities. The *Financial Times* was the leading financial paper and in the magazine field, the Iliffe Press, wholly owned by Kelly's Directories, published the leading periodicals in many great industries.

I do not think that at this time William had given much thought for the future control of what might be called the imperial provinces. He hoped that my brother and myself would eventually form a partnership as close and sustaining as his had been with Gomer but, being so used to being the senior partner himself, he had not worked out how the empire might evolve.

An impetus came, I think, from Gomer's second wife, Edith, whom he had married in 1931. Edith was French and had been married to a Dutchman. She was well known in Paris and liked entertaining. She now found herself married to a very rich newspaper man who controlled no newspapers and had no great social position.[1] Unlike Gomer's first wife, who had died of cancer in 1928 and who, having lived through the early, precarious and anxious life of the brothers, had no further ambitions for her husband, Edith was understandably anxious for him to become someone in his own right. Everyone knew that the Berry brothers acted, and had always acted, as one. Everyone knew, too, that Gomer was 'No.2'.

After all, of the many companies and their subsidiaries that the brothers controlled, William was always Chairman and Gomer Deputy Chairman. The only company of which Gomer was Chairman was the

---

[1] Nor had he any decent house, either in London or in the country, though he did rent Lord Burnham's fine pheasant-shoot, Burnham Beeches, near Beaconsfield, Buckinghamshire.

St Clements Press,[2] a subsidiary of the *Financial Times*. Who was Chairman of the *Financial Times*? Why, William!

It may also have been a source of irritation when the third member of the triumvirate, Edward Iliffe, had been made a peer in 1933, even though this was 'for political services'. In addition to giving up his safe parliamentary seat to Sir Arthur Steel-Maitland, he had been President of the Associated Chambers of Commerce and had served on many Government advisory committees. It was true that Gomer was already a baronet, but this had been due to good works outside newspapers: his pioneering work for the Infants Hospital and the King Edward VII Hospital at Windsor. Moreover, Colonel Fred Burnham, the Manager of *The Daily Telegraph*, whom he saw every day, was heir to the Burnham barony.

No doubt through the indirect prompting of his sister-in-law, William now set about getting a peerage for Gomer. He himself had obtained his own in 1929 through John Davidson,[3] at that time Chairman of the Conservative Party.

The latter recorded on 6 March 1929: 'I lunched with Sir William Berry ... At the end [after a long discussion on Conservative ministers] he asked me whether now his brother is dead it would be possible for him to be considered for a peerage ... For many reasons I felt it would be better if it were after the election ... and he entirely agreed. I think, however, that he certainly ought to get it in June.' He did.

Now he again approached Davidson, who had by 1934 become Chancellor of the Duchy of Lancaster. In November of that year he extracted a half-promise from Stanley Baldwin, leader of the numerically stronger element in Ramsay MacDonald's Coalition Government. Like all Baldwin's decisions,[4] it took a long time coming through and had to be pressed through Davidson.

The issue dragged on. On 12 March 1935 William wrote to Davidson: 'I saw SB this morning and had a very interesting talk on political affairs generally. He did not make the slightest reference to the other matter. I can only assume it was definitely arranged.' To which Davidson replied: 'I gather from a talk I have just had with him your interpretation

[2] After the split, I was myself a director. Most of the time at directors' meetings was spent in deciding which of the debtors could be pressed hardest.

[3] Davidson was exceptionally intimate with Baldwin. As a young man he had been Private Secretary successively to Lord Crewe, to 'Lulu' Harcourt and Bonar Law. Becoming an MP in 1920, he was Parliamentary Private Secretary to Bonar Law, then to Baldwin and to Bonar Law again when he was Prime Minister.

[4] Baldwin obtained a viscountcy for Lord (Hamar) Greenwood in 1937. The latter knew nothing about it until he read it in *The Daily Telegraph*. Baldwin later explained he had not bothered to tell Greenwood he was putting his name forward since he knew that he wanted it.

of the situation is the right one.' The last record of the series is a note from William: 'Very many thanks for your note. I am very pleased and so is Gomer.' The satisfaction was premature. Baldwin wrote on 12 May 1935 that Ramsay MacDonald, still Prime Minister, 'has not found it possible to include your brother's name', but that 'when the responsibility lies with me, I will submit Sir Gomer's name'. The peerage was not gazetted until January 1936.

Then there was the question of Gomer's six sons, three of them now of employable age. The eldest was already an assistant general manager in Manchester, a second was in Kelly's, while a third, who had had to abandon an apprenticeship in Lloyd's Paper, when William sold it, was working editorially in Glasgow. Meanwhile another nephew, by William's sister, Beta, was managing director in Newcastle. I think it was Gomer's idea to bring the 'Glasgow son' on to *The Daily Telegraph*, where my elder brother, Seymour, was already playing a large part, which engendered William's realisation that 'something must be done'.

In theory, a split was not too difficult as it could be arranged by 'swaps' without much money passing. The difficulty was that, while *The Daily Telegraph* was privately owned, all the other companies were public, with many shareholders whose interest must not only be protected, but be seen to be protected. William, as the re-creator of the *Sunday Times* and *The Daily Telegraph*, was concerned to keep the two, where they were in any case complementary, and would have been prepared to let everything else go. But how to do it? The *Sunday Times* was the flagship of Allied Newspapers. How enormous a price would William have to pay to justify its detachment? Anyway, where else could Gomer hoist his flag? The only other national papers, the *Sunday Graphic* and the *Daily Sketch*, were 'picture papers', already losing supremacy in their field. According to Sir Denis Hamilton, Editorial Director of Kemsley Newspapers (who must be regarded as a hostile witness in that Gomer did nothing for senior staff when selling out to Roy Thomson), Gomer told him: 'Lady Kemsley says that, without the *Sunday Times*, I am nothing.'

After some months, a general arrangement was worked out, though the financial details were still being discussed two days before New Year's Day 1937. An announcement, whose secret had been observed, was made on Tuesday 5 January.

Gomer sold out of *The Daily Telegraph*, the *Financial Times* and the Amalgamated Press to William. William sold out of Allied Newspapers to Gomer and out of Kelly's to Edward Iliffe. Edward also kept 10 per cent of the *Telegraph*, to which he had become sentimentally attached, but later sold out by mutual agreement.

Gomer thus became Chairman of all the Allied Companies and immediately appointed himself Editor-in-Chief of the *Sunday Times*. Edward Iliffe stepped up to be Deputy Chairman at Allied and was happy to become Chairman of Kelly's, which owned his old family firm of the Iliffe Press.[5]

The day before the 'split' was announced, William wrote to all the Allied directors, but it was his parting with the *Sunday Times*, now entirely in the *Telegraph* building, which really hurt.

Its editor from 1932, and the man who had recommended him for journalism all those years ago at the Merthyr school, William Hadley, wrote:

> I soon learned that you had made [the *Sunday Times*] what it is. *Your* initiative and *your* judgment was stamped on every page of it and there is no great newspaper (except the new *Daily Telegraph*) which is so much the product of one man's thought and will ... the impress of your mind will long be on the paper ...

William replied in a handwritten letter (rare for him), thanking him for 'a very charming letter':

> It would be silly of me to conceal the very patent fact that my separation from the *Sunday Times* is a most painful wrench. I have lived with the paper for nearly twenty-two years and I know it like a mother knows her child. Life will seem quite different now that I am divorced from it ... I am sure you will be very happy with Lord Kemsley – and our 'romance' goes on.

Almost equally gratifying, since he was not musical, was a letter a month later from Ernest Newman, the eminent music critic since 1920: 'It has always been a pleasure and a pride to me to be on the *Sunday Times* but, over and above all that, the personal element, if you will let me say so, counted for a very great deal ... at the moment, things somehow do not seem quite the same.'

Another letter which he kept came from Beverley Baxter, MP, engaged

---

[5] Gomer at this time was prepared to have a larger share of the empire than he actually received. He would liked to have had the *Financial Times* and when, a year later, Edward Iliffe, unhappy with the new set-up, withdrew from Allied, Gomer accepted a deal to take over Kelly's. His wife, thinking him already fully extended, persuaded him to abandon it. Whereupon, to Iliffe's dismay, he passed the deal on to William who incorporated Kelly/Iliffe in the Amalgamated Press. The latter's directors were delighted to have quality periodicals complementary to their mostly mass-market magazines, while Edward Iliffe was annoyed to have his old family business swamped in a much larger organisation. He could have spared himself. William always ran the two companies separately and the two managing directors were responsible directly to him.

as 'Atticus'[6] when he lost his job as Editor of Beaverbrook's *Daily Express* (he was a stimulating writer but a poor editor):

> For some curious reason I found your leadership inspiring. It may have been imagination but I felt absolutely in tune with you in your attitude towards journalism, politics and life. It is a great joy to write under such conditions ... I shall never forget your kindliness to me at a time when my career had become unpleasantly complicated. My deepest respect goes out to you as a man and a journalist.

*   *   *

The loss of the *Sunday Times* meant that he now had more time to give to the *Financial Times*. It was perhaps high time. The *Financial Times* had been so long pre-eminent in its field that he had been paying little attention to it. Its competitor, the *Financial News*, owned by the Crosthwaite-Eyre family and chaired since 1928 by their nominee, Brendan Bracken, MP,[7] had always trailed far in the rear. During the Great Depression, it had almost foundered. First Rothermere and then Beaverbrook had been invited to take it over. When Beaverbrook was prepared only to put £10,000 into it, Bracken lost heart. Threatening to liquidate the business, he concluded gloomily: 'I daresay the Berrys will pay us a sum for the copyright and goodwill ... I feel I must give up the House of Commons ... a person who can't run a small business is hardly fit to play a part in managing the country's affairs.'

Somehow, however, the *Financial News* staggered through. When financial advertising began to pick up once more, Bracken, who had clung on to his parliamentary seat and had become a faithful lieutenant of Winston Churchill, appointed a brilliant twenty-eight-year-old editor, Maurice Green.[8] The paper became, editorially, much more talked about. It was perhaps over-weighted with bright young economists, whereas the *Financial Times* was much more market-oriented, with more emphasis on what William called 'bread and butter' City matters.

The top three positions at the *Financial Times* were occupied by men who had all been very good in their time but were by now well into their seventies. R.J. Barrett, the Managing Editor, had been transferred

---

[6] Before the 'split', Baxter had been available for other papers in the Allied group. In 1936, when I was a gossip writer on the *Daily Sketch*, I heard that Baxter was booked for the celebrity-strewn maiden voyage of the *Queen Mary*. Through the picture editor I arranged for him to be supplied with a flash camera and a crate of carrier pigeons. A pigeon duly arrived with a roll of film. When developed, all it showed was Baxter in his cabin bunk. He explained that he had a cold, while still in pigeon range, and the photograph had been taken by a steward.

[7] Minister of Information in the wartime Coalition.

[8] Editor of *The Daily Telegraph* 1960–70.

from the *Financier* when that paper was absorbed. He had been commissioned to write a weekly column for the *Sunday Times* and placed on the board of Allied Newspapers when that company was formed. He was a superb advertising canvasser[9] but now did little editorial work and left most of the managing to the company secretary. He was on poor terms with the editor, who had an adjoining room with a glass panel above the partition. He made both of them ridiculous when he installed a redundant GPO telephone box on his side of the partition so that he could conduct confidential conversations without any word penetrating to the editor. Now seventy-four, he had had a serious operation and was becoming forgetful. The editor had been in the chair since 1924 and had made his name in the pre-First World War rubber boom.

William made a clean sweep. The editor, managing editor and company secretary were all retired. His appointment as editor, however, was surprising; perhaps an answer to the appointment of Maurice Green.

The choice for a successor to Hunter lay between a newly joined leader-writer, Archie Chisholm, and A.G. Cole, the man who had been holding the paper together under Hunter's failing hand. Cole, in his late forties, had been a staff member since 1910 (apart from war service, when he lost a leg) and was the obvious choice. He was typical of the pre-Second World War working journalist, leaving school at sixteen, with only natural flair and experience as the qualifications for the highest editorial desk jobs. He had an all-round knowledge of the City, could turn his hand to anything and was easy to get on with. On the other hand, though perfectly presentable, he did not look like the ideal image of the editor of the leading financial journal.

Chisholm, on the other hand, was a tall, slim, well-dressed man of thirty-four, with a patrician air. He seemed a 'personage', who could be imagined to confer on terms of equality with the highest in the Square Mile. He wore, it is true, an eyeglass, through weakness in one eye, which might have been expected to raise William's hackles – he was allergic to all affectations, including beards.[10] Chisholm's experience was minimal. He had had a couple of years on the *Wall Street Journal* and then six as a junior executive with the Anglo Iranian Oil Company

---

[9] Barratt's forte in later years was collecting advertising at £3,000 a time from foreign governments for inserted supplements on Mondays. When I took over his office I found one drawer of his desk filled with foreign medals, like the Order of the Nile, 4th Class. After his retirement, the first one on the stocks was found to be an Italian supplement, whose editorial had all been contributed by Mussolini's corporative ministers and which had to be substituted by more objective writers.

[10] He never could be persuaded that beard wearers might have sensitive skins. He perhaps remembered a story about Northcliffe's order to his secretary when meeting a bearded man emerging from *The Times* building: 'Find out what that man has to hide.'

(now British Petroleum) in Iraq and Kuwait. He had, however, one advantage for an editor, shared only by Maurice Green on the *Financial News* and Geoffrey Dawson on the *Times*: a first-class Oxford degree.

Though William had always regretted not having gone to a university, indeed not having any higher education at all, I do not think he had until now felt a degree to be an important part of a curriculum vitae. Most of the desk staff recruited to *The Daily Telegraph* had come from other national or provincial papers and their qualifications were their achievements there. Not until after the Second World War did I ever hear him enquiring how many of the staff on *The Daily Telegraph* had degrees (nowadays of course, with greater affluence, the burgeoning of universities and the lessening of the need to 'earn' by teenagers, the answer would be 'most').

The choice was Chisholm, with Cole as 'Associate Editor'. Without any clear directive, a division of duties emerged: Chisholm was in charge of the leader page and features and Cole in charge of the markets, with myself,[11] a chicken of twenty-five, as Managing Editor working with the news editor. It worked quite happily and we never let the *Financial News* creep up. Our circulation was never less than three times theirs until the war.

Meanwhile, William brooded over all. His early-morning routine, which had been to mark with pencil crosses numerous items in the *Telegraph* and *Daily Sketch*, then translated for his secretary into editorial notes, now extended to the *Financial Times*. His was the initiative which pioneered our campaign against the infamous National Defence Contribution (taxing only those companies whose profits increased), introduced by Neville Chamberlain in his last budget of 1937 and withdrawn in July.[12] He, too, caused the starting of a City gossip column, 'City Men and Matters', on the same lines as the *Telegraph*'s 'Peterborough'.

*　　*　　*

Of the relentless rise in the *Telegraph* circulation, much had come from the *Daily Mail* (with more solid, middle-class readership than the *Daily Express*) and from an increase in multiple newspaper buying. Very little had come from the other two quality papers, *The Times* and the *Morning Post*. The latter, the oldest daily paper in Britain, started when the

---

[11] I was not entirely green. I had been given a three months' crash-course in the *Telegraph* City office, and before that, with some editorial experience in Aberdeen, Glasgow and Manchester, had been Editor of the Scottish *Sunday Mail*, admittedly a popular paper.

[12] The *Financial News* at first raised no objection to it.

United States were still the thirteen colonies, had, however, been known to be short of money for some years.

The *Morning Post* had had a strange career. After a patchy first half-century, during which it had counted among its contributors Coleridge, Southey, Charles Lamb and Wordsworth, it had been edited by members of the Borthwick family for three generations. The second Borthwick, Algernon, had established the reputation of the *Morning Post* in the 1850s when he was an intimate of Palmerston and brought off a coup with an interview of Napoleon III, just before he seized the crown. By 1882 its circulation had sunk to the ridiculous figure of just short of 4,000 copies daily. This enabled Borthwick to buy the paper himself, whereupon he reduced the cover price of 3d. to 2d. The sales shot up to 30,000, the revenue increased tenfold, and more could be spent on the editorial. The standing of the *Morning Post* further increased under the third Borthwick, Oliver (it was he who sent the young Winston Churchill to the Boer War), and by the first decade of the new century it was outselling *The Times* and making a decent profit to boot. Oliver died before his father, who had by now become Lord Glenesk, and in 1908 ownership passed to Glenesk's daughter, Lady Bathurst. Lady Bathurst gloried in the political name of 'die-hard' and in 1911 appointed an editor of the same persuasion, H.A. Gwynne, a protégé of Joseph Chamberlain. Public taste, after the First World War, passed them by. Moreover, the *Morning Post*'s speciality, social news, with its attendant large volume of domestic jobs advertising, was no longer a pulling feature. Lady Bathurst, dispirited by Baldwin's new, 'progressive' Conservatism and the coming into power of the first Labour Government, gave up and sold out to a political syndicate of Tory 'die-hards', headed by the Duke of Northumberland. She was pained that the editor might imagine that she would 'sell the *Morning Post* to Lord Rothermere or the Jews'. Under the new ownership, Gwynne had continued 'agin everyone'.

In 1926 the *Morning Post*, too, had tried the ploy of reducing the price from 2d. to 1d. This had had the effect of doubling the circulation, which continued, even while the *Telegraph* was moving ahead so fast, to a plateau of 135,000 between 1933 and 1935. (In that year Lord Apsley, Glenesk's grandson, resigned from the board: 'The newspaper was continually taking the [National] Government to task over political issues ... rather in the nature of "red herrings" or journalistic stunts.') There was then a slow decline to 116,000 and increasing losses were being made. Now the annual loss to 30 June 1937 was estimated at £40,000.

Sometime in the early spring of 1937, the general manager of the

Morning Post approached his opposite number, Colonel Lawson, on the *Telegraph* to 'discuss whether Lord Camrose would be interested in its purchase'.[13] It transpired that the approach was out of turn. The Chairman of the *Morning Post*, Major J.S. Courtauld MP, was already in negotiation with a 'saviour'. He was now put in touch with William. He had been negotiating with Rothermere's son Esmond Harmsworth 'over the last six months'. The idea had not envisaged the passing of control, but a capital injection as well as 'more money from the shareholders'. Even so, he 'realised what a shock it would be to have the name Harmsworth associated with the *Morning Post*'.

William saw Courtauld again on 31 May, and Gwynne, ten days later. Negotiations with Harmsworth were at an end and the Editor realised that 'a comparatively small amount to keep the paper going' was no solution. There must be 'substantial money' to 'spend enterprisingly'. That meant an outright sale.

Thereafter, events moved fast. On 15 June William made an offer of £220,800 (£4 a share) but payable only in $3\frac{1}{2}$ per cent notes redeemable over five years, ending in 1943. Evidently it was his intention to pay the whole amount from *Telegraph* profits. There could be no realisation of assets, which consisted almost entirely of 'goodwill' (the earning power of a familiar title), since the building and printing plant had been flogged earlier to provide working capital.

Deferred payment did not appeal to the long-suffering syndicate shareholders and, after discussion, a new offer was made on 9 July of £193,000 in cash (£3.15s. a share) plus £20,000 of directors' loans to the company.[14] William sent his son, Seymour, round to see the chief general manager of the National Provincial Bank who, unlike modern bankers, promised £200,000 (now about £4.5 million), without wanting to see any figures.

Though the forty-six shareholders, in the letter making the offer, had been asked to 'prevent' it 'being made public at present', William's control must have become known from early August. It was assumed by many, including the editor of *The Times*, that an attempt would be

[13] Lord Burnham, *Peterborough Court*. There is no evidence that William had previously contemplated an offer. There is a list among his papers of the shareholders of the *Morning Post* as at December 1934 and 1935, obtained from Companies House. This may have been part of his normal habit of obtaining the balance sheets (in this case unpublished, since the *Morning Post* was a private company) of all newspaper companies.

[14] The shareholders were certainly a hungry lot. Unwilling to wait for separate distribution from a single *Telegraph* cheque, they insisted on separate banker's drafts for each of them. William having left for Paris, the company secretary pursued Seymour to Croydon airport whence he was going to join his father. All forty-six of them had to be signed at the departure desk.

made to keep the *Morning Post* going as a separate title. But, as Lawson observed:

> The editorial staff had been numerically so depleted in the interests of economy as to be almost on a care and maintenance basis. To build up again would be a long and very expensive matter. Camrose had his own very definite ideas of what a good newspaper should be, and the result would not have been sufficiently different from *The Daily Telegraph*.

In modern jargon, the *Morning Post* and the *Telegraph* would both be competing for the same public in what was then thought to be a limited quality market.

But there were two reasons for delay. First, compensation for the breaking of the printing contract[15] had to be negotiated, and second, the future of the staff had to be considered. The offer document, signed by William, had mentioned almost conversationally that 'the importance' of this aspect 'is very apparent to me, and my general idea is that we would be willing to accept the guidance of Mr Gwynne'.[16]

The decision was taken to amalgamate on 1 October 1937, and no attempt was made to 'stuff the letter boxes'[17] – substituting the *Telegraph* without warning for the now absent *Morning Post*. After the first edition the night before, an announcement was made to the staff. Gwynne's recommendations had been worked out in complete detail. Each member was handed an envelope setting out whether he was offered a job at the *Telegraph* (about half of them), or how much compensation he was entitled to, or whether he was to be put on pension. The *Telegraph* took over the existing pension list and assumed a double commitment. Gwynne himself was retired on full salary, while the City editor was given the sinecure of 'associate City editor'. Next day the *Telegraph* displayed the title 'The Daily Telegraph' with 'and the Morning Post', in its own version of Gothic type, almost equally large underneath.[18]

---

[15] It ran until December 1938 and a claim, according to Courtauld, might amount to £45,000.

[16] Gwynne had expressed anxiety about the staff. Most of them had been recruited, and all top staff promoted, by him.

[17] This method of combining sales in a fused paper was used by Roy Thomson to get the *Sunday Times* past the million mark. The *Sunday Times* had the detailed distribution lists of the *Sunday Graphic*, a paper in the same group. On the night of fusion a similar number of extra copies of the *Sunday Times* was printed and distributed without warning. The newsagents duly substituted, as rival papers had had no notice. In the event the appeal of the two papers being different, not many stuck, but the trick was done.

[18] The size of 'The Morning Post' gradually sank over the years but William, while he lived, would never allow it to disappear altogether. When H.D. Ziman, later Literary Editor of the *Telegraph*, met one of the Russian judges at a party during the Nuremberg Trials, he told him that he represented the *Telegraph*. 'And the Morning Post', retorted the Judge.

William expected a good chunk of the *Morning Post* readers to move over, but not an almost 'clean sweep'. Geoffrey Dawson, Editor of *The Times*, was equally doubtful. He thought the *Telegraph* 'too parvenu and frivolous'. It 'was not so much a matter of political preference as one of social values'. He persuaded his board to spend £10,000 to catch the dispossessed.

The result was without any modern precedent. The 112,000[19] or so readers went over in a body – and stayed. The *Telegraph* circulation figure for October seemed too good to be true and was shown only as 'in excess of 630,000', an apparent advance of 104,000. The November figure, however, confirmed the good news. Whereas a 20,000 increase on September might normally have been expected, the certified increase was 120,000. 100,000 had joined and some of the rest, like libraries and institutions, may hitherto have been buying both.

The second half of the 1930s were halcyon years for the *Telegraph*. As William had said, he had the field almost to himself for serious readers, hungry for objective reporting. This was the period of important constitutional events at home (often celebrated with twenty-four-page, half-size picture supplements) and international crises abroad. Abyssinia (1935), the death of George V and the Abdication (1936), the Coronation (1937), Eden's resignation, the Austrian *Anschluss* and Munich (1938), Prague (1939) and the looming of war, all provided immense stimulation of newspaper readership. An annual increase of 20,000–30,000 soon gave way to some 50,000 or 60,000. By the last month before war broke out, the circulation figure, which had been 84,000 in December 1927 (and 530,000 at the time of the 1936/7 'split'), was now, twelve years on, 756,000.

So much for figures. It is now time to survey the whole period, to describe William's changing life style and his part in the great events of the time.

---

[19] This was the *Morning Post* figure for each of July and August. There are no figures for September 1937.

CHAPTER FOURTEEN

People, Politics and the Abdication

BEFORE THE GREAT War, William's friends had been drawn from the world of Bohemia – publicists, freelance journalists, advertising men, commercial artists. The twelve men who gave him a lunch to celebrate his baronetcy in 1921, on his forty-second birthday, were largely the same as those who had attended his bachelor party fifteen years earlier. Yet they gradually moved apart, for their life styles were changing. Only Herbert Morgan and Ted Hunter remained close friends for life, with Van (Count Vanden Heuvel) on the periphery.

William's own life style began to change in the early 1920s. At first his children were too young to give him companionship and my mother was reluctant to spend many evenings in London, leaving her own widowed mother to baby-sit. All this gradually changed. Some of the old friends came to his new country house, but they mingled with neighbours and new acquaintances from the wider London world. Summer holidays, which before the First World War had been by the sea with the families of Seymour and Gomer, he now took in rented houses, with rough shooting, in Scotland. His own family, which completed its 'quiver-full' of eight by 1923, was enough to fill the houses; his eldest daughter brought friends home and the two elder sons were now old enough to shoot and receptive enough for him to talk business and newspapers to, or play billiards with, after dinner. Family bridge became a cult when a friend of his eldest son taught them all Contract. Sometimes the whole family played Roulette, with dried beans as 'chips'. William's lightning calculations as croupier were sometimes thrown out by my mother's habit of gaily biting her chips in half to restock her kitty.

* * *

It is perhaps appropriate here, though out of chronology, to describe his progress in property-owning. Barrow Hills, near Chertsey, I have already described in Chapter 8. It was a comfortable house set in 200 acres, but hardly a fine or memorable house, being already on the fringe of London suburbia, and without a shoot, then the desideratum of any affluent country house owner fond of entertaining. In 1935 he had the chance of getting a really noble house, in 'real country' – Hackwood Park, Hampshire, dating from 1688, with 3,000 acres. Apart from its beautifully proportioned rooms and a number of Grinling Gibbons carvings, it boasted the magnificent eighty-acre Spring Wood (now listed Grade 1), also dating from the seventeenth century. It had long been in the ownership of the Bolton family, though the then Lord Bolton had not lived there since the turn of the century. It had been let on long leases to Lord Curzon when he returned after being Viceroy of India and, after his death, to his widow. The purchase nearly fell through when William's son, Seymour, discovered that (Eric) the third Earl of Dudley, was intending to bid for it. Dudley had sent his factotum to view the property and reckoned that by clear-felling the Spring Wood and stripping the roof lead he could make a killing. It so happened that Dudley was inclined to be frightened of William, as well he might. He was a non-executive director of the Westminster Bank and was known to have quantified William's overdraft at a dinner party.

William moved into Hackwood at the end of 1936. By now, half of his children were married with their own children, so that at weekends the house was filled with them and other couples invited for the shooting. They often sat down to a meal more than twenty.

In London, too, he had moved, this time because he had to. He discovered that his house at Seamore Place, in a pleasant cul-de-sac, was to be demolished in order to extend Curzon Street into Park Lane. He was lucky, therefore, when again his son, Seymour, discovered that there was a fine house going in St James's Place, a cul-de-sac off St James's Street, fronting on to Green Park. He had to hurry as a prospective purchaser was Olive Bailey, the American heiress, whose trustee was fortunately away in America.

*　　*　　*

If his personal expenditure had now reached its highest level, so too his generosity continued in abundance. Like his brother, Buckland, he established no charitable foundation but gave freely when the occasion arose. I have already written of his large and frequent contributions to Merthyr hospitals, which had to come to an end when the National Health Service was founded. A £25,000 promise to Basingstoke Hospital was aborted for the same reason. He and Gomer provided a new organ for the Merthyr Market Square Chapel, and in newspaper files are mentioned frequent gifts to schools in South Wales. In the Depression he and Gomer had kept Merthyr pits going.

Soon after coming to Barrow Hills he bought and presented to the Chertsey Council the twenty-four-acre beauty spot, St Ann's Hill (threatened by builders), where, according to the local paper, 'Some of the most beautiful views in the County of Surrey can be obtained.' Later, he gave a valuable site in the centre of Basingstoke as a football ground. In 1939, when the last of his four sons left Eton – after a continuity of seventeen years – he set up the Camrose Bursary which is now the largest of all the school's bursaries.

A great deal of his giving – which he represented as 'loans' without interest but rarely got them back – was personal, to friends who had been speculating or were down on their luck. One of his largest creditors was Sidney Carroll, who lost thousands as an impresario. Carroll at first tried to finance his enterprises by borrowing heavily from his magazines, which themselves got into trouble. William and Gomer jointly guaranteed one of his company overdrafts and rescued him from moneylenders. Each year, though always saying they would not do it again, they paid off the losses of Carroll's Regent's Park Open Air Theatre.

William's own biggest guarantee was to Lord McGowan, Chairman of ICI, whose speculations in the 1937 recession led to a scandal which prompted a popular press headline: 'Boomster Peer may quit ICI'. The directors called in Sir William McLintock, the eminent accountant, but refrained from calling for McGowan's resignation when he reported that William had guaranteed him for £60,000 (now about £1.4 million). The guarantee continued until 1951.

His 'loan accounts' in 1941 amounted to £105,000 for twelve recipients. In addition there were fifteen covenants. On one occasion he paid £5,000 from his own pocket to a managing director whose surtax bill had suddenly risen by that amount owing to a change in the company's accounting year. He was always embarrassed when such largesse was mentioned and said to one, whose debts he had paid and whose wife and daughter he had endowed: 'The thing about making money is that you can make slaves of your friends.'

* * *

His budding friendship with Birkenhead led to his breakthrough from acquaintanceship to intimacy with the 'men of influence', by his election in 1926 to The Other Club, a fortnightly, single-table dining club. He attended almost every dinner and there met, on equal terms, politicians like Lloyd George and Churchill, Robert Horne and Hamar Greenwood, Eddie Winterton, George Lloyd, Freddy Guest, James de Rothschild and J.H. Thomas; fellow newspapermen like Rothermere, Beaverbrook, Riddell, Dalziel and Garvin; artists like Orpen, Munnings, William Nicholson, Lavery and Lutyens; authors like Arnold Bennett, H.G.

Wells, A.E.W. Mason and P.G. Wodehouse; businessmen like Harry McGowan, Lord Ashfield and Norman Holden; and a host of other well-known names.

In the same year he bought the 550-ton, semi-diesel yacht *Sona* from the executors of the great sailing man, Lord Dunraven[1] (I say 'great' as he had twice challenged for the America's Cup, sailing the challenger himself). Two years later he, together with Sir Mortimer Singer the industrialist, accepted a challenge from New York for a 21-metre race series in 1929. While the two defending boats were being built the American challenger went bankrupt and the two defenders were relegated to the Big Class, mostly of 23-metre boats or their equivalent. Though they received a handicap, neither of the newcomers achieved much success and after two years William sold his yacht, *Cambria*, as a cruiser.[2] (The idea of a racing yacht was not quite dead. When Sir Thomas Sopwith returned from his own America's Cup challenge in 1934, he said that he had approached William as a partner: 'It was a very near thing.') Though William had experience neither in sailing nor helmsmanship, he had made many new friends, both in the Solent, the 'headquarters' of sailing, and in the various ports where racing took place.

In 1930 he was elected a member of the Royal Yacht Squadron. After the war, he was the first non-sailing man to be chosen as Vice-Commodore, in 1948, where he made himself responsible for the finances of the Club. His partnership with the Commodore, Sir Ralph Gore, was a natural fit, for Gore, though the best helmsman in the 12-metre class, had no flair for organisation. William was held in some awe by the younger members and remained Vice-Commodore until his death.[3]

* * *

I turn now to politics, from the General Election of 1924 to the National Government of 1931, and the part the Press played in it.

Though William saw much of Churchill at The Other Club, he was not as yet, and was not for some years, a political admirer of his. Though he had come to Churchill's aid in 1923, when he provided a platform for his return to politics (see Chapter 10), he still regarded him as the adventurer he had condemned in the *Sunday Times* on his readmission to Government in 1917, and as the political buccaneer,

---

[1] Dunraven had built it as an excellent 'sea-boat', with the high-bowed line of a trawler. According to Beaverbrook, in the *Evening Standard*, the boat was built for £100,000 and sold for £52,000.

[2] The boat, though no longer with a racing rig, is still afloat in the Mediterranean.

[3] Nowadays the officers of the Club have multiplied and are elected for a fixed term. In addition to the Commodore and Vice-Commodore there are two Rear commodores.

'always out for office', he described to J.C.C. Davidson in March 1929.[4] After the General Election, which the Conservatives lost in May of that year, Davidson reported to Baldwin in October: 'From a talk I had with Bill Berry, it looks as if Winston, while giving lip service to loyalty, is inclined in his cups to give expression to his innermost thoughts.'

Churchill, however, was only the first to lose confidence in his leader. By 1930, most of Baldwin's colleagues were similarly doubtful. Though personally still popular in the country and on the backbenches, he had lost two general elections and, in debate, was too inclined to see the Government's point of view. The Party had no policies. Baldwin was waiting for the newly formed Research Department to produce them.

Meanwhile, the Conservative Party was split into several pieces by the antics of Beaverbrook's Empire Crusade; by Rothermere's equivocal support for it (to Rothermere the Empire meant India); by other 'protectionist' lobbies, and by Churchill's flirtation with his old hero, Lloyd George.

William himself had been highly supportive of Baldwin and the Conservatives at the 1929 General Election. Davidson had told him of a two-hour conversation with Thomas Marlowe, an ex-editor of the *Daily Mail*. Marlowe had described how Rothermere was in Beaverbrook's political pocket. They had devised a scheme to give half-hearted support to the Conservatives in the run-up to the election and then to switch suddenly to Lloyd George, who was preparing a well-researched policy document, with the assistance of J.M. Keynes and Walter Layton, Editor of the *Economist: The Yellow Book – Britain's Industrial Future*, soon popularised as a pamphlet: *We Can Conquer Unemployment*. According to Davidson, William volunteered 'a two months' campaign of an intensive nature' of all the newspapers under his control against Lloyd George's onslaught, long before the dissolution.

In retrospect, the document can be seen to be of much more substance than generally thought at the time and to be similar in many respects to the New Deal by which President Roosevelt cured America's Depression by trial and error from 1933 onwards. At the time however, it seemed to have only a political dimension – that, since the Liberal Party was of no current significance and led, in Sir Robert Horne's *mots*, 'by a crook with no flock', it would lead only to a split in the anti-Socialist vote.[5] Later, after the election, which resulted exactly as

---

[4] See Chapter 10, pp. 130–1.
[5] The Labour Party was still widely regarded as a revolutionary party even though the extremist Independent Labour Party had been defeated at the Labour Party Conference in 1928.

predicted, Baldwin nevertheless wrote to thank William and his brother for their support:

> I want to thank you warmly for the unswerving support you have given me during a difficult time.
> I do this the more because I recognise in you and your brother (as I felt with Buckland) men who act in honest conviction. I should have regretted your opposition but I should have respected it, for I know that you would direct your policy as you thought right. Your support therefore has been doubly welcome and I appreciate it.

William replied:

> We have the satisfaction of giving our assistance to somebody for whom we have the greatest respect and in whose honesty of purpose and singleminded devotion to the welfare of the community ... You had inspired in my brother Buckland a great affection and there is not the smallest doubt that had he been living the result would have been different in at least three seats in South Wales.

Eighteen months after the election William, too, was beginning to have his doubts of Baldwin's grip.

At this time William had been asked by Beaverbrook to enlist *The Daily Telegraph* and the *Sunday Times* under the banner of Empire Free Trade but had replied with a gem of prevarication:

> My personal feelings and political thoughts have been up to now of an opposite character to those which you hold on the great question with which you are concerning yourself; but they are not of a rigid and rabid Free Trader and I feel that the general question ... is one which has to be studied afresh ...

His refusal to 'sign up' was based not only on the danger of being led into extremes (he knew from experience that Beaverbrook was incapable of running any campaign without descending into personalities), but also by the vagueness of the Empire Free Trade concept. It was not a programme in any detail, more a worthy attitude. The trouble was that the Dominions, of which Beaverbrook knew only Canada, were lukewarm about it. Unlike 1903, when Joseph Chamberlain had launched his similar campaign, they were now building up their own basic industries and saw no benefit for themselves in giving a preferential tariff to British manufacturers. A preferential tariff for Empire food meant a British tax on foreign food, which Northcliffe had damned as a 'stomach tax'.[6] Hence the 'programme' finally boiled down to a preferential rate for Canadian wheat only and the encouragement of the export of Welsh anthracite. Beaverbrook, denied William's general support, asked at least for an article in *The Daily Telegraph*, lauding anthracite. William found this request easier to refuse. He pointed out that his financial interest in coal, either personal or as trustee for Seymour's family, made it impossible.

Beaverbrook at this time was on reasonably friendly terms with Baldwin. He was still a paid-up member of the Conservative Party. His campaign, however, which had started only as a Conservative 'ginger group', soon became vituperative. Having involved Rothermere, he was anxious to keep him and the support of his newspapers' still-enormous prestige.[7]

Rothermere, on the other hand, ever since his snub from Bonar Law, had hated the Conservative leadership in general and Baldwin, Law's successor, in particular. Beaverbrook stumped the country (he was a first-rate platform speaker) and quickly the campaign became a vendetta against Baldwin. Rothermere called publicly for his replacement by Beaverbrook. The latter acknowledged the compliment by saluting Rothermere as 'the greatest trustee of public opinion … in the history of journalism' (he had made the same salute to Rothermere's brother, Northcliffe, in 1922).

William reacted to 'the press lords' campaign as a journalist. It was not that he tore into the campaign. Beaverbrook wrote to him that 'he had treated him much better than *The Times* … Don't hesitate to hit me hard when you think I deserve it. But the occasional touch of human understanding is a bond between us.'[8] But professionally he was appalled that such a large section of the Press should so prostitute itself for personal reasons, turn themselves into propaganda sheets whose 'stunts' monopolised their presentation of news and editorial criticism of

---

[6] The whole problem of 'preferences' was immensely complicated, understood only by economists and those politicians like Leo Amery, who had made a life study of it. Two years later, when 'preferences' were being 'studied afresh' by the Ottawa Empire Economic Conference, Amery complained that William's views on the subject were 'very muddled'. Well might this be. The complexity of the negotiations resembled those when Britain entered the Common Market after the Second World War. In addition, Amery was a bi-metallist.

[7] Though he recognised its continuing prestige, Beaverbrook regarded the *Daily Mail* as 'a bad newspaper'.

[8] Rothermere showed no such magnanimity. When the St George's bye-election (see below) was at its height and the *Telegraph* and *The Times* were backing Duff Cooper, the London *Evening News* wrote: 'Which of the candidates has the backing of the largest and wealthiest Croesi [sic]? These [William and Major Astor] presumably "insolent and irresponsible plutocrats" [Baldwin's phrase] are probably both wealthier than either Lord Beaverbrook or Lord Rothermere, neither of whom incidentally is anything like as rich as some people imagine.'

unreported speeches. Apart from his own revulsion, he sensed a strong public reaction which, he thought, would welcome an objective alternative. He had always wanted a London evening paper and still regretted his chance of obtaining the *Evening Standard*, of which Beaverbrook had 'robbed' him in 1923.

It was at this time that William became friendly with Neville Chamberlain, who had just been made Chairman of the Conservative Party by the wily Baldwin, to lock the 'heir apparent' into the organisation. They had first met as man to man in the middle of 1930, when Edward Iliffe gave a men's dinner party and 'placed Lord Camrose next to Neville Chamberlain'. On 22 November, Chamberlain recorded in a letter to his sister: 'I lunched with Camrose who is beginning to think of starting an evening paper in London, a procedure which I did my best to encourage as being likely to keep my volatile friend in order.' This was at the nerve-wracking time when the decision had just been taken to reduce the price of *The Daily Telegraph* to one penny, when, whatever the financial future, the strain on the *Telegraph*'s cash flow would be accentuated. Moreover, the sale of the *Telegraph* was still so low as not to provide much public goodwill capable of transfer to another publication from the same stable.

Thus, there need be no surprise that the project was still only in the discussion stage when Chamberlain recorded in another letter, of 21 February 1931:

I dined alone with Lord Camrose. The purpose of the dinner was the starting of an evening paper about which he had spoken to me before. But I found that he had begun to have doubts as to whether it would be a success because of the want of faith in the party in their present leader. He said he himself had a great regard and respect for SB but was coming definitely to the opinion that he could never bring his party to victory. He said that if I were leader he thought confidence would come back and he as good as said that I should leave the Central Office which he evidently thought was standing in my way. I said that I was not yet ready to leave the CO unless I did with the deliberate intention of taking SB's place and that I could not entertain. He seemed disappointed but said he didn't believe SB would go on for much longer anyhow.

We got along extremely well together and before leaving I asked whether if I would get him £150,000 he would go on with the paper. He said he probably would, so next day I sent for David [Davidson] and asked if he could help.[9] [J.C.C. Davidson, whom Chamberlain

[9] I have recorded the discussions with Davidson in Chapter 13. Baldwin told Tom Jones, Deputy

had ousted from Central Office, was Baldwin's most intimate political friend.]

... I believe David to have real gifts for raising money – his trouble is that he doesn't know how to spend it.[10]

Just as almost all his contemporaries recognised William's personal integrity, so I think he had usually the most acute perception of that quality in others. He would surely have been shocked to know that while Chamberlain was expressing loyalty to Baldwin he was just a week from organising his deposition. He then sent to Baldwin a memorandum, afterwards declared by Central Office officials to be deliberately exaggerated, by Robert Topping, Chief Agent[11] of Central Office, reporting a disastrous decline in Baldwin's popularity in the constituencies, and accompanied by the recommendation of principal colleagues that he should resign. Just at this moment, Beaverbrook put up an anti-Baldwin candidate at the St George's by-election and Chamberlain 'reluctantly' had to put the full support of Central Office behind their own candidate.

Ruefully, Chamberlain reported to his sister:

... Just at the moment when the train was laid and the match actually lighted Max has once more blundered in and upset the apple cart ... it is going to involve me more deeply with [Baldwin] while Winston who has left the sinking ship[12] ... will remain unaffected ... [But] once you take away the anti-Baldwin irritant his followers would shrink to a handful.

Whether or not Baldwin learnt later of Chamberlain's double-talk I do not know, but certainly he had no knowledge of it at the time, for his first reaction to the recommendation for his resignation was to accept but then to go back on it and offer to be the official candidate himself.[13] The news was picked up by the *Telegraph*'s political correspondent and Arthur Watson, the Editor, queried the story with Davidson, saying that Lord Camrose would oppose it.

In the event, Baldwin was persuaded not to stand himself. Two days before the poll, he delivered the famous rebuke to the press lords: 'Power

Secretary of the Cabinet, who commented that 'the news made me feel that SB was still counting on holding the leadership'.

[10] The letter quoted above has not, as far as I am aware, been unearthed before. The Neville Chamberlain papers have not been published in full. They occupy an entire wall of the Heslop Room in Birmingham University Library.

[11] The title was later changed to Director.

[12] Churchill had resigned the Whip over the India issue.

[13] Vainly Chamberlain remonstrated: 'Think of the effect on your successor.' To which Baldwin, realising at last Chamberlain's ambition, replied: 'I don't give a damn about my successor, Neville.'

without responsibility – the prerogative of the harlot throughout the ages'. (Voice: 'There goes the harlots' vote.') The whole speech was the most splendid piece of sustained invective since Lloyd George's Newcastle speech in 1909.[14] As Lady Diana Cooper, the candidate's wife, wrote: 'I saw the blasé reporters, scribbling semi-consciously, jump out of their skins to a man.' Beaverbrook himself had already written: 'He always beat me – the toughest and most unscrupulous politician you could find – cold, merciless in his dislikes.'

Duff Cooper, the official candidate, won handsomely (there was no Labour nor Liberal candidate). Beaverbrook quickly recognised that he had been wrong-footed: 'We were wrong to fight on India and the leadership ... The issue might have been the policy of Empire Free Trade and unemployment.' By the end of the month he had agreed a joint statement of policy with Chamberlain. The Empire Crusade as a political movement was dissolved. This did not prevent Beaverbrook complaining to William that *The Daily Telegraph* had declared the statement a defeat, a complaint impossible to sustain since the statement referred to tariffs (Chamberlain was a strong 'protectionist'), but contained no mention of the Empire.

Moreover, Chamberlain had kept William fully in touch with the moving situation:

I should like to tell you the full story of the negotiations with Max ... Sam Hoare suggested it to me that it might be useful if I were to see Max again before I give up the Chairmanship of the Party. At first I was reluctant ... I saw him ... and, to my great surprise, found him willing to come all the way into our camp ...

The first question you will naturally put to me is how long will the agreement last? Already there have been departures from the spirit, though not strictly from the letter, of it; and no one who knows Beaverbrook well can expect that he will ever cease from troubling ... Perhaps we can fix up a meeting.

The Conservative leadership confirmed, the governing Labour Party was meanwhile becoming terminally sick. Through the summer of 1931, Labour wrestled unavailingly with the mounting economic crisis – an unbalanced budget, the collapse of exports, mounting unemployment, culminating in a run on the pound.

An American loan became essential, but could only be obtained if

---

[14] The best-remembered highlight from that speech attacking the House of Lords, the dukes in particular, who were opposing land taxes in the Budget, is: 'A fully equipped duke costs as much as two "dreadnoughts"; they are just as great a terror and they last longer.'

the Government agreed to a cut of around £100 million – more than 10 per cent of its entire budget – in national expenditure. (Hence the expression 'Bankers' Ramp'.) More than half of this was to come from a cut in the dole, a measure which most of the Cabinet and almost all backbenchers would not tolerate. In normal times, the obvious solution would have been a general election. But the crisis, which blew up in August, would not wait upon it. Only coalition would solve it – but what coalition? Ramsay MacDonald was ashamed to offer himself as leader without his party; Baldwin, having broken a coalition in 1922, was reluctant to assist in the formation of another, while the Liberals (or most of them) were historically averse to revenue-raising tariffs which the Conservatives would demand. The solution had to be sought among the leaders – a political quadrille. Even if opinion polls had existed at that time, they could have had no chance to mirror the result.

Here *The Times* had an enormous advantage over all other papers. *The Times* was still regarded as the principal organ of political influence. It was to that paper which the 'greats' confided their feelings and to which lesser men wrote letters for publication. It has to be said the political competition was not great. The *Telegraph* was still in a con- valescent stage, the *Morning Post* had become impossibly 'die-hard' and the *Daily Mail*, under Rothermere's erratic hand, lost all 'weight'. The Editor of *The Times*, Geoffrey Dawson, too, had the advantage of long occupation of the editorial chair – he had been Editor since 1912, except for a two-year interval during Northcliffe's final mad spell. He had got off to a flying start through his fellowship of All Souls, Oxford, and his secondment from the Colonial Office to Lord Milner's 'kindergarten', which was reconstructing South Africa after the Boer War. In his diary for 1909 – the year William gave up the *Advertising World* – he recorded, during a visit to England, breakfasting or dining with Lloyd George, Bonar Law, Smuts, Brand (the international banker), Dr Jameson, Leo Maxse and F.S. Oliver (the historian).

As early as 1923, he had been consulted by the King's Secretary, Lord Stamfordham, about the choice between Baldwin and the acting Prime Minister, Curzon, to succeed the dying Bonar Law. Now, he was consulted by Baldwin, Chamberlain, Reading (for the Liberals), Snowden (the Chancellor), MacDonald and even by Sir Clive Wigram, the King's new Secretary, who wanted his advice as to how MacDonald could be brought up to scratch.

It was thus fair for Evelyn Wrench to write, in his biography of Dawson, that '*The Times* under Dawson played a very important part in making possible the formation of the National Government in 1931.'

William, and the *Telegraph*, at this time played next to no part in the drama. He was not yet equipped to do so. He had met most of the leaders but was not in a position of influence. He controlled no paper of great influence, nor yet was he a 'political animal'. When he saw politicians he did so as a journalist, not to press his own opinions but to gather background which might steer his papers' presentation of the news. As the *Telegraph* and the *Sunday Times* added authority to commercial success, so he too enlarged his personal involvement in the crises to come. In this one, he played no conspicuous part. Caught on his yacht in this crisis he saw no reason to be daily at his Fleet Street helm and followed it by telephone from the various British ports at which he purposely put in. (He was in good company, for Baldwin himself did not return from his holiday abroad until two days before the formation of the National Government in August 1931.) He allowed Edward Iliffe, as an old parliamentarian and President of the Chamber of Commerce, to decide the economic policy of the paper with the editor, the political correspondent and J.B. Firth, but this was of small importance.

The main constituents of a recovery programme were not difficult to identify. The difficulty was to find the leaders willing to cooperate to carry them out, all previous combinations notwithstanding.

I will leave appeasement, the great issue of the 1930s, to later chapters. Meanwhile, I turn to the Abdication crisis, in which the *Telegraph* was a major player.

* * *

In retrospect, one of the most curious aspects of the Abdication crisis of 1936 must seem to be the almost uniform silence of the British Press until only a week before it had been resolved. The popular press of 1936 was no less irresponsible than the Press of today, though it did not indulge then in brazen vulgarity. Nor did it have today's obsession with sex, when the presumed affairs of anyone from a duchess to a footballer can be headlined as national events. Its stunts were often as lightly based as today's, but the bribing of restaurant waiters, when divorce was more difficult, was the practice only of private detectives. The first sign that Rothermere's *Daily Mirror*,[15] now controlled by its staff, was going 'pop', was not the unearthing of some great scandal but a gossip paragraph that Queen Mary had been seen in 'peep-toe' shoes. It did not, then, even occur to the popular press that the King's taking of a new mistress was 'news'.

---

[15] Rothermere had dribbled out his shares on the Stock Exchange so that, by 1936, there was no large holder or proprietor.

Even before George V's death in January it had been known in café society that Mrs Simpson had supplanted her fellow American, Lady Furness, as what the new King's Secretary, Major Hardinge, called 'the lady of the moment'. But, in public, she had always been accompanied by Mr Simpson.

In the two previous years they had both been included in holiday parties to Kitzbuehl, Vienna, Budapest and Biarritz. It was not until 10 July that the King had given a dinner, recorded in the Court Circular, when Mrs Simpson had been present without her husband. What set tongues wagging was her inclusion, alone, in the King's party when he chartered the yacht *Nahlin* for a summer cruise in the Adriatic, attended by two destroyers and the American press corps.

Before the trip started, Buckingham Palace had issued a request to the Press, usual since Victoria's reign, not to intrude on the royal holiday. Almost all the British papers respected the embargo. The *Telegraph* even went so far as to strike out the name of Mrs Simpson from the *Nahlin*'s guest list. Only the Cooperative Society's (Sunday) *Referee* gave a series of pictures, while the *Daily Sketch*, part of Allied Newspapers, which printed one American agency picture of the pair together, was told by William not to do it again. The *Daily Express* printed a similar picture but cut out Mrs Simpson from the frame. Though the King made a number of official visits to presidents and prime ministers, arranged by the Foreign Office,[16] everywhere he went he was photographed with Mrs Simpson in attitudes of obvious infatuation.

Not so, of course, the American press. Their sensational papers 'went to town' on the running story. It was not that they suspected, or even inferred, a royal 'romance', but that it was an extraordinary reversal of normally stuffy British court manners. They were fascinated that the King should be flaunting an American divorcee[17] mistress in the course of a series of official talks.

Not all the American press followed suit. Their quality newspapers remained silent. The *New York Times* never mentioned the subject until almost the end. Similarly, the Dominion papers followed the British lead. When the New Zealand Prime Minister, M.J. Savage, and the South African General Herzog were asked for their formal view on a morganatic marriage, they had to ask the governors-general who Mrs Simpson was.

The King's intentions only became suspect when, in the first half of October, he requested Walter Monckton, the Attorney-General of the

---

[16] To their consternation, he invited Kemal Atatürk on a state visit to London.
[17] Simpson was her second husband. The first was still living.

Duchy of Cornwall, to start a divorce action on behalf of Mrs Simpson. He denied wishing to marry her himself, saying he was only acting as a friend. First to hear that the petition had been put down was the editor of the *Evening Standard*, who asked Beaverbrook's approval to print the news in his gossip column. Beaverbrook rang Theodore Goddard, the solicitor handling the case, who assured him of the King's non-involvement. Goddard reported the enquiry to Monckton, who told the King. Whereupon the King sent for Beaverbrook to ask him to get the whole Press not to mention the impending action. Beaverbrook was not at that time a confidant of the King. He delayed answering the summons for two days, pleading non-existent dentist's appointments. He used the interval to meet Ernest Simpson to find out the background. He then, with Monckton, saw Esmond Harmsworth who, though dominated by his father, Rothermere, was Chairman of the Newspaper Proprietors' Association. A meeting of the NPA Council was called at Harmsworth's Warwick House (coincidently a stone's throw from St James's Palace), when all the proprietors were nobbled with the exception of *The Times*, *Telegraph* and *Morning Post*, who would not care to be dictated to on an editorial matter but who could be expected to keep silent. They all agreed to keep mum until the King should release them from their bond. The King had also asked that Beaverbrook use his influence similarly to muzzle the American press. Beaverbrook knew that such an attempt would be futile and did not attempt it.

By now Baldwin, the Prime Minister, was becoming alarmed and, prompted by Hardinge and Davidson, saw the King for the first time on the subject. He handled the meeting with such exaggerated tact that the King hardly realised that he was receiving an ultimatum. Baldwin thought that he could defuse the crisis if he could persuade the King to stop the divorce or, if that were not possible, Mrs Simpson to leave the country for six months. After making suggestions for improvements in the herbaceous border, he left the King to think it over. There was no admission that marriage was in the air.

While the King played for time and Baldwin did nothing, hoping for a cessation of 'conspicuous behaviour', the divorce went through on 27 October, preceded by a day by the firm prediction in Randolph Hearst's *New York Journal* that 'EDWARD WILL WED WALLY'. It was taken seriously in London because it was known that Hearst, whose papers had not so far been foremost in playing up the scandal, had recently visited Fort Belvedere, the royal weekend house which the King had bought when Prince of Wales.

The Times and the *Morning Post* were now becoming anxious to publish. Gwynne, Editor of the latter, wrote directly to Baldwin saying he 'cannot long remain silent' unless the Prime Minister gave some guidance. Baldwin seems to have replied through Tom Jones[18] that he could tell him nothing currently. To Dawson of *The Times*, who called on Downing Street, he answered that any immediate publicity would be bound to be interpreted as a direct attack on the King. The King was due to pay two, two-day visits: to the Fleet at Portsmouth and to the Distressed Areas in South Wales. If the publicity were before the Fleet visit it might be construed as an attempt to reduce his popularity; if after the visit to South Wales, as an attempt to minimise his influence.

According to Dawson, Baldwin 'wondered vaguely ... what machinery was available to explain [the position] to newspapers as a whole' should 'it ever become necessary' for him to use it. He cannot have been given a satisfactory answer since Dawson made it clear to his diary that *The Times* 'must be the first to speak', and that 'the rest of the Press had quite openly been looking to us for a lead'. The only evidence for the latter assertion is that Gwynne had met him by appointment at the Bath Club and given the impression that he would not 'go' before *The Times*.

The first crunch – or 'false dawn', according to which way you look at it – in the crisis came when Hardinge, with Baldwin's approval, sent a tough letter to the King saying that the Press would not stay silent much longer, nor the Government be kept from resignation, unless Mrs Simpson were to 'go abroad without further delay'. The King, at last admitting his determination to marry, summoned Baldwin and told him flatly that he would abdicate. Baldwin, by now suspicious of his old friend, asked Dawson to see him immediately after the audience and told him 'nothing definite' except that he was to see the King 'again within a week'. 'Any Press comment at this moment might weaken his influence.'

All was to begin again when Rothermere, through his son Esmond, mooted to Mrs Simpson the idea of a morganatic marriage[19]. This was followed by a leading article in the *Daily Mail* praising the King's famous promise to the unemployed in Dowlais, South Wales:[20] 'Something must

---

[18] Jones had been Deputy Secretary at the Cabinet and still saw Baldwin frequently.

[19] According to Brian Inglis, who quotes John Connell, a writer on Rothermere's *Sunday Despatch*, the idea came from the editor of that newspaper, citing an uncle of Queen Victoria, heir-presumptive until the Queen had children. He was refused royal assent and his wife became Duchess of Inverness. If Mrs Simpson could not be Queen, she was prepared to settle for Duchess of Cornwall.

Later, when it became clear that Mrs Simpson did want to be Queen, Beaverbrook suggested sardonically that she should marry Rothermere and become Queen of Hungary.

[20] This was the same Dowlais that George V had visited in 1911 when William's father was Mayor of Merthyr (see Chapter 1, p. 2) and which Seymour had done so much for in the 1920s.

be done for these men.' The *Mail* leader, headed 'The King Edward Touch', though not overtly mentioning the crisis but quite obvious to those in the know, contrasted the constructive energies of the King with the nerveless failures of his Government. To this, at least, *The Times* was the first to reply, pointing out that if the monarch were to disassociate himself from some of the actions of his ministers, by inference, he must take responsibility for all the rest.

There is no record of when William first sought official information of what was happening. He had been aware for some months that the King, as King, was behaving in an irresponsible manner. Lord Wigram (who had been Private Secretary to George V) had told him that he did not 'do his [Government] boxes'. He often took weeks to return them. When Wigram had visited Fort Belvedere he had found them open on the hall table with the breeze, between the open front door and garden doors, blowing the papers about. Wigram probably did not know that the Foreign Office had been similarly informed and had become selective in what was included.

During the 1930s, William had a habit of making notes, for his file, of all important interview, but there are no memoranda of his of any sort relating to the Abdication. There is, however, a memorandum of 27 November in the Davidson papers: 'I went to see Lord Camrose at 10 o'clock this morning at his house,' (25 St James's Place). The next sentence, 'His reaction following his conversation with the Prime Minister was very definite', suggests that, like Gwynne and Dawson, he had been to see Baldwin on his own initiative and had got the same, vague answers. Now, knowing that Davidson always had his finger in every Baldwin pie, he had asked the former to come and see him. The interview is worth repeating in full:

> He held the view that the country would not stand for marriage. He took the line however that if he were advising the King, without any care for the public interest but with the object of getting the best terms for the King, he would suggest procrastination, separation from Mrs S. and marriage after the Coronation. He asked me what would be the position if HM said, 'I am going to carry on with the Coronation, but I am not going to decide finally on marriage till after I am crowned.' If HM were to govern well for a month, and face the Government with a *fait accompli* of marriage, a most difficult and dangerous situation would be created.
>
> My answer was that I did not believe the King was in love with the lady. No doubt Lord Camrose and I, being normal people, would be prepared to face six months' separation from the women we loved,

but not so the King. If he were prepared to let Mrs S. go abroad for six months, and live a normal life, the public might have far greater sympathy with him later on; but that did not appear possible. [This is what Beaverbrook wanted him to do, but, to his credit, the King never contemplated that solution. He was aware of the sacred element in the Coronation ceremony and commented melodramatically later that he 'could not live a lie'.]

Lord Camrose had heard about the Esmond Harmsworth plan, which he regarded as fantastic. He then cross-examined me on the constitutional position, and it was impossible for me to plead ignorance.

I told him that in my view, assuming the King supported the Harmsworth plan, it would have to be considered in specific terms by the Government and that obviously if it were put forward seriously, it would also have to be considered by the Dominions; that a vague idea was hopeless, and the scheme would have to be worked out, if not in detail, at least under some definite headings.

Lord Camrose regards the whole position as one of immense gravity. He does not think the Press has anything to go on yet, and therefore will keep silent; but he believes that the great silent mass of the people will be definitely shocked at the thought of marriage, and that if a constitutional crisis were to be faced, the King could no longer rely upon the individual support of the public at home and in the Dominions. If by any chance the King were to be so mad as to force an election it is possible he might obtain quite a number of votes, but the great mass of the country would vote against marriage with Mrs S. The very contemplation of an election makes me shudder.

I listened most carefully. He expressed the view that the Crown would recover rapidly; were the tradition of the last twenty-five years re-established.

It is part of history – 'what every schoolboy knows' – that the Bishop of Bradford, who had never heard of Mrs Simpson, was the unwitting catalyst to cause the whole Press to break silence simultaneously. His address to his Diocesan Conference, prepared six weeks in advance, was an attack on the maverick Bishop Barnes of Birmingham, who had urged that the Coronation, fixed for the following year, should be a secular ceremony and have no religious content. Bishop rounded on bishop. The monarch had need of God's grace at the climax of the ceremony, adding, for good measure, the wish that the King 'gave more positive signs of his awareness'.

Dawson has left the only record of what happened next:

I took the (to me unprecedented) course of ringing up Camrose of the *Telegraph* and Gwynne of the *Morning Post* and asking them plainly what they meant to do about it. My talk with Gwynne on November 16 [the Bath Club meeting] had given me an excuse so far as he was concerned; but he had left the office before dinner, giving instructions that nothing was to be said. I had also met Camrose lately dining with Abe Bailey [South African industrialist], so that it was quite easy to have a word with him. He was reluctant, he said, even to report the Bishop's address, which indeed, as I told him, I myself had not yet read fully; but he begged me to do so at once and to let him know my decision. After thinking things over therefore, and concluding that it was not a bad thing that the break had come in the Provinces [the *Yorkshire Post* in the Bradford circulation area], I told him (1) that it was quite impossible in my opinion to withhold publication of a pronouncement which would certainly become historic, and (2) that I had made up my mind to refrain from comment until the following day. He said he would take the same course; and, since it was certain that the Rothermere and Beaverbrook organs would not explode, I felt pretty confident now that the whole London Press was safe.

When, the following day, 3 December, the national Press at last broke silence, Harold Nicolson recorded in his diary:

The storm breaks. A fine leading article in the *Telegraph* and a confused muddled jumble in *The Times*. I suspect that when Geoffrey Dawson sees a vital crisis he writes the leader himself, and the result is an amalgam of tortuous and pompous nothings. The other papers write in sorrow rather than in anger.

Nicolson's comment on *The Times* leader was not surprising. Dawson had for some time been putting down 'first thoughts' on the subject either to show his proprietor, Major Astor, or his deputy editor. When the time came, he recorded: 'I put together a leader on "King and Monarchy" from fragments already written.' The fragments, it seems, did not mention the name of Mrs Simpson. Nor did the leader. 'A paragraph to explain why, as King, he could *not* marry her ... I deliberately kept for the next day.'

Dawson, while claiming a special, 'foot-in-the-door' relationship with Baldwin, was evidently a little hurt that *The Times* had not played a special role:[21] 'The PM probably saw a great deal more of me at this

---

[21] Perhaps it was because of his frustration that Dawson authorised in *The Times* two news items, next to each other, which Tom Driberg, gossip writer in the *Daily Express*, described as 'feline malice

time than any other journalist, but that was due rather to an old friendship and habit of discussion ... He never in fact told me any secrets.'[22]

Meanwhile the King, warned by Beaverbrook, who always regarded *The Times* as a monument to priggery, became alarmed that Dawson would make a vicious attack on Mrs Simpson. He asked Baldwin, in Dawson's words, 'To find out, and if necessary stop, what was going to appear in *The Times*. He "instructed" the Prime Minister to forbid [a personal attack]. In vain SB had explained that the Press in England was free ... In the late evening he [Baldwin] rang me up twice himself – the only time, I think, that I ever heard his voice on the telephone ... When he spoke to me, full of apologies, the second time, it was to say that the King would now be satisfied ... if [the Prime Minister] would read the article for him. Could I possibly let him see it for the sake of peace ... Towards midnight I sent a proof by messenger to Downing Street and heard no more about it.' Actually, Baldwin had gone to bed.[23]

The King did not go at once. Nine days were to pass before his departure for France. During that time, William kept close with Davidson, though Davidson claimed credit for the liaison:

[The Times] lost its character and even its information became about forty-eight hours out of date. I thought it was essential that one respected newspaper should be properly informed so that it could give the nation a lead; I accordingly saw to it that *The Daily Telegraph* was kept completely informed ...

The confidence I placed in the Proprietor was not misplaced; nothing secret was disclosed, and of course I made no attempt to influence the newspaper's attitude. But it was very striking how accurate was the information carried by the *Telegraph* and how out-of-date was that carried by *The Times*.

and vulgar frivolity, that can scarcely have been paralleled in the worst of the gutter press' – one of Mrs Simpson's 'renunciation' of the King; the second that 'Thelma, Viscountess Furness, arrived at Southampton on the liner *Queen Mary* yesterday from New York.'

[22] Throughout the crisis, Baldwin confided in as few as possible. Only the inner circle of the Cabinet was kept up to date – Chamberlain, Halifax, Ramsay MacDonald, Simon and Runciman (because of his Methodist connections). 'You can't,' he told Tom Jones [no longer Deputy Secretary of the Cabinet but still one who saw Baldwin whenever he wished], 'tell a thing like that to the whole Cabinet. Out it would come ...'. He unburdened himself only to his immediate staff – Horace Wilson, Dugdale (Parliamentary Private Secretary) and to the Davidsons.

[23] G.M.Young, in *Stanley Baldwin*, wrote that 'he had gone to bed, as he had on the night of the General Strike ... Barrington-Ward [Deputy Editor] agreed with me that he never read it.'

Davidson concluded: 'One of the most interesting features of the crisis was that it was the making of the *Daily Telegraph*.'

Of the popular press, Beaverbrook and Rothermere fought an unavailing battle for the King. Both were partly inspired by hatred of Baldwin. Beaverbrook's object, Randolph Churchill reported him as admitting, was to 'bugger Baldwin', while more soberly he admitted that Baldwin's departure from Downing Street would have been 'a welcome by-product'. Rothermere continued to press his morganatic solution long after it had been abandoned and made an idiot of himself by writing two letters to himself, published on the same day. The first, in the *Daily Mail*, contended that the King's abdication would hit recruiting, already bad, thus making conscription inevitable; the second, in the (London) *Evening News*, maintained that the King was being forced to abdicate because he was too sympathetic to South Wales.

The King did not thank them for it. After the war he sent his solicitor, the same respected solicitor who had represented him throughout the crisis, to see William. He was anxious to place his book, *A King's Story*, before the *Telegraph* readership. William, without looking at it, replied that he would not print and it would be more dignified not to publish the book at all. This was a hard saying, too hard for the Duke, who always seemed to be short of money. Between America and Britain he earned £1 million[24] (some £15 million today) from the book. In England Beaverbrook published it in the *Sunday Express*, which put on 750,000 copies, the largest increase owed to a single serialisation in the history of British journalism.

---

[24] The American proceeds were not taxed at source, nor were they in France, where the Duke of Windsor was domiciled, on the ground that the money had been earned abroad.

Hunting with Seymour. William, my mother, and (Gladys) Lady Buckland at a meet at Seymour's house in Breconshire, of the Galligren and Talybont hounds. Seymour's eldest daughter, Eileen (he had five daughters and always regretted not having a son, whereas his two brothers had ten between them), was Master at age thirteen.

Shooting with Sir David Llewellyn (Seymour's coal mining partner) in Glamorganshire. Right is Sir John Beale who became Chairman of Guest, Keen and Nettlefold's after Seymour's death.

Below left Dining at Cannes.
Left to right, Mary, Mrs. McNair Scott, William's eldest daughter, my mother, Ronald McNair Scott, Sheila, Lady Birkenhead, second daughter, William.

Below Backgammon. Playing with his grandson, Robin Furneaux. Though they did not play for money, William's was a gambler's style – a trail of blots to get home first.

Christmas party, 1913, at JMB's house at Merthyr.
Back row William, Molly (with Sheila, aged six months), Jack Jones, married to Beta (William's elder sister), Gladys' wife of Seymour, Doris (daughter of Beta), Gomer, Ewart (son of Beta and Jack).

Middle row Lillian (wife of Gomer), Denis (Gomer's second son), the author, Eileen (Seymour's eldest daughter), JMB, Lorraine (Seymour's second daughter), my Grandmother, Seymour (William's eldest son) Mary (William's eldest daughter), Lionel (Gomer's eldest son).

Above left Barrow Hills. William's first house in the country. Even though the suburbs were encroaching, it was convenient for London to which he commuted by train. A mock-Tudor house built on high ground with 200 acres, it was very comfortable but lacked the amenities for much entertaining.

Left Hackwood. Bought from Lord Bolton in 1935 and first occupied in 1937, after much rewiring and plumbing. The main part of the house was built in 1688 and stood among 3000 acres. Boasts an eighty acre ornamental wood, listed as Grade 1.

Christening group of the youngest child, Diana, 1924, at Barrow Hills.

Back row: Seymour, monthly nurse, Canon Tringham ('the saintly Canon Tringham' as Mary called him, who persuaded my parents to become regular Anglican churchgoers). Herbert Morgan (godfather), William, Mary, Nurse Grocock (who came in 1910 and was on pension when she died aged 101), the author.

Front row: Third son, Rodney, Phyllis (my mother's sister), my mother with Diana, my grandmother (Agnes Corns).

Sitting below: Sheila, second daughter, Julian, fourth son (later Colonel of the Horse Guards), Patricia, third daughter.

Christmas 1938, at Hackwood.

Back row: Ronald McNair Scott (married to Mary), Freddie Birkenhead (married to Sheila), the author (with his son, Adrian, aged one and a half, on his shoulder), Seymour, Rodney, Diana, Julian, Lady Chetwode (mother-in-law to Patricia), Roger Chetwode (married to Patricia).

Front row: Mary, Pamela (wife of author), Molly, William, Sheila (with her son, Robin, aged two and a half), my grandmother, Patricia (with her son, Philip, aged two).

On ground: Three of Mary's children, Gillian, Thomas and Linda.

William's two yachts.

Above Sona, 550 tons, was bought from the executors of Lord Dunraven in 1925. She was an excellent 'sea boat' as she was built on the lines of a fishing trawler. She was requisitioned in 1939 but not much use in convoy as she was unable to steam at variable speeds. She was eventually sunk by a freak bomb which dropped straight down the funnel.

Below Virginia, 750 tons, was bought from the Admiralty after service in the Red Sea. She had to be largely gutted, at a cost of over £100,000 before being fit for service as a pleasure boat. William took a party across the Atlantic to the Caribbean in 1949. Sold, after his death, to the President of Liberia where it sank on the rocks of Monrovia.

CHAPTER FIFTEEN

Appeasement I – Why William So Long Doubted Churchill's Genius

AFTER WILLIAM'S DEATH in 1954, people often said to me, remembering that he had been Churchill's closest non-political friend for the last fifteen years of his life, that they supposed William had always followed his star. That was not so at all. It is true that William, not being a political animal, was never concerned that Churchill had been a turn-jycoat, not once but twice. If he thought about it he would have accepted Churchill's explanation that the parties, not he, had changed their philosjyophies. The social philosophy of Asquith and Lloyd George in 1906 had become the social philosophy of Baldwin. In his 1924–9 Government, Churchill had introduced no fewer than twenty-five bills of social reform, for which Churchill as Chancellor and Neville Chamberlain as Minister of Health both claimed credit. Even so, bearing in mind the suspicion and hatred which old-timers still nourished against Churchill until his final retirement, William was a little surprised to be told by him with glee a couple of years into his last administration, and prodding his left palm with his right forefinger: 'I've got the Tory party there!'

I have already described William's early antipathy to Churchill the politician as a 'gambler' (after Antwerp and the Dardanelles), an 'office-seeker' in 1929, and his witness as a man of poor judgment later in the same year. He was by that time a friend, in so far as he found him a scintillating fellow-diner at The Other Club and an occasional bridge companion.

As soon as he lost cabinet office after the General Election of May 1929, Churchill sought to 'replenish his exchequer' by writing and in one year, 1931, earned the then enormous sum of £35,000 (now about £800,000) from his pen.[1] His first assignment was a series of articles for

---

[1] Of the several books that Churchill serialised in newspapers (he did not have an agent) during the period it is notable that he negotiated with William in respect of the *Telegraph* or the *Sunday Times*, but that with *The Times* his dealings were not with the editor but with the general manager. When it was a matter of complaint, as when the *Daily Mail* published a major article by him on the same day as the first of a previously advertised series of four, Colonel Lawson was deputed to deal with it.

the *Sunday Times* on the American scene, where he went directly. While there he was badly injured when he stepped into the path of a taxi, and eight of his friends organised a £15 a head subscription to buy him a £2,000 Daimler to meet him at the station on his return. William was not one of the organising committee but among more than 140 who subscribed. In 1931, Churchill gave a twenty-first birthday party for his son Randolph. He had the happy idea of making the centrepiece speeches by famous fathers and their sons. The diners included Rothermere and Esmond, Lord Hailsham and his son Quintin, Lord Reading and his son Lord Erleigh, and the new Lord Birkenhead, whose father had died the previous year. William himself was not included as a speaker, but he was delighted when his son, Seymour (aged twenty-two), was called on without notice and did as well as those who had long burnt the midnight oil. William was also delighted with a 'sketch' of the proceedings he commissioned for the *Sunday Times* by Seymour's Oxford friend, the twenty-three-year-old Basil Dufferin,[2] who thereafter became a family friend and almost another son.

To return to politics. We are now approaching the long period when Churchill, almost alone, first sensed the German menace and during which he received very little personal support either in Parliament or Press. In general, his position has been very well described by Robert Rhodes James in his book with the challenging title: *Churchill – A Study in Failure 1900–39*:

By the end of 1933 Churchill was widely regarded as a failed politician, in whom no real trust could be reasonably placed; by June 1935 these opinions had been fortified further. His habit of exaggerating problems, and in clothing relatively minor questions in brightly coloured language, had the effect that when a really major issue did arise there was no easy way of differentiating it, either for orator or audiences.[3] His sense of the dramatic had ceased to excite the emotions as it had once done – and was to do again in 1940. His few political friends were neither collectively nor individually impressive nor influential. Many who were coming to agree with him on fundamentals were alienated by his assertions on particulars. Others were affronted by his conception of total personal and political friendship. Some

---

[2] Dufferin had just succeeded his father in the marquesate, on the death of the latter, Speaker of the Northern Ireland Parliament, in an air crash. He was later a junior minister in the National Government. When he was killed in action in 1945, William found he had been nominated as an executor.

[3] Baldwin, who like everyone else was momentarily dazzled by these pyrotechnics, remarked that if one instead read them in Hansard it was like watching a conjuror in slow motion.

questioned whether the campaign was national or personal, and shared the view of T.E. Lawrence that 'if Winston's interests were not concerned in a question, he would not be interested'.

Certainly, his stand on the issue of dominion status for India, which he chose as a pretext for leaving Baldwin's shadow cabinet,[4] was as much anti-Baldwin as it was constitutional. His charge that Baldwin had committed the party to a socialist measure without consultation was a central part of his initial attack, supported by the *Morning Post*, what are now called the Cheltenham Colonels and the usual immoderate enthusiasm of Lord Rothermere. According to Tom Jones' diary, Churchill also 'canvassed the support of *The Daily Telegraph* and *Sunday Times*', but the moment was inauspicious. This was just the time William was thinking of starting an evening paper against Rothermere and Beaverbrook.

The campaign took most of Churchill's energies over long years to 1935, but he rarely got the better of exchanges with Baldwin, so much the better debater, or with Sir Samuel Hoare, the master of detail. He was rolled over by Leo Amery, as sound an Empire man as himself, when he foolishly invited Amery, a classical scholar, to translate the well-known tag *Fiat Justicia ruat coelum* and bought 'If I can bring down Sam, the [National] Government's bust.' As the Bill reached its closing stages, he accused Hoare of having doctored the evidence of Lancashire textile manufacturers and was humiliated by an adverse report from the Committee of Privileges.[5] Outside the House of Commons, his interventions were as maladroit. He could have postponed his great attack on the India Bill at the Albert Hall, which coincided with the eve of the St George's poll and with the massed placards of the Rothermere press, 'Gandhi is watching St George's.' The whole campaign seemed an attempt to substitute himself for Baldwin, confirmed in retrospect by a letter to his wife: 'There is no doubt that the whole spirit of the Conservative Party is with me, and that much of their dissatisfaction with SB turns itself into favour with me.'

If the campaign to bring Baldwin down could not succeed, Churchill was still anxious for office. The vehemence of his attacks on the Government noticeably cooled as the 1935 General Election loomed and the cynical quickly deduced the reason. His nadir came in the Abdication crisis in December 1936, when he was howled down in the House of Commons and seemed to be offering himself as head of the

---

[4] Then called the Business Committee.
[5] Martin Gilbert, the official biographer of Churchill, makes a good case for the thesis that Churchill was right but he had next to no supporters at the time.

King's Party, even after the King had decided to go. The King, in his agony, managed an excellent imitation of Churchill: 'We must have time for the big battalions to mass. We may win; we may not. Who can say?' Only with disappointment that he could not lead the fight did he accept Beaverbrook's assurance that 'Our cock won't fight.' He did not realise the depth to which his reputation had sunk when he persuaded Leslie Hore-Belisha, a member of the Cabinet, to plead his case when Chamberlain took over from Baldwin in June 1937: 'If I take him in ... he will dominate it; he won't give others a chance of even talking.'

*   *   *

If Churchill's record out of office in the 1930s can be shown as erratic and self-centred, his periods in office during the 1920s were as music to the pacifists – not, of course, in pursuit of pacifism, but of economy. First as Minister of War and Air 1919–21, he had reduced the home Air Force to only three squadrons while keeping up strength in the Middle East and the Northwest frontier of India, where a few light bombers (much cheaper) could do the police work of large numbers of troops. Then, as Chancellor 1924–9, he risked the resignation of the whole Board of Admiralty in trying to cut the cruiser replacement programme and did succeed in cutting the estimates of the other two services to the bone in every financial year.

The result was the emasculation of the armaments industry. He justified himself by persuading Baldwin to extend the Ten Year Rule, according to which a threat of war was assumed negligible, not just in the decade of the 1920s but by a rolling ten years from whatever the current date might be.

Churchill in office had always been totally dedicated to the interests of his own department – when he was not interfering with those of others. Now, out of office since 1929, he took several years to discover a new cause, beyond resisting Indian reform. He had approved Austen Chamberlain's 1925 Locarno Treaty, whereby France, Belgium and Germany signed a non-aggression pact, their frontiers guaranteed by Britain and Italy, and Germany was admitted to the League of Nations. In foreign affairs thereafter he had become a 'League Man', with the proviso that France should remain the strongest military power in Europe. Even in November 1933, the month after Hitler had seized absolute power and left the League again, he commended[6] the Government's refusal to extend obligations in Europe.

Do not meddle in the Continent more than you are involved already.

[6] Speech to the Devonshire Club, reported in the *Daily Telegraph*, but not *The Times*.

Do your part in the League of Nations ... and fulfil your obligations as they are. Do not add to these obligations by pressing countries which are in great danger to weaken their defences [through the Disarmament Conference] ... or you will usually find yourself dragged into a continental struggle ... with allies you have ... weakened ...

We have done enough. I hope I may live the rest of my life in an England which will not be called upon to face the horrors of another war.

The first test of the League was not in Europe but in the Far East, where Britain, America and Holland had extensive interests, and it failed miserably. Japan, a League member and late ally of Britain, had invaded Manchuria in 1931 and Shanghai, where a battalion of British troops were stationed, in January 1932. Sir John Simon made unavailing efforts at Geneva to invoke sanctions but gathered no support since President Hoover, whose country was not a League member, was still more interested in making her fleet stronger than the British. The main lesson learnt was the appalling weakness of the Air Force. The permanent secretaries of the Foreign Office and the Treasury, Sir Robert Vansittart and Warren Fisher respectively, were added to the Committee of Imperial Defence.[7] Their recommendations included extra squadrons for home as well as for Far East stations, and the Ten Year Rule was cancelled.

Nothing happened until the end of 1934 since Neville Chamberlain, the Chancellor of the Exchequer, pleaded the need for economy, with more justification than Churchill during his period in that office. But meanwhile Fisher and Vansittart leaked the facts – Fisher to Churchill, who had been his political chief, and Vansittart to Lord Trenchard, the 'father of the RAF', who had retired in 1929. From these seeds grew the public campaign for rearmament in the air.

Not until 1934 did Churchill wake up to the defenceless state of this country, which was his own legacy. Nor was he the first to recognise it. The first public man to propagand for rearmament in the air was Rothermere, all of whose other campaigns were so futile – anti-waste, Hungary, Beaverbrook for PM, Mosley, etc. Churchill could write to him in April 1935:

For two years or more you have shown the danger of air power. Now when it is admitted, you come out with fulsome praise of the ministers responsible. At the same time you continue to quote figures [of

[7] To form a Defence Requirements subcommittee.

German air strength] ... which are so fantastic that they simply deprive you of the enormous credit.

And to Mrs Churchill at the same time:

Rothermere rings me up every day. His anxiety is pitiful. He thinks the Germans are all powerful ... He proposes to meet this situation by grovelling to Germany. 'Dear Germany do destroy us last!'

Rothermere paid for the prototype Blenheim light bomber, which was used as a night-fighter carrying radar when the equipment was air-portable.

To Churchill and Trenchard, the next war would be the war of the bomber: not pin-point bombing (that was not yet possible), but area bombing of 'targets containing military facilities'. They did not admit it, but in practice 'area bombing' amounted to 'terror bombing'. It was assumed that France, the great land power, would be our ally, holding the Low Countries, and that therefore the requirement would be for long-range bombers on either side. Aircraft would not trouble European soldiers as opposed to disorganised tribesmen and, as for the other services, Churchill no longer believed in tanks, his own brain-children ('the poor tank cannot carry thick enough skin to stand up to [the anti-tank rifle and the anti-tank gun]', nor in submarines.

It was therefore on air rearmament that he concentrated and to which the Government, with oh-so-slow steps, gradually moved (fortunately they concentrated on fighters; four-engined bombers were not ordered until 1938 nor entered service until 1942). He misunderstood the purpose of the expanding German air force – a short-range force to co-operate with, and blast the way for, armoured battle groups. In fact, the Germans never built a heavy bomber. The 'V' weapons were afterthoughts.

Trenchard, for his part, leaked to William, with whom he had formed a friendship at The Other Club and whose brusque elimination of corruption and ill-discipline from the (London) Metropolitan Police Force (he had been made Commissioner in 1931 after retiring from the RAF) he was fond of describing. William, too, therefore campaigned for a larger Air Force, though without comprehending that Trenchard's idea of the next war was a competition in killing civilian populations.[8]

Thus, when Churchill wrote to William in May 1935:

I am sure you will feel, as I do, grave continuing anxiety at the disclosure of the way in which the Germans have turned the tables

---

[8] The justification of 'area bombing' was still being maintained in 1942, when it was argued that large movements of populations would negate the Gestapo's records on possible dissidents.

upon us in the air. Air parity can never be attained by England alone
... I do trust you will continue to watch with vigilance the development
of this lamentable affair.

William was able to reply:

You can rely on us to do all we can in respect of air parity. You will
doubtless have noticed we have kept up well with this subject in *The
Daily Telegraph*.

But it was only on rearmament that they agreed at this time. Earlier,
William, in acknowledging a presentation copy of the *Life of Marlborough*, had written:

Although we differ in politics today I treasure the hope that the ever
changing current of events may some day bring us together again,
and I am sure that meanwhile 'no rancour or asperity'[9] will interfere
with our friendship.

They continued to differ on League matters. In principle, Churchill
was always a 'League Man'. Even after Munich, in October 1938, he
declared to the House of Commons:

I have tried my best to urge the maintenance of every bulwark of
defence – first, the timely creation of an Air Force, superior to anything
within striking distance of our shores; secondly, the gathering together
of the collective strength of many nations and thirdly the making of
alliances and military conventions, all within the Covenant ...

Where their difference lay was in the importance of maintaining the
authority of the League, so that its threat of the 'big stick' would always
be credible. William felt that if British foreign policy was to be based
on the Covenant – like NATO today – then it should be consistent.
Churchill agreed in principle, but in practice found consistency inconvenient.

Thus in the Manchurian affair, while the *Telegraph* supported the
Government's attempt to invoke the Covenant, Churchill condoned
Japanese action on the ground that the territory annexed had been
under Communist control. To oppose it would strengthen China's allies,
the Soviets. There was still a chance that Germany might go Communist.
A Communist Germany, as Lloyd George declared, would be infinitely
more formidable than a Communist Russia.

[9] A reference to the last clause of The Other Club rules (written jointly by Churchill and
Birkenhead): 'Nothing in the rules or intercourse of the Club shall interfere with the rancour or
asperity of party politics.'

Similarly, it was Britain's part in betraying the League, on the signature of the Hoare-Laval pact, which brought forth the *Telegraph*'s condemnation. Briefly, Hoare, the Foreign Secretary, had gone to Geneva following the Italian invasion of Abyssinia, another League member, and made a clarion call for League sanctions. France agreed but would not include oil, Italy's one vital requirement. Moreover, it was found that the British Mediterranean Fleet, which would have had to block the Suez Canal, had hardly any ammunition and no air cover. Hoare then went to Paris and negotiated a deal with Pierre Laval[10] (who, it turned out later, had already given 'the green light' to Mussolini) whereby Italy was ceded two-thirds of Abyssinia, which was to retain only a corridor, but no railway, to the sea[11] (the one railway was owned by the French, at Djibouti, who now gave a small part of its ownership to Italy).

The pact was leaked in the French press. Since Baldwin disclaimed responsibility, Hoare was made to resign by a press campaign, from which only Beaverbrook, who already saw Hoare as his new Bonar Law and the eventual successor to Neville Chamberlain, dissented.[12]

By now, it was clear to all that Germany was rearming rapidly and would soon be a formidable world power, in spite of the restrictions imposed by the Treaty of Versailles. On the other hand, Hitler at first played his hand skilfully, persuading many that Germany had been treated too harshly. Hence the policy of 'appeasement', by which it was hoped Germany would see reason if offered treaty revision before too much head of steam had been built up. Appeasement would lead to Containment, safeguarded if necessary by the League. Here arose a fundamental difference. Churchill and Vansittart, the chief author of the Hoare-Laval pact, were convinced that Germany was the only strong threat to European peace. Every effort must be made to unite all the nations against the German threat, even if some of them violated the peace. Had not Italy, by moving troops to the Brenner, single-handedly prevented a 1934 Nazi coup in Austria after the murder of Chancellor Dolfuss? It was not a matter of the democracies against Fascism, but of all countries uniting to hold Germany in check. It was essential to

---

[10] It was pointed out at the time that Laval's deviousness was illustrated by the ability of his name to sound the same whether read forwards or backwards. For his collaboration during the war he was condemned to death by a French court in 1945.

[11] The tartest comment was in *The Times*, written by Colin Coote, who succeeded Arthur Watson as Editor of *The Daily Telegraph* in 1950. The leading article was titled: 'A Corridor for Camels'.

[12] Two years later, Beaverbrook began to pay Hoare an annuity of £2,000 p. a. (now some £50,000) 'so that he could remain in politics'. Soon back in the Cabinet, Hoare was Beaverbrook's constant informant. When Chamberlain succeeded Baldwin, Hoare repeatedly tried to have Beaverbrook put in the Cabinet.

keep the other dictator power on the side of the democracies. Hence Churchill, after praising Hoare's original 'clarion call' at Geneva, was privately supportive of his volte-face. The League, in the short term, could go hang.

When non-oil sanctions were at last abandoned, he praised Mussolini for his 'amazing qualities of courage, comprehension, self-control and perseverance'. Similarly, during the Spanish Civil War (Spain was also a League member), he condoned the continued presence there of Italian 'volunteers' (long after their promised withdrawal) while Eden, the new Foreign Secretary, resigned because Chamberlain wished not-withstanding to make an agreement with Italy, League or no League.

The argument of the rest, to which William subscribed, was of course that, while Germany was certainly the greatest threat, if League members were allowed, without any action against them, to attack other members, the League itself would prove a paper tiger when its authority was invoked. Probably it was always destined to be a paper tiger, but no one – not even Churchill – ever said so.

*   *   *

When Baldwin took over the office of Prime Minister from Ramsay MacDonald in June 1935 he did not offer Churchill a Cabinet post but he did authorise, in spite of Chamberlain's opposition, his co-option to an Air Ministry advisory committee and his science 'guru', Professor Lindemann, to its scientific subcommittee.[13]

He was also tolerant of Churchill's use of civil servants to build up his own intelligence staff, which, by the outbreak of war, numbered some twenty. As Vansittart more and more found his advice rejected by his political superiors, he too fed Churchill with information. He relied on his own network, which he called the 'Z' organisation, including a contact within the German air ministry and the head of SIS (secret service), unbeknownst to his staff.

Before the General Election, Churchill's information had not been very accurate and, in April 1935, he was glad to circulate to his political friends detailed figures from *The Daily Telegraph* on the respective German and British air forces. These had been obtained in odd cir-cumstances. Sir John Simon, the Foreign Secretary, and Anthony Eden, Minister of State for League of Nations affairs, had paid the first official government visit to Hitler. They had gone to negotiate a kind of Locarno

---

[13] With disastrous results, since 'the Prof.' would insist on sidetracking the subcommittee from its primary role, the development of radar. Eventually its Chairman, Prof. Henry Tizard, disbanded the subcommittee and reconstituted it without 'the Prof'.

air pact, promoted by the French, at a time when Germany had just boasted of the existence of an air force, prohibited by the Versailles treaty. Simon had reported the negative results of the visit in the House of Commons, but had omitted Hitler's boast that he already had air parity with Britain. Victor Gordon Lennox, Diplomatic Correspondent of the *Telegraph*, discovered the boast from the Foreign Office, published it and elaborated it with figures, not exactly accurate but very close to those checked by the Air Ministry.

Simon and Eden had not been impressed by Hitler, in one of his less excitable moods. Eden had read *Mein Kampf*, but had not realised that the English edition had been expurgated, as had been the French, to the extent that Hitler's ambitions in the West went unmentioned. He was therefore able to describe him to the King as 'an Austrian Joan of Arc with a moustache'.

In the following year, William was able to form his own impression when he had an hour with Hitler in Berlin (attached as an Appendix to this chapter, pp. 216–19). It was not, as he explained, an interview but a series of monologues contained in only five replies. The main conclusion he formed was that the hopeful idea of 'moderates' surrounding Hitler was nonsense. He was the unchallengeable master of his country. This led William in the months to come to discount the pleas of the faint-hearted that strong/soft words would decrease/increase the power of non-existent moderates to influence German policy. History proved him right. The few brave 'moderates' there were had no influence and were shot or hung after the July 1944 plot. The only moderates in the army were those who doubted from time to time whether the forces available were capable of the tasks allotted them.

*   *   *

During what I here call the 'appeasement period' (that is to say, from 1933 to the outbreak of war, though it is no part of my story to describe it in sequence), William had a habit of recording important conversations he had with political leaders and diplomats, British and foreign.

His main informants were Chamberlain, whom he saw formally every three to six months; Eden while he was Foreign Secretary; Lord Tyrrell, one-time Head of the Foreign Office and Ambassador in Paris; Trenchard, and Vansittart, whom he continued to meet even after he had been 'kicked upstairs'[14] (largely sidetracked by Chamberlain and given

---

[14] Vansittart was sidetracked not so much for his erratic advice but for his manner of giving it. Cadogan's No. 2, Sir Orme Sargent, told the second Lord Birkenhead, researching his Life of Lord Halifax: 'Vansittart used a terrible style in his minutes to the Cabinet, violent, facetious and fizzing

the courtesy title of Chief Diplomatic Adviser, yielding the permanent secretary's job at the Foreign Office to Sir Alexander Cadogan). Cadogan he knew socially, but Halifax hardly at all.

All of this was, of course, 'for background'. Only rarely did William steer the conversation so as to emphasise his own point of view. When he did, he always seemed to pick on the issue of the moment. One such occasion was an interview with Chamberlain on 26 April 1938, after the Austrian *Anschluss* and some nine months after Baldwin's retirement:

> We talked for a long time about the Air question, and I think I made some impression on him ... My general impression was that the facts had only recently come to his knowledge and that he has not yet fully made up his mind on the steps he will have to take ... He did not demur in the least to my statement that the Air question was the most important matter in this country at the present time and that he will have to concern himself with it, and that without delay.

Whether William's criticism of the personalities involved was well-founded is now, with hindsight, open to question. He strongly attacked the Air Minister, Lord Swinton, as being 'very unpopular' and suggested Kingsley Wood as his successor. 'While it was perhaps natural for the Air Minister to have his enemies at the present time, Swinton's unpopularity was a very general thing.' Lord Weir, his management adviser (he had been a star of the First War Ministry of Munitions), 'was looked upon as a man who was past his prime'. Swinton, though notoriously both conceited and abrasive, was the man who had ordered the Spitfire and the Hurricane 'off the drawing board' when the fighter force consisted of bi-planes. He was about to do the same with four-engined bombers whereas, when he took office in 1935, the only bomber in service had a top speed of 73 mph and a height limit of 7,000 feet. There were a number of light and medium bombers under development, but their range was too limited for deep penetration.

As well as encouraging research on radar, he had conceived the idea of 'shadow factories', which would vastly increase the rate of production in a crisis, but in this had fallen out with Lord Nuffield,[15] an important

with bad epigrams and they simply would not read them ... A big man without hysterics and Van's lack of subtlety ... could have fought Horace Wilson [Chamberlain's advisor at No. 10].'

[15] Nuffield seems several times to have been snubbed. There is a note on William's 'interview file' of a conversation with Sir Wyndham Portal, the industrialist, eventual trustee of Lord Nuffield's scheme of assistance for Special Areas and afterwards Minister of Works in the Coalition Cabinet. Portal spoke of a meeting in Sir Horace Wilson's room at 10 Downing Street attended by Nuffield, Portal and Frank Hodges, the trade union leader, at the time of the Abdication. The charm of the story is that Wilson, Chief Industrial Adviser to the Prime Minister, was supposed to be 'the great conciliator'. Afterwards he was foreign affairs *eminence grise* to Chamberlain as Prime Minister.

participant. His disappointing production figures were misunderstood. All the talk, at least until 1938, was of numbers of 'first line aircraft', irrespective of quality and capacity for future production. Swinton had deliberately slowed down the production of obsolete aircraft to await the new.

A month after William's interview, following a stormy debate in the Commons in which Lord Winterton (Swinton's deputy – his title was an Irish one and did not entitle him to sit in the Lords) was continually harried on 'numbers' by Churchill and Sinclair (for the Liberals), Swinton himself resigned and was replaced by William's nominee, Kingsley Wood. (Wood made peace with Nuffield.)

Churchill then ate his words in a public speech: '[Swinton] worked night and day. He accomplished a great deal, and his contribution was far greater than that of some others who now hold high office of State.' (One reason for the resignation was an adverse report by the Cadman Committee on Civil Aviation, for which the Air Ministry was also responsible.)

This episode shows the pitfalls deliberately placed in the path of the newspaper proprietor trying to see clearly the background to the problems on which he has been seeking to rally public opinion. In giving the impression that the 'facts had only recently come to his knowledge', Chamberlain himself, Chancellor from 1931 to 1937, concealed his prime role as a perpetual brake on expenditure,[16] just as Churchill, in less hazardous times, had been in the 1920s, and Sir John Simon was to be until the war.

Only a month before, the Cabinet minutes had recorded that 'the Cabinet were reminded that at the present time the Defence Services were working under instruction to cut estimates'. He also persuaded William to adopt his argument that 'the Government has been wise not to concentrate so intensely on the production of munitions as to cripple trade and industry which [is] the foundation of its staying power'.

Nor had Churchill, with his special sources of information, been any

They discussed a scheme for the Distressed Areas. Nuffield asked if there was anything of a concrete nature available. Wilson's reply was that, while they had nothing which might be described in that way, there was a strong feeling in the country and in ministerial circles that, Lord Nuffield having made so much money, it was up to him to give a very large sum indeed for the aid of the Distressed Areas. Nuffield left the room in high dudgeon.

After the Abdication, he offered £2 million through Portal, adding that he would not have done so while the late King was on the throne because he (the King) would have claimed that it followed as the result of his visit to South Wales.

[16] His often-quoted boast to his sisters that 'unhappily it is part of my nature that I cannot contemplate any problem without trying to find a solution to it', was made in the relation of defence expenditure to general finances. A month later, in June 1934, he wrote in his diary that he proposed to 'bring 5 years' expenditure down from £75 million to £50 million'.

more helpful. He still swopped figures with Rothermere but seems to have given no confidences to William – though they had both attended a dinner given by Trenchard in October 1937 for General Milch, German Air Minister, and his research expert, Colonel Udet, together with stalwarts like Leo Amery, Sir Robert Kindersley (Chairman of Lazards, bankers), D'Arcy Cooper (Chairman of Unilever) and Weir. Milch was on an official German air mission[17] to check the optimistic findings on British air preparedness by Field Marshal von Blomberg when he had represented Hitler at the Coronation. The only message Churchill had passed was to congratulate William on a *Telegraph* leader drawing attention to the 'lag'.

*   *   *

So far, I have discussed the role of William and the *Telegraph* during the whole 'appeasement period' only in the context of the Air and the League. In the following chapters I deal with the *Telegraph*'s role in the dance macabre.

---

[17] Adam von Trott, an anti-Nazi in the German Foreign Office, executed after the attempted assassination of Hitler in June 1944, said in June 1939 that the mission reported: '[The British] had shown them nothing presumably because [they] had nothing to show.'

———

Notes of an Interview with Hitler
Berlin, 12 August 1936

Whatever opinions the German people may hold of the Nazi Government, there is one thing of which they are absolutely and definitely convinced, and that is the entire sincerity of Adolf Hitler. In private conversations they may criticise all the other leaders who have helped to bring about the revolution ; but, whether they agree or not with what Hitler has done and the way in which he has done it, they never doubt in the very slightest degree Hitler's absolute sincerity of purpose.

An interview with him makes this quite understandable. One single hour is not a long time in which to form a reliable impression of such a man, but it is sufficient to make one feel why the German people have that opinion of him.

Hitler occupies the very large and impressive room set aside for the Chancellor. His desk is set at the far end from the entrance, at the side of one of the windows. He is dressed in the khaki jacket of the Party, with no insignia of any kind, wearing black trousers and patent leather shoes. Somehow or other he gives one the impression that the surroundings are not congenial to him, that he is not of the room, as it were, that he does not feel comfortable in it. He greets his visitors cordially but stiffly, giving one the feeling that he is on the defensive. He takes a seat in an easy chair and sits clumsily and awkwardly.

To formal greetings through an interpreter (Hitler speaks no English but is said to understand a little) he bows his acknowledgement. To a second question, bringing in the matter of arms, he replies volubly. Perhaps 'volubly' is not a correct description, for Herr Hitler speaks for something like ten minutes without the slightest pause. His pace increases as he proceeds and he uses his hands in short upward motions to emphasise his points.

In the course of the hour's interview, Hitler makes five replies, three of which are at least eight to ten minutes in length. At the beginning of these monologues his eyes are fixed on a spot on the carpet a yard or two away, but, as he gets warmed up, he lifts them to regard the ceiling at the end of the room.

The interview consists, as, I am told, most interviews with him do, of a series of monologues. Once started in speech, he seems to find it difficult to stop – not, indeed, surprising when one realises that he has been in the habit for many years of making speeches of two or three hours or more in length, and often two such speeches in a single day.

Hitler is a man full of vitality and energy. He is undoubtedly obsessed with the idea of a mission, and is a man with whom it would be difficult to carry on an argument for any length of time. He strikes one as being a visionary and a dreamer but with an overwhelming love of power. That he can be ruthless his history proves, and no one observing him, even for a short time, at close quarters could have any doubt of his character in this direction.

That he is intellectually strong or well balanced may be doubted. One is rather forced to the feeling that he has won his way to power by a great and overwhelming power of speech and by the use of what is unquestionably a magnetic personality. His sense of humour is not great except in a sardonic way, but his smile is charming and almost like that of a gracious woman.

The supreme and undisputed chief of the German nation, one gets the impression that he is a little lost and somewhat irritated in that position, that he was happier and more at home when he was fighting his way. Ribbentrop is said to have great influence with him. If my diagnosis of his character is at all correct, this is easily understandable. Ribbentrop is of an entirely opposite character; he loves analysis, likes expressing his views at great length in private conversation, but is not at all excitable or impetuous. One can well believe that he acts as a foil to his chief and disputes with him only in the mildest way. The two are said to hold very lengthy conversations together, and the British Ambassador told me that at critical moments, particularly in foreign affairs, he had known them to walk for hours in the Chancellory gardens, talking together in the most intimate way.

As for what Hitler said, it is difficult to give anything but the crudest summary. Despite the efforts of a most able interpreter (Dr Schmidt, a man famous in that capacity, who has served several German Chancellors) Hitler's speeches were so long and took so much translation that anything in the nature of a conversation was impossible. He spoke at great length about Communism and Bolshevism, said that the latter was the danger to the world.

What would happen if we allowed it to take root in India or other parts of the Empire? A strong British Empire was desirable from everybody's point of view, but if we played with the fire of Bolshevism the Empire would be destroyed.

What he had done in an extremist way would not be understood in England. Germany was on the very brink of ruin. He had but a short time to act. The Bolshevists had overrun the country; they had committed innumerable acts of bloodshed and violence, the last of which was the burning of the Reichstag. On the other hand, his had been a bloodless revolution in which not a single life had been lost. The German people were different from the English; they were romantic and had no historical bonds of unity. In England at a time of crisis the Government could rely on the sanity and the unity of the people. We had disarmed, but our national spirit and organisation were such that we could quickly put ourselves in a state of preparedness. It was only by the steps he had taken that Germany could become a strong and united nation again.

He had completed the first part of his work and Germany was strong enough to take her proper place in the world. Now he desired to live in peace with his neighbours and in free competition with a Europe in which each country was content in its own borders.

Asked what he meant by free competition – did it include arms – Hitler said he meant friendly rivalry in culture, in the arts and in sport, such as we had seen in the Olympic Games – among the nations of the West.

With Russia that was impossible. Russia was out to destroy the world. People had talked about the size of the German Army. The Russian Army in proportion was much larger and more powerful and its purpose entirely sinister. Germany had been the barrier (the interpreter used the word 'barrage') against the barbarians of the East for many centuries, the Huns, the Goths, &c., and they would have to face those enemies again. The whole world had got to realise that Russia and Bolshevism were the enemies of mankind, and sooner or later they would have to be fought and destroyed. They in Germany knew that there was no hope for them or for civilisation unless Bolshevism was utterly destroyed. He returned again and again to this topic.

A final question as to the freedom of the Press brought the reply that he did not think the time had come for that in Germany. English people did not understand how the Press in Germany had been used in the past to promote Bolshevism and Communism, and the same would happen again to-day if the newspapers were allowed to say what they liked. France had just adopted a measure, giving workmen a 40 hour week and 15% increase in wages. Germany could not afford yet to increase wages. What would have happened if the Press had been allowed to taunt the Government? The trouble in Germany had been largely created by the lies printed in the Press. As it was, there was no active Government censorship in Germany to-day; the control was exercised by the newspapers themselves through their own (what the interpreter terms) Trade Chambers.

To a remark that, as a newspaper proprietor, the question naturally interested me greatly, Hitler said that he had been a newspaper owner himself – eight out of the nine papers he had started had been suppressed – so he understood the feelings of the proprietor quite well from personal experience.

CHAPTER SIXTEEN

Appeasement II –
Early Attempts to Control the Press

IT IS FUTILE to evaluate national attitudes in the run-up to the Second World War without first examining the legacy of the First World War.

The Treaty of Versailles, largely dictated by Clemenceau, established a Carthaginian peace – not as drastic as the Morganthau plan of 1944 but designed to render Germany incapable of making war again for fifty years. It was understandable. France was exhausted. It had suffered far more casualties than any other belligerent and its northeastern *departments* had been uniquely devastated. Alsace and Lorraine, the former with a German majority, were taken back and a fifty-kilometre strip of land to the east of the Rhine was decreed to be demilitarised: to harbour no troops nor fortifications. In middle-Europe, the Austro-Hungarian Empire was dissolved and replaced by what Lloyd George helplessly described as 'a [surrounding] mob of small states, many of them consisting of peoples who have never previously set up a stable government for themselves, but each of them containing large masses of Germans'.[1] East Prussia was separated from the Fatherland by a Polish corridor and the German city of Danzig declared a League of Nations mandate. Germany could have no air force, only a coastal navy, and an army, without conscription, of 50,000 men. On top of this, impossible reparations were demanded which, when unpaid, led to the occupation of the industrial Ruhr by French troops for six years. And then came the Great Depression, wherein Germany suffered desperation whereas France was little affected.

Even some of the victors had their grievances. Italy had been brought into the war in 1915 with handsome promises. President Wilson's insistence on 'self-determination' baulked that. Various territories, including Albania, on the Adriatic were denied to her while ex-German colonies and ex-Turkish provinces were for the most part divided up

---

[1] Jan Masaryk, Czechoslovakian Minister in London and son of Thomas Masaryk, first President, claimed that his father had blamed Lloyd George for insisting on the inclusion of Germans.

between France and Great Britain. In the Far East, Japan got practically nothing.

The other legacy of Versailles was the universal assumption that wars, and the Great War in particular, are caused by neighbouring states being armed to the teeth. Explosives are piled up, sparks fly, a general conflagration is bound to result. Hence, the way to permanent European peace was to disarm. Germany, who had belatedly been brought back into the fold by membership of the League and who, by the Treaty of Locarno, accepted the new territorial rearrangements, was to be allowed gradually to arm up to a new maximum.

The assumption was doubly misconceived.

Firstly, examination by historians of German Foreign Office papers of the First World War, following their capture after the Second World War, has shown conclusively that Germany deliberately started the First World War in fear of Russia. European Russia had been the last country to enjoy an industrial revolution. Economic strength enables military strength. In 1914, the German establishment calculated that in a few years' time the Russian hordes might be too well armed to be resisted. The murder of the Archduke at Sarajevo seemed heaven-sent. Germany incited the Hapsburg government to send a note to Serbia so humiliating that it could hardly be accepted. But accepted it was. Hence the message of 'capitulation' was not shown to the Kaiser, swashbuckler though he might be. The German-propelled engines of war began to turn and country after country was drawn in.

Secondly, and fortunately, the French would have nothing to do with halving their own army while permitting the German to be doubled – what Anthony Eden, Foreign Under-Secretary in 1933, in reply to Churchill, called necessary 'appeasement'.[2] Nor could the East European countries be persuaded to lay down their arms in confrontation with a resurgent Soviet Union, itself a fleeced victim of Versailles.

Thus the Disarmament Conference, spurred on by Ramsay Mac-Donald, who took foreign affairs into his own hands more than any other pre-war prime minister before Chamberlain, continued year by year at Geneva. The only positive result, as detailed in the last chapter, was the continual disarmament of Britain, not only in the air but in the other services.

*   *   *

[2] This, on 23 March 1933, was the first time the word 'appeasement' had been used in the House of Commons. Ironically, it was the same day as the German Reichstag voted Hitler full dictatorial powers.

In the run-up to 1939, it has been said that 'The Press, in its support for Chamberlain and appeasement, was dangerously out of step with public opinion ... one of the most telling polls revealed [in the wake of Munich] that 86 per cent of the population did not believe Hitler's protestations that he did not have any more territorial ambitions.'[3] If the Press was to be judged only by its leading articles, that accusation may well seem true, even in the case of *The Daily Telegraph*, until the Munich crisis began to blow up. But where did the population get its information on which to base such a firm opinion? The first duty of a serious newspaper is to inform and, in respect of the *Telegraph*, its reporting was extensive and thorough. It had for long been the boast of the paper that it employed more foreign staff correspondents than any other British paper and, unlike those employed by *The Times*, their despatches were not toned down before publication.

I have not checked day by day the reports in other newspapers of the rise of Hitler: his street-fighting campaigns; his harrying of the Jews; his murder of social democratic politicians in their beds; his setting up of the first concentration camp; his mass arrests of Austrian dissidents. But certainly, in the *Telegraph*, they were very full.

My own attempt to learn German in Munich in October 1933, some six months after Hitler assumed total power, came to an abrupt end when the *Telegraph*'s 'stringer' correspondent led the paper with reports that storm troopers were drilling in nearby woods in contravention of the Versailles restrictions on the army.[4] The stringer was arrested and I myself, as a son of the proprietor, was fetched home. Thereafter the *Telegraph* suffered more than its fair share of correspondents expelled. Irrespective of the caution – until 1938 – that might be advocated in the leader columns, the policy was always to report the news straight and it was usually this that gave offence to the dictators. William's policy from the start was that there must be no 'editorialising' in the news columns. News and views should never be mixed.[5] (*The Times*, at least until the *Anschluss*, seemed to follow a similar policy, but its purely factual account of the German experimental bombing of the undefended Spanish town of Guernica in 1936 aroused dictatorial ire. Geoffrey Dawson complained of the criticism: 'I should like to get going with

[3] Some of them may have been influenced by the *Telegraph* which printed, on the day the Godesberg terms were discussed in Cabinet, a list of Hitler's broken promises to date.

[4] When the British Ambassador protested two months later, Hitler informed him that the SA (storm troopers) and the SS were 'like the Salvation Army'.

[5] Nowadays, this encomium is often carried to ridiculous extremes. One can hardly read a statement of policy by one of the political parties without its comprehension being muddled by insertion of instant quotes from other party leaders predictably 'rubbishing' it. This is not balance, but over-balance.

the Germans. I simply cannot understand why they should be so much annoyed with *The Times* ... I spend my nights in taking out anything which I think will hurt their susceptibilities and in dropping in little things which are intended to soothe them.') The foreign correspondent, who by tradition always wrote anonymously,[6] was encouraged to send the background to the news by memorandum to Fleet Street for the guidance of leader-writers but eschewed not to let their personal views permeate their news reports.

There was one case of a recalcitrant correspondent which, first aired in the *Daily Worker*, generated a correspondence in the *New Statesman* in 1939. Eric Gedye, a most knowledgeable Germanologist (he had served in the Intelligence and in the Allied Commission in the Rhineland before becoming a Central European journalist) had been expelled from Austria after the *Anschluss* (he had reported very factually the arrival of the Gestapo before the German troops and their searching of, and arrests on, double-length trains with fleeing Austrians aboard. *The Times*, by comparison, merely reported cheering crowds, without noting that they had largely been imported from Germany and that protesters would hardly be likely to show themselves).[7] Garvin, in the *Observer*, put the rape to music: 'The majority of the Sabine victims felt the call like magic, and gloried in the espousals.'

After Vienna, Gedye was moved to Czechoslovakia, which everyone realised would now be under threat. No complaint of his reporting was made by head office, until, without warning, a publisher's advance publicity foretold a forthcoming book by Gedye as telling 'the uncensored truth' about all things Nazi including humiliating criticisms of Chamberlain. On seeing this, Arthur Watson wrote to him and explained that he could not remain a *Telegraph* reporter and at the same time give vent to extreme views on countries on which he was supposed to be writing factually. Watson did not make the comparison, but implicitly he was making the point that it was open to Churchill, who was now writing fortnightly for the *Telegraph*, to write things which could not come from the pen of a reporter. Gedye offered to resign but his resignation was refused: nevertheless, when the book came out it was found that the tirades had by no means been modified and he was sacked with six months' compensation.

---

[6] The based staff correspondent was by-lined 'From Our Own Correspondent', the stringer 'From Our Correspondent' and the roving staffer, 'From our Special Correspondent'.

[7] *The Times* correspondent reported privately to Geoffrey Dawson: 'In my wildest nightmares, I had not foreseen anything so ruthless, so strong ... The vital thing to remember is precisely the destruction of England.'

As Hugh Carleton Greene,[8] who had temporarily replaced him, remarked, Gedye was 'a wonderful reporter [but] he sometimes allowed his crusading instincts to run away with him'. I have the feeling that the affair had, for some time, been blowing up. As long before as February 1934 there is an item in William's editorial notes: 'Is Gedye giving us the news? I have rather the feeling that he is influenced by political aspects too much.'

*　　*　　*

William never saw himself as a political thinker. He had firm political principles but they did not in themselves make a political credo. He had no illusions about the separateness of the Fourth Estate. Newspaper proprietors could not serve in the Executive (if they did, as Rothermere had done in the First World War and Beaverbrook did in the Second, they were supposed to cut themselves off from their newspaper). A newspaper in its opinion columns must therefore travel in the same direction as one of the political parties. As he had written when he first took over the *Telegraph*, he supported the Conservative Party in general terms, with the duty to differ on specifics. In the mid-1930s there seemed no other option. The tiny Liberal Party was still headed by Lloyd George.

Once William's hero, he now seemed irrelevant.[9] The Labour Party was still avowedly socialist. On rearmament, which, with foreign affairs, now began to dominate political discussion, it was crudely partisan. As late as 4 March 1938 (when the Austrian crisis was already blowing up) it was still opposing rearmament on the grounds that it 'permits private manufacturers to make huge profits out of the nation's need', although Attlee, the leader, was only reluctantly supportive.[10] Peace could only be maintained by collective security through the League without 'immense armaments in defiance of election pledges'. Until 1935 it had been 'virtually an article of faith that for Britain to rearm in competition with another major country was a certain step toward war'. In the 1935 General Election, Labour had campaigned with an anti-Tory poster showing a baby in a gas mask.

William was a fervent believer in the superiority of capitalism over

---

[8] Greene, a brother of Graham Greene and after the war the liberalising Director General of the BBC, was for some years *Telegraph* chief correspondent in Berlin. He was expelled in April 1939 as a tit-for-tat concerning a German correspondent in London.

[9] After a visit in 1936, he had prounounced *Mein Kampf* a German Magna Carta and Hitler as their Resurrection and the Way.

[10] The *Telegraph* parliamentary sketch writer had ealier recorded: 'The Socilaist leader, Mr Attlee, is generally at his best on the subject of defence but [he] was heard even by his own party with an obvious lack of interest.'

socialism,[11] in Samuel Smiles with a soft spot for the underdog, in a strong country without European entanglements but, above all, in the importance in life of strong leadership, integrity, absence of humbug and the power of decision. He thought he saw all these qualities in Chamberlain, while he had a poor opinion of the colleagues. Hoare was a smarmy and self-important poseur; Simon a brilliant lawyer, but weak and vacillating;[12] Inskip another lawyer but less distinguished; Eden, a politician whose sole experience had been in foreign affairs; Hore-Belisha 'suffering from an inferiority complex [partly because of his race] and too fond of the limelight to settle down to tackling awkward problems.'[13]

There was really no one else but Churchill and he still seemed too unstable to be trusted with the top job. As Lord Riddell had written of him in 1915: 'He is like a wonderful piece of machinery with a fly-wheel which occasionally makes unexpected movements.' In the 1930s his fly-wheel had malfunctioned regularly, and he had never acknowledged the defect. In 1936, for instance, he had advocated to Hankey, the Secretary of the Committee of Imperial Defence, that the Navy should detach a permanent squadron for service in the Baltic.[14]

What William did not realise in Chamberlain's make-up was his pig-headedness and a confidence so great that it degenerated into vanity. Chamberlain, though respected by all, was incapable of making friends. He shot and fished at weekend parties – he stayed at Hackwood in 1937 – but otherwise did not mix socially. Unlike Baldwin he was not a 'good House of Commons man'. He did not sit through long debates or mingle in the Smoking Room. He had no intimates among colleagues but poured out his innermost thoughts to his two sisters, in weekly letters, with unfailing regularity, of eight, ten, or twelve pages in his

[11] Tom Jones recorded in his diary for 21 October 1936 a dinner by Sir Abe Bailey of '30 or 40' to meet the American ambassador: 'I listened to some dialectics between Camrose and A.V. Alexander [Secretary of the Cooperative Party and First Lord of the Admiralty in the Coalition Government] on the respective merits of the Capitalist and Cooperative Systems. This was my first meeting with Camrose, tall, successful, genial, generous.'

[12] Lord Greenwood had told William that Simon expected to be regarded as Chamberlain's successor and wished to be made an honorary member of the Carlton Club. David Margesson, Conservative Chief Whip, was said to favour Inskip as heir apparent.

[13] William recounted that Hore-Belisha, as a minister, did not come to his department until noon, when his first appointment was with his publicity adviser.

[14] There was a feeling that Churchill actually enjoyed war, or at any rate, its direction. A.P. Herbert wrote at the time: 'I never liked Mr Chamberlain (I hardly knew him): but I admired him. For more than twenty years I had adored (that is the right word, I fear) Mr Churchill ... I did not think, as so many thought in those days, that he was brilliant, resourceful, brave, but nearly always wrong. I thought he was nearly always right – right for example about the Dardanelles, right about Antwerp, in both of which affairs our Division (the Royal Naval Division) was involved. But I did think that he rather enjoyed a war: and, after three years in the infantry, in Gallipoli and France, I did not.'

own handwriting. As they were both local Birmingham councillors, where he had acquired his masterful ways in his formative years, he could happily discuss with them the minutiae of politics and even House of Commons procedure. 'I know that I can save England, and that no one else can,' he quoted Pitt the Younger. 'Hore-Belisha has sent me a bust of Pitt. He thinks I am the heriteur.'

Not long after he had taken over from Baldwin in May 1937, the latter had told him, 'I made peace at home. It may be you will be able to crown that with peace abroad.'

As soon as he entered No. 10 Downing Street this became his obsession. He would do it alone. He conceived the idea of a 'General Settlement' in which Germany could be tamed by the relaxation of her Versailles bonds in Europe, and most of her colonies restored while Mussolini, in spite of his Abyssinian and Spanish adventures, could be flattered into counterpoise to Hitler. He would never desert France, but because of her succession of weak governments, he would have to be the leader of the democracies. France, he wrote, 'can never keep a secret for more than half an hour, nor a government for more than nine months'.

Not much of this emerges from William's notes of his meetings with Chamberlain. William went as a journalist, trying to find out what was going on and not with any intention to argue. They began regularly in 1936 (he made no record of his first long conversation in which they had taken to each other in 1931), but during Baldwin's time most of the news was of when the latter would finally retire.

So many books have been written on the appeasement period that it is sometimes difficult to remember the extraordinarily short period the Chamberlain phase occupied. Chamberlain became Prime Minister at the end of May 1937. Sixteen months later, during which we sat on our hands while Germany raped Austria and then abandoned Czechoslovakia to her fate, came the Munich agreement. Only another eleven months, and we were at war.

We can now plot with some accuracy the painful steps – all by secret diplomacy – taken down the slippery slope to abasement or war. On the few occasions when the diplomatic cat jumped out of the bag, it was put back by bland denials, not from the Foreign Office News Department but by the press officer at No. 10.

As far as William himself was concerned, he derived some scanty information from Chamberlain himself – there are three recorded meetings between May 1937 and Munich – robust views from Vansittart and the extreme appeasers' case from Lord Astor (proprietor of the *Observer*) and Lord Lothian (key member of the so-called Cliveden Party with

Geoffrey Dawson and Dr Gilbert Murray). At his first meeting with the new Prime Minister, in his room at the House of Commons on 8 November 1937, he learned that Chamberlain had lost confidence in the Foreign Office because of its 'methods and the way they work in grooves and [unsuitable] channels ... they have the most determined prejudices' and with the Foreign Secretary (Eden) himself. He was particularly annoyed with Eden for an impromptu attack on Mussolini, whom Chamberlain was now intending to woo as a counterweight to Hitler. William had twice seen Eden before this interview when they had talked about nothing but Italy and her refusal to withdraw her 'volunteers' from Spain and Majorca (the latter to the annoyance of the French). Chamberlain, on the other hand, was anxious to arrange a four-power conference (Britain, France, Italy and Germany but 'without the presence of Russia') to achieve his General Settlement. Though he did not say so, this would mean short-circuiting the League as a negotiating body. It was on this issue that Eden, feeling Chamberlain, with Sir Horace Wilson, was conducting his own foreign policy behind his back, resigned in February 1938 and got no support from the *Telegraph*.

In retrospect, the most important part of the interview was discussion of the impending visit of Halifax (Lord Privy Seal, in the Cabinet without portfolio but acting, by agreement, as a deputy to Eden) to Hitler.[15] William was not told that the visit had been opposed by Eden and Vansittart because Halifax would be manoeuvred into suggesting undesirable compromises. Chamberlain did, however, say that Hitler had an agenda since he (Chamberlain) had seen the notes of an interview between the Aga Khan and Hitler – 'very stiff terms but something to talk about'. The terms, in short, were:

1. The division of Czechoslovakia as Ireland, the German part working closely with Germany but not actually allied.

2. Non-opposition to commercial and social links with Austria but not actual annexation. [This was contrary to the Treaty of Versailles. A 'customs union' had been vetoed by France, with British support, in 1931, before Hitler came to power.]

3. In return Germany would re-join the League and sign the Covenant.

[15] The visit was to arise out of an invited visit to Berlin to see a hunting exhibition. Chamberlain had encouraged the Ambassador to arrange a meeting with Hitler though it was announced to the Press that Hitler had suggested a meeting. This fiction was exposed by the diplomatic correspondent of the *Daily Telegraph*.

These ideas seemed to William to make constructive sense and, until the actual invasion of Austria in March 1938, he caused the *Telegraph* to support Chamberlain's foreign policy.

What actually happened at the Halifax/Hitler meeting was exactly what Eden had feared. According to Andrew Roberts, latest biographer of Halifax, Hitler began the talks with 'his customary line about the unfairness of Versailles and went on to waffle in a pseudo-intellectual way about the rule of higher reason ... But as he had nothing substantial to offer, he cannily allowed Halifax the floor'. Halifax was thus bamboozled into making a general statement of:

> possible alterations in the European order which might be destined to come about with the passage of time. Amongst these questions were Danzig, Austria and Czecho-Slovakia. England was interested to see that any alterations should come through the course of peaceful evolution and that methods should be avoided which might cause far-reaching disturbances.

Roberts continues his summary, no hint of which was published or made known at the time:[16]

> Of course Halifax hedged his message with qualifying phrases ... but Hitler had little difficulty in seeing through the diplomatic language ... so far as the British Government were concerned, parts of [the Treaty of] Versailles could be up for review, so long as force was not concerned.

Halifax himself believed he had 'squared' Hitler. Chamberlain wrote to his sister that the visit had achieved its object, 'that of creating an atmosphere in which it was possible to discuss ... the practical questions involved in a European settlement ... I wanted ... to convince Hitler of our sincerity and to ascertain what objectives he had in mind'. What he actually achieved was to show that Britain was prepared to renegotiate Versailles without the threat of military action. Hitler was to tell Schuschnigg, the Austrian Chancellor, just before the *Anschluss*: 'I shall always get my way because I am ready to run the risk of war but my opponents are not.'

Moreover, Halifax, perhaps unwittingly, revealed that England would seek no alliance with the Soviet Union, since he congratulated Hitler in keeping Communism out of his country and blocking its progress to the West.

---

[16] Roberts also comments that the notes made by Halifax's interpreter, Ivone Kirkpatrick (who acted as interpreter), were pretty similar.

How secret were the details of this meeting, which Chamberlain refused to discuss in the House of Commons, was shown by an entry in Harold Nicolson's diary for 10 March 1938:

lunched with Leo Amery ... for Franckenstein, the Austrian Minister[17] ... We congratulate him on Schuschnigg ... being so brave as to stand up to Hitler. He confirms that Hitler ... lied to Schuschnigg in telling him that Halifax had told him England did not mind if Austria was absorbed.

*   *   *

After seeing Hitler at his mountain retreat, Halifax moved on to Berlin where he had tea with Goebbels ('I couldn't rather help but like the little man'). Goebbels asserted that the British Press correspondents in Berlin were 'dishonest and unfair'. Challenged as to why he had not complained before, he explained 'with a charming smile': '... because Germany was not rearmed ... now are we strong enough'. Halifax, as usual seeing two sides to every question, welcomed 'the desire to avoid the Press in either country making mischief ... HMG would do everything in their power to influence our Press to avoid unnecessary offence.'

What particularly enraged Goebbels was the work of the British cartoonists. Their stock-in-trade was to hit below the belt, his own speciality. It was to these that Halifax, not yet Foreign Secretary, at first addressed his emolliating effort. The most brilliant were David Low of the London *Evening Standard*; Will Dyson, of the *Daily Herald*, and Wyndham Robinson of the London (Evening) *Star*, a sister paper of the *News Chronicle*. Halifax himself saw Lord Southwood, Chairman of the *Herald* holding company, who was reluctant to admit Dyson's savage style was anything more than symbolic, and Sir Walter Layton, Editor-in-Chief of the *News Chronicle*. With the *Standard*'s Managing Director, Mike Wardell (no doubt with Beaverbrook's approval), he was more successful. Low was the wittier of the draughtsmen. For a time he agreed to tone down his satire and instead invented a comic pair, Hit and Muss, who were always getting into scrapes.

As soon as Halifax succeeded Eden in late February, there was direct

---

[17] Austria had then only a legation, not an embassy.

pressure on Sir John Reith,[18] who was persuaded to drop planned BBC talks on the subject of German colonial claims.[19]

The talks would have been awkward for Chamberlain, who was planning an offer of *Lebensraum* in Africa in return for abandonment of German *Lebensraum* in Central Europe. The idea had its origin in a talk Halifax had had with Dr Schacht, the German economic 'wizard' who had complained of Germany's lack of raw materials. Chamberlain converted this into a plan to transfer virtually the whole of West Africa, from South Africa to the Sahara, to a trust territory, Germany having the controlling interest. The colonies were currently the property of France, Belgium and Portugal, with a small British contribution. The idea, put to Hitler by Henderson, fortunately found no favour, as the others had not been consulted.

These were the first 'fruits' of the Halifax mission. Chamberlain, in commending it to the House of Commons on 21 December 1937, had finished with an appeal:

> for the exercise of restraint and toleration by the Press of all countries when dealing with foreign affairs, whether they are presenting their account of current events or commenting on policies or personalities. The power of the Press for good or for evil in international relations is very great, and a judicious use of that power, accompanied by a full sense of responsibility, may have far-reaching effects of creating an atmosphere, favourable for the purposes at which we are aiming.

The Foreign Office enjoyed a prolonged Christmas holiday that year. It was not until 5 January that Henderson's attention was drawn to Chamberlain's statement. He was instructed to give Goebbels the usual bromides about the difficulty of controlling the British Press (only the theatre could be censored); to point out to him that Hitler, though Head of State, must be open to criticism as 'an active politician', and in particular to invite him to send in any complaints about the British Press.

Henderson, much to the annoyance of the Foreign Office when they discovered the omission at the end of February, sat on the instruction but continued to bombard London with complaints, some of which,

---

[18] Comically, the Foreign Office minute recommending such persuasion was careful to emphasise that Reith himself, rather than the department concerned, should be approached. Chamberlain knew where the power lay. Shortly afterwards he 'promoted' Reith to be Chairman of Imperial Airways.

[19] These were to have been on the same lines as two articles in the *Daily Telegraph* by Victor Gordon Lennox in December 1937, which had provoked an angry despatch from Henderson complaining of 'immense harm'. According to Halifax's private secretary, 'Reith asked Halifax whether the Government wished to stop them. Halifax replied "Yes", but would deny it if challenged in public.'

he said, were supported with 'indignation in certain English circles'. Eventually, on 3 March, the message was delivered personally to Hitler, together with the Colonies proposals, just when Hitler was working himself up about the iniquities of the Austrians. In the meantime, he had been raging about Press treatment of the squalid manner in which he had made himself Commander-in-Chief.[20] At the same time, he had forced the top service chiefs to swear oaths of allegiance to him personally.

Eden does not seem to have concerned himself with these matters but Halifax, on succeeding, attempted not only to act in relation to the Press but also to be seen by the Germans as acting. Against the advice of the News Department, he instructed Henderson to pass on his actions under three headings. The information was to be conveyed in confidence as otherwise 'there might be trouble in the House of Commons':

1. The terms of reference to the newly-formed Vansittart Committee. The Committee's object was to propagate news of Britain in conjunction with the British Council.

2. Text of what Halifax would say to the Press. (An earlier plan for Chamberlain and Halifax together to see the Chairman of the Newspaper Proprietors' Association seems to have been abandoned.)

3. Outline of what he would say to Sir John Reith concerning BBC bulletins on German and Italian affairs, bearing in mind 'the extreme sensitivities of Hitler and Mussolini'.

The text of Halifax's address, listened to, as he later told Ribbentrop, the retiring ambassador (he was to succeed the 'moderate' von Neurath) by 'about 80 Press representatives' – too large an assembly to be attended by proprietors or editors, was:

> We live in a free country with a free Press and none of us would wish to change in any way that happy state of affairs. Freedom implies freedom to criticise and I would not dream of asking you to cease from exercising that right. But it also implies responsibility and when

---

[20] Field Marshal von Blomberg and his Chief of Staff, General von Fritsch, had both been removed by Goebbel's machinations. Blomberg had married his secretary, to the fury of other generals' wives, though Hitler and Goering had both acted as witnesses. Goebbels invented a police record for her and a report of homosexuality for Fritsch. The report, in fact, applied to another officer with a rather similar name. Thus, at one blow, the 'moderate' generals, who felt no bond between the army and the Nazi Party were removed. Blomberg, in interview with Major-General Temperley, the *Telegraph* Military Correspondent, at the time of the Coronation, had several times referred to 'my army'. Temperley had heard the same Blomberg phrase from the C.-in-C. of the Lithuanian army.

it comes to unguarded criticisms of other countries, specially of the head of the State or the Government, it may be a big national responsibility.

I presume that we are all agreed that in the present state of Europe nobody here wishes to make the situation worse by needless provocation ...

On matters of importance the British Press will wish to express disapproval, but disapproval is a very different thing in its effect abroad from abusive criticism or pinpricking or from too great a readiness to accept and publish rumours before their correctness has been verified. All these things do great damage not only to our reputation abroad, but seriously impede any official effort to remove misunderstandings and improve relations ...

Throughout the spring and early summer, the Foreign Office was made to repeat these emollient gestures and obediently to investigate any charges made in German newspapers. When Hitler made his usual speech attacking 'lies spread by Jewish international poisoners', instancing the *News Chronicle*, the Foreign Office hierarchy (all most distinguished and later to be ambassadors or better)[21] conducted a three-day passage of minutes, culminating in Sir Charles Peake's magisterial judgment: 'There is a Jewish element in the M/G [*Manchester Guardian*], though the proprietors who direct the policy are extremely[22] Aryan. The N/C [*News Chronicle*] is, so far as I am aware, free of all Jewish influence.'[23]

As if to emphasise the iniquity of the *News Chronicle*, the Berlin Embassy sent a telegram a little later entirely on this subject: 'Ministry of Propaganda has started special weekly *Stamtisch* [regular table] in one of the principal clubs. *Daily Telegraph* and *News Chronicle* correspondents, not invited.' A further telegram reported the *Telegraph* 'in particular comes under drastic censure' for reporting the supersession of Austrians by Prussians in the best jobs, based on a Paris press conference with 'Jewish-Marxist' Viennese *émigrés*.

The most ridiculous of the Foreign Office's enquiries was of a double-

---

[21] I give their later titles – Sir Frank Roberts, Sir Ivo Mallet, Lord Strang, Sir Charles Peake, Sir Orme Sargent, and Sir Alexander Cadogan.

[22] To be fair to Peake, he finally crossed out 'extremely' and substituted 'entirely'.

[23] Hitler's obsession with Jews had its counterpart in Britain. A.J.P. Taylor, in *Beaverbrook*, quotes a 'deplorable' letter to Frank Gannett, the American newspaper proprietor, after Munich: 'The Jews have a big position in the Press here. I estimate that one third of the circulation of the *Daily Telegraph* is Jewish. The *Mirror* may be owned by Jews. The *Daily Herald* is owned by Jews. And the *News Chronicle* should really be the *Jews' Chronicle*. Not because of ownership but because of sympathy.' Yet Beaverbrook was not normally anti-Semitic.

page spread, in the *Sunday Graphic* (now part of Gomer's stable), printing an 'exclusive' interview with Hitler. The Germans complained that Hitler had given no interview. It seemed odd that the tone had been mild and that no mention had been made of Czechoslovakia nor of the 'criminal' President Benes. After a long correspondence, it emerged that the editor had been sold a pup by an American agency. The interview had taken place two years earlier and had already been printed at that time.

I do not think William was ever aware of this abject posturing and futile pen-pushing. In the run-up to Munich I can find no evidence, either in his papers or in *Telegraph* files, of any further government warnings of the sensitivities of the dictators. It was not until Sir Samuel Hoare was put in charge of soft-soaping the proprietors, of which more later, in September, that any attempt was made to influence the direction – though, as we shall see, Chamberlain was guilty of some misinformation.

The only other record of political pressure on the Press before that time is the post-war revelation of a despatch to Berlin by the German embassy press attaché (who claimed he was often given 'leaks' of Chamberlain's thoughts by George Steward, Press Officer at No. 10) in which he refers to 'Chamberlain's interview with representatives of the British Press on Wednesday evening' (1 June). That interview, the attaché alleged, inspired a leading article in *The Times* pressing a series of ethnic plebiscites[24] on the Czechoslovak government.

It seems much more likely, however, that the inspiration came from Halifax who, though following Chamberlain blindly[25] until the eleventh hour of Munich, seemed himself to lead Geoffrey Dawson, Editor of *The Times*, by the nose. This procedure had begun early in Halifax's tenure of the Foreign Office. Immediately after the rape of Austria, Oliver Harvey, Halifax's Private Secretary, told his diary: 'The Press is unanimous in condemning Germany's behaviour. Even *The Times*, though reluctantly so, but H had spoken to Dawson, who will do whatever H tells him.' Dawson regularly lunched and dined with Halifax and, according to Andrew Roberts, was sent sensitive Foreign Office

[24] If those plebiscites had taken place, Czechoslovakia must immediately have fallen to pieces, without thought for the identity of the succeeding states. The population was approximately 7.5 m. Czech, 3.25 m. German, 2.5 m. Slovak, 500,000 each Hungarian and Ruthenian and 80,000 Polish. Today, the country is just as mixed. When Pope John Paul visited it in 1989 he delivered blessings in one single town of Moravia in Czech, Slovak, Polish, Hungarian, German, Ukranian, Byelorussian and a few other languages.

[25] William Strang, head of the Foreign Office Central Department told Lord Birkenhead Halifax's attitude seemed to be, 'Here is the Prime Minister. He has got his own policy. Let us get along with him.'

memoranda. When the post of Ambassador to Washington fell vacant, Halifax told Cadogan to find out whom Dawson recommended.[26]

Where pressure was undoubtedly applied was in the giving out of news from the Foreign Office and other departments.

Newspapers, of course, cannot comment intelligently unless they are able to gather the day-to-day news to supplement the background obtained from, perhaps, partial sources. At the time of appeasement the old method of individual pressmen cultivating individual ministers (or, as often, vice versa) and senior civil servants was passing away. In its place had come the 'press officer', with his own rooms, who held regular mass meetings of all the newspaper specialists. This practice was introduced by Ramsay MacDonald in 1929 to prevent 'leaking' from sources other than 10 Downing Street and was developed when Baldwin became Prime Minister again in 1935. Ministers themselves often took the meetings, but what was divulged was, by the rules, 'non-attributable' so that ministerial pronouncements could only be referred to as 'authoritative sources' or a 'well-placed observer', of whose identity only the already informed were aware. Traditionally, the Foreign Office has always been suspicious of, and antagonistic to, No. 10. Consequently, the Foreign Office in 1935 established its own News Department, headed by Rex Leeper, a protégé of Vansittart. Thereafter, those diplomatic correspondents who could be trusted were fed what the Foreign Office considered the facts, while No. 10 touted what it would like them to be.

The 'trusties' were Victor Gordon Lennox of the *Telegraph*, Voight of the *Manchester Guardian*, Vernon Bartlett[27] of the *News Chronicle*, Ewer of the *Daily Herald* and Tower of the *Yorkshire Post* (a paper of considerable influence but with only 30,000 readers). Chamberlain extended the system of briefings by Conservative Central Office at St Stephens, across the road from the Houses of Parliament. These might be taken by Topping, the Director, or by Sir Joseph Ball, an ex-MI5 man and head of the Research Department. Close though Ball was with Chamberlain – they were fishing together when the news of the invasion of Prague was announced – too much importance may have been

---

[26] Dawson was a life-long friend of Halifax, having met him first when he was a secretary to Lord Milner in 1901. Both were Yorkshiremen, Fellows of All Souls, Fellows of Eton, High Anglicans, who rode and shot together. As Lord Brand, who had known them from earliest days, wrote: 'Baldwin, Dawson and Halifax all had this in common. They were all English country gentlemen, all good public school men, and all good Churchmen. They seldom visited Europe or knew what Europeans were like. None of them could have had the slightest conception of the enormity of Hitler. Their whole upbringing conspired against understanding that such people could exist and that the Nazi state was a lunatic state.'

[27] Bartlett left the team soon after Munich, when he won a by-election as an Independent.

THE CANNIBAL SHIP.

A 1930 cartoon by Low in the *London Evening Standard* on the British press during a period of amalgamations. William, labelled 'Berry Press', is digesting 'Burnham' (*Telegraph*). The *Morning Post* is already under threat but its pursuers are unidentified. On the bow the *Daily News* is eating the *Westminster Gazette*. Near the funnel lurks the *Daily Chronicle*, soon to be amalgamated with the *Daily News*. Ironically *The Times*, here bound up as a mummy and marked 'Not edible', has changed hands twice since then.

A 1929 cartoon in *Truth* by Strube showing a slanging match with Rothermere. Beaverbrook is shown with his hands on the wall, apparently impartial. I do not know who the figures in the windows are.

   A variety of 'free gifts' offered by the Rothermere papers is behind him. Top of the pile is 'free meals', ridiculed by Allied Newspapers as connoting soup kitchens and the dole.

   Rothermere had boasted of never closing a paper down. At far left is reference to the Staffordshire *Sunday Sentinel* which had folded after nine months.

THE DIGNITY OF THE PRESS.

Rothermere, right, with his son, Esmond, who succeeded him in control of the *Daily Mail*. Eleven years older than William, he seemed, after his brother, Lord Northcliffe's, death in 1922, to regard the rise of the Berry brothers in newspapers as an insult as much as a challenge.

Opposite A map first published in the *Daily Mail* and *Daily Mirror* showing Rothermere's plans for his evening papers. The first tranche were to be in those cities ringed, except London where he already had the *Evening News*. Of these only Newcastle and Bristol ever got started.

Those cities underlined were to be the second tranche.

A specially taken photograph for William's fiftieth birthday dinner in 1929, given him by the directors and staff of Allied Newspapers at Claridge's Hotel. The occasion was only a fortnight after he had received a peerage: the time, at the height of the battle with Rothermere. His health was proposed by Edward Iliffe.

A studio portrait of Edward Lord Iliffe, who, as Sir Edward Iliffe, knighted for war service, became a partner of William and Gomer in 1922. 'He had many industrial contacts and a high reputation in the City ... Though he lacked William's dash, Iliffe was a good judge of men, of great shrewdness, with a Midas touch.'

After their first meeting, Iliffe became a director and shareholder in all of William's businesses until 1937, including a thirty per cent interest in the *Daily Telegraph*. He was responsible for the 1930 Telegraph building in Fleet Street, now owned by Goldman Sachs.

attached to this departure from precedent. As the meetings were avowedly 'conservative', they cannot have influenced Opposition papers like the *News Chronicle*, the *Daily Herald* or the *Manchester Guardian*.

Already, in late February 1938, Voight is recorded in a Foreign Office minute as complaining that 'under the new regime at the Foreign Office [he] no longer received from official sources material for his anti-German campaign'. From then on there is continuing evidence that Leeper was instructed not to say anything on some new development but to leave it to No. 10 and the lobby correspondents. Finally, at the beginning of August, Gordon Lennox, Voight and Tower sought an interview with Halifax on the subject. He expressed 'sympathetic interest' but nothing was changed – except when Sir Alexander Cadogan was on holiday and Vansittart reintroduced what the correspondents described as 'a cool detached view'.[28]

*　　*　　*

Chamberlain and Halifax's campaign to soothe Hitler's sensitivity came to an abrupt end with the rape of Austria on 11 March 1938, though in the months to come every effort was made to look at the slide to Armageddon through Pangloss' glasses. But the brutality of the SS, let loose for the first time outside their own country, was not to be concealed through any tints. As Churchill was able to sum up in the *Telegraph*:

> It is easy to ruin and persecute the Jews, to steal their private property; to drive them out of every profession and employment; to fling a Rothschild into prison or a sponging house; to compel Jewish ladies to scrub the pavements; and to maroon clusters of helpless refugees on islands in the Danube[29] ... And it is not only the Jews. It is part of the policy of German Nazism to treat with exemplary rigour persons of German race who have not identified themselves with Nazi interests and ambitions.

[28] The *Yorkshire Post* Diplomatic Correspondent, John Tower, wrote to his editor that the Foreign Office was providing 'information necessary for guidance' to four responsible newspapers: *The Times, The Daily Telegraph*, the *Manchester Guardian* and the *Yorkshire Post*. 'There is no desire whatever that the four papers ... should display a false optimism. But the desire is expressed that they will allow the information coming from Germany to reach the public gradually without giving it immediate panic-character.' No attempt was made to discourage 'popular journals' from talking rather more optimistically, 'the explanation ... being that if they were warned off that line they would immediately become sensationally pessimistic and create in advance the very conditions of popular panic upon which the Nazis are known to reckon as one of their weapons'.

[29] Churchill was quoting from a report in the *Telegraph* of 2 April that several hundred Austrian Jews, fleeing across the Danube, had been refused entry to both Czechoslovakia and Hungary. They had been marooned on marshy islands and robbed of all property and valuables.

CHAPTER SEVENTEEN

Appeasement III –
From the *Anschluss* to Berchtesgarten

WILLIAM HAD JUST arrived in South Africa when news of the *Anschluss* came through. He had planned the ten-day visit since early February, partly to see the country and its leaders, partly to let a sea trip (fourteen days each way) give some relief to his gout. One of his feet was severely swollen, enabling only a hobble. As he wrote when the trip ended: 'I left South Africa, as I arrived, on my back ... the trip was seriously interfered with.'

That first weekend he stayed with Sir Abe Bailey. General Smuts, Deputy Leader of the governing United Party, came to dinner on the Saturday night (12 March, the day of the *Anschluss*) and they had 'a long talk'. Smuts viewed the situation 'with gravity, not because of the act but because of the way it had been done. England, he felt, had the duty and the position to be the arbiter and the arbitrator'. As he had urged on the British Government a few months back, if France was not prepared to fight for an Austria which was German in race, 'we should have told Germany our views and made our relations with Germany easier and (potentially) more influential'.[1] He thought Chamberlain was 'a good man' as did Smuts' leader, Herzog, who came to lunch the next day. On the strength of these and other conversations, William was able to send Chamberlain birthday greetings from his home-going ship:

ALL SYMPATHY AND GOOD WISHES ON YOUR GREAT RESPONSIBILITY STOP EVERYONE I SAW IN SOUTH AFRICA FROM PRIME MINISTER DOWN HAS FAITH IN YOU.

For it *was* a great responsibility. All eyes were now turned on Czechoslovakia, whose unfortified southern frontier with Austria was uncovered. Churchill was calling for a Grand Alliance – a Franco-British alliance with all the smaller states of Eastern Europe to be drawn in, at first

---

[1] Smuts also said that Germany had, on the same day as the *Anschluss*, repudiated an agreement he had made personally that the inhabitants of Southwest Africa should owe allegiance to the British Crown.

economically, and later militarily.[2] France already had a treaty obligation
to aid Czechoslovakia if the latter were attacked. Was Britain to be tied
in with an ally weakened by the Maginot concept who had refused to
act against a far weaker Germany when it occupied the Rhineland two
years earlier, without total mobilisation of France and Britain on land,
on sea and in the air? Was Russia to be drawn in, as she herself
proposed but Churchill still objected to as the 'Bolshevik menace'?[3]

Chamberlain's answer was his first use of what he called 'the guessing
game'.[4] In the debate on Czechoslovakia 24 March 1938, he cautioned:
'Obligations imply the purpose and power to fulfil them.' Therefore,
our armament programme would be accelerated. But 'If war broke out,
it would be unlikely to be confined to those who have assumed such
obligations.' It was to a forecast of the speech that William wirelessed
to the office:

BELIEVE ASSUMED DECISION WILL SATISFY DOMINIONS WHICH
ALMOST VITAL STOP TO UNDERTAKE POSITIVE COMMITMENT MEANS
ALSO TIE UP WITH PARIS DIPLOMACY AND UNKNOWN STALIN
STOP THESE MY THOUGHTS BUT KNOWLEDGE INSUFFICIENT TO
DOGMATISE NEAR EQUATOR ...

As soon as he hobbled off the boat on 1 April, William found waiting
for him a letter, of which he had been warned while still at sea. It was
from Churchill, offering him a fortnightly article for the *Telegraph*. This
had been carried for the last two years at £70[5] a time by Beaverbrook's
Evening Standard but, on the day of Churchill's Grand Alliance speech,
had been terminated, as 'Your views on foreign affairs and the part
which this country should play are entirely opposed to those held by
us.'

William immediately accepted the offer as an 'experiment for six
months ... if the period were longer our policies might well be at serious
variance'. In fact, the 'experiment' (Churchill recognised it 'could not
continue indefinitely') was extended to fourteen months, ending in May

---

[2] Garvin, in the *Observer*, was his most scathing critic. 'What we are really asked to guarantee is
the racial ascendancy of the Czech minority over the rest ... Call the League together and see what
happens. Not a quarter of it will agree now to stake themselves in arms for Czech domination.'
Garvin warned against Churchill's 'gorgeous sophistry and air-rapt visions'.

[3] Chamberlain was of the same view for a different reason. He had written to his sisters, 'The
Russians are stealthily and cunningly pulling all the strings to get us involved in war with Germany
(our Secret Service doesn't spend all its time looking out of the window) ...'

[4] The phrase had been coined by Eden during the Baldwin regime, when he declared in November
1936: 'Nations cannot be expected to incur automatic obligations save for areas where their vital
interests are involved.'

[5] Plus £140–150 from syndication.

1939, when the articles were transferred to the *Daily Mirror* at the time the *Telegraph* was starting to campaign for Churchill's inclusion in the government, suggesting that the *Mirror* offered more money.[6]

Picking up the threads, William first saw Churchill, then Vansittart and finally Chamberlain himself.

In Vansittart, who seemed, with William, to keep his 'fizzing epigrams' to himself, he found some hope still left. Unlike Smuts, Vansittart felt it would be 'fatal to our prestige' to make approaches to Germany. 'Events have proved that any approach to them is hopeless and only tends to deepen their conviction that we are becoming afraid of their might':[7]

On the other hand, he is convinced that Germany is bluffing very hard, that she is not at all ready for war on a big scale, that there was a good deal of trouble with their motor equipment in the descent on Austria, and that their raw materials are still scarce.[8] All depends on the way in which the people in this country are kept informed of the seriousness of the position and the way in which our rearmament programme is achieved.

I have already quoted from the interview William had with Chamberlain on 26 April,[9] six weeks after the *Anschluss* (at William's house, 25 St James's Place, presumably because of his foot). Chamberlain was perhaps less than frank about rearmament in the air. While agreeing that 'the Air question was the most important matter in the country at the present time', he had given the impression that current deficiencies 'had only recently come to his knowledge'. We now know that, since 12 March, no fewer than four cabinets had discussed the matter and

[6] In his letter signalling the end of the *Telegraph* contract, Churchill wrote to William: 'I hope you have been satisfied with the character of the articles. Alas, they have mostly only proved too true.'

[7] Vansittart did not refer to it but he had no doubt seen Henderson's despatch on his fruitless pre-*Anschluss* interview with Hitler. Henderson had reported: 'He inveighed vigorously against the intrigues of the Press, the meddling of bishops and the iniquities of Bolshevism ... Germany would allow no one to interfere in the settlement of her relationship with "countries ... with large German populations".'

[8] At this time there was much evidence of Germany's 'Guns not Butter' policy having resulted in a shortage of foreign exchange. The word *'ersatz'* (substitute) has now passed into our own language. There were many bad jokes about German army units having to shelter in doorways during rain storms, otherwise their uniforms would fall to pieces. The known shortages led to an exaggerated evaluation of blockade in the event of war.

[9] See Chapter 15, p. 213.

that the Cabinet Committee of Chamberlain, Simon, Inskip[10] and Swinton was to recommend the very next day an accelerated programme. But it was not to include compulsory double-shift working and 'dilution of labour', which the air staff considered essential. This had already been turned down by an earlier cabinet, with only Duff Cooper dissenting. It would make trouble with the trade unions, who 'might demand that the Government should undertake to use the arms in support of Czechoslovakia or insist on the question being dealt with by the League of Nations'. (The history of the time is curious in the enormous importance credited to the trade unions while the Labour Party was treated with disdain. For instance, during the Abdication crisis, Baldwin had only a short interview with Attlee, among others, whereas he had asked Sir Walter Citrine, the thirty-five-year-old General Secretary of the TUC, to lunch at Chequers alone and had spent the whole afternoon with him.)

Such obfuscation, of course, made the task of the Press as watchdog next to impossible. The Press, even in confidence, had been given no figures of what increased expenditure would produce in terms of numbers. Even the Government did not know. At its meeting of 29 April, the Cabinet authorised the Air Ministry to negotiate with individual firms to produce 'as many aeroplanes as they could'. It was hoped to produce 12,000 aircraft of all types, with first-line strength of 2,373 but only if expenditure did not exceed the authorised upper limit of £1,650 million over five years. All this did not help to explain to readers, in Vansittart's words, 'the way in which our rearmament programme is achieved'. For the time being Chamberlain had to be taken on trust.

The other major subject discussed was Czechoslovakia. The trouble, Chamberlain said, was that until the coming of Hitler there had been 'unfair and unwise treatment of the German minority' (rather like the treatment, he might have said, of the Roman Catholic minority in Northern Ireland under Stormont). 'He has advised the Czechoslovakian authorities to leave no possible loophole for any real complaint on the part of Hitler. He does not place any reliance on Russia.

'He feels the Germans would be very reluctant to do anything which they felt with any degree of certainty would bring us into the picture.' He based this opinion partly on his reading of the German action in Austria. Chamberlain was persuaded that the invasion was decided on a whim, without consultation. 'The ultimatum was only decided at the

---

[10] Sir Thomas Inskip, Attorney-General, had been appointed to the new post of Minister for the Coordination of Defence in 1936, immediately following the remilitarisation of the Rhineland. Unlike a Defence Ministry, which had been expected and for which Churchill had hoped, the new minister had only an advisory role.

very last moment by Hitler himself under the excitement of the crowd outside the hotel in Linz.'

A week after Austria, Chamberlain had written to his sister on 20 March:

> I have abandoned my idea of giving guarantees to Czechoslovakia or to France in connection with her obligation ... My plan is to say to Hitler: action over Austria makes it impossible to talk colonies. Tell us exactly what you want in Czechoslovakia ... If reasonable we will urge it on the Czechs ... Then I might be willing to join in some joint guarantee with Germany over Czechoslovakia.

To put the ball into the German court might have been a good business plan but the Foreign Office was given no instructions on it. A month later, on 22 April, Cadogan confided to his diary that that was what he had been advocating for two years but, 'I appear to be the only one thinking along these lines.' When the French came to London on 29 April demanding the 'grand alliance' and staff talks, Cadogan persuaded Chamberlain, Halifax and Vansittart to adopt his plan, selling it with the phrase: 'German demands, like mushrooms, grow in the dark – they are always higher next week.' The French were delighted and, at last, on 3 May, six weeks after Chamberlain had thought the plan his own, Henderson was instructed to act.

It was far too late. Hitler had, as usual, outsmarted the West. Germany would make no demands at all: all the demanding must come from the German minority, apparently independent of the German state. Germany would only act if the minority's own patience was exhausted or, preferably, if the Czech government was responsible for some atrocity.

Meanwhile, President Benes had not been idle. Whether or not influenced by French and British prodding, he produced a draft National Minorities Statute intended to meet all Sudeten (German minority in southern Czechoslovakia) grievances. On 28 March, Konrad Henlein, an earnest young ex-gymnastics instructor, leader of the largest Sudeten party, supposedly independent, was summoned to Berlin and given his instructions. These, in brief, were to negotiate with the Czech government but never to make an agreement: 'Do not be satisfied with any compromise agreement.' Meanwhile, he was to report to the German minister in Prague for any further instructions – ironic, since one German plan provided for the minister's assassination in order to make an 'incident'. (A later plan provided for Henlein's own 'assassination'.)

On his return Henlein dutifully rejected the draft Czech statute and promulgated his own eight-point 'Karlsbad Programme'. In effect, the

Programme envisaged a totalitarian German province, including one million Czechs, inside Czechoslovakia (the Czechs to be responsible for defence but not police) with a rider for a revision of Czech foreign policy (i.e., abandonment of its treaties with France and Russia).

Thus, when Henderson at last asked Ribbentrop (now German Foreign Minister) for details of German demands, the latter was able to reply smoothly that Karlsbad seemed a reasonable basis for internal discussion. Pushing his luck, Ribbentrop arranged, through Vansittart of all people, for Henlein to be invited to London. Though, as a matter of protocol, he could not see ministers, there he was able to persuade the Foreign Office and even Churchill (who gave him lunch at his house) that he was genuinely independent,[11] so much so that Cadogan could not tell Henlein 'to come off his eight points altogether' as Berlin would 'think we are double-crossing them'. The Czech government naturally rejected Karlsbad but the French and British governments both pressed President Benes to go as far as he could.

Meanwhile, Hitler overplayed his hand. Goebbels turned on the full power of his propaganda machine, alleging the usual atrocities, culminating in German 'spring manoeuvres' with four motorised divisions on the Czech border.

It seemed evident that Hitler, though not yet ready for a contested operation, thought he could motor into Czechoslovakia without opposition. The Czechs 'partially mobilised', the French government, now resolute, said they would march if a single German soldier crossed the border, and Halifax gave the German chargé d'affaires the usual 'guessing game' threat of, 'It would be impossible to say we should not be drawn in.' Russia announced she would stand by France and Czechoslovakia in compliance with treaty obligations. Hitler withdrew in a rage, and Chamberlain wrote to his sister a month later that Hitler had 'missed the bus'.[12] In case the Press might draw a lesson of 'standing up to the dictators', Halifax saw the diplomatic correspondents and urged their papers 'to adopt a moderate line'.

Indeed, instead of claiming a 'famous victory', Chamberlain and Bonnet (who had become French Foreign Minister only in April) seemed to have had a genuine fright. Perhaps Germany had not really intended an invasion and they had been stampeded by Czech propaganda into the most fearful risks, which their general staffs were agreed they

[11] According to Harold Nicolson, who gave a small tea party of MPs for him, Henlein did not believe in Nazi 'anti-God and anti-Semitic measures'. In 1939, Hitler made him *Gauleiter* of the Sudetengau, where his atrocities were as bad as any of his tin-pot colleagues.

[12] This was his first recorded use of the term. The second, inexplicably, was after Munich and the third, which came back to haunt him in 1940, was after the late arrival of the Germans in Norway.

should not have taken. Both governments now put renewed pressure on President Benes, the French government going so far as to say that if Benes were 'unreasonable [it] might well declare that France considers herself released from her bond'. It seems never to have occurred to the British government that Henlein was really Hitler's puppet (he had been on the German Foreign Office payroll since 1937 and in the same year had written to Hitler suggesting he should take over the whole of Bohemia), even when he gave a highly indiscreet interview to Rothermere's roving correspondent, G. Ward Price.

He said there were three choices to the solution of the Sudetenland:

1. Give the Sudetens all they wanted
2. A plebiscite on secession
3. Simpler still – war

Report of the interview was banned in the German Press and in the German-language papers of Czechoslovakia. Even so, until a fortnight before Munich, the Foreign Office was still treating Henlein as an independent, and leading the British press to make the same assumption.

From 'the coup that wasn't' of 21 May, Henlein's 'negotiations' continued in Prague during the whole of June and July. First Benes was pressured into accepting Karlsbad as a basis for negotiation. At the beginning of July, Henlein put it out in London that the Czechs were being 'deliberately dilatory'. Benes, he said, was not taking pressure from Britain and France seriously: 'He thought he could fool them.'

Halifax was taken in. On 14 July he instructed the British Ambassador in Prague that, if Henlein's report was correct, he should warn Benes that 'British public opinion would not think a plebiscite an unreasonable request'. No inkling of this got to the ears of the Press except to Geoffrey Dawson at *The Times*.

Chamberlain, seeking to break what to him looked like deadlock, now proposed to Paris that an Anglo-French arbitrator be sent to Prague. The French pointed out that this would put Benes in an impossible position – if he refused he would be branded as intransigent; if he accepted, he would be bound to accept the arbitrator's finding in advance. The title 'arbitrator' was therefore withdrawn; a 'mediator' was substituted in the shape of Lord Runciman (whom Chamberlain had described to William in the previous year as, 'a weak head of a department'). Benes objected strongly and only accepted when he was told that otherwise Britain would disinterest herself in Czech affairs.

At the same time, Goering arranged that Hitler's adjutant, Captain Wiedermann (he had also been adjutant of Hitler's battalion during the Great War), should visit London. The ostensible purpose of the visit was to sound out whether Goering himself would be received in London as an extra-special ambassador. (Halifax, who had described him during his German visit as 'a mixture of the Duke of Devonshire, his head gamekeeper and Al Capone, all topped off with a schoolboy', even envisaged that he might shoot with the King at Sandringham.)

After conferring with Chamberlain and Horace Wilson, Halifax (with Cadogan as interpreter) saw him at his house. Wiedermann seemed to give the assurance that Germany would take no aggressive action in Czechoslovakia, providing there were no 'incidents' for six months or a year. Halifax pointed out that, in the pursuit of a peaceful solution, such incidents (which were being blown up by the German Press most days of the week) should be taken in their stride, as Britain had taken the bombing and sinking of red-ensign merchant ships off the Spanish coast. Chamberlain made the same point to the German ambassador next day, saying that 'not even 500 Sudeten deaths' should form a *casus belli*.

At the close of the parliamentary session, Chamberlain told the House of Commons on 26 July that Britain was not 'hustling' Benes, that the latter had asked for the mediator and that there was a general relaxation of tension. 'We have been very happy to receive assurances,' he said, 'from the German government of their own desire for a peaceful solution of the Czechoslovakian dispute.' The first two statements were flat lies, while the last was fanciful. Ever since Austria there had been feverish activity on the Siegfried Line fully visible from the French bank (10,000 men working round the clock with arc-lights at night – £750 million had been spent by the end of the next month) and there were already 1.5 million men under arms. The Press was given guidance that they were conducting 'the usual peace-time manoeuvres'.

The following day Chamberlain saw William and gave him the same 'sunny-Jim' story for which William, like the House of Commons, seems to have fallen. Chamberlain repeated what he had told the German ambassador about his 500 Sudetens and believed that Kingsley Wood was making a great success on the Air about which they had talked so much at their April meeting. He was highly criticial of Hore-Belisha at the War Office who 'was in a highly nervous state and incapable of tackling any serious problems', and said, without withdrawing the canard of Benes' 'invitation', that the calling-in of Runciman was his own idea.

William seems to have accepted all this, but waited to make his own contribution and with such tact that Chamberlain was able to minimise its importance. To effect faster and more balanced rearmament, William had caused the *Telegraph* to call for a Ministry of Supply in May 1938 (and was to do so again after Munich). Chamberlain never said so, but it was clearly his bad relations with the Opposition that made it impracticable. Such a ministry, he thought, would have needed some compulsory powers which the trade unions, without a broader-based government, would have resisted with all their might. Chamberlain did see the TUC leaders but nothing emerged from the conversations.

I told the PM that I thought he had had a very successful Session, and that the only flaw in it was that the Opposition seemed to be antagonistic to him personally. I suggested that he could remove this very easily if he chose to do so. He admitted with a smile that he had been rather hard on the Opposition, but claimed that it was very difficult for a man of his temperament to refrain from giving them some of their own medicine. He admitted, however, that it might be wise for him to handle them a little differently, and believed that he could get across to the back benches, particularly the trade union people, without kowtowing to the front bench, whom he regarded as dangerous in the extreme. He admitted also that other people had said the same thing to him, and claimed that he gave one sop to the Socialists in his speech on Tuesday.

William may not have known the full background, but was certainly aware that there had for some months been murmuring against Chamberlain's rigid right-wing, seemingly arrogant, stance. According to Keith Feiling, Chamberlain's biographer, 'He realised it was inevitable that he should lose some of Baldwin's liberal support, but he hoped to recoup it by energising his own party.' Almost the first to realise the fact was Baldwin himself. He had been shaken by Eden's resignation. Though Eden's resignation speech had been so diffuse that few could grasp the principles at stake, Baldwin felt that he represented the main link of a *national* government. He was horrified by the one-man leadership now becoming evident – conducting the Government on pure Tory Party lines and destroying its national character he regarded as his life's work. 'All my work to keep politics national, instead of party, undone.'

After his resignation, Eden had left for a prolonged holiday in the South of France. There he saw a lot of his old chief, Baldwin. Baldwin, now well informed of the political atmosphere at home, began feeding the Editor of the *Yorkshire Post*, Arthur Mann, through a third party, with anti-Chamberlain propaganda. Even in the dark days of 1930 Baldwin's support had been staunch in the North, while Eden's father-in-law, Gervaise Beckett, had persuaded Mann to accept the editorship in 1919. Eden himself had worked briefly on the paper and retained a friendship with the Editor. From this time, the *Yorkshire Post* became consistently anti-Chamberlain (temporarily modified at the moment of Munich, on his chairman's[13] appeal), as much on the personal as on the anti-appeasement tack.

Eden himself, while not criticising Chamberlain until after Munich, began to make speeches on internal – as opposed to foreign – affairs. Horrified by the reactionary views of backbenchers, his text was that the Tory Party must be progressive or succumb. How else, the inference was, could the Tories get working-class support for rearmament?

Chamberlain, as his remarks to William made clear, had been aware of his unpopularity, except with the broad Tory mass of silent back benches, for some time. He had got Horace Wilson who, after all, was Baldwin's protégé, to ask the latter to make a speech in support, 'as he was having such difficulty'. Baldwin had replied that 'he could hardly believe any speech from him was necessary in view of the powerful support they were getting from Lord Beaverbrook'.[14]

As to his earlier remarks in his talk with William, Chamberlain had not been trying to deceive when he said that the Czech crisis had calmed down, though he did not repeat his phrase that 'Hitler had missed the bus.' He genuinely believed that Runciman would come up with a plan to save every face. A fortnight later Halifax wrote to Henderson that 'a large part of German policy might be bluff or fear'. It was not until the middle of August that the awful realisation dawned. Henlein was not negotiating at all. His minions had been talking endlessly to Benes. Now they rejected, without any counter-suggestions, three plans, each more submissive than the last. Finally, Benes summoned the Sudeten leaders, gave them his pen, told them to write their own terms and he would accede to them in advance. When they proved dumbfounded, he wrote them down to their own dictation. 'My God,' cried one, 'he has given us everything!'

Henlein's answer was to move to Germany while Goebbels whipped up the German press and radio: every disturbance, however trivial, was an 'atrocity'. At last it was clear. Henlein was just Hitler's puppet. The progressive stages of ineffective negotiation were just the backdrop to Hitler's forthcoming tirade at the Nuremberg Rally.

No inkling of this seems to have reached the Press. At the *Telegraph* it was still assumed in mid-September, as they had been assured in May,

[13] The chairman, following Gervaise's death in 1937, was now his younger brother, Rupert Beckett.
[14] The above information is derived from Oliver Harvey's diaries. Harvey, post-war Ambassador in Paris, had been Private Secretary to Eden. Though he transferred to Halifax when Eden resigned, his first loyalty was to Eden, whom he regarded as 'the one man who commands the sympathy of the Left and could lead an All-Party team'.

that Henlein was his own man and might even be out of tune with Hitler.

The Times now published what has been called the most disastrous leading article ever printed. Whereas Henlein 'had always maintained that he only demands full rights within the framework of the Czechoslovak Republic', even Hitler had not yet demanded what was now suggested: that 'the Sudeten fringe' be ceded to Germany, 'thereby making Czechoslovakia "a more homogeneous state"'. It was disastrous because *The Times* had for long been regarded at home and abroad as the voice of the Foreign Office. It produced strong reactions in Prague and Berlin. The Foreign Office immediately denounced the idea, but it soon became known that Halifax himself by no means deplored it. In Geneva, where a Foreign Office team had gathered on League affairs, the diarist Chips Channon heard that Halifax had dined with Dawson two nights before.[15]

The Times then wrote in a similar vein the next day. When William's son, Seymour, saw Halifax a week afterwards, he 'did not react one way or the other'.

During 'these awful days' (to use Cadogan's expression) of early September, no inkling of crisis was given to the Press. It was suggested in the Foreign Office that a statement should be made endorsing Benes' plan, but the idea was rejected after strong representation from Henderson, and Newton in Prague. Similarly, an intended warning to Hitler, leaked to the *Daily Mail* and picked up by the *Telegraph* in late editions, was withdrawn on Henderson's objection and the notion officially denied by the Foreign Office. On the urging of Churchill and Eden, and after consultation with leaders of the Opposition, Halifax persuaded Chamberlain to issue a statement to the Press on 11 September, the day before Hitler's speech at the Nuremberg Rally: 'Germany cannot with impunity carry out a rapid and successful military campaign against Czechoslovakia without fear of intervention by France and by Great Britain.'

Bonnet, French Foreign Minister, immediately had all French diplomatic correspondents advised to minimise the importance of Chamberlain's statement. He had good reason. All summer it had been Foreign Office policy to maximise to Germany Britain's resolution but to minimise it to Paris and Prague. And when, the day after, Bonnet asked Halifax bluntly whether Britain would march with France, Halifax fell

---

[15] This may not have been true. Dawson, in his diary, recorded: 'The Foreign Office went through the roof – not so, however, the Foreign Secretary, who came and lunched with me at the Travellers, and had a long talk.'

back upon his usual verbiage of 'hypothetical circumstances'.

This was the moment at which the crisis entered its final phase. It was also a most unfortunate moment for William. He had never entirely thrown off his fits of gout. Through Professor Lindemann there now appeared at his service a doctor recently escaped from Vienna, claiming to have perfected a cure. The cure, however, had not been field-tested – as it would be nowadays – so that it was not known whether it had side-effects. Nor was the doctor aware that William had twice had attacks of jaundice. The result was catastrophic. For twenty-four hours William was in delirium, half his liver was destroyed, and he was found to have become permanently diabetic.

As such, he was for some weeks physically weakened while his correct dose of insulin could be determined, but his mind was not affected. Reading was no difficulty and it had been said that he was born with a telephone in his hand – but it could only be used from his bedroom at Hackwood, fifty miles from London.

Chamberlain's statement of 11 September had seemed to indicate a resolute British stance, but now it had been announced he was to fly to meet Hitler[16] face to face (in those days heads of government very rarely met and an air journey for a sixty-nine-year-old who had never flown before was a most daring escapade). Evidently some radical reassessment was in the wind. William therefore asked his twenty-nine-year-old son, Seymour, who had been some six years on the paper and had often acted in the proprietorial role in his father's absence, to see Halifax.

Seymour also had the advantage of being friendly with two of the younger and more robust Cabinet members, Duff Cooper and Oliver Stanley. The interview was at 7 pm on 15 September 1938. Chamberlain was at that moment at Berchtesgarten. It was the day the attitude of the democracies fatally changed. Before it they were prepared to back the Benes plan – autonomy of the Sudetenland within Czechoslovak boundaries. After that day they became committed to its incorporation in the German Reich.

---

[16] The flight had been announced at 9 pm on 14 September though Dawson had been told of it in the afternoon by Halifax. According to Chamberlain's letter to his sister, 'It was so unconventional and daring that it rather took Halifax's breath away.'

CHAPTER EIGHTEEN

Appeasement IV –
Munich and the Press

HALIFAX'S WORDS TO Seymour were an accurate forecast of what actually happened. In his own, cynical way he enlarged on what he had conceded to Hitler in November 1937 and this time brought in the irresolute French government to emphasise its inevitability. (The text of the interview is given in Appendix A to this chapter, pp. 257–8.)

Seymour had started by repeating the rumours of French defeatism and backsliding. They were contrary to reports from the *Telegraph*'s Paris correspondent. The latter's information, which turned out to be correct, was that there was a strong Resistance element in the French Cabinet and that the feeling in the country was at least resigned.[1] However, Halifax was able to evince the effect on French morale of a recent report by the American Colonel Lindbergh, reinforced, though he did not say so, by the chief of the French air staff, on the immense superiority of the German air force. Meanwhile, Bonnet had discovered that there were no civilian gas masks in France.

On the prospects for Berchtesgarten, Halifax was despondent. He rightly thought Chamberlain would have little chance of getting Hitler to accept 'autonomy' and that he would instead insist on transfer of territory through plebiscites, in spite of all the difficulties of mixed populations.

Halifax could not, of course, describe the mood of Berchtesgarten, as Chamberlain was still there, but the *Telegraph* leader next day in no way reflected his fatalism. It did not even mention the possibility of plebiscites, or the carve-up of a sovereign state. Instead, it presumed that Chamberlain would maintain the 11 September declaration. The 'supreme merit' of Chamberlain's visit, it considered, was that there was 'no room for doubt in any quarter as to the attitude of the Government and people of this country towards the use of force ... the mission gave

---

[1] Cadogan, not trusting Sir Eric Phipps, British Ambassador, later instructed him to obtain evaluations of French opinion from all British consuls and to have them sent direct to London so that they could not be 'doctored' in Paris (Oliver Harvey's expression).

Herr Hitler the opportunity to consider the advantages of a course of moderation. No man could have done more.' Meanwhile, it called for an armistice not only in the Sudetenland, but also of German propaganda and in the mobilisation of troops.

It was a feature of the Munich crisis that the Press was kept so long in the dark. From Chamberlain's return on 16 September to 26 September when Hitler's 'memorandum' (Chamberlain called it an ultimatum) at Godesberg was published, no account of to-and-fro was released. Rumours, of course, abounded but, as a *Telegraph* leading article reported, 'The velocity of events is such that it is hardly possible to know at one moment what the next may bring.'

Even the British Cabinet was starved of immediate information. It was usually called only to hear the decisions of the Inner Cabinet (Chamberlain, Halifax and the two ex-Foreign Secretaries, Simon and Hoare), grandly named by Hoare as 'the Big Four' (usually joined by Wilson, Vansittart and Cadogan). By what channels I have been unable to discover, there was by now considerable pressure by the Press for information. Hoare states in his Notes that 'as a result of F.O. Press Department' (this can be taken as reference to the muzzling of Leeper's department by Chamberlain), he was deputed to brief the Press at the suggestion, though Hoare does not say so, of Beaverbrook, the arch isolationist, who had Hoare, literally, financially, in his pocket. Beaverbrook assured the Prime Minister that 'given guidance ... the newspapers of the right and left will go with you in your decisions'. It was not difficult to imagine the unctuous tone of the 'information' Hoare might impart. From his own notes it seems that his whole intention was to induce calm and fatalism.

In William's absence, it fell to Seymour again to represent the *Telegraph*, on Sunday 18 September, when the Big Four, together with Daladier, the French Prime Minister, and Bonnet, were discussing the Berchtesgarten demand at Downing Street. He found Hoare finishing dinner with Sir Philip Sassoon,[2] and was allowed fifteen minutes over coffee before driving back to the conference with him.

Seymour was given the now familiar propaganda about Czech maltreatment of the Sudetens in the past; the weakness, both political and military, of the French, and the yearning of the British people for peace. As the basis for a leader Hoare suggested 'three points could be usefully emphasised':

1. Chamberlain should be regarded as the only man who can check Hitler. He had made a great impression on him. Hitler had stated

[2] First Commissioner of Works, what would now be called Environment Minister.

249

frequently that he wanted none but Germans in the Reich. But for the interview, there would have been war last week.
2. The British must not be thought to have influenced France.
3. The importance of a peaceful solution.

The one positive statement was that 'we should, of course, be stronger in a military sense in the future'.

What Hoare told Seymour he had no doubt just been telling, though in more detail, in the same way to his host, Sir Philip Sassoon. Oliver Harvey wrote in his diary the same day: 'AE [Eden] had just heard all about the meetings from Philip Sassoon who had had Sam Hoare dining with him. Sam had been in his smuggest and most complacent mood . . .'

The *Telegraph* next day reflected none of this. It remarked acidly that the 'Anglo-French plan' (not published, but in fact a recommendation to Benes to accept Hitler's Berchtesgarten demands, together with a French-suggested Anglo-French guarantee of the Czechoslovakian rump, which would at least commit Britain irrevocably to abandonment of the 'guessing game'), 'does not imply that it is acceptable either to Germany or to the Czechs'. The leader went on to devote half its space to the stream of vicious propaganda issuing from Germany, 'as grave an impediment to the cause of peace as the original dispute itself'.

As the week progressed the *Telegraph* grew more and more exasperated at increasing German demands – 'a far cry from what Germany was demanding only a week ago'. The Czechs must have 'definite assurance not only of their military security but of their political, economic and cultural independence'. 'There is talk of separating Slovakia', and of break-off of Hungarian and Polish areas. 'If so, it is no settlement at all.'

On Thursday 22 September, Seymour saw Hoare for a second time, now with the Editor, Arthur Watson. Their object was to find out what Chamberlain expected to get from his second visit to Hitler, at Godesberg, whither he had departed that morning. The ostensible object was to convey Anglo-French acquiescence to the Berchtesgarten demands and to agree methods of implementing them. Hoare was now a little less defeatist. Godesberg was the final test of Hitler's good faith. If he only wanted the Sudeten areas, then there were no means of stopping him, though Chamberlain would insist on certain undefined conditions. Thereafter Britain would be morally committed to a guarantee of the dismembered state, joined by France, Germany and Russia. However, the guarantee would not be operative unless all four agreed to its implementation.

Of the outcome at Godesberg, 'he was neither optimistic nor pessimistic; but if Hitler proved sincere it might be the basis of a European settlement which could include the discussion of all outstanding grievances'. (The text of the interview is given in Appendix B to this chapter, pp. 259–60.)

The *Telegraph* next day (23 September), conceded that 'all we know for certain is that ... the discussions will open on the basis of the Czech surrender of the Sudeten lands. What remains to be determined is the contribution Herr Hitler will make ... in return for this tremendous concession. If that contribution is to satisfy the anxious expectations of Europe it will need to be of very substantial dimensions.'

At 10 pm the same evening Halifax, having been given a summary of what further demands Hitler was now making, cabled Chamberlain in Godesberg: 'Public opinion as expressed in Press and elsewhere mistrustful of our plan but perhaps prepared to accept it with reluctance as an alternative to war. Great mass of opinion seems to be hardening that it is up to the Chancellor to make some contribution.'

The reference here to the Press must, I think, refer to the *Telegraph* and the *News Chronicle*, though the latter, which had been consistently anti-appeasement, but also anti-rearmament, was soon to be muzzled by its Editor-in-Chief, Sir Walter Layton, who had several times seen Hoare.

On this day, Seymour was called up to join his territorial anti-aircraft battery. Thereafter Arthur Watson, though he left no written notes, must have represented the *Telegraph* alone to receive Hoare's briefings. Hoare recorded in his notes[3] that he was seeing 'the big Press men'. 'Camrose ill with jaundice.' 'Snow White and the 7 dwarfs' (this was a reference to the recently enobled Lord Southwood, publisher of the *Daily Herald*), 'Max' (Beaverbrook). The date of this entry was the second day of the Cabinet's deliberation on the Godesberg's ultimatum, which demanded much greater cession of territory and populations than had been embodied in the Berchtesgarten proposals.

Hoare was one of those who backed Chamberlain in recommending acceptance[4] (going back on what he had told Seymour). It must have been the Godesberg issue which caused Oliver Harvey to write in his diary of 'the disastrous effect Sam Hoare had had on Camrose when he tried to swing him during the [Munich] crisis'. From that time on, William had detested Hoare. He once sprained his ankle turning sharply

---

[3] Hoare's notes appear to have been written some time after the events described. They seem to be paragraph headings for a full subsequent account.

[4] Andrew Roberts, *The Holy Fox*. Hoare's 'notes' record the opposite.

to avoid him as he saw him precede him to Grillon's dining club, and returned home. He had always disliked Hoare. While recognising his ability as an administrator, he could not abide his mincing speech, too-obvious ambition and craving for publicity.[5]

Hoare put immense application into anything he tried. Without overmuch talent he made himself a good tennis player and ice-skater. Edward Iliffe had once recorded in his diary a professional skating exhibition before which Hoare, as a guest, had insisted on doing a circuit of his own.

The rest of the story up till the Munich agreement on 29 and 30 September is soon told.

When Chamberlain, overborne by Halifax and half the Cabinet, persuaded by the French and a now-confident General Gamelin (the half-completed Siegfried Line will be like marmalade, he said), at last issued a firm statement: 'The transfer of Sudeten areas is already conceded but if there is a German attack France will come to Czech assistance and the United Kingdom and Russia [this was the only reference to Russia throughout the crisis] will certainly stand by France', the *Telegraph* was emphatic, now, that Hitler's demands had at last been published:

> [Mr Chamberlain's explanation] elevates the whole question from a category of a mere local dispute in which the British Empire could have no direct concern to one of basic principle from which it would be impossible to hold aloof ... Study of Hitler's map shows a new Czechoslovakia where the state is cut in two by a narrow and untenable frontier at the centre, for the purpose of a German stranglehold going far beyond the rectification of Sudeten grievances ... Hitler's interest is the destruction of a state whose bare existence is a stumbling block to his dreams of paramountcy from the Rhine to the Black Sea – and beyond.

It is nowadays represented that the Munich agreement was a capitulation to all Hitler's demands. A comparison of the Godesberg and Munich maps shows very considerable difference. Whereas Godesberg was as described above, the Munich territorial cessions were very much reduced and were, moreover, to be made over ten days rather than one. Nevertheless, the *Telegraph* observed:

---

[5] Owing to their previous closeness, William may have heard the story from Beverley Baxter, 'Atticus' of the *Sunday Times*, of Hoare's approach to the latter in 1937. He had tried to persuade Baxter that Eden, as Foreign Secretary, was worn out and that he, Hoare, was ready to take the job on again.

If we could accept [Hitler's promises] that latest territorial demands in Europe were at an end ... the declaration would not survive a repetition of the policy of threats and 'surprises' which has just brought all Europe to the verge of a general conflagration.

No one could then foretell that the British and French ambassadors to Germany, now nominated as Allied administrators of the territorial arrangements, would be so out-manoeuvred as to yield back unprotestingly all those cessions cancelled at Munich and to acquiesce in a final solution (as described in the next chapter) far worse than Godesberg itself.

*　　*　　*

Chamberlain, on his return from Munich, had claimed 'Peace with Honour'. In the debate that followed he descanted on 'the real triumph': it had shown that four great powers could agree on 'a difficult and delicate operation by discussion instead of force [averting] a catastrophe which would have ended civilisation as we know it'. Now that 'the most dangerous' threat had been removed, further progress must be made 'in the removal of ... suspicions and animosities'. Meanwhile, 'deficiencies ... in our armaments' must be filled up until the removal of hostility between nations enabled them to 'feel that they can safely discard their weapons, one by one'.

This was what the frightened backbenchers – Churchill called them 'this over-whipped crowd of poor whites' – wanted to hear. They had not after all, it seemed, been craven. They had known all along that the Germans, though a little excitable, were a civilised race whose wild talk had been no more than bluff, now called. The snarling, guttersnipe language of Hitler, Goering and Goebbels was just part of the act. A little more money on armaments, even though money *was* tight in a new depression, and all would be well. Meanwhile, their Prime Minister had promised to devote 'what energy and time may be left to me before I hand over office to younger men'.

This preposterous scenario is not what the men of Munich remembered in later years. They justified their support of Chamberlain with the assumption that Britain was too weak to go to war in 1938 and that the achievement of the Munich surrender was that another year gave us the time to catch up, so that, for instance, we could win the Battle of Britain, whereas in 1938 only half the fighter squadrons were equipped with Hurricanes and the Spitfire was not even in service. Certainly Chamberlain himself never used that argument and his letters to his sister in the month after Munich show his attitude more clearly than any of his later speeches:

Oct. 15, 1938.
One of my colleagues and an important one [Halifax] is pressing me to broaden the base at the Cabinet offering to take in Labour and also Anthony ... [but] he is really dead against making terms with dictators ... I fear if he were again a member of the Cabinet he would do what he did before, always agree in theory but always disagree in practice ... I see Labour men forming a group with him ... running fight ... that would soon make my position intolerable.

Oct. 22.
I believe I have convinced everyone that it would not do to invite either Labour or Anthony or Winston to join the Cabinet ... whether we want a Minister of Supply and one of National Service ... it could possibly begin by slowing things down and certainly create a lot of friction and though in the end it might increase output I wonder whether by then we might find that the need was slowing off ... A lot of people seem to me to be losing their heads and talking and thinking as though Munich had made war more instead of less imminent ... The papers are largely responsible for it and I want to try to get them back to the view that though there are gaps to fill up we need not believe that we have got to have huge additions to the programme now being put into operation.

November 6.
I don't believe there is a menace to European peace any longer. I was unable to see the *Sunday Times* men this week and they have a perfectly fantastic article on alleged Air Force programmes. Nothing could be more unfortunate when I am trying to represent that we are only perfecting our defences ... my policy is summed up in the old trinity of Faith, Hope and Charity.

He had quite ignored the fateful message he had received from Baldwin on the evening of his return from Munich: 'You have everything in your own hands now – for a time – and you can do anything you like. Use that time well, for it won't last.' And in the House of Lords four days later, Baldwin had been more specific: 'Class barriers are breaking down in the face of common danger and there should be neither party nor trade union opposition ... Put industry on a war footing: mobilise it tomorrow.'

It was not just this wishful thinking that the *Telegraph* had warned against when the convening of the Munich conference was announced:

It is clear that Hitler was not very earnestly seeking a settlement ... the present respite must be hailed with a certain reserve though it does not diminish the gratitude due to Mr Chamberlain's persistence ... the danger against which [he] must be vigilant is that the Munich conference does not result, a few months hence, in a revival of all the present trouble.

As a curtain-raiser to the Munich debate, the warning was reinforced:

The moral is clear. Failing an immediate agreement on disarmament we must rehash our defensive effort, especially in the air. It has been proved that when sufficiently provoked our nation will rise as one man to make ready its defences. But improvisation at the last moment is utterly inadequate ... the Munich agreement has provided us with a respite. It remains for us not to neglect the chance.

The striking omission from Chamberlain's thinking was any compassion for the victims. Even when war had seemed inevitable after Godesberg, he had only been able to talk of 'a quarrel in a far away country between people of whom we know nothing'. And when he had discussed them with Hitler at their first meeting at Berchtesgarten, he had confided to his diary: 'I said ... on principle I didn't care two hoots whether the Sudetens were in the Reich, or out of it ...'. There was no talk, as in 1914, of 'gallant little Belgium'.

This the *Telegraph* put straight the morning after Chamberlain had spoken in the debate:

It is never to be forgotten that if a war has been averted a great injustice has been suffered by a small and friendly people and there must be a sense of humiliation that we should have had to urge on that nation such proposals ...

The *Telegraph* can thus be excepted from the general verdict of W.W. Hadley, still Editor of the *Sunday Times* under Gomer's control, that 'the free press of this country has never been nearer to complete unity than in the chorus of praise and thanksgiving that followed Munich'. It was certainly true of *The Times*:[6] 'No conqueror returning from a victory on the battlefield has come adorned with nobler laurels.' Rother-

---

[6] During the House of Commons Munich debate, Dawson perpetrated a gross breach of journalistic etiquette. Because he had himself heard Duff Cooper's resignation speech and found it 'not very impressive', he altered the 'sketch' of it by his Lobby Correspondent, Anthony Winn, who had described it as well received. Dawson altered the 'sketch' to describe the speech as a 'damp squib', with a sneering reference to Duff Cooper's opportunity to devote more time to literature, but still kept the by-line 'From our Lobby Correspondent'. Winn resigned and immediately joined *The Daily Telegraph*.

mere, who had at the beginning of the year telegraphed Chamberlain that he had 'instructed my newspapers to lend their full support to the only person who could save the peace', telegraphed again more economically: 'You are wonderful.'[7] The *Daily Mail* leader was accordingly titled 'With Honour'.[8] Beaverbrook triumphantly added to the *Daily Express*'s banner line: 'There will be no European War This Year', a new tag 'or next year either'. The *News Chronicle*'s critical leader by the editor was rewritten on the instructions of Walter Layton (who had seen Hoare four times during the crisis) in the opposite sense. The editor of the *Daily Herald*, whose hitherto resisting diplomatic correspondent had decided in May that the Sudetenland must be given up, was already under instruction from Southwood that 'an anti-Chamberlain line was likely to drive away some public and advertising support'. Now Southwood himself toned down the leading article which the editor had written.

Gomer's *Daily Sketch* sent an instruction to the editor of its Manchester edition to put out a news-bill 'with the most flattering picture of Hitler, headed by the one word "Peace"'. Even Mann of the *Yorkshire Post* was temporarily cowed by his chairman and wrote in praise of Chamberlain's efforts, though 'We have yet to fathom all the consequences.'

On Sunday 2 October only the Cooperative Society's *Reynolds News* denounced Munich. It seems that Garvin, Editor of the *Observer*, would liked to have done the same, even though he had been preaching appeasement throughout the year. With Dawson, Lothian and other members of the Cliveden set, he had been dubbed one of 'the shiver sisters'. Now he praised Chamberlain's statesmanship in print, though telling his notebook of 'hysterical raptures ... a debauch of delusion about things and consequences ... a smokescreen of hypocrisy'. Owing to his consideration for the national interest, 'we have written under the strictest reserve ... comments on many aspects must be rigorously postponed'. His proprietor, Lord Astor, who had lately cured himself of the appeasement bug, observed drily that Garvin's obfuscations in the leading article were at least more realistic than the 'inspired dope in the *Sunday Times*'.

---

[7] President Roosevelt's telegram was even shorter: 'Good man'.

[8] In December 1937, Rothermere had retired from the chairmanship of Associated Newspapers, owners of the *Daily Mail*. He had said that control would now be exercised by his son, Esmond, but at least in 'foreign affairs' he carried on as before.

APPENDIX A TO CHAPTER 18
(MR SEYMOUR BERRY)

———

Notes of Conversation with Lord Halifax at Foreign Office – 7 o'clock, 15 September 1938

I explained that Lord Camrose was ill and had asked me to seek an interview with him.

We had heard surprising rumours about the plebiscite project and that the French, through Bonnet, had sent us a telegram in the previous two or three days, asking us to secure any agreement which would enable them to evade their Treaty obligations to Czecho-Slovakia; I had heard this from a friend in the city, who stated that he had obtained this information the night before at a dinner party at which Lord Halifax was present. I explained that it would be a great help to us if he could tell me anything for guidance as the *Daily Mail* and *Times* line seemed calculated to make it difficult for H.M.G. to maintain their firm attitude.

He said he would be frank and tell me all he knew! For some time (about six months) he had been asking the French Government if they realised the military problems and general obligations of their Czech guarantee. Until recently they had refused to admit that these presented great difficulties; but, in the last two or three days, the Foreign Office had had the most pressing telegrams, urging the necessity of finding a solution that would not involve the French military guarantee. Halifax said that within a few weeks of outbreak of war the English and French would find themselves faced with the complete conquest of Czecho-Slovakia, and that even if they won the war they would not wish to redraw the Czech borders as they are now.

The French had been affected by a report drawn up by Lindbergh, who said that the Germans were greatly superior in air strength and that the French Air Force was in a very bad condition. These messages had come from Bonnet, who was not perhaps a perfect Minister. It might be that Bonnet and/or other members of the French Cabinet would resign, but so far as the British Government were concerned, the foregoing was the attitude of the French Government.

As regards the Czech problem itself, the plebiscite proposition would be very difficult to refute, although there were many objections. Self-determination was the principle on which the British Empire was based, and the Dominions, or at least, their peoples, would be sympathetic to the idea. Were we to go to war to prevent self-determination or were we to acquiesce in this bullying? In any case, he felt that the age-old problem of the two races – the Slav and Teuton – grinding harshly against each other, had constantly resulted in war but had never been solved by war. Indeed, the problem was nearly insoluble. The use of force to alter territorial boundaries was as old as history. No country would give up land except by threat of force or force itself. Therefore changes of this sort (the cession of Sudetenland) should not be unduly lamented because the threat of force had been the cause. Until human nature altered – which it showed no sign of doing – this would appear always to be the habit of things.

The plan for Berchtesgarten was to point out that the plebiscite presented great difficulties ('awfully difficult'), and that Hitler should tell the Henleinists to accept the Carlsbad points and agree to have a plebiscite later. If this were refused – which he thought it probably would be – we should have to try and arrange some kind of plebiscite. It would be very difficult to have a properly conducted one at the moment. Perhaps in outlying districts, where the minorities were balanced, the previous communal vote would count. It might be possible to transfer the population into the predominant Sudeten German areas. The anti-Nazi minorities in Sudetenland would affect public opinion here, and it might be possible to 'opt' them out and to 'opt' in pro-Nazis from outside. (He used a sentence which I thought meant that the whole rearrangement could be said to have the appearance of readjusting the Versailles Treaty).

The Prime Minister's approach to Hitler in a personal conversation might improve the position. He would point out that we did not wish to obstruct Germany's economic rights in East Europe. They had always wanted friendship with the British Empire, and it was not impossible. The general arguments about force, etc. might seem cynical, but he did not feel we should throw the Empire into war on these grounds.

Halifax did not react either way or the other when I mentioned the *Daily Mail* and *The Times* attitude as having been disastrous. I said I thought we should not advocate a plebiscite as that would obviously weaken the Prime Minister's hand. He saw this point but without enthusiasm and said that if the papers here were too firm, this intransigence would be used in France to embarrass the French Government. He instanced the *News Chronicle*.

Notes of Conversation with
Sir Samuel Hoare at Home Office –
12.15, 22 September 1938

Watson and I saw Hoare at the Home Office.

The Prime Minister's second visit to Hitler was the final test of the latter's good faith. He had repeated frequently at the Berchtesgarten interview that he was only interested in the Sudeten Germans ; he did not intend to press his claims towards the others. The Prime Minister's task was to ascertain if Hitler had changed his demands. If so, his sincerity could definitely not be relied upon.

I asked about the conditions on which Chamberlain might be insisting, and instanced *The Times* report today that demobilisation and other measures would be sought. Hoare gave no details of these but inferred that the Prime Minister had a number of considerations which he would present as the occasion arose. At the meeting on Sunday the French – and particularly Bonnet – were panicky.

He admitted we were morally committed and would have a positive commitment for the dismembered State. If the Germans marched now or without a settlement the thought we should be involved. He repeated that the military authorities did not consider that the Sudeten mountain frontier was really defensible, and it would probably only serve to delay the Germans for two or three days. The Germans ought never to have been included in Czecho-Slovakia, and recent events made it obvious that they could not remain in the Czecho-Slovakian state.

Watson asked if a new guarantee, possibly involving France, Germany, Russia and ourselves, would be joint or several. He said it would be a joint guarantee, and did not agree with Watson's suggestion that this would be valueless.

Mussolini seems definitely to have decided to act with Hitler. The Poles and Hungarians had a very bad record in regard to minorities, but would be troublesome. He was sceptical about Russia's assistance. He was neither optimistic nor pessimistic about the outcome of the Godesberg interviews ; but if Hitler proved sincere it might be the basis of a European settlement, which could include the discussion of all outstanding grievances.

CHAPTER NINETEEN

Appeasement V –
From Munich to the War

THE TELEGRAPH'S ATTITUDE to Munich and Chamberlain upset Edward Iliffe, who, with 10 per cent of the ordinary shares, was still a director. 'I suppose,' he wrote to William, 'if I advocated in public my line and the DT took another my association with the paper would become embarrassing and I should have to resign my directorship. That I don't want as I value my association with you.' He advanced the usual defence of his old friend Chamberlain, and put all the blame on Baldwin: 'I should like to see *The Daily Telegraph* a little kinder to Neville, who I believe was right.' William conceded that Chamberlain had inherited only small armaments[1] ('I do agree with you, however, that Baldwin was really the man as much as anybody responsible for our present difficulties, and to many people the annoying part is that Winston Churchill and even Rothermere, were in the right'); but that the subsequent speed of rearmament had been too slow. In particular there was still no Ministry of Supply, first demanded after the crisis of May, which could take special powers to hurry things on and through which we should 'be reaching for the offensive as well as defence'.[2] He summed up: 'I think you have formed a wrong impression of the *Telegraph*'s policy since it criticised the Prime Minister. We criticised him very directly, and since that time have left the matter alone.'

That last sentence epitomised William's concept of how a serious newspaper should be conducted. In the fluidity of action, reaction and interaction, as in the recent crisis, it was right to declare strong views every day. This the *Telegraph* had done from the Berchtesgarten meeting on 16 September down to 7 October, when the four-day Commons debate finished. But it should not be continued into a campaign. The

[1] This was not entirely fair. The decision to triple the strength of the RAF had been taken in August 1935.

[2] This phrase, repeated in the paper, makes a turning point in thinking. Hitherto, the Army had been much more neglected than the Air Force or the Navy. After Godesberg, all that had been promised to France was 150 aircraft and two infantry divisions, leading to the gibe that Britain would 'fight to the last Frenchman'.

crisis period was rounded off with a selection of the 3,000 letters to the editor (against the usual 600 a week). Whereas most of the letters had been anti-Government, 'as far as humanly possible we have kept the scales even'. (This even-headedness did not prevent a 'flurry of letters' to Dawson at *The Times* alleging, according to one, that it 'was so obvious that *The Daily Telegraph* is working to bring down Chamberlain and put in Eden, Duff Cooper and Churchill that he [the reader] had dropped it in favour of *The Times*'.

Neither German actions nor Chamberlain's self-satisfaction made it easy to 'leave the matter alone'. It soon emerged that the machinery devised at Munich to settle the exact boundaries of occupation was totally misconceived. It had been left for the ambassadors of the four powers, plus a representative of the Czech government, to delineate them. No census of the areas could be found later than 1910, when they had been part of the Austro-Hungarian empire, and the Western ambassadors had agreed its use. The result was, as the *Telegraph* wrote:

> Herr Hitler has obtained, through the machinery at Munich, a still larger slice of Czechoslovakia than he had sought by the method of ultimatum at Godesberg. To add to their troubles the Czechs are now confronted with an expensive reconstruction in the country left to them. Pilsen is cut off from its water supply, Prague from electricity and Bruen from its railway connection with Prague.

Nor had any provision been made in the Agreement for an orderly transfer. Those who had elected to move from one sector to another had to leave without their property and, if they were farmers, without their stock. There were no arrangements for compensation. A number of Sudeten Germans who had fled to non-German areas were ruthlessly returned by the Czech government, who were in no mood to pick a new quarrel with the usurpers. As Stephen Koss (in *The Rise and Fall of the Political Press in Britain*) has observed: 'Camrose's *Telegraph* paid increasing attention to German moral transgressions. At most it gave stinted praise to Chamberlain's diplomacy, and its comments were often double-edged ... in terms of practical politics, the equivocations of the *Telegraph* were more damaging than abuse from predictable sources.'

The odiousness of Nazi 'moral transgressions' was now becoming obvious to the 'man on the Clapham omnibus'. At the end of October the German government decreed the expulsion of all 20,000 resident Polish Jews 'amid terrible scenes of brutality and hardship'. This provoked the seventeen-year-old son of one of them to shoot a junior German diplomat in Paris. The murder led the Nazis to visit their wrath in a country-wide pogrom: *Kristallnacht*, it was called, the night of breaking glass. Synagogues were set on fire, homes wrecked, hundreds savagely beaten, at least eighty killed outright and many more sent to concentration camps. A few days later Goering, whom Halifax, a year before, had thought almost 'a joke figure', ordered all Jews to cease their trading or professional business by the end of the year; Jewish property was seized to pay for a £80 million fine imposed on the whole Jewish Community, while those still at liberty and whose houses had been gutted were ordered to restore them at their own expense.

As one result, public adulation of the Chamberlain Government cooled. Whereas, after the Munich debate, the Government did well in by-elections, now the mood, though not reversed, was changing. The dissidents, who were at first harried by their constituency associations, now found themselves in demand as public speakers. It was not, however, a triumph for Churchill. The Churchillites in the House of Commons numbered only four or five and were far outnumbered by the Edenites, who sought to stiffen the Government from within. As Harold Nicolson, one of the latter, observed: 'Winston gives the impression of being more bitter than determined, and more out for a fight than reform.' What Churchill feared was a 'coupon' general election in which the dissident Conservatives would be forced out by the machine. However, Chamberlain, who had been met by Halifax on the return from Munich, and admonished not to take advantage of the moment by calling a snap election, now let it be known that the Government would carry on.

Otherwise, Chamberlain was still 'on a high'. He refused Halifax's suggestion to broaden his Cabinet. His only idea was to offer a place to Lord Samuel, who had surrendered the Liberal leadership to Sir Archibald Sinclair on his elevation to the Lords: 'He made an excellent speech the other day in my support ... would be a nasty smack for Master Archie.' (Samuel refused.)

He had long ago given the promise: 'no conscription in peacetime'. Now he reiterated it, linking it to a decision that the Government did not envisage a continental army. Nor would he have either a compulsory National Register, for which Halifax spoke in the House of Lords, or even a voluntary one, until driven to it on 2 December.[3]

Nor did he, in face of the mistrustful Opposition parties and TUC, dare decide on a Ministry of Supply.[4] By mid-November, Harvey was

---

[3] Leo Amery told his diary: '[It] is really typical of the half-heartedness of Government policy in every sphere. Why a compulsory register should be impossible in peace because it has to be kept up to date and why a voluntary register should not require keeping up to date passes my comprehension. I am glad to see *The Daily Telegraph* expressed its disappointment in the strongest possible terms.'

[4] Harold Nicolson discovered another reason. In his diary he recorded meeting Inskip's parliamentary private secretary, who had talked with Kingsley Wood. The latter 'had admitted frankly

recording in his diary: '*The Daily Telegraph*, on Camrose's orders, is now demanding [the Ministry] daily and fiercely.'

As the weeks passed it became increasingly clear that Chamberlain, far from seeing Munich as a respite for much greater effort, was positively enthusiastic of its outcome. He summed it up in a letter to his sisters:

> I begin to feel at last that we are getting on top of the dictators. The solution is well put by Scrutator in the *S. Times* today. They missed (or rather Hitler missed) the bus last September ... we have seen where our weak points were and have strengthened them so that they could not make nearly so much a mess of us now as they could have done then while we could make much more a mess of them. It is the same with the French.
>
> Point two ... the people have looked at war and didn't like it. If they thought they were being brought near it again they would protest very violently and all the more because they believe that Mr Chamberlain is a nice kind old gentleman who would not want to treat Germans roughly and unfairly.
>
> Allied to Point two: The economic situation in Germany is bad and everyone knows it. That's not a position in which to start a deathly struggle ...
>
> Point four is that ... it would not take much to bring the US in on the side of the democracies.
>
> These points ... enable me to take that 'firm line' in public which some of my critics have applauded without understanding the connection between diplomacy and strategic strength ... my policy [is] steadily succeeding.

Of course he was never quite so naïve in public, but this attitude could be perceived generally from his complacent speeches. As for rearmament in the air, Horace Wilson was sent to see Kingsley Wood, the new Air Minister, and explain to him why his plans for accelerated output were politically impossible: 'The Ministry's proposed increase in the production capacity equal to the estimated German capacity could not be accepted because Germany would take it as a signal that we have decided at once to sabotage the Munich agreement.'

He seemed to have the knack of the most complacent utterance immediately before a disaster. Twenty-four hours before *Kristallnacht*, but after the expulsion of the 20,000 Polish Jews, he told the Lord

that we can do little without a Ministry of Supply, but that to appoint such a Minister would arouse the anger of Germany'.

264

Mayor's guests at the Mansion House banquet: 'You can all look forward to a Happy Christmas.' And just six days before Hitler committed the rape of Prague on 15 March 1938, Chamberlain summoned the lobby correspondents, without the knowledge of the Foreign Office or the Foreign Secretary. He told them that once the Spanish Civil War had been settled, the next step would be a halt in the armament race.[5] Much depended on Anglo-German relations but the position was more promising.[6] He asked Hoare, too, to make a confident speech in his constituency, which turned out to be rather overdone. Hoare foresaw 'a Golden Age' in which:

> The long period of preparation [of armaments] having come to an end, a Five Year Plan would raise standards of living to heights we had never before been able to attempt. [The builders were to be] five men in Europe, the three Dictators and the Prime Ministers of England and France ... These five men working together might make themselves the eternal benefactors of the human race.

And this from the man who had said during the Munich debate that the guarantee of the new Czechoslovakia would render her 'as safe as Switzerland had been for many generations'.

Shortly after Czechoslovakia had ceased to exist, Harvey met William at the house of his daughter and son-in-law, who was Parliamentary Private Secretary to Halifax:

> We dined last night with the Birkenhead's and met Camrose. Latter was very critical of the PM and said he would never lead a really All-Party Government or carry compulsory powers as Labour did not trust him.

No sooner had the Prague coup been digested than there were rumours of German troop concentrations on the Polish border. Chamberlain, in conjunction with the French, on Friday 31 March, issued a statement guaranteeing Polish independence. Most of the Press, except *The Times* and the *Express*, naturally assumed that the statement meant that Britain and France would go to Polish assistance if its territory were attacked. *The Times*, as usual, had a different interpretation. The guarantee was not, it seemed, of the present frontiers but of its independent government. Thus, the guarantee had not 'effectively given the control of British policy to Poland'.

---

[5] Cadogan described it as a 'ridiculous rainbow story – much too optimistic'.
[6] The press conference was 'on lobby terms' and could not be attributed to the Prime Minister. The *Telegraph* identified its source as 'unofficial and semi-official contacts'.

There was no 'encirclement' of Germany. For once *The Times* had itself been used. Cadogan had seen L. Kennedy, their leader-writer, and 'gave him the low-down – hope I can trust him'. As might have been expected, 'the Poles at once took fright', and 'Chamberlain had to issue a *démenti*'.[7] Chamberlain, however, showed his complicity to his diary when he 'stressed the important point perceived alone by *The Times* ... it is we who will judge whether their independence is threatened or not'.

The following Sunday, 'Scrutator', of Gomer's *Sunday Times*, joined in playing down the importance of the guarantee to Poland. It was well known that Hadley, Editor of the *Sunday Times*, saw Chamberlain before most weekends. Thus the blast which the *Telegraph* now delivered can be taken as much as a caution to Chamberlain as a rebuke to the *Sunday Times* for its Munichois faint-heartedness, taking a new speech by Hitler as its text:

> [Hitler] repeated for the 100th time the wearisome story of Germany's alleged wrongs, and served up once again all the familiar jargon about 'living space', 'vital rights', 'the place in the sun', 'encirclement' and the rest ... It will be noted that Herr Hitler made no reference of any kind to Poland. It is part of his technique to be silent about the thing most immediately occupying his mind ...
>
> All the more is it necessary to deprecate the blatant crudity of a Sunday newspaper which detects evidence of a climb-down in certain phrases ... it has been asserted for instance that [the guarantee] 'involved no blind acceptance of the status quo' and its essence is that 'independence in negotiation must be restored to the weaker part ...' [The argument] can mean nothing less than that if Germany puts in a demand for Danzig or the Polish corridor, our role as guarantor of Polish independence is to negotiate these territories away.
>
> There must be no shadow of doubt.

As soon as the guarantee had been published, the *Telegraph* had noted:

> A more complete reversal of a policy tenaciously adhered to over many decades it would be impossible to imagine ... The military commitment which we refused even to France before 1914, after 1918 and right down to January of this year, we now grant outright to a

---

[7] Harvey's diaries. The wording of the guarantee had been agreed by Chamberlain, Halifax and Cadogan, then referred to 'the Big Four' and finally to the full Cabinet. A study of the papers seems to show that Chamberlain and Cadogan intended 'the low-down' but Halifax did not. Cadogan, who was also responsible for rebuffing Russian attempts to set up a conference with eastern states, was subsequently unrepentant. He does not mention the *démenti* in his diary and three weeks later wrote, 'I hinted to the Pole [Polish ambassador] that they must not be intransigent about Danzig.'

Letter of January 5, 1937 to W. Hadley, editor of the Sunday Times. The occasion was the split of publishing interests between William, Gomer and Edward Iliffe. William had retained ninety per cent of the *Daily Telegraph*, a private concern, but had had to yield the *Sunday Times* as part of a publicly-owned company. To justify to the shareholders the separation of their 'Flagship', the *Sunday Times*, William would have had to pay an absurdly high price.

Hadley had been the man who had first steered William's way to journalism by judging a school competition, giving thirteen-year-old William first prize, and marking his paper: 'This boy should go into journalism.' Hadley had been recruited by Leonard Rees, the editor of the *Sunday Times*, as assistant editor. When Rees died suddenly in 1931 William appointed him editor.

REGENT 5208.

25. St. James's Place.
S.W.1.

5th Jan 37

My dear Hadley

Thank you for a very charming letter. It would be idle of me to conceal the real satisfaction from the 'appreciation' by a friend. Since ... a most grateful words. I have lived with the paper by nearly 22 years and I know if I like a bit the ... to ... (J.C.) first ... I'll accept your ... now that you ... from it

I shall use your confirmation that our congratulations and it into re-arranged to make the re-arrangement is any other way that ...

[closing]

With all my good wishes
Yours
[signature]

The front page of *The Daily Telegraph and Morning Post*, London, Friday, October 1, 1937, London Late Edition, One Penny.

Above The front page of the *Daily Telegraph* for October 1, 1937, the first day that it had amalgamated the *Morning Post*. William had bought the *Morning Post* several months before but could not keep it as a separate publication since it was losing money heavily and to reorganise it according to his own newspaper lights would have meant both papers being too similar. The result was almost unique for a newspaper amalgamation: almost the whole of the *Morning Post*'s circulation was added to the *Daily Telegraph*.

The *Morning Post* is set in its own individual Gothic titling: the size dropped considerably over the years (see opposite, two years later), but the title was always retained on the front page during William's life-time. Even after the war, he felt that the *Morning Post*'s goodwill lingered on.

Opposite On Tuesday, April 25, 1939, the *Telegraph* put news on its front page for the first time. All papers do it now of course, but at the time it was an innovation and also a risk. Hitherto page one had been dominated by announcements of Births, Marriages and Deaths (BMDs). The *Telegraph* carried at least three times as many BMDs as any other paper. Many readers were thought to buy the paper for BMDs alone and there was a danger that they might drop off and that the announcements, even though they were charged at a very low rate, might go elsewhere.

Of the other main London papers at the time only the *Daily Express*, which had started that way in 1900, carried news on the front. The *Mail* carried a single advertisement on page one, at a special solus rate. The *Mail* was forced to change to news on the front during the war when it was reduced to four pages. *The Times*, which had similar money problems in that it printed its valuable Personal advertisements on page one, did not follow suit until June 1966, six months before it was sold to Roy Thomson.

Note the extraordinary number of modern standards (nineteen not including the news summary) of separate news stories and the double column 'sub-editor's introduction' of many of the stories on the page.

The idea behind the front page, from then on, was to be the shop window of the paper. A reference was to be made to every important news story of the day, even if it were only a reference to a longer story inside.

The absence of a front page picture on this very first occasion was probably due to the desired insistence to concentrate on news.

The Daily Telegraph and Morning Post

NO. 26,175 TUESDAY, APRIL 25, 1939 LONDON LATE EDITION ONE PENNY

IRTHS, MARRIAGES, DEATHS & IN MEMORIAM NOTICES, PERSONAL AND CONCERTS, TOURS, CRUISES, &c. ON BACK PAGE

RITISH AMBASSADOR TO WARN HITLER

IR N. HENDERSON'S MISSION IN BERLIN

NSCRIPTION IN ENGLAND IF PEACE PLAN IS REJECTED

UMANIA SEEKS CREDIT TO BUY ARMAMENTS

Sir Nevile Henderson has returned to his post as nbassador in Berlin with instructions to make important presentations to the German Government before Herr ler speaks on Friday.

The Ambassador will urge the acceptance by Germany President Roosevelt's peace plan and

Emphasise that were it to be rejected, the British vernment, in carrying out its non-aggression policy, uld be forced to introduce conscription.

In London yesterday the Rumanian Foreign Minister, Gafencu, saw Mr. Chamberlain and Viscount Halifax, e Foreign Secretary, and will continue his talks to-day. ne of his objects is to obtain credits for the purchase of ns in England.

The Soviet Vice-Commissar for Foreign Affairs, M. temkin, who has been appointed to undertake a special ssion to Turkey, last night arrived in Rumania.

EHRER'S VIEW OF BRITISH STRENGTH

BY OUR DIPLOMATIC CORRESPONDENT

Nevile Henderson, British assador to Berlin, who re- ed unexpectedly to his post on day, has important functions to harge before Herr Hitler esses the Reichstag on Friday. st there be any doubt in the of the German Government, ill stress to Herr von Ribben- the Reich Foreign Minister, other members of the Govern- , that Britain will have no native to pressing on with her nt policy in the absence of uring statements and action ermany.

y will be told that Britain aligns lf four-square with the stand by President Roosevelt in the he addressed to Germany and -a fact which has been made tantly clear to Washington in tches from London.

Nevile is expected to convey that Herr Hitler reject the Roose- appeal, it would not be possible e British Government to resist onger the rapidly growing public nd for compulsory military ser- and the necessary legislation have to be introduced soon s there was abundant evidence of nge of heart in Germany.

MAN CLAIMS

ic Approach Desired

h evidence might take the form thdrawal of German men and from Spain, cessation of the campaign against Britain, and an tant measure of demobilisation. many will doubtless also learn t is the British Government's to see a practical and pacific ach made towards solutions of ions claimed to be outstanding. is the British Government pre- to acquiesce in any statements Britain has turned a deaf ear to an claims for easier access to materials. Germany will be re- ed that Britain has often invited o enter on discussions on such ts.

tical discussions of considerable tance for the future security of e were conducted in London ghout most of yesterday between h Ministers and officials on the and and M. Gafencu, the Ruman- oreign Minister, and his experts e other.

AFENCU'S DAY

With Premier

ount Halifax the British gn Secretary, accompanied by Sir ander Cadogan, Permanent Head e Foreign Office, Mr. Maurice m, head of the Southern Depart- and Mr. William Strang, head of estern Department, received M. cu at the Foreign Office in the ng, the conversations lasting for than one and a half hours.

the official luncheon given by Halifax at the Foreign Office M. cu was seated between the gn Secretary and the Prime ter. At the end of the meal Lord ax introduced Mr. Churchill, Mr. and Mr. Attlee, Leader of the ition, to the Rumanian Foreign ter, who had long conversations each in turn.

urther formal meeting was held afternoon in the Prime Minis- room at the House of Commons, Halifax, Sir Alexander Cadogan ther officials again being present. night the two Foreign Ministers had further opportunities for conversation at a dinner given by Lord Lloyd, as chairman of the British Council.

The conversations will be continued to-day.

The British Ministers were anxious to hear from M. Gafencu whether he had formed any fresh impressions on German intentions as the result of his talks in Berlin last week with Herr Hitler and his associates.

It seems that Herr Hitler pronounces himself scornful in the extreme of Britain's ability to lend practical help to any other country, being unable, in his view, even to protect herself. I gather from other sources that German diplomats in many important centres have been instructed to harp on this theme.

ARMS ORDERS

British-Backed Credits

The German annexation of Czecho-slovakia was a severe blow for Rumania, since she was relying on the Skoda works for the bulk of her military equipment. Although Germany has undertaken to ensure that the Rumanian orders will be executed punctiliously, Bucharest is unwilling to rely a second time on German-made armaments after her experience in the last war.

The same thought has been present in the mind of the Jugoslav Government, which, I gather, has been pressed by Berlin to accept a £12,000,000 five-year credit for armaments of all kinds, including aircraft.

It may thus be assumed that M. Gafencu will seek to obtain British Government-backed credits for orders which his Government wishes to place with British armament firms. In Bucharest even more importance is attached to this than to the economic matters which are being discussed there with the mission headed by Sir Frederick Leith-Ross, British Chief Economic Adviser.

AXIS TACTICS

Sidelight on Albania

An interesting sidelight on Italo-German relations reaches me in reports of the circumstances in which the Italian invasion of Albania took place.

Certain circles in Paris are saying that Rome learned that King Zog, acting as Germany's agent, had been asking for Italian troops to suppress a rising in Northern Albania, with the object of getting them involved in frontier incidents with Jugoslavia, thus providing an excuse for German intervention in Jugoslavia in support of the Axis partner.

The reports add that the Italian Government was greatly incensed by this disclosure of tactics.

CIANO VISIT CANCELLED

From Our Own Correspondent

BERLIN, Monday.

Count Ciano, the Italian Foreign Minister, will not, after all, visit Berlin this week for the Reichstag meeting on Friday.

Page 13:
France Wants Conscription in Britain
British Ambassador in Berlin.

Page 11:
Gibraltar Food Supplies.
Japanese View of Soviet Pact.
Rome Expects Prince Paul

From to-day THE DAILY TELEGRAPH AND MORNING POST *will print news on the front page.*

The daily news—home and foreign—is now so vital in the national life that it is obviously wrong that the most important page, the one which is seen first by the reader, should be occupied by advertisements.

Actually the custom of printing advertisements on the front page of daily newspapers has for many years been peculiar to this country: in every other country the contrary has become the invariable rule.

We believe that the new arrangement will be found both convenient and appropriate.

In every other respect **THE DAILY TELEGRAPH AND MORNING POST** ***remains exactly the same paper as before.***

Births, Marriages & Deaths and all other advertisements formerly on the front page will, in future, be found on the back page.

SOVIET ENVOY TO TURKEY

SENT ON SPECIAL MISSION

FROM OUR OWN CORRESPONDENT

MOSCOW, Monday.

The most important development here in the last 24 hours has been the departure of M. Potemkin, Vice-Commissar for Foreign Affairs, for Angora on a special mission to the Turkish Government.

The significance of the mission is that the Anglo-French-Turkish talks are nearing conclusion, and the purpose of M. Potemkin's journey is therefore obvious.

M. Maisky, the Soviet Ambassador to Britain, left for Finland to-night on his way to London. From Helsinki he is expected to fly again via Stockholm, where he stopped last week when coming to Moscow to report on his talks in London with Lord Halifax.

There have been no new direct Anglo-Russian diplomatic exchanges here since Monday.

The Soviet Press makes no comment whatever on Russian policy. To-day's semi-official "Journal de Moscou," however, again praises Mr. Roosevelt, and declares that Jugoslavia is the next objective of the Axis Powers.

JOURNEY BY WAY OF RUMANIA

A SIGNIFICANT ROUTE

From Our Own Correspondent

BUCHAREST, Monday.

M. Potemkin, Soviet Vice-Commissar for Foreign Affairs, arrived this afternoon at Tighina, on the Rumanian frontier, on his way to Angora. The Rumanian Government put a saloon car at his disposal.

M. Potemkin will arrive in Bucharest at 7.15 a.m. to-morrow and will remain till 2 p.m., when he leaves for Sofia. This is the first occasion on which a high Soviet official has travelled through Rumania.

So far, no appointment has been made for M. Potemkin in Bucharest. It is, however, very significant that he is travelling to Turkey by way of Rumania, instead of taking the direct route by sea from Odessa.

He will stay for a very short time in Sofia. The main object of his visit to Angora has not been disclosed.

U.S. AMBASSADOR NOT RETURNING

HITLER'S MOVE AWAITED

From Our Own Correspondent

WASHINGTON, Monday.

Mr. Wilson, the United States Ambassador to Germany, is not returning to Berlin for the time being. He was recalled to report after the German pogroms of November.

The decision regarding his return is expected to depend on the nature of Herr Hitler's speech on Friday.

If the Fuehrer gives some hope of a peaceful approach to world problems, in line with President Roosevelt's message, Mr. Wilson will return to Berlin.

Officials here do not share the alarm expressed by some London correspondents of American newspapers over the return of the British and French Ambassadors to Berlin.

It is realised that this does not imply approval of previous German policies. American Ambassadors still remain in Tokyo and Rome, despite Washington's disapproval of the recent policies of Japan and Italy.

ENVOY'S RETURN TO BERLIN

STATEMENT BY PREMIER

The Prime Minister, replying to a question by Mr. Attlee, Leader of the Opposition, stated in the House of Commons yesterday that there was no special significance in the return to Berlin of Sir Nevile Henderson, the British Ambassador.

He was called back to report. After he had made his report he was given a short period of leave, which expired after Easter, and he was therefore going back in the normal course of events.

Mr. Wedgwood Benn (Soc., Gorton): May I ask whether the Government has decided to recognise what has been done with Albania?

The Prime Minister: No, not decided.

Mr. Boothby (Cons., Aberdeen): Are we to understand that in sending Sir Nevile Henderson back to Berlin it in no way denotes that his Majesty's Government accepts the annexation of Czechoslovakia?

The Prime Minister: Certainly not—in no way. (Cheers.)

CABINET HEAR TO-DAY'S BUDGET PROPOSALS

Sir J. Simon to Speak For 90 Minutes

DEBATE MAY LAST TILL 11 P.M.

Socialist Questions On Mediterranean

By Our POLITICAL CORRESPONDENT

The Cabinet met in the Prime Minister's room at the House of Commons last night to consider the Budget proposals.

Sir John Simon, the Chancellor of the Exechequer, will rise at approximately 3.45 p.m. to-day to present the Budget, which will be the second since his appointment as Chancellor.

Questions will be taken for the first hour as usual, and there will be a crowded House to hear his statement.

It will, however, be nearly five o'clock before Sir John reaches that part of his speech which discloses the closely-guarded secrets concerning new taxation proposals.

MR. CHURCHILL MAY SPEAK

This delaying procedure is always adopted, because such statements must await the final closing down of Stock Exchange dealings for the day. The whole speech is expected to last approximately an hour and a half.

When the Chancellor has finished, Mr. Attlee, Leader of the Opposition, will speak for about 20 to 30 minutes. Then Sir Archibald Sinclair, Leader of the Opposition Liberals, perhaps Mr. Winston Churchill, and some back benchers will continue the debate.

In recent years the House has risen somewhere about 7 p.m., and the debate has been adjourned until the following day. There is, however, no reason why back benchers should not continue the debate until 11 p.m.

If the debate finishes by dinner time the Opposition, according to present plans, intend to raise the subject of the situation in Spain on the motion for the adjournment.

MR. BURGIN AT CABINET

The Socialists have many questions to ask the Foreign Office spokesman concerning Gen. Franco's activities and the strategic position in the Mediterranean resulting from the Spanish Government's adherence to the Anti-Communist Pact.

If this debate takes place the House may not rise until 11 or even 11.30 p.m.

Mr. Burgin was present at yesterday's Cabinet in his new capacity as Minister without Portfolio, and Capt. Euan Wallace was present for the first time as a Cabinet Minister.

Since Capt. Wallace was already a Privy Councillor it was not necessary for him to take the oath at a Privy Council meeting. Yesterday morning, however, he attended the India Office to swear before the Marquess of Zetland the oath undertaking to carry out faithfully his duties as Minister of Transport, and this entitled him to be present at the Cabinet meeting last night.

CABINET AND COMPULSION

APPROVAL IN PRINCIPLE

A decision in principle, I understand, was taken at the Cabinet meeting that in certain circumstances the country would be asked to accept a measure of compulsory military training.

The decision will be announced at an early date if no change in the international situation renders postponement advisable.

The Ministry of Labour has worked out the numbers in the 18-20 age groups which would be affected by a mobilisation of those groups for military training, after exemptions for work of national importance such as munitions, naval shipbuilding and so on. Possibly 50 per cent. of each group would become temporary soldiers.

In Continental countries where conscription is the rule, 48 per cent. of each group is the average number called to the colours for training. On this basis about 150,000 men in each group would be affected.

To-morrow, in the House of Lords, Lord Buckmaster will move that it would be in the best interests of the country if a measure of compulsory national service, including service in the Forces, were adopted. In political circles last night it was debated whether Lord Halifax would express the Government's attitude plainly.

EGYPT'S FAITH IN BRITAIN

PROMISES CONFIRMED

From Our Own Correspondent

CAIRO, Monday.

The Premier, Mohamed Mahmud Pasha, made a reassuring statement in the Senate to-night on the country's measures for defence.

He assured the Egyptian and foreign residents that they might have perfect confidence that the Government would take all necessary measures to safeguard order and security, and all precautions to ensure essential supplies during any emergency.

He spoke of the close co-operation which existed between Egypt and Britain, and said that the Egyptian Government had been repeatedly assured by Britain that her military, naval and air forces would support the Egyptian army in ensuring the country's safety.

Britain's actions, he added, confirmed her assurances.

M. COULONDRE'S PLANS

From Our Own Correspondent

PARIS, Monday.

M. Coulondre, the French Ambassador in Berlin, will leave Paris for Berlin within the next 24 hours.

Officially M. Coulondre will be resuming his duties after a period of "leave." Actually there is no doubt it has been felt desirable that the presence of the British and French Ambassadors in Berlin should synchronise.

News Summary: Other Pages

NEW AMBASSADOR TO U.S.

APPOINTMENT OF LORD LOTHIAN

The Marquess of Lothian has been appointed British Ambassador in Washington in succession to Sir Ronald Lindsay, it was announced last night. Sir Ronald, who is 61, is retiring this summer.

Lord Lothian, who is 57, is a Liberal and has been a frequent speaker in the House of Lords and an energetic member of his party.

He owns about 28,000 acres, which include land in the Dalkeith area, where oil-boring experiments are taking place.

THE MARQUESS OF LOTHIAN.

Lord Lothian is the head of an ancient Border family, with seats at Blickling Hall, Norfolk, Newbattle Abbey, Ferniehurst Castle, and Ancrum Castle.

Newbattle Abbey is now used as a college for adult education, and Ferniehurst Castle by the Scottish Youth Hostel Association, movements with which Lord Lothian has been associated as a generous benefactor.

Lord Lothian, as Mr. Philip Kerr, was with Lord Milner in South Africa after the Boer War and was one of the motive forces of the Union.

He was one of Mr. Lloyd George's secretaries during the Great War, and afterwards had a considerable share in the peace negotiations.

Lord Lothian has been Chancellor of the Duchy of Lancaster and Parliamentary Under-Secretary to the India Office. He is unmarried.

He opposed Lord Tweedsmuir, the present Governor-General of Canada, when, in 1937, the latter was elected Chancellor of Edinburgh University, and in the following year flew to Australia to attend a conference to review problems of the British Commonwealth, economic, strategical and political.

U.S. WELCOMES THE APPOINTMENT

OPINION IN CAPITAL

From Our Own Correspondent

WASHINGTON, Monday.

The appointment of the Marquess of Lothian as British Ambassador is warmly welcomed in official and diplomatic quarters here, and will do much to mitigate the regret in the capital at the loss of Sir Ronald Lindsay after nine years' service.

Lord Lothian already has a wide circle of friends here in official, journalistic and university circles. Editorial comment to-morrow will praise the wisdom and imagination shown by his appointment.

GERMAN WARSHIPS OFF SPAIN

SEEN FROM LINER

From Our Special Correspondent

ABOARD THE RANPURA, Monday.

While rounding Cape Finisterre, North-West Spain, at noon to-day, in the P. & O. liner Ranpura bound for Gibraltar, we passed four German destroyers, part of the fleet that left Germany for Spanish waters last week.

The destroyers were carrying out fuelling exercises with two tankers about 12 miles off the Cape. They were too far away to be identified in detail, but the swastika flag could be seen flying at the stern of each ship.

Cape Finisterre is about 600 miles from Gibraltar.

CRUISER AT BILBAO

BARCELONA, Monday.

The German 10,000-ton battleship Admiral Scheer, with a crew of 900, has arrived at Bilbao where she will remain until Thursday.—Exchange.

20 WAR CANOES TO MEET KING'S SHIP

Red Indian Welcome At Vancouver

PLANS FOR BRITISH COLUMBIA VISIT

FROM OUR OWN CORRESPONDENT

OTTAWA, Monday.

Twenty war canoes, manned by Indians in tribal regalia, will welcome the King when he arrives at Lions Gate, outside Vancouver, aboard the Canadian Pacific steamship Princess Marguerite on May 29.

According to latest details of the western section of the tour, just issued, their Majesties will leave Banff on May 28 and arrive at Vancouver on the following morning.

They will be received by the Socialist Mayor, Mr. Tellford, at the City Hall. This will be followed by a 50-mile drive round the city before the departure by steamer for Vancouver Island.

At Victoria the King and Queen will be received by the Lieutenant-Governor, Mr. Eric Hamber, and will spend the night at Government House. On the following day the ceremony of the presentation of the King's Colour to the Navy will take place. The King will broadcast at a luncheon.

THE RETURN JOURNEY

On May 31 the Royal party will leave by the Canadian National steamship Prince Robert. They will land at Vancouver and start their return journey eastwards the same afternoon from New Westminster.

They reach Niagara Falls on June 7, and will cross the American border at 9.30 the same evening.

The Canadian Navy has arranged to send out the destroyers Skeena and Saguenay to meet the battleship Repulse, with the King and Queen on board, at Cabot's Strait, at the mouth of the St. Lawrence.

The same vessels will escort the Repulse 100 miles out to sea on her final departure from Halifax.

On the West Coast, the four destroyers Fraser, Ottawa, Restigouche and St. Laurent will escort the vessels in which the King will travel.

NAVY'S SEND-OFF FOR THE KING

CHANNEL TRIBUTE

When the King and Queen steam down Channel in the 32,000-ton battle cruiser Repulse on May 6, escorted by the cruisers Southampton and Glasgow, they will be met by a miniature fleet which will steam out of Portland to bid them God-speed on their voyage to Canada and the United States.

Official notification of this tribute was made in the following statement last night from the Admiralty:

> On the conclusion of Easter leave the Home Fleet will assemble at Portland on April 28 and 29. Certain units of the Fleet will participate in the departure of their Majesties in H.M.S. Repulse for Canada.
>
> Subsequently the Fleet will carry out the usual gunnery practices from Portland.

THE DAILY TELEGRAPH learns that the ships which will greet Repulse will consist of four battleships, the remainder of the Second Cruiser Squadron—of which the two escorting cruisers are a part—and a flotilla of destroyers.

As the vessels meet Repulse all will fire a Royal salute, crews will muster on deck, and, in naval language, "have a chuck-up," that is, wave their hats and cheer.

EARL OF PERTH LEAVES ROME

CIANO BIDS FAREWELL

From Our Own Correspondent

ROME, Monday.

The Earl of Perth, the retiring British Ambassador, left here for London by the Paris express this morning. The Countess of Perth and their youngest daughter were with him.

Count Ciano, Italian Foreign Minister, and the staff of the British Embassy were among the many distinguished people who saw Lord and Lady Perth off.

DUKE OF ALBA'S RETURN

The Spanish Ambassador, the Duke of Alba, yesterday returned to London, having visited Burgos and attended Holy Week at Seville.

RACE TO FINISH WORLD'S FAIR THIS WEEK

ONLY FIVE DAYS OFF OPENING

MANY SECTIONS NOT READY

AMUSEMENT CENTRE DELAYED

FROM OUR OWN CORRESPONDENT

NEW YORK, Monday.

With only five days left to finish the great exhibition which New York has been preparing for the past two years, activity at the World's Fair has risen to fever pitch.

Grandiose opening ceremonies, in which President Roosevelt is taking part, are prepared for next Sunday, when, if the weather is good, a crowd of 1,000,000 may swarm over this 1,200-acre "world of to-morrow."

Meanwhile a huge job remains to be done, and in spite of the optimism of the Fair's officials, it is obvious that it will not be entirely completed on time.

According to these officials, "nearly all" the buildings in the main exhibit area will be fully equipped by the end of the week, but only 55 out of 70 proposed concessions in the amusement area will be ready for the public.

CLOSING THE GAP

The old boast that the Fair would be in working order a week before it opened has been conveniently forgotten, and those in charge, realising the supreme effort necessary, confidently predict that "miracles" will be performed in closing the gap which still exists.

Many foreign pavilions, including the French and Russian, are clearly lagging behind schedule, but the British Pavilion, which is the biggest foreign one, has reached an advanced stage and looks as though it will be complete in every detail by next Sunday.

Disputes with unions over electrical work, plumbing, and the employment of foreign workers had caused a certain amount of delay, especially in a number of foreign pavilions, notably the French one.

During the past week 16,000 workers have been engaged in the Fair grounds earning more than £200,000 in a single week. But from this morning onwards the number of those engaged will be increased to 25,000, and work will be carried on day and night.

DOZENS OF CARGOES

It is estimated that another 35,000 workers in New York factories are busy putting finishing touches to exhibits. A steady stream of lorries is carrying these exhibits to the grounds.

Dozens of ships are bringing large cargoes from countries in all parts of the world. Already advance sale tickets, which cost 3s each, have passed the £600,000 mark.

Although the Pacific Fleet has been ordered back to its bases on the West Coast, 38 warships are arriving in New York harbour for the opening. The city will play host to 12,000 officers and men.

Hardly less anxious than Mr. Grover Whalen, president of the Fair, is Billy Rose, the impresario, who is trying to settle the strike of 250 chorus girls and swimmers taking part in his huge water spectacle "Aquacade."

They have stopped work, after five and a half weeks' rehearsal, because the American Federation of Actors insists that they should be paid £7 instead of £6 a week, and demands payment of wages for a part of the time spent on rehearsals.

SHOWS HELD UP

While this dispute seems likely to prevent the "Aquacade" being ready for the opening of the Fair on Sunday, a survey of the amusement area indicates that several other important shows, including a Wild West one, will not function for several weeks.

This backwardness is mainly due to the fact that exhibitors felt that the financial conditions laid down by the Fair authorities were not sufficiently attractive. They therefore failed to sign contracts until the last moment. Work is now proceeding at full speed.

FIRE IN FRENCH SHIPYARD

OLD LINER DESTROYED

From Our Own Correspondent

PARIS, Tuesday Morning.

Fire last night destroyed the old liner Anger, 9,847 tons, which was in process of being broken up at the Vanacker Shipbreaking Yard at La Seyne-sur-mer, Toulon, across the harbour and opposite the naval dockyard.

For a time important petrol stores near by were threatened by the flames. The firemen, however, protected the stores with their hoses until the danger was over.

In view of the fire which destroyed the liner Paris at Le Havre last week, the naval authorities have opened an inquiry.

A French police official at La Seyne stated last night that the police did not suspect arson to be the cause of the fire.

FLEET EXERCISES IN MEDITERRANEAN

CALLS AT GREEK PORTS

The Admiralty announces that the first summer cruise of the Mediterranean Fleet to the Eastern Mediterranean will include visits by units of the Fleet to ports in Greece, Cyprus, Palestine and Egypt.

On the conclusion of these visits it is probable that the Fleet will carry out exercises in the Eastern Mediterranean.

Picture—Page 18.

SPINSTERS AND PENSIONS

The Committee on Pensions for Unmarried Women, which issued its report yesterday, expressed the view that if pensions were granted to spinsters of 55, it would be impracticable to withhold the demand from other classes of insured women of that age.

Details of report—Page 16.

William, and his two elder sons, Seymour (left) who is modestly walking out of the picture, and the author. They were returning at the lunch hour from the Law Courts when William was the principal in a libel suit against Sir Oswald Mosley's weekly paper, *Action*.

Mosley had attacked three newspapers in turn for not reporting the political, as distinct from the rowdy, content of his meetings. He then turned on the *Telegraph*, implying in the Judge's words, that William was 'a Jewish international financier with no loyalty to the Crown and no sense of patriotism ... where [his] treasure lies [his] heart will be'. William was awarded £12,500 damages and the *Telegraph* £7,500.

William leaving his London house on the morning when his suit against *Action* began. He is carrying the morning's newspapers marked by him earlier, indicating that he is going first to the office.

country at the other end of Europe. Thus we have finally broken the last link with the nineteenth century era of 'splendid isolation' and now for the first do we assume military as well as political engagements on the Continent ...

A further guarantee was granted to Greece when Mussolini jumped on Hitler's bandwagon and invaded Albania. Rumania, too, was added to the list after new Hitlerian threats.

A grand show of bellicosity had been made, but where were the troops and where were the arms to justify it? Already, before Prague, Hore-Belisha, in his Army Estimates, had outlined his 'Field Force for the European Theatre'. Instead of the two divisions promised to the French at Munich there were now to be nineteen, nine of which were to be from the (part-time) Territorial Army. Two new AA divisions were to be formed for home service. All remained on paper. The money was voted, the method of recruitment unspecified and the means of multiplying arms sixfold unmentioned. All pointed to conscription and a Ministry of Supply, both Chamberlain's political bugbears. He was still arguing to his sisters that the conscription issue would 'show the Germans we were fiercely divided ... the mere suggestion [might be] enough to inflict a serious check on aeroplane production ... can only be done by agreement with at least the TUC'. But cold necessity and desertions by senior colleagues forced him along.

Hore-Belisha, as Minister for War, played the politically hazardous leading part and got most of the credit from Churchill. Halifax was the staunchest of the Big Four, joined reluctantly by Simon and even Hoare, leaving Chamberlain alone. The Ministry of Supply was the more easily granted. Half its impact was lost, however, when, instead of Churchill, who might have exercised his dynamism without attempts to dominate the Government, the minister chosen was Leslie Burgin, a competent solicitor, who happened to be a National Liberal.

The battle for conscription was helped on by a plea from the French Prime Minister, Daladier. When at last it came, on 27 April, it was a sickly child. Only men of twenty and twenty-one were to be called up and then only for six months. There was to be a curb on armament profits but the Labour Party and, at first, the Sinclair Liberals, were no more susceptible to their own appeasement than the dictators against whom they were still crying 'Stand up'. Labour held up conscription through seventeen divisions.

From the documents of the period I do not get the impression that the Press in general, nor the *Telegraph* in particular, in hammering away for the twin objectives, enjoyed much influence on the principal actors.

The classical balance of power between the Executive, the Legislature and the Press had been quite undone. Beaverbrook, who had been politicking ever since he arrived in Britain in 1909 as a millionaire on the political make, put it almost fatalistically to Harold Nicolson, a member of the Eden group:

> You must realise that politics have ceased to exist. In the old days active people in the House of Commons or men like myself who control great press interests were able in such matters to render their views effective. Today we are living under despotism by consent. The opposition is too futile to oppose and your little group, which is the only one hitherto who has effectively criticised the Government, are rightly deterred by patriotic feelings from giving the impression abroad that the country is not united. The result of this is that the Prime Minister has been able to establish a personal rule under which Parliament is practically ineffective and under which the Civil Service is silenced by the imposition of Horace Wilson. The power of the latter can scarcely be exaggerated. It is he who has maintained Hore-Belisha in his position, who has appointed John Anderson,[8] Chatfield,[9] Burgin and Perth,[10] even the most minor appointments are contrived to fortify his position. The country ... is being ruled from the ante-room of Downing Street.

The Press, nevertheless, may have engendered a public opinion quite altered since Munich, which, in turn, influenced members of parliament. Chamberlain was no longer seen as 'the nice old gentleman' he imagined but more as a ditherer, who comforted himself: 'Badgered by the two Opposition parties and Winston, everywhere I go the people collect in crowds to give me their good wishes'. Before either decision had been made or even the guarantee given to Greece, Cadogan wrote in his diary: 'Corbin [French Ambassador] is in league with the DT who will have an attack on the Government tomorrow for "indecision". (Seems they are running H against PM – Silly).' This was hardly a correct anticipation. The leader, when it appeared, implicitly excepted Halifax from the 'indecision' but it did not call for a change of leadership. That, in any case, was not William's way. He did not see himself as a latter-day Northcliffe, a maker or breaker of governments – not that, for all his Olympian conceits, Northcliffe had ever brought down a party

---

[8] Previously Permanent Secretary to the Home Office, the Governor of Bengal, now Lord Privy Seal.

[9] Admiral Lord Chatfield, now Minister for the Coordination of Defence.

[10] Lately Ambassador in Rome and beyond retiring age, now brought into the Home Office to set up a Shadow Ministry of Information.

leader. Both Rothermere and Beaverbrook had tried it in their crude ways, but both had seen ranks close against them. To members of parliament, newspapers were outsiders. They could be very effective in advocacy and exposure but they had no place nor vote in the smoke-filled rooms.

William got the impression now that, once conscription and a Ministry of Supply had been achieved (or, at any rate, had been set in train), Chamberlain was settling back into his old optimism. Indeed it was true. 'I believe,' he wrote to his sisters on 29 April 1939 (two days after the Conscription Bill had been introduced but not yet passed), 'every month that passes makes war more unlikely.'[11]

He was therefore annoyed when the BBC on the same evening interpreted the Polish guarantee as enabling Poland 'alone' to judge when it applied. His answer was to send a precautionary message to Warsaw and at the same time to persuade *The Times*, through Horace Wilson, to declare that 'Danzig is not worth a war.' This latter leader happened to coincide with a strong leader in the *Telegraph*:

> ... Hitler dreaming of the partition line of 1772–1795 ... Herr Hitler speaks in *Mein Kampf* of the 'boundless humanity' of the Treaty of Brest Litovsk, which annexed to the Reich the whole of Russia's shares of partition Poland. Poles will not readily forget his assurance that once the German Sudetenlands were restored he would have no further interest in the Czech state. He had already given precisely the same assurance on March 7, 1936 (Rhineland) ... Once in control of Danzig the Reich would be in a position to exert stranglehold on Poland's economic life line.

Evidently Chamberlain sensed that William was once more in his post-Munich critical mood. He now tried an oblique approach through R.A. Butler, Halifax's under-secretary who answered for foreign affairs in the House of Commons. Butler, the arch-appeaser whom Chamberlain regarded as one of his few dedicated supporters, even if an 'uninfluential' one, was deputed to get Halifax to reason with William 'not to allow such "provocative" leaders[12] in the *Telegraph*'. But, 'when I heard of it,' wrote Harvey (remembering the Sam Hoare pre-Munich episode

---

[11] He gave the same message in an 'unattributable' address to selected lobby correspondents. James Margach (recently joined correspondent of the *Sunday Times*) wrote later: 'The worst was over and there would be no more shocks or surprise coups by the dictators – he was convinced of their good intentions ...'.

[12] Cadogan had summed up the difficulties of the Press. 'If you are too bellicose you provoke the dictators into doing something irrevocable If you are too passive, you encourage them to think they can do anything.'

quoted in Chapter 18), 'I impressed on him how sound Camrose really was, pro-H, though anti-PM, robust and not defeatist.'

Halifax seems to have got the point and to have confined himself to listing the obstacles to an Anglo-Russian agreement advocated in one of Churchill's articles for the *Telegraph*.[13]

While Chamberlain believed that the prospect of war had now receded, a small section of the public saw it as inevitable, while Churchill, in the early summer, put the odds to Harold Nicolson as 60–40 on. A larger section was inclined to doubt Germany's economic ability to withstand a long, all-out conflict. Some bankers were predicting a financial collapse. To test the question I commissioned a series of four articles in the *Financial Times*, describing 'Germany's endeavour to make herself economically self-sufficient, a study important in considering whether she can risk provoking a major war'. The articles, published in May, concluded that 'a political solution ... involving war' could only be avoided by a currency inflation or large-scale conversion of armament industries to peace-time activities – neither of which, though the articles did not say so, seemed likely. William liked the articles but thought their conclusions unnecessarily alarmist. That, I think, fairly summed up his view. The danger was very great but might still be avoided by resolution. Harold Macmillan of the Eden group, put it succinctly: 'The only thing which can prevent war is to convince them that we shall make it.'

At the end of June the Eden group at last decided they must be more active. Hitherto, as Harold Nicolson recorded, they had done little but talk and were more an irritant than a threat to the Government. '[The whips] respect Eden, Duff Cooper, Amery and the big bugs. But they are terribly rattled by the existence and secrecy of the group itself. They know that we meet, and what they do not like is that we do not attack them in the House. It is no use our saying that we are not plotting ... that we are too patriotic to demonstrate disunity abroad, and that we are in fact merely a ginger group, discussing ginger ...'.

Now there were strong fears that Hitler would take Danzig. If he played his cards as at Munich he could, by involving Chamberlain in negotiation, get the Poles to surrender bloodlessly on the threat of being abandoned by Britain. The Group decided that, 'The easiest way to convince Hitler that Chamberlain will fight for Danzig is the immediate

---

[13] Britain's approaches to Russia had always been half-hearted. During the Munich period Russia, though Litvinov, Foreign Minister, had gone through the motions of support for the Anglo-French initiatives, he had been rebuffed. Now, with Germany immensely stronger, Russia had its price – the Baltic States for a start. At the beginning of May, Litvinov was replaced by Molotov which, in retrospect, can be seen as the time that Russia abandoned the idea of a pact with the West.

inclusion in the Cabinet of either Churchill, Eden, Duff Cooper or Amery.' To this end they deputed Macmillan and Nicolson 'to go and see Camrose and ask him to help in *The Daily Telegraph*'.

Nicolson, though he knew William, evidently didn't know him as well as he knew Beaverbrook and sought to arrange a meeting through Tom Martin, the *Telegraph* Lobby Correspondent. The story is best told through Nicolson's diary, showing its usual facility for total recall:

TM telephones later to say that Camrose is very anxious to see us and that Eden will probably be coming himself.

Party assembles in DT hall: Eden, Lord Astor, Balniel ('representing the good Tory'), Harold Macmillan, Tom Martin and HN [Amery is ill]. Anthony is terrified of being recognised and keeps his head bowed under a big hat.

Astor says that Hitler will occupy Poland, Hungary, Rumania and the Ukraine this autumn so that he can stand a long war. Ribbentrop has convinced Hitler Chamberlain will do another Munich. Says that group, including Trenchard, should create War Cabinet, hold autumn manoeuvres in France and send large part of Air Force. We then discuss how far PM would be opposed to bringing in Churchill and Eden. Eden offers to withdraw from room.

Camrose says that Winston is the vital figure since Eden's inclusion is likely to follow in any case. The difficulty is that the PM himself, as well as Hoare and Simon, are terrified of Winston and will put up the strongest resistance. It would be much easier for them to accept Anthony, Amery, or Duff Cooper. 'Yet you must have Winston.'

We agree that any movement openly originating from the Eden group or the anti-Munich people would be regarded as an intrigue against the present Cabinet and would be bound to fail.

We show Camrose our draft letter [by Macmillan]. He points out that such a letter can't be anonymous and it would require many days to induce elder statesmen to sign. He feels the campaign should be opened by a leading article which would suggest that this idea was already in the PM's mind and would promise him full support.

Astor offers immediately to have such an article written in the *Observer*. Camrose at that rises like an enormous salmon and says, 'Not at all, the scoop must be mine.'

In the event, Lord Astor did not keep mum and there was a leader in the *Observer* that Sunday, advocating Churchill's inclusion in the Government. But it was written without great apparent enthusiasm and withdrawn by next week: 'The time is not ripe.' The *Telegraph*'s leader,

Nicolson noted, caused 'considerable excitement in the lobbies ... The DT has come beautifully up to scratch.'

The leader in the *Telegraph* did not, as promised, quite affirm that the inclusion of Churchill 'was already in the Prime Minister's mind'. As part of the preamble it produced an unconscious parody of Disraeli's famous likening of the government front bench to a row of extinct volcanoes: 'It is no disparagement of His Majesty's ministers, individually or collectively, to say of them that they do not exhaust the list of those best qualified to decide upon fateful issues or to plan strategic strokes ...', winding up that Churchill's inclusion 'would profoundly impress the Axis powers', and suggesting that 'this most popular step' would 'enhance [Chamberlain's] stature and influence far from diminishing them'.

According to the diarist 'Chips' Channon, who saw a lot of Chamberlain in preparing his notes for parliamentary questions, the full-length leader in the *Telegraph*, occupying a column and a half, 'is quite threatening, the PM is taken aback by it. All day David [Margesson, Chief Whip] had been sending for me.' However, writing five days later to his sister, Chamberlain seemed relaxed.

This has been a comparatively quiet week only enlivened by the drive to put Winston into the Government ... I am vexed that Camrose who used to be such a firm supporter should now have committed himself. As soon as I saw the leader in the *Telegraph* I sent for him and explained just why I was not prepared to invite Winston. I did not convince him, but perhaps the interview was useful as at any rate I was assured that there was no bitterness in his mind. But since his illness Camrose is a changed man.[14] I fancy he is a good deal influenced by his son who is always about with Randolph [Churchill].

William's own account of the interview, made on the same day, is too long for reproduction in this narrative (it is attached at Appendix A to this chapter pp. 278–9), but two points may be singled out. The first is that Hitler could have secured Danzig without opposition from Britain if he had been prepared to play his usual 'salami' tactic and put off a direct attack on Poland until the spring. This time, evidently, he could not wait. His lack of raw materials was too pressing.

The other point of immediate interest was Chamberlain's acknowledgement of William's critical attitude to Munich and the shyly expressed hope that bygones could be bygones.

---

[14] This was the same argument as used by Rupert Becket about the fierceness of his editor, Arthur Mann. He put his obstinacy down to his mental exhaustion.

The 'Bring in Churchill' cry was taken up by most of the London press during the week of the *Telegraph*'s leader, where it was followed, notwithstanding the meeting with Chamberlain, by political news stories and in the correspondence columns. The exceptions were Beaverbrook's *Evening Standard* (Chamberlain will stand fast against this 'terrible barrage from the newspaper artillery'); the *Sunday Times* (there was never any likelihood of the campaign's success), and *The Times*, which made a public fool of itself.

On the morning of the *Telegraph*'s leader, *The Times* published a letter from J.A. Spender, an Asquithian Liberal and Editor for a quarter of a century of the *Westminster Gazette* until it folded in 1922, attacking Sir Archibald Sinclair for his criticism of Chamberlain. Leading Liberals, including Asquith's daughter, Lady Violet Bonham Carter, then sent a reply asserting loyalty to Sinclair and ending with a plea that Churchill be included in the Government. *The Times* refused to print the letter unless the reference to Churchill was cut out. Whereupon Lady Violet, that formidable controversialist, took the letter round to the *Telegraph* with an explanatory covering letter.

In vain, Dawson and his correspondence editor went down to the House of Commons to persuade the Liberal chief whip to withdraw the letter. Lady Violet was not to be denied. The *Telegraph* published both letters while other papers gave the facts on their main news pages. Harold Nicolson tells the story in his diary: 'Camrose rings me up and is obviously chuckling over *The Times*' discomfiture.'

Meanwhile Chamberlain ignored the in-fighting. For three weeks from 15 July he was writing his regular letters to his sisters, confident that the crisis was over. There was no need to bring Churchill in 'to frighten Hitler'. Hitler already knew we meant business:

All my information indicates that Hitler now realises that he can't grab anything else without a major war and has decided therefore to put Danzig into cold storage. On the other hand he would feel that with all these demonstrations here, mobilisation of the fleet, territorials and militia men training, bombers flying up and down France, he must do something to show he is not frightened. I should not be at all surprised therefore, to hear of movements of large bodies of troops near the Polish frontier, great flights of bombers and a crop of stories of ominous preparations, commandeering of buildings and cars, warning of doctors, calling up of civilians and so forth. That is part of the war of nerves and no doubt will send Winston into hysterics. But to summon Parliament to ask questions and to demand counter measures is to play straight into Hitler's hands and give the world the impression that we are in a panic.

His concept was that the West was bound to win by Fabian tactics:

... what Winston and Co. never seem to realise. You don't need offensive forces sufficient to win a smashing victory. What you want are defensive forces sufficiently strong to make it impossible for the other side to win except at such a cost as to make it not worth while. ... Even Camrose has dropped the Winston idea.[15]

The only papers that opposed Churchill's inclusion in the Government on principle were Gomer's. Gomer himself had been in search of a journalistic and political coup since late May. At that time he had come across a piece of German propaganda which he mistook for a genuine attempt to cool international tension. Dr Dietrich, Goebbels' Director of the Press, had published an article describing an offer made to 'a group of American papers'. The offer, the article said, was 'to put the entire German press at the disposal of the best American writer' on condition that an informative article about Germany was put in the group of American papers. The American had rejected the exchange for fear of being 'reproached by his competitors as being under German influence'. There is no evidence that the offer had ever been made, that 'the American' existed, or that the whole idea was not just a ploy to convince the German public and the neutrals of the Anglo-Saxon 'destructive attitude of mind'.

Gomer, nevertheless, jumped in with both feet. He telegraphed Dietrich: 'On behalf of the *Daily Sketch* and my important group of London and provincial morning and evening newspapers I shall be glad to accept this offer for publication on the same terms. Full liberty of comment to be reserved on both sides.' Dietrich, alarmed at what he might be letting his masters in for, prevaricated for two months and finally invited Gomer 'urgently' to come to discuss the details, with the promise of a meeting with Hitler himself. There, on 27 July, he presented himself 'not [as] a diplomat or a politician, but [as] a newspaper proprietor and a businessman. If this were a problem in his business he would certainly see if some move could be made.' He found Hitler doubting Chamberlain's durability because he might at any time be ousted by the war-mongering Opposition, in alliance with Churchill. Gomer thus put himself in the anomalous position of arguing with the

[15] Actually, the 'Winston idea' was still being pursued in the *Telegraph* letters columns.

Nazi leader whether Churchill mattered or not.[16] He made no reference to the articles and instead asked Hitler what proposals he had 'for a better understanding'. Hitler replied that 'each country should put down his demands on paper', but did not elaborate. Nevertheless, Gomer 'left with the clear impression that the Fuehrer felt that he had made a definite move'. Gomer gave a written report (reprinted in full in Appendix B to this chapter, pp. 280–2) to Chamberlain on his return and, according to Cadogan, 'was made to write to Dietrich to ask Hitler [for] his desiderata'.

This interview, though Cadogan regarded it 'as harmless and as useless, as most such', led Gomer to exaggerate the influence of the press proprietor. In January 1940, after the war had started, Mrs Robin Barrington-Ward, wife of the deputy editor of *The Times*, 'found Kemsley full of the belief that, if it had been left to him, he could have managed Hitler and he could have stopped the War.'

* * *

As July faded into August, the prospect of war became ever more likely. Alone among the rest, the Beaverbrook press tried to spy through the gloom and polled its twelve European correspondents, ten of whom reported, 'There will be no war this year.' The *Daily Express* resurrected its slogan of the previous year: 'Britain will not be involved in a European war.'[17] Even *The Times* had forgotten its haste to cede Danzig. When Hoare, at the suggestion this time of Chamberlain and Sir Neville Henderson, was once more seeing the Press almost daily, seeking to lower the temperature, he only recorded one meeting with Geoffrey Dawson. In his notes, against Dawson's name he wrote the one word – 'Futile'. Nor, this time, could Hoare bring over the *News Chronicle*. Against Layton's name Hoare wrote, 'rather restless. Will it be another Munich?'

Another proprietor seen was Gomer. No comment was made against his name. The *Sunday Times* remained faithful to Chamberlain to the last. When, on Saturday 2 September, the now-famous cry went up

---

[16] Two days earlier Gomer had seen Dr Rosenberg, the Nazi ideologist. He told him, 'You worry much more about [the Opposition] than we do ... You never seem to appreciate that virulent attacks are made even on the Prime Minister – sometimes much more serious than the references to Germany ... You will never understand England unless you think of Neville Chamberlain as our Fuehrer, as we have to think of the Fuehrer as your Neville Chamberlain.'

[17] In 1943 Beaverbrook wrote to Hoare, now Ambassador in Madrid, that this headline, caricatured by Noël Coward in *In Which We Serve*, had been put in 'from time to time' at the invitation of 'the Government ... the purpose being to influence opinion favourably, so that there might be delay and time for consideration'.

(from 'Bob' Boothby, or was it Leo Amery?[18]) to the leader of the Opposition: 'You speak for Britain' (Chamberlain had announced no decision on war), Harold Nicolson recorded next day: 'The *Sunday Times* makes no mention of last night's demonstration. It shows that the Tory line is to forget all about it.'

There is no mention in Hoare's notes of meetings with William or the editor of the *Telegraph* – 'meetings with [unnamed] editors' probably referred to independent provincial editors. Nor, after Hoare's performance before Munich, was there likely to have been. They did not, in any case, miss anything. There is hardly any information in his notes. His effort seems to have been entirely to take the bite out of all comment – 'Go quietly ... Don't assume ... Don't dramatise ... Don't emphasise ... Don't disparage ...'. Of background news there was none, except what the diplomatic correspondents could get out of the Foreign Office.

As for the Foreign Office, the attitude of Sir Charles Peake, the new head of the News Department who had succeeded the too-forthcoming Leeper, is a classic in 'how not to'. Peake had been asked to advise on a Beaverbrook suggestion that the Prime Minister should regularly meet newspaper proprietors 'for guidance', as had been done 'by Bonar Law and Ramsay MacDonald but abandoned by Earl Baldwin'. His reply is worth quoting almost in full:

> I should not be in favour of the institution of a regular conference of the newspaper proprietors with the Prime Minister. This would be a bore and a further and unnecessary burden on the Prime Minister's shoulders. But I would much like to feel that we have the chance of cracking the whip at the newspaper proprietors, and that they could be summoned when necessary and told to mind their 'p's and q's'. This might be done either by the Prime Minister or the Secretary of State.
>
> To establish ourselves in this position it might be worthwhile calling them together at a time when they have done nothing particularly foul, and give them a little background ... This would break the ice and help to provide that basis of mutual confidence which would enable us at a later date to chastise them with scorpions when they needed it, which they frequently do.

Notwithstanding the 'boredom' for the Prime Minister, he did see

---

[18] The cry has been attributed to both. Nicolson's recollection that it was Boothby is the more likely to be correct. Boothby sat for an Aberdeen constituency. English MPs would have used the name 'England'.

some newspaper proprietors (among whom, probably, was William, as a friend of the host) when Roderick Jones, head of Reuters, gave a dinner for them, attended by Chamberlain. When he heard of the dinner, Peake minuted: 'We might ... ask the PM to give a homily on "leakage" and its prejudicial effect on negotiations.' This Chamberlain seems to have done, deploring also 'critical articles'. As the Government gave no background news, almost everything that was not a communiqué was classed as 'leakage'. Even in the dark, penultimate hours before the German ultimatum was issued to Poland – which was never told its terms – Chamberlain could preface his speech to the House of Commons with a call to the Press for 'the utmost restraint – a few thoughtless words [may] wreck the whole [government] effort'. 'A rather unnecessary attack on the Press', commented Harold Nicolson in his diary.

When war began, the Press Office at the Ministry of Information was manned from the Foreign Office. Harold Nicolson recorded in his diary on 12 September: 'The newspaper proprietors have protested to the Ministry of Information against the senseless restrictions ... they have to confine themselves to communiqués and are therefore all the same.' And on the next day: '[John] Gunther [US Correspondent] asked for a copy of one of the leaflets we have dropped over Germany. He was told he might not have it since it would "convey information to the enemy".'

Notes of Lord Camrose's Conversation with Neville Chamberlain

3 July 1939

The Prime Minister said that he had not yet given up hopes of peace. He had now reason to believe that Hitler was aware, to some extent, at any rate, of the resolution of this country, and steps were being taken all the time to further inform him of it. If Hitler were asking for Danzig in a normal way it might be possible to arrange things, as Beck[1] had intimated when he was over that if full protection could be devised and faith could be placed in German undertakings, Danzig should not be an insuperable problem.

He had, of course, read the leader in *The Daily Telegraph* and thought he would like to see me on it to explain his point of view. This was to the effect that while he appreciated Churchill's ability, his own experience in Cabinet work with him had not been such as to make him feel that his (Churchill's) inclusion in the Cabinet would make his own task any easier. He admitted that Baldwin had not attempted to control his Cabinet, and that therefore Winston had had a much freer rein than he should have done. In any case, however, the result was that Winston's ideas and memoranda tended to monopolise the time of the whole Ministry. If you did not agree with him he was liable to lose his temper in an argument and a number of his colleagues had found that the easier way was not to oppose him. Personally he had had two discussions with him which had ended in rather violent disagreement; but in each case he found that in a week's time Churchill had forgotten the matter and had some fresh idea which he regarded as being more important. His own personal relations with him were quite cordial and they had never had any lasting differences.

His own responsibility at the present time was so onerous that he did not feel that he would gain sufficiently from Winston's ideas and advice to counterbalance the irritation and disturbance which would necessarily be caused.

In our article we had suggested that other names came readily to the

---

[1] Polish Foreign Minister.

mind. One was, of course Anthony (Eden). Well, Winston was Public Enemy No. 1 in Berlin, and Eden was the same in Italy. Their inclusion in the Cabinet might strike both ways. So far as the latter was concerned, he still clung to the idea that Italy being the weaker and now the unwilling partner of the Axis, we ought not to eliminate all idea of being able to seduce her away from her present entanglement. Eden's appointment might have a detrimental effect on such a chance.

To my suggestion that all the present members of the Cabinet were not popular and that some, including Simon, were definitely distrusted, he replied that he knew very well that Simon was not liked or admired.

We agreed that the question of Eden ('while he has a following in the country') was not of the same consequence as that of Winston. He did not strongly demur to my emphasis of the psychological effect Winston's inclusion would have on the country, but he was the only person who could properly judge the question from every angle. Simon's judgment, and Hoare's, might have been wrong at times, but Winston's was notorious. As a recent instance, on the Saturday after the Italians marched into Albania the latter warned them persistently ('he was on the doorstep all day') to at once seize Corfu as the essential and immediate counterstroke. He emphasised the privacy of this statement.[20]

Salisbury[21] was asked whether he could not find some means of getting Randolph back. S replied, 'If you have once got rid of a carbuncle do you make an effort to get it back?' He told me this as an amusing remark, not seriously applying it to the present situation.

He (C) was a man who was slow to make up his mind, and equally slow to change it once he had made his decision. He would not say that he would never ask W to join the Cabinet, but at the moment he did not intend to. Circumstances might arise which would make him feel that W could be of positive help to him – he did not rule that out. In the event of war W would, of course, be in the Cabinet and in the War Cabinet itself.

At the outset of his remarks on Winston he said, rather enigmatically, that although we appeared to have had some differences last year ('I have read of them') these matters were now over, and he had hoped that we should understand each other again and 'be like we used to be'. I formed the conclusion that he was a little nervous in making this statement and phrased it badly in consequence.

---

[2] Martin Gilbert, in *Winston S. Churchill*, writes that this is misleading. Churchill did not go to Downing Street that day. He had telephoned twice and sent a letter by hand.

[3] The third Marquess of Salisbury, Prime Minister in 1886, at the time of Lord Randolph Churchill's resignation (as Chancellor of the Exchequer).

Notes of Lord Kemsley's Conversation with Hitler, Bayreuth – 27 July 1939

Dr Dietrich opened the interview by explaining to Herr Hitler the reason of Lord Kemsley's visit to Germany. Herr Hitler replied that he hoped some good could come of it as he personally had never been anything but friendly towards Britain. In this connection he referred to his many friendly allusions to Britain in his speech of April 28. Lord Kemsley said that he would only be too pleased if as a result of his visit a better understanding should come about between the two countries.

Lord Kemsley thought that the contest between the Rothermere papers and his own could be compared to the present position between England and Germany. That fight cost one side over £4 million and the other £$2\frac{3}{4}$ million. The conflict was a very severe one and the outside competitors were watching it very closely, hoping that one day either one or both of the opponents would be so exhausted that it would be a great opportunity for third parties to step in. Eventually through the intervention of a friend knowing both parties very well the conflict came to an end. Though the two concerns have been friendly since then, competition between them has been as keen as ever, but it has been of a legitimate kind with no unfair advantage taken by either side.

Herr Hitler appreciated the analogy and said that he was afraid that we were drifting towards war. He considered that up to a few months ago slightly more than 90% of the people had been behind him in Germany, but as a result of the English pacts the minority had joined him and he now held the entire 80 millions of the German people.

In September he would have 2 million men mobilised, and would also have a very large Air Force. Lord Kemsley said that nowadays one had become accustomed to gigantic figures. After all, in England this year we were spending £730 million on armaments and surely we should have something very substantial to show as a result of this huge expenditure. Herr Hitler said that the next war would be quite different from the last as far as Germany was concerned, because there was no Bethmann-Hollweg now. He went on to say that he thought Germany would win but on the other hand he was quite sure that Lord Kemsley would say that Britain would win. But the real point of the matter was that whichever side won there would be no real victory ; and that both combatants would be weakened so much that it would afford an excellent opportunity for Japan.

Lord Kemsley said that he was the owner of a large number of newspapers in England, and had used all his influence in consistent support of the Prime Minister. He had met Mr Chamberlain a short time after his return from Munich and he was absolutely convinced that Mr Chamberlain attached tremendous importance to the document which had been signed by Herr Hitler and himself. He looked upon the Munich Agreement not merely as a settlement of the Sudeten matter, but as the forerunner of a different relationship with Germany in the future.

In Lord Kemsley's opinion no section of the English people had any intention of arming to attack Germany. But he believed that if the Prime Minister considered that Germany had done something so serious as to affect the security of the world, and announced in Parliament that he had decided to declare war on Germany, then the whole House would rise in support. It was none the less true that if the Prime Minister were to announce that he had come to an agreement with Germany, the whole Parliament would show just as much enthusiasm. He thought a factor which would carry the greatest psychological effect would be a reduction in armaments, but it was of no use nowadays to talk of total disarmament.

Lord Kemsley also pointed out that the people of England were showing that they were now prepared to make any sacrifice whatever the cost.

Herr Hitler talked about the strength of the Opposition to the Prime Minister, and referred particularly to Mr Winston Churchill and his powers of expression. Lord Kemsley replied that in his opinion far more notice was taken abroad of the Opposition than in England and whilst giving every credit to Mr Winston Churchill for his ability as a writer and as a speaker, he reminded Herr Hitler that Mr Churchill had been unfortunate in his campaigns on at least four occasions in the past, starting with the Abdication of King Edward VIII.

Lord Kemsley said he was not a diplomat or a politician, but a newspaper proprietor and a businessman. He said that if this were a problem in his business he would certainly see if some move could be made. Had it not been for Czechoslovakia his first thought would have been whether a meeting might not have been arranged between Herr Hitler and Mr Chamberlain.

As regards Czechoslovakia, Herr Hitler said that it was impossible to allow that country to be a spearhead pointing at the heart of Germany. He remarked that he had dealt with this very fully in his speech of April 28. So long as anything he did was not in conflict with British interests he could not see any justification for England wishing to interfere. He considered that Britain's attitude towards Poland etc., was very unfair and unreasonable ; and Britain had made a pact with Poland just when Germany was about to conclude a special trade agreement.

They were more or less self-supporting in Germany but they were a nation of 80 million and *must have foreign trade*. At the present moment that was impossible.

He went on to say that every country – even small countries like Belgium and Holland – had their colonies, and it was ludicrous that a great country like Germany with its 80 million people should be without. They must have colonies ; they would prefer the ones they previously owned but this was not essential so long as they had some. He mentioned the Wohltat-Hudson talks ; these did not interest him because Germany was not after money.

They must also have the cancellation of the Versailles Treaty.

In response to Lord Kemsley's enquiry as to whether Herr Hitler had any proposals to make for a better understanding, he suggested that each country should put its demands on paper, and that this might lead to a discussion. Herr Hitler further said that what they wanted were (a) colonies and (b) the cancellation of the Versailles Treaty.

The interview concluded with Herr Hitler expressing his pleasure that Lord Kemsley was going to lunch with Dr Goebbels, and Lord Kemsley left with the clear impression that the Fuehrer felt that he had made a definite move.

CHAPTER TWENTY

War I – Ministry of Information

WHEN HOSTILITIES AGAINST Germany began on 3 September 1939 there was a great deal more fighting at the new Ministry of Information than in any theatre of war: Geoffrey Dawson, who may be taken in this context as an impartial witness, reported in his diary:

> *Tuesday 5 September.* Information and Censorship were committing incredible follies, a budget of letters testified to the ineptitude of the nonstop BBC bulletins.

> *Friday 8 September* ... more struggle with the censorship which develops new follies daily.

The most extraordinary blunder came three days later, when Radio Paris announced the deployment of the British Expeditionary Force in France, news of which had been previously banned in London. The text of the French message was now released by the Ministry of Information with the agreement of the War Office. This was obviously big news for the morning papers and the BBC. Just before midnight Hore-Belisha, the War Minister, decided that too much detail had been given out and reimposed the ban. Police confiscated printed papers in Fleet Street, at stations and even from the hands of bewildered motorists who had bought first editions. New editions, without the news, were prepared, but at 2.55 am the ban was lifted *in toto*.

Because of its name, the Ministry of Information took the public blame. The blame really lay with those who had planned its organisation. As long before as 1935, the Committee of Imperial Defence (CID) had been deputed to prepare a plan for a modern ministry in the light of experience from 1918. In reality, it was no experience at all. A Ministry of Information had been formed and headed by Beaverbrook in February 1918 but its remit had been information only to neutral and allied countries – enemy propaganda was reserved for Northcliffe, to give him some active job and to stop him attacking Lloyd George[1] in his

---

[1] Beaverbrook said that Northcliffe had so much confidence in Wickham Steed, Foreign Editor of *The Times* and an expert on Italy, that he insisted on keeping that allied country. Beaverbrook in return took Turkey, an enemy.

newspapers. There had been a Press Bureau for Censorship but no organisation to supply, nor further to control, the British Press.

The CID had concluded delphically that a ministry should 'present the national case to the public at home and abroad ... and for the control of information ... as may be demanded by the needs of security'. The Home Secretary, Sir Samuel Hoare (who after the Hoare–Laval fiasco had been readmitted to the Government as First Lord of the Admiralty and then succeeded Simon at the Home Office in 1937) was made responsible for planning. His first choice as a director-general (designate) made sense in so far as he was a man with some knowledge of publicity. It was Sir Stephen Tallents,[2] then in charge of public relations at the BBC. The Censorship Department had been mobilised at the time of Munich and the Earl of Stanhope, President of the Board of Education, made Minister of Information (Designate). Tallents resigned at the end of the year for lack of support from the Home Office.

Thereafter three directors-general with no publicity experience followed in nine months, the last one Sir Findlater Stewart, being seconded from the top civil service job at the India Office a week after the war had started.

Hoare was advised by Beaverbrook, who seems to have mistakenly identified the new Ministry with his own of 1918. Hoare at first asked Beaverbrook to take it on as Minister, and when he refused on the ground of asthma,[3] Sir John Reith. He too refused, because of 'the chaotic state of its planning'. The Ministry did not have a head until after the outbreak of war. Harvey, in his diary, recorded that Hoare wanted the job for himself but there is no contemporary evidence to that effect.

On 28 July 1939, Hoare announced his plans for a wartime Ministry of Information in very general terms, concentrating on press and censorship. 'The press side,' he said, 'would be able to operate quickly and efficiently.' In retrospect, it seems that Hoare had not concerned himself with the source of news but only with the rules of censorship and the staff to enforce it.

A minister was not appointed until the day after the outbreak of war, in the unlikely shape of Lord Macmillan, a Scottish Law Lord. To all

---

[2] Tallents had been a pioneer in the field of government public relations, at first with the Empire Marketing Board, and latterly with the Post Office's film unit which, among other outstanding productions, made the deservedly famous *Night Mail*.

[3] After the war had started, he wrote to Hoare on 30 October, 'I would have been the best man for the job. [But it] has now been stripped of its function.' At the same time, Churchill was trying to persuade Chamberlain to take in Beaverbrook as Minister of Food. 'In all the Press you have never had so consistent a supporter.'

but Hoare he seemed an extraordinary choice. He was not, however, a stranger to 'information'. As well as being highly articulate he had been an assistant director of Intelligence in Beaverbrook's ministry of 1918. Beaverbrook, who must have known Macmillan[4] was advising Hoare, wrote in June 1939 that, under Arnold Bennett, 'Lord Tweedsmuir [John Buchan] supplied us with our information.' Along with Lord Macmillan, he 'keynoted' the propaganda. He followed this with the prescient observation: 'The dissemination of information by officials does not suit the genius of the British race. As long as possible, news and opinion should be left to flow in the natural channels.'

Immediately war came, the existing system of 'dissemination of information' was abruptly ended. The Lobby system, by which journalist specialists had regularly been fed news, either on or off the record, by government departments, was discontinued. Instead, all news, whether political or military, was supposed to be given out by the Ministry of Information to a collection of general reporters, home and foreign, with no background knowledge of the subjects. Ministry officials were naturally cautious in such company. In any case, the Service Departments treated the Ministry with contempt. They either issued the most anodyne communiqués or kept anything interesting for their own Ministers in Parliament, sometimes days after the event. What newspapers could collect for themselves had to be submitted to an erratic censorship (operating in eight-hour shifts of 100 censors on duty at a time) with a list of ninety taboo topics drawn up in the most general terms by the departments and the Home Office.

In short, as Duff Cooper, who was glad to become Minister of Information in May 1940, observed a year after taking office: 'The MOI is a misbegotten freak bred from the unnatural union of Sir Horace Wilson and Sir Samuel Hoare (considering the progenitors I wonder the offspring is not even more revolting) but I have tried to straighten the freak's limbs and make it serve some useful purpose.'

In the planning stage, Hoare had set up a Press Consultative Committee, headed by Esmond Harmsworth, but it seems never to have been convened. Instead, the (National) Newspaper Proprietors' Association (of which Harmsworth was also Chairman), as soon as the futility of the Ministry became evident, sent a letter of protest to the Prime Minister.

It is not clear from William's files what happened next. On 10 September he received a letter from Sir Findlater Stewart, Director-General, that Macmillan would like to have his advice upon 'one point

---

[4] In the previous year, Macmillan had been in correspondence with Tallents.

in particular' and proposing a meeting next afternoon. On 14 September, Chamberlain, probably by telephone, asked him to go to help Macmillan and on 15 September William called at the Ministry. There, Macmillan seems to have thought all would be well if he could have a highly respected press lord in the 'at once dignified and authoritative' post of News Controller,[5] responsible for the two divisions (out of twelve) of News and Press Relations and of Censorship. William baulked at a letter of appointment in these terms, presumably because he could not on his own put the system right unless he could persuade Macmillan to thump the Cabinet table. Three days later, on 18 September, an amended letter of appointment was issued making William 'Chief Assistant'[6] to Macmillan 'as Minister of Information and Controller of News Relations'.

There is little documentary of William's reorganisation at the Ministry as he infuriated the civil servants by tearing up all internal correspondence or notes of conversations save memoranda to the Minister himself, usually signed unbureaucratically, 'Yours truly'. His first endeavour was to get the Minister to get the news from the Service Departments, where he found the worst offender was the Admiralty.

Churchill, who returned to the Admiralty on the outbreak of war (he had left in dudgeon in 1915), had defined the division of responsibility for news three days after he got back there: 'It is for the Admiralty or other Department to purvey to the MOI the raw meat and vegetables and for the Ministry to cook and serve the dish for the public.'

Churchill was perhaps thinking of his days at the Ministry of Munitions in 1918, when the MOI was issuing half a million fortnightly foreign news letters in almost literally every language under the sun, except German. Now he, whose department was the only one which had any successes to record, kept all the meat for the House of Commons.

Four days after his appointment, William was belabouring Macmillan to make the Ministry's position clear:

23rd Sept., 1939

Dear Macmillan,

The reasons which prompted me to suggest that you should speak in the House of Lords on Wednesday next have become much more

---

[5] He may have got the idea from Hoare. Tom Jones, in his diary, recorded that Hoare had offered him 'Publicity' in the MOI in June. 'Luckily I was able to plead the impending operation. For press work I urged Camrose on him.'

[6] The German radio commented: 'It is hoped in London that more life will be brought into the British Propaganda Ministry by the appointment of a subordinate liar.'

definite. I see there are several questions being asked in the House of Commons, some of which plainly indicate the confusion which runs in the public mind as to the functions of the Ministry.

I find also among some of my newspaper friends a similar misunderstanding. All these people believe that it lies in the power of the Ministry of Information to issue news how and when it pleases; further that the Ministry has in the past deliberately withheld news from publication, for the reason that it considered such news was not in the public interest to print. In other words, both public and Press are firmly of the opinion that the Ministry of Information has been created for the purpose of deciding what news of the fighting services shall be published, and what shall not. Unless this idea is uprooted, and the public told what are the true functions of the Ministry, we are going to be continually and persistently attacked.

I am taking what steps I can to inform the newspapers privately, but it does seem to me essential that in your speech you should give the public a definite and clear idea of the functions of the Ministry. Moreover it is urgent that this should be done before news starts to come from France. Whatever news is supplied from there, there is sure to be criticism and discontent, and this will be exaggerated all the more if the public are allowed to keep it in their heads that there exists a Ministry in London in whose power it lies to withhold or publish news on its own decision ...

And the same day, he dealt with Hoare:

23rd September, 1939

Dear Macmillan,

Further to my letter enclosed, there was a happening last night of which I think you should have immediate information.

Sir Samuel Hoare made a broadcast address last night. The representatives of the newspapers were all at the Ministry of Information to receive the manuscript. Nothing turned up there. Instead it was given out direct by Sir Samuel's own people. This, as I understand it, is a direct infringement of the rules laid down by the Cabinet, and results in some scores of newspaper men, who had been kept hanging about for the story, venting their anger on the Ministry of Information as a totally incompetent body.

You will remember that one or two similar cases arose during the week, which you were going to take up.

Yours truly,

On 27 September he turned his searchlight on Churchill:

27th September, 1939

Dear Minister,

Mr Churchill's speech in the House of Commons yesterday focuses in a definite and public way the impossible character of the task which the Ministry of Information is at present attempting to perform.

On the one hand the public and the Press are charging the Ministry with suppressing vital news concerning the doings of the fighting forces; on the other, the Press is complaining bitterly of the work of the censors.

In his speech Mr Churchill gave to the House of Commons the following items of news:

1. The story of the way in which the *Courageous* [aircraft-carrier] was sunk – how she was attended by four destroyers, that two had to go to hunt a U-Boat attacking a merchant ship, that when she turned into wind at dusk in order to enable her own aircraft to alight upon her landing-deck, she happened on a 100 to 1 chance to meet a U-Boat on her unpredictable course.

2. German captain signalled to Mr Churchill personally, *and is now in our hands*.

3. German ships have deliberately sunk themselves to avoid capture.

4. We have seized and converted to our own use 67,000 tons more German merchandise than have been sunk in our own ships.

5. We have lost 60,000 tons of oil.

Some of these stories have been public property for days and have been struck out of messages submitted to the censors by newspapers. All of them should have been published through the Ministry if they are considered to be suitable for publication. Contrast the details concerning the *Courageous* given by Mr Churchill with the bare communiqué the Ministry was given to issue.

Equally, the speech contains the following statements, every one of which the censors are bound to suppress by the rules laid down for them by the Admiralty.

1. Our merchant vessels and fast liners are armed with defensive armament.

2. For a fortnight past armed (merchant) ships have been continually leaving the harbours of this island in large numbers. Some go in

288

convoy, some go independently. This applies not only to the United Kingdom but to our ports all over the world.

3. The Mercantile Marine are ready at the various arming stations.

4. All the guns and equipment (for arming merchant vessels) are ready at the various arming stations.

5. Two or even one destroyer can maintain a prolonged and relentless pursuit.

6. RAF and Fleet Arms are directing the hunting destroyers and also attacking the submarines.

7. Air-carriers are being used while more ships are under construction.

Under the censorship rules all references to the matters above are forbidden. In literally scores of messages submitted by the newspapers and periodicals any matter even remotely suggesting any of these things has been rigorously eliminated. Indeed, had Mr Churchill's speech come before the censors, they would have been compelled, under the Admiralty regulations, to cut out a very large part of it.

We cannot go on with our present policy without making the Ministry of Information a laughing stock. Mr Churchill ended his speech with a promise to the House that he would take other opportunities of making similar statements to the House. Mr Hore-Belisha and Sir Kingsley Wood will probably follow suit. You cannot be surprised at any minister saving his titbits so as to make a nice, juicy statement to the House of Commons; but is it possible for the Ministry of Information to acquire any useful reputation in such circumstances?

You may appeal to the Defence Forces, as you promised in the House of Lords yesterday, to become publicity-minded, but you have no chance of success unless the Prime Minister himself will persuade or instruct his colleagues to release the news when it happens and not save it for use in impressive House of Commons speeches.

So far as the censorship is concerned, we are bound to encounter a constant series of humiliating and irritating incidents unless we insist on an immediate and drastic revision of the rules of each of the fighting services.

The Ministry is already firmly established in the public mind as a bureaucratic and vicious institution. It has been made the scapegoat of other departments (witness the incident concerning the Queen and the Paris Embassy yesterday). Unless firm measures are taken immediately it can never recover.

It seems to have been a hopeless battle. There is no record of whether Macmillan formed up to the Prime Minister, but the matter seems to have been solved when the Chairman of the Lobby wrote to Chamberlain at the end of September asking for a return to the Lobby system. A statement agreeing to it, prepared by Sir Horace Wilson and sub-edited by William, was made by the Prime Minister on 3 October. At the same time, the censorship, some of whose over-rigid rules William had been 'successful in getting cancelled'[7] ('and I am hoping to get the removal of a good many more') was transferred *en bloc* to the responsibility of the Ministry of Home Security.

The censorship was now put into the hands of Sir Walter Monckton, whose emollient genius made him the ideal choice.[8] I think the choice must have been made by William, as the Ministry's parting gift. For Monckton thought it necessary to explain his new system to Sir Horace Wilson, to whom he wrote: 'The Press is like a young horse to be ridden with good hands and a light curb.' His method was the 'D Notice system', which continued for many years after the war was over. Instead of taboos, the Press was given a list of subjects which *might* be dangerous. Editors could still publish if they thought right but they were thereby warned that they *might* be prosecuted for breaking the Official Secrets Act. Even so, except in the most scandalous cases, there was no question of the confiscation of their newspapers.

Although during the war there were only four prosecutions under this new arrangement, *The Daily Telegraph* was only saved on one occasion by Churchill himself, when Prime Minister.

In May 1943, the Army Council and the Air Council wrote officially to Brendan Bracken, now Minister of Information, asking him to prosecute the *Telegraph* for publishing the news of the escape of three RAF pilots from Germany, in contravention of a D Notice on escapes. 'This,' said Brendan's private secretary to Churchill, 'is the twelfth occasion this year ... the *Telegraph* is one of the most persistent of all offenders ...'. In reply to which, Churchill minuted to Bracken: 'Considering what a friendly paper this is and that Camrose is a patriotic man, would it not be well to see him first and explain that we have no choice unless he can give absolute assurance for the future. However I leave it to you to do what you think fit.'

*   *   *

[7] William Will, Chairman of the (Provincial) Newspaper & Periodical Emergency Council: 'Since you went there ... I find now there is a different atmosphere about the place [MOI] altogether.'

[8] During the Abdication crisis, Monckton had advised the Duke and Duchess of Windsor and had been equally respected by Baldwin.

William had now, as he said, 'organised himself out of a job'. The conception of the Ministry as a communicator of news had been abandoned and, having no background information, it was clearly unsuited to censor what the newspapers found from their own sources.

Before he left, Macmillan asked him to make a general review of the remaining organisation, which he had already damned in a private letter to Lord Derby[9] who had written to him on his appointment, hoping he get some sense into the Ministry:

The whole Ministry is one vast 'bloomer', the work of our friend, Sir Samuel Hoare, when he was at the Home Office. He and his officials consulted the Press, but in most instances studiously ignored their advice. Hoare worked through one or two Civil Service officials, none of whom had the slightest idea of how the vast machinery which they were setting up would function. I have been at the Ministry for nine days and I have never seen anything to equal it. Macmillan had not the vaguest idea of what he was taking on and I doubt whether even today he knows what he is up against.

William's remit was not to make the organisation work but to see whether it could function if properly directed, with the right people in the right places. Each of the directors of the twelve divisions was responsible to the Director-General and the Minister. It was for them to get on with it. He found much duplication and reduced the staff of 600[10] by 30 per cent, particularly unpleasant because most of them had not sought jobs but had been individually recruited by Home Office officials, or by the directors.[11] Mostly by amalgamation, he reduced the number of divisions to eight, abolishing the Collecting Division completely. This was supposed to report weekly, through regional committees, on the state of morale of the man-in-the-street or public house. 'I have not the slightest idea what useful purpose [they] can perform: they were set up by Hoare with the idea of supplying information to the Government about the feelings and conversations of people in the provinces. To my mind they were intended to be

---

[9] Derby was uniquely informed on opinion in Lancashire, where he wielded immense benign influence.

[10] The full staff, before the Censorship Division was split off, was 999 which, when announced in the House of Commons, had excited great derision.

[11] H.V. Hodson, Editor of the *Sunday Times* after the war and later Director of the Dytchley Foundation, was at this time head of the Empire Division. He told Birkenhead that, when William 'was grilling him about the kind of people he had', William said: 'When I want an historian I hire one.'

largely espionage centres. They are costing a tremendous amount of money ...'.[12]

William announced his resignation in a debate on the Ministry on 25 October, just five weeks after joining. He received a nice note from Chamberlain, who made no mention of Hoare, but afterwards Halifax told Sir Alexander Cadogan, Permanent Secretary of the Foreign Office, that the Prime Minister was thinking of abolishing it altogether:

> We are all most grateful to you for stepping in at such an exceedingly awkward moment and carrying through so successfully work which must, I know, have been distasteful.
>
> I hope the Ministry will gradually emerge from the storms which have raged round it with such violence ever since it was first created.

William was less sanguine. He replied to Rothermere,[13] who telegraphed to his 'old friend' on his 'disentanglement from the futilities of a much criticised department':

> Between ourselves, Macmillan has really not the faintest idea of how he should function as Minister or what his Ministry should do ... I have blessed him to the extent of seeing that he now has a chance to do something but, privately, I have the most serious doubts as to his future performance.

There was an important omission from William's terms of reference. Apart from the Enemy Propaganda Division (responsibility for which was later shared with the Foreign Office and the Ministry for Economic Warfare), he was specifically precluded from examining the Home Publicity Department (HPD), partly the responsibility of the Home Office, and charged with the definition of War Aims, a matter for the Cabinet. The HPD was especially charged with maintaining civilian morale and quickly became the Aunt Sally of the Ministry, satirised in Evelyn Waugh's book with the telling title, *Put Out More Flags*. Its campaigns excited more ridicule than any other division. As the historian of the Ministry, Ian McLaine, has written:

> The higher officers, because of their class blinkers, tended at first to look upon the mass of the population as beings to be hectored, cajoled and placated, infirm of purpose and likely to turn defeatist while their masters were resolved to stand firm against Nazism. As the war

---

[12] The idea, but not the method, was revived when Duff Cooper became Minister in 1940. He employed teams of investigators of morale. They were dubbed by the *Daily Herald* and the Beaverbrook press as 'Cooper's Snoopers'.

[13] Rothermere was by now a sick man, with only a year to live.

progressed, the same officers came to see that explanation and honesty were far more effective devices in the maintenance of morale and in furtherance of the war effort than were campaigns which insulted the intelligence and courage of the meanest citizen.

Sir Kenneth Clark,[14] Chairman of the Home Morale Emergency Committee, finally conceded, 'It was a perfectly useless body.'

As to Clark's Deputy Chairman, Harold Nicolson, he was described by a colleague:

He was a wonderful gossip but seemed to know hardly anyone outside Westminster, St James's and Bloomsbury. He was quite ignorant of the habit and attitudes even of the middle classes. As for the working classes he seemed to regard them as barbarians to be feared, admired and placated. Never was there a man who represented so fully completely in himself the distinction between Us and Them.

William's 'reconstruction' was not universally acclaimed. The *New Statesman and Nation*, at that time a thoughtful radical periodical, commented that it had been 'little more than a massacre of the innocents. He [has] decimated the ranks of the experts but left safe in their posts most of the "high-ups" who planned the Ministry before the war and ran it into trouble in the first weeks.' But this was to misunderstand the remit – not to judge the quality of the people but to slim down the organisation so that a job *could* be done without duplication. William had specifically commented:

I am forced to the conclusion that the structure on which the Ministry was formed and the selection of its personnel will stand in the way of its proper functioning unless the Minister can satisfy himself, by a more detailed scrutiny, division by division, than was possible in the time available to me, that the members of the staff are fitted for the work required of them, and that the responsible heads of the divisions understand his policy and can be trusted to carry it out adequately.

Thus he departed. He had nothing more to do with the MOI until four years later, when Beaverbrook himself prevented his appointment as Minister.

---

[14] Lately Director of the National Gallery.

CHAPTER TWENTY-ONE

War II – Politics

IN MARCH 1940, William, at the invitation of General Lord Gort, undertook a tour of northern France with Victor Gordon Lennox, the *Telegraph*'s Diplomatic Correspondent. He found his status now very different from that of the conducted tour as the Managing Editor of the *Sunday Times* in 1916.[1] Now everyone wanted to talk to him – Reynaud, the new Prime Minister; Mandel; Monnet; Leger (the legendary head of the Quai D'Orsay). He commiserated with Frossard, head of the newly constituted Ministry of Information. He missed General Gamelin, but dined with the French Army group commanders. He went as far south as the great Maginot fort near Strasbourg and peered across the Rhine at the German sentries. On the British front he went up to the Belgian frontier and visited Generals Gort, Dill (very impressive) and Montgomery, and Air Marshal Barratt (Air C.-in-C.).

There were varying views of the next stage of the war but on the British side there was universal satisfaction at the dismissal of Hore-Belisha (one of his many publicity stunts had been the suggestion that the British embryo fortifications should be called the Belisha Line). On his last night (April 3) at British GHQ he heard on the 9 o'clock news that Hoare had been made Secretary of State for Air in place of Kingsley Wood and appears to have kept his own counsel among the soldiers. Nor did he offer any comment when, on a final visit to Leger, the latter 'made the enigmatic remark that we English must think Hoare a very wonderful man'. It was not so on his last night, when he gave a dinner for Oliver Harvey (Eden and Halifax's Private Secretary, now Councillor at the Embassy); de Margerie (Chef de Cabinet to Reynaud); the British Air Attaché, Gordon Lennox and an American woman journalist.

All of them, even the Air Attaché, were violently anti-Hoare and William evidently joined in, concluding in his account of the tour: 'The party was Lennox's idea and a great success, the conversation being certainly the most interesting of all the dinners of the trip.' Harvey recorded in his diary that 'Camrose was outraged' by the reshuffle. 'Camrose would like the PM to stay on but to jettison his unpopular

[1] See chapter 7, pp. 94–5.

colleagues', but of course he was speaking in front of the principal aide of the French Prime Minister. He had already heard the story from Gordon Lennox of Chamberlain's lukewarm war aims (later confirmed by the publication of a letter to his sister in February): 'It would be a mistake to beat the Germans too hard and create chaos which would open the door to Bolshevism.' (As the futility and muddled direction of the Norway campaign became clear at the end of the month, the *Telegraph*, in 'Chips' Channon's description, grew 'mildly critical [of Chamberlain] but stayed their hand'.) However, Harold Nicolson recorded: 'I can see [Camrose] has been much shaken and he admits if we have to leave Narvik, Chamberlain will fall.'

As William had landed at Heston at 3 pm on 5 April he had found a message saying the Prime Minister would like to see him.

Went straight to Downing Street and was shown in at once. The PM told me that he had been trying to get hold of me early in the week to tell me of the proposed appointment of Sir Samuel Hoare as Air Minister, but that the announcement had now been made.

He also told me that at one time he had almost decided to make no change at all, but he could not adhere to this decision because of Kingsley Wood. The latter told him that he felt he had done as much as he could in that particular position, that he was feeling the strain of such a heavy task ...

He asked my opinion of the Hoare appointment. When I reached Paris on Thursday everybody I met was full of it. Opinion in both places was vehement – not a single voice in favour. I told him this and added that my own opinion was the same, furthermore that the public opinion of Hoare was so unfavourable that many people felt that the war would never be efficiently conducted so long as he remained in the Cabinet. He said rather petulantly that he was not surprised as I had always been prejudiced against Hoare.

(Actually he had himself on more than one occasion concurred mildly in my opinion of Hoare but had always said that he was popular with his colleagues and stood high in the party councils.)

He went on to say that while it was easy to criticise it was not so easy to find a man capable of doing the job. He had been through the lot a dozen times (he had told me this before also). Winston, who was no friend of Hoare's, had warmly approved the appointment.

I said at once that there was one outstanding person in my mind who could not only fill the position but whose appointment would arouse confidence and enthusiasm in the RAF, and that was Trenchard. His first reply was that he was too old (68) and when I countered that he said Trenchard would not have taken it unless the Cabinet agreed to accept his policy.

I retorted by saying he ought to have sent for Trenchard, told him that it was his absolute duty to take the position, and as for his policy he could fight for that as a Minister but could not lay down its acceptance as the condition of taking the position, and that I would also have told him that if he refused the appointment on those terms I would label him as a traitor to his country.

He so far acquiesced in the idea as to say that the time might come at any moment when this policy could be adopted and he had it in mind that sooner or later Trenchard might be the man to whom he would offer the position.

Breaking the text of William's memorandum here for a moment, it should be observed that Marshal of the RAF, Viscount Trenchard, was a dyed-in-the-wool 'win the war by bombing' man. He had been almost disappointed, as C.-in-C., Royal Flying Corps, when the First World War came to a quick end. He had planned a massive raid on Berlin in 1919 (with the then puny bombers), which he felt sure would have broken German morale. Moreover, on the insistence of the French, Britain had now agreed not to bomb the Ruhr,[2] nor even to mine the Rhine, for fear of retaliatory raids on French undefended towns. To brand the supremely patriotic 'Boom' Trenchard, 'Father of the RAF' and scourge of the London police, a traitor, would have been a formidable mission, even for a Prime Minister.

William's memorandum continues:

I went so far as to say that a continued use of Hoare would end in the public thinking that he was completely tied to Hoare, a remark which caused him to shake his head gravely.

Generally in regard to the new Ministerial arrangements he said he had not expected enthusiasm for it, but he himself was satisfied that he had greatly improved the working of the War Cabinet and of the other Ministries by the new arrangement which had been made.

He told me that Winston was in the seventh heaven of delight on his appointment as Chairman of the Cabinet Military Co-ordinating Committee. He emphasised that Winston would have no executive authority, but that recommendations from the Committee would be brought to the War Cabinet by him and that, therefore, he would in future have to bear some responsibility attaching to all the Service

---

[2] Even the Black Forest, with its invaluable timber and munition dumps, had been sacrosanct. To Leo Amery's inquiry Kingsley Wood had replied; 'Are you aware it is private property?'

Departments as well as to the Ministry of Supply ...

We parted on good terms, but it was the most unfriendly interview I have had with him, except perhaps on the occasion when we discussed Munich.

PS Saw Trenchard a few days after and he told me that Hoare had come down to him in the country and had asked him to come to the Air Ministry with him. Trenchard flatly refused, although Hoare pressed him very hard indeed.

A month later, Trenchard's 'patriotism' *was* put in question, with explosive results. On 22 May 1940, after Churchill had taken over and appointed Beaverbrook Minister of Aircraft Production, William recorded that 'Trenchard called to see me in a state of some agitation.' He had seen Beaverbrook, 'who appealed to him on the grounds of patriotism'. He wanted Trenchard to take on 'the job of Civil Defence in regard to aerodromes, an impossible job – you could not separate aerodromes from factories, open spaces'; a job which could only be a smaller part of a bigger organisation. Trenchard hotly replied that 'Beaverbrook had no right or title to ask him on such grounds to yield to a course which his own better judgment told him was wrong in the interests of the country' and a good deal else.

Two days later, on 24 May, Trenchard told William of a dinner at Downing Street at which only Eden, Mr and Mrs Churchill, and their ATS daughter, Mary (now Lady Soames), were present. This time Trenchard fell out early with Eden, who criticised the training of RAF pilots in ground attack. Next, Churchill, in a discussion in which 'both ladies took part quite freely', 'demanded to know in a very heated way what he proposed to do about the office of GOC for Home Defence which had been suggested to him'. Trenchard had replied that it was 'a sheer waste of time to appoint a GOC who had to consult the staffs of the Services, then the Ministers and then the PM'. For good measure he replied to Churchill, who had 'complained of the way certain people were working', that 'while it might be convenient and perhaps necessary for the Prime Minister to sleep two or three hours in the afternoon and work at night, it was impossible for everybody else engaged in the war to arrange their doings accordingly'.

This not very jolly dinner ended abruptly while Churchill was out of the room, when Mrs Churchill turned on him and 'wished that he [Trenchard] and Roger [Admiral of the Fleet Keyes, VC, liaison officer with the King of the Belgians, already turning defeatist] could be sewn up in a bag and thrown into the sea'.

Even so, it was Trenchard who wrote a letter of apology. He was longing to serve in a worthwhile job.

* * *

To return to April 1940. Kingsley Wood may have been 'feeling the strain', but he was still up and running. Chamberlain had given him Hoare's old job of Lord Privy Seal without departmental responsibility, after Air. He was soon to be Chancellor of the Exchequer in the Churchill Coalition. A three-cornered conversation at a lunch with Beaverbrook, just before the Norway debate brought down Chamberlain, is interesting. William's note on the subject reads:

Friday, 3 May 1940:

Went to lunch with Beaverbrook ... Kingsley Wood there. B raised the question of who would be Neville's successor if latter 'went under the bus next week'.[3] B's prophecies were in following order: first, Halifax, as compromise man under whom Labour would work; second, Sir Samuel Hoare, as Neville's natural successor in the leadership of the Conservative Party. If not Hoare, 'then you, Kingsley'.

Winston he would not admit to be even a possibility. The people would never trust him as leader in view of his record in the last war and the way he had been wrong so often in Home Affairs. Kingsley and I disagreed and put Winston first if a compromise leader was not sought; but we could make no impression at all on Beaverbrook.

He added as an additional reason why Winston would not be acceptable that his name was synonymous in the public mind with war and that he was looked upon as a war-monger. He reminded me of what he had said in 1939 when I was advocating Winston's return to the Cabinet, to the effect that if Neville took him in it would mean war for a certainty. Germany would be bound to take it that way.

Beaverbrook's gift of prophecy proved awry. A week after this conversation much had happened, including the shattering of Chamberlain's prestige in the Norway debate and the German invasion of the Low Countries. It can only be concluded from the evidence that his hopes now were guided by the main chance. He had not had a 'good war' so far. The immediate occasion for war, the pledge to Poland, had been a grievous error, he maintained. 'The *Daily Express*,' wrote his official biographer, A.J.P. Taylor, 'became the channel for every sort of

---

[3] An unfortunate metaphor. Chamberlain's jibe that Hitler 'had missed the bus' over Norway was used against him in the debate which brought him down.

William and Churchill playing gin rummy in a private plane en route from Marrakesch to London via Bordeaux in 1948. Churchill, William complained, usually won because he kept changing the rules. Behind is Churchill's doctor, Lord Moran. The photograph was taken by 'the Prof', Lord Cherwell. The plane was paid for by Henry Luce, proprietor of *Time–Life*, partner in the serialisation of the War Memoirs. Luce, of course, had dollars.

1946, at the fiftieth anniversary dinner of the birth of the *Daily Mail*, at which Churchill, now in opposition, was principal speaker. 'All Fleet Street' attended.

Above William playing croquet with his two oldest friends, Ted Hunter (centre) and Herbert Morgan.

Above right On left is William, on the same occasion. He is wearing a favourite grey flannel suit, which he found suitable for travelling – it would do as well in town as in country.

Left In the same flannel suit, on his yacht, in a typical alert attitude.

Below William and Molly on the poop of *Virginia*, a sheltered spot outside the saloon (sitting room).

With Sir Ralph Gore, Commodore of the Royal Yacht Squadron. William was elected Vice Commodore after the war. They made an ideal match. Gore was a first rate sailing man but no organiser. William, though never a helmsman, took the management of the club in hand.

William and Molly ready to receive guests at the first *Telegraph* General Election results party in 1950. The *Telegraph* took all the public rooms at the back of the Savoy Hotel. Before the days of mass television, individual results were displayed on 7-foot-long revolving three-sided drums. 6,000 people of every political persuasion, or none, were invited. 2,000 came. Most wrote 'thank you letters' but as many wrote letters for publication to *The Times*.

Receiving an honorary degree from Churchill, the new Chancellor of Bristol University, 1951. In most universities it is customary for a new Chancellor to make his own list of recipients of honorary degrees, independently of the governing body.

At Chartwell, Churchill's house near Westerham, Kent.

Left to right: William, Churchill, his actress daughter, Sarah, and his son, Randolph.

Below: Churchill speaking, after unveiling a plaque to William, in the crypt of St Paul's Cathedral, 1956. The occasion was a year after Churchill had retired as Prime Minister. The plaque was designed by Sir Albert Richardson, at the suggestion of Brendan Bracken, another old friend.

Inset. My mother arriving for the St Paul's ceremony.

IN MEMORY OF
THE RIGHT HONOURABLE
WILLIAM EWERT
VISCOUNT CAMROSE
BORN 23RD JUNE 1879
DIED 15TH JUNE 1954

grumble and grievance. It campaigned against rationing, against the blackout, against increasing the army, even against buying aeroplanes from America.' In March 1940 he was flirting with Maxton's Independent Labour Party, offering to pay their by-election expenses on a programme of a negotiated peace – the Empire retiring behind its frontiers 'leaving the Continent to work out its own destiny'. True, on 10 May 1940, the Germans had started the war in the West and Churchill could no longer be dubbed a 'war-monger'. But the other objections to him had also melted away. So, too, had Beaverbrook's support for Hoare or Kingsley Wood. Now, on the day that Labour refused to serve under Chamberlain, he lunched with Churchill and by his own account[4] made his peace, perhaps mindful that Churchill had twice recommended a place for Beaverbrook in Chamberlain's Government.

Beaverbrook's account of his lunch proceeds:

I asked – do you intend to serve under Halifax? He answered – I will serve under any Minister capable of prosecuting the war. It was a disappointment for I had hoped C would lead us ... the choice of Halifax would simply mean the continuance of the present Administration.

It was not too late. Halifax, though preferred by almost all including the King, recognised his impossible position in the House of Lords, unanswerable to the almighty Commons. Churchill therefore succeeded Chamberlain and had nominated his chief office holders, including Beaverbrook[5] as head of the new Ministry of Aircraft Production,[6] by midnight on the afternoon of kissing hands. It was not only a Coalition Government, but a 'ministry of all the talents', with businessmen included, as well as the nominees of all the political parties. I have no reason to believe that William was in any way jealous of the preferment of Beaverbrook who, though he had no experience of executive government, proved an immense success (his attempt to boost tank production by the same methods in the following year as Minister of Supply was less successful). He may, however, have been surprised as, according to Taylor: 'Beaverbrook [now that his subsidised hero, Hoare, had been packed off to Madrid, as Ambassador] clearly intended to be the man behind the scenes, an expert adviser, perhaps only on publicity.' He dallied four days before accepting the job.

[4] Taylor wrongly attaches the date of this meeting to the previous day.
[5] Churchill overrode the objections of the King, who thought the appointment would be unpopular in Canada.
[6] Split off from the Air Ministry.

William had had a long talk with him on 11 April:

I have recently spent some time with Beaverbrook and dined with him last night.

He has aged considerably in the last year, possibly as a result of the asthma from which he now suffers; but he also impressed me more than ever with the changeable character of his opinions and with the extremely voluble way in which he expresses them.

He has now got into the habit of repeating sentences and phrases in the manner often used by a public speaker to keep the flow of his ideas going. His views vary from day to day and are expressed with a maximum of criticism of anything and everything.

There is a great deal of 'posing' and I begin to feel that he is intoxicating himself with his own acting.

What William might have wished for, though he never breathed a word to his family, was the Ministry of Information. This went to Duff Cooper who, having been a Chamberlain minister throughout the period of appeasement, had earned a spurious reputation for his resignation at the time of Munich. Despite his fighting resignation speech, it had transpired that the 'resignation' was not over the Munich terms but over the way all the decisions had been taken by the Big Four and not by the Cabinet. After Munich, therefore, he had tried to withdraw but Chamberlain, piqued, would not allow it. He was a fine orator (his broadcasts vied with Churchill's for effect), a Francophile, a scholar, but no administrator. Moreover, though Churchill liked him, he never, as minister, got his ear – in William's view, reiterated in a 1941 speech in the House of Lords, the minister could achieve little unless he could fight his corner in the Cabinet (not just 'sit in') or, better still, badger the Prime Minister himself, now that he was also Defence Minister. Duff Cooper wrote to concur directly after the speech but the Ministry never had the essential right of extorting war news until Brendan Bracken, who lived at 10 Downing Street for the rest of the war, succeeded Duff Cooper in July of that year. A petulant minute by Churchill to Bracken survives: 'Now please leave off scolding me on paper, and if you have any griefs come and beat me up personally. You know perfectly well that you can see me almost any time.'

Some recognition for William's part in anti-appeasement and the campaign for greater preparedness – though no consolation for the lack of a war job – came in Churchill's first Honours List in the New Year of 1941. William was created a Viscount and there were Companionships of Honour for two editors, Arthur Mann of the *Yorkshire Post* and J.L. Garvin of the *Observer*. The comment of Gomer's *Sunday Times*

was a little churlish for its virtual founder: 'We of the *Sunday Times*
remember gratefully Lord Camrose's distinguished association with this
paper over a long period.'

*   *   *

A quarter of a century after Churchill's death, it is difficult to recall
how nearly he faltered in the winter of 1941/2 and how insidious was
the campaign against him. The campaign had started in the autumn
when Russia was seen to be reeling in face of Hitler's surprise offensive.
Oliver Harvey (now returned from Paris after the fall of France and
once again Private Secretary to Eden, who had succeeded Halifax at
the Foreign Office) noted in the Diary on 10 October 1941:

> Outcrop of Press attacks on the Government for doing so little over
> Russia [Actually, the delivery of vast quantities of tanks, aircraft and
> raw materials had already been agreed to the extent of all that had
> been asked for] ... AE wonders if there may be a plot to weaken the
> PM by striking down his lieutenants [Eden, Ernest Bevin and Mor-
> rison, Home Secretary] – much as the Fifth Column did in France,
> Flandin and Co. attacked Daladier and Reynaud for negligence, lack
> of energy in order to get in themselves and make peace ... on the
> ground that further warfare was impossible.

Harvey described it as a campaign begun by Dawson in *The Times*,
persistently pursued in the *Mail*, *Herald* and *Evening Standard*: 'A
deliberate campaign by Rothermere [Esmond Harmsworth, who had
succeeded his father in 1940] and Southwood [*Herald*], hunting in couples
as they always do, with the Beaver possibly in the background'.

The *Telegraph* took no part in this campaign nor did it feel it necessary
to come in on the other side, as a letter from William to his eldest son,
Seymour, on 14 November makes clear:

> 'I sat next to our friend [at The Other Club] last night. He seemed
> to be quite optimistic ... Moscow is not likely to fall ... He feels that
> the country had settled down and is no longer resentful about the
> absence of the Second front ... I had arranged for the *Telegraph* to
> send me a message immediately they received the result of the
> Nationality Act at Washington [an amendment to the Act would
> allow US merchant ships to be armed, taking the load off British
> shipping]. I passed it across the table to Fred Lawson (who was in
> the Chair) to announce ... it was received with great enthusiasm and
> Winston was highly delighted ... I could see he feels it cannot be
> many days before America is finally in the war'.

Soon America *was* in the war, but not in the way expected. Instead of becoming an immediate asset she was forced back onto the defensive and all British possessions in the Far East came under Japanese attack. This time the *Mail* (inspired by Beaverbrook, Brendan Bracken thought, as it had so often been in the time of the first Rothermere) led the pack, first against Churchill's lieutenants and then against Churchill himself. As the menace to Singapore grew clearer the *Mail*, which up to the middle of December had been shouting for more armaments to the eastern front, switched tack in a night and now, far too late, blamed the lack of tanks and aircraft[7] in Malaya on their diversion to Russia.

'A catalogue of catastrophes', as many papers called it, followed. Singapore fell; Burma was threatened; the Libyan offensive turned into a retreat and the invasion of Sicily had to be abandoned; the toll of the U-Boats rose rapidly; two German battlecruisers escaped from Brest and ran the Channel gauntlet in broad daylight[8] ... Churchill told the King that 'Ceylon, Calcutta, Madras and part of Australia might fall into enemy hands.' Meanwhile, General Wavell reported from the Far East and General Brooke, CIGS, opined from the centre of his web in Whitehall, that somehow British troops lacked fighting qualities. As Churchill put it in his *War Memoirs*: 'I felt the sense of an embarrassed, unhappy, baffled public opinion, albeit superficial, swelling and mounting on me on every side.'

The *Mail* attacks continued on the line that there were two Churchills: 1. The Inspirer of the Nation. 2. The Controller of the War. The nation, it said, was perplexed by 2. Churchill had 'laid down the doctrine that it was the duty of Parliament and Press to maintain the Government with the implication that any weakening of his own position would be a weakening of our cause ... no man is indispensable'. *The Times* was more lofty. It spoke of 'putting the office of Prime Minister into commission'.

Most of the criticism by the Press, however, was against the administration and the generals, not against Churchill himself.[9] Almost alone, the *Telegraph* supported the team in a succession of leading articles: 'The form of support which consists in profession of admiration for Mr Churchill with criticism of his Government at large recalls Roosevelt's warning [concerning] Hitler sowing mistrust and suspicion ... Profession

---

[7] Sir Keith Murdoch, the renowned Australian journalist, wrote at this time that the Australian government had specifically asked for battleships, rather than aircraft, for the defence of Singapore. Two of Britain's newest battleships were sent and, without fighter cover, sunk.

[8] 'Vice Admiral Ciliax,' wrote *The Times*, 'has succeeded where the Duke of Medina Sidonia failed.'

[9] Oliver Stanley, a government minister, satirised the critics' position: 'They are backing the jockey but not the horse.'

of trust in Mr Churchill's leadership with distrust of the way he leads is not a rational statement.' There was also specific praise for Beaverbrook and several others.

A particular thorn in the Churchill flesh was the *Daily Mirror*, now controlled by its management, the first Rothermere having sold his controlling interest in small packages on the Stock Exchange. Its main theme was that the series of military disasters was not due to Churchill imagining himself the embodiment of his great ancestor, the Duke of Marlborough, and overriding his service advisers, but to the social system over which the Tories presided. Its constant refrain was that all the generals were useless and that top jobs in the army could only be obtained by those born a Lord or with some other golden spoon in the mouth: 'The accepted tip for army leadership would in plain truth be this – all who aspire to mislead others should be brass-bottomed boneheads, socially prejudiced, arrogant and fussy ...'.

The *Daily Mirror* continued in this vein for some weeks, culminating in a cartoon of a shipwrecked merchant seaman alone on a raft in a stormy sea, with the caption, 'The price of petrol has been raised by one penny.' Labour members of the Government were as outraged as their colleagues; Bevin, Minister of Labour, in particular, judged the message a deterrent to men joining the Merchant Navy, for their efforts were interpreted as a means to keep up the profits of the oil companies. Churchill and Bevin were for closing the paper down under the Defence Regulations but Morrison, the Home Secretary, elected only to issue a warning for 'systematic publication of matter calculated to foment opposition to the prosecution of the war'.

Immediately there was an outcry from most of the national papers, sensing an attack on the freedom of the Press. The *Mail* 'abstained', but the *Telegraph*, the prestigious provincials – the *Birmingham Post* and the *Yorkshire Post* – supported the warning. William, alone of the press barons, spoke on it in the House of Lords.[10] '[The warning] will be sufficient: on the other hand it will not cause the reservoir of honest criticism to show the slightest sign of running dry.'

Churchill felt the pain of the turbulence. At lunch with *The Times*, where Robin Barrington-Ward had succeeded Dawson:

---

[10] Lord Simon, the Lord Chancellor, put the matter magisterially, citing Milton's pamphlet *Areopagitica – A speech for the liberty of unlicensed printing*: 'Milton never confuses the principle that the Press is a free instrument of expression of opinion with the totally different suggestion that there is some unlimited license given to those who edit publications to say whatever they like in all circumstances, whatever be the extent of the danger to the State itself which might be involved in their publication ... the noble Lord who introduced this matter ... does not dispute this proposition. Nobody can ... The fearful injury ... on discipline, confidence, energy and unity ... strikes too deeply at ... essential national requirements.'

He had no complaint against sober reasoned criticism of *The Times* and *Manchester Guardian*: it was the campaign in the *Daily Mirror*, *Daily Mail* and *Daily Herald* which was calculated to undermine the army to which he was opposed ... Winston said, 'I am an old man (he didn't sound it) ... I may be seventy before this war ends ...'. His utter absence of pomposity is engaging ... Ate heartily.

There is no doubt that Churchill himself now almost gave up. He had suffered his first heart attack in Washington, where he had gone directly after Pearl Harbor. Returning to an atmosphere of growing criticism, Brendan Bracken found him 'most depressed, saying he could only go on for another month and then he would be finished ... the chiefs of staff are at sixes and sevens, the soldiers and sailors quarrelling, and the PM is no longer able to grip the thing'. He shocked Captain Pim, RN, in charge of the No. 10 Map Room, saying 'he was tired of it all and he was seriously thinking of handing over his responsibilities to other shoulders'. Captain Pim replied stoutly: 'My God, sir, you cannot do that ... the loudest shouts ... come from those who ... hope to be in the running for some greater or smaller Government position.'

It is doubtful that Captain Pim was pointing the finger at Beaverbrook, though the latter was fitting the description had Pim known it. While whipping up Rothermere and not restraining the *Express*, he was expressing undying loyalty to Churchill and persuading him to make him Minister of War Production, controlling all other war ministries including Bevin's Ministry of Labour.

When the Labour ministers would not agree to it he walked out of the War Cabinet *à la* Michael Heseltine, explaining next day his asthma made further service impossible. (Lord Moran, his doctor as well as Churchill's, who was never bothered by the Hippocratic Oath, later declared: 'I did not accept that [his] asthma was an adequate explanation.') True, he did not then hold a press conference attacking his colleagues, but he began publicly campaigning at mass meetings for a Second Front,[11] knowing that the Chiefs of Staff judged it impossible for 1942.[12] On the anniversary of Hitler's attack on Russia (21 June), which was also the day of the ultimate disaster of 1942, the fall of Tobruk, he made a broadcast charging that 'people in high places' had

[11] 'Strike out to help Russia! Strike out violently! Strike out even recklessly!'
[12] They caused a plan, favoured by the Americans, to be made to land seven British divisions in the Cherbourg peninsula for the winter, to be reinforced in the spring. The planners reported it would be suicidal. As Professor Lord Cherwell, Churchill's scientific guru, observed to Harry Hopkins, Roosevelt's confidant: 'You are arguing against the casualties of the Somme.'

opposed helping Russia in 1941.[13] The *Economist* commented: 'This is plain mischief making … it is hard to avoid the view that these attacks have some … political purpose …' A week later, according to Ernest Bevin, he was conspiring to oust Churchill himself.

In an account that Bevin gave his staff, Beaverbrook asked Bevin to go and see him. He 'expressed the opinion that Churchill was on the way out and started to sound Bevin on the formation of an alternative Government'. Bevin cut him short, went straight to Churchill and told him. He was shocked when Churchill did not take the matter seriously. His explanation was: '[Churchill] is like a man who's married a whore; he knows she's a whore but he loves her just the same.'

For Churchill, fatigued though he was by constant troublemaking, genuinely regretted the end of his partnership with Beaverbrook. He told W.P. Crozier, the Editor of the *Manchester Guardian*: 'I didn't want him to go. He was good for me! Any number of times, if things were going badly, he would encourage me, saying, "Look at all the things on your side. Look what you've accomplished. Be of good courage!" and he put courage and pep into me.'

Though Beaverbrook came back into the Government, but not the War Cabinet, as Lord Privy Seal (without departmental responsibility) in September 1943 he was never, until the General Election, quite so close to Churchill again.

* * *

It was at this time that William became especially close to Churchill. His file of memoranda are bespattered with little nuggets of their conversations but now there was a new closeness. He often lunched at Downing Street and at The Other Club, normally a sit-as-you-please, one-table dining club, now always sat next to Churchill, the surviving founder. It was not that William in any way resembled Beaverbrook. Churchill did not take him, as Attlee had said of Beaverbrook, 'as a kind of stimulant or drug'; nor, as Oliver Lyttelton put it, as 'a mixture of enthusiasm and cynicism, of kindness and harshness, above all an original twist, astringent and exhilarating'; nor for 'the emotionalism and buccaneering spirit common to both', which Sir Robert Bruce Lockhart[14] perceived. But William did have what Bruce Lockhart described as Beaverbrook's 'agile brain which the Englishman likes to

---

[13] Churchill had had to insist on his leading the military mission to Moscow rather than Eden. He wrote to Beaverbrook on 30 August 1941: 'It is our duty and our interest to give the utmost possible aid to the Russians even at serious sacrifices to ourselves.'

[14] Consul and special agent in Russia during the Revolution. Memorable for his *Memoirs of a British Agent* (1932), he was a journalist who, during the war, worked in Foreign Office propaganda.

use as a whetstone on which to sharpen his own remarkable wits'. William, moreover, always took 'the long view' and his wide knowledge and judgment of men was invaluable. After the war, as Vansittart, who, though to some extent discredited as unbalanced, knew everybody, remarked to Malcolm Muggeridge: 'Camrose is the only person who has any real influence on Churchill.'[15]

Closeness with Churchill, however, made his exclusion from any job connected with the war doubly galling. His chance came suddenly in September 1943 but disappeared again only twenty-four hours after it had appeared. The Chancellor, Kingsley Wood, had died. Churchill wished to have a major reconstruction which 'would liven up the Government'. 'Except for you and me,' he said to Eden even after it had been done, 'this is the worst Government England ever had.'

Kingsley Wood had died in the night of 20/21 September. It was probably a coincidence that Churchill had invited Beaverbrook to lunch on the 22nd. The latter had put down a motion on the Second Front to be debated the next day in the House of Lords and the lunch was probably to get him to withdraw it. As it was, Churchill was able to silence Beaverbrook by offering him a non-departmental job, not in the War Cabinet but as Lord Privy Seal and Leader of the House of Lords. Beaverbrook, for his part, no doubt reiterated the proposal which he had already made by letter in July that Brendan Bracken, with his excellent Press contacts, should supplant the 'aristocratic' Halifax as Ambassador to Washington and that his job as Minister of Information should be filled by Bonar Law's son, Dick Law.

Oliver Harvey tells the story of how the reconstruction developed:

After lunch today (23 September), A.E. called in Alec C. and myself to tell us, most confidentially, that a major reconstruction was to take place as a result of Kingsley Wood's death. The P.M.'s idea was this: [Oliver] Lyttelton to become Chancellor of the Exchequer, [Sir John] Anderson to become M. of Production, Attlee to become Lord President of Council and nothing else, [Lord] Cranborne to return to Dominions Office where Attlee was a failure, Beaverbrook to be Lord Privy Seal and Leader of the Lords, Bracken to go to War Office, Dick Law to be M. of Information and Duff Cooper to be Assistant Minister at F.O.

A.E. asked us what we thought of this. We both immediately shook our heads at the idea of Duff coming and Dick going. We both said we liked Duff but he was far too lazy and indeed incapable now

---

[15] Churchill, immediately before the 1945 General Election, saw much of Beaverbrook, whom he regarded as a great political tactician, but afterwards they drifted apart.

of hard work at the F.O., whereas Dick was invaluable here. Nor would Dick be likely to prove a good M. of I. Could not Bracken remain at M. of I. and Dick become the Assistant Minister here? Here A.E. explained that the insufferable [Sir P.J.] Grigg was to be demoted to a civil servant again and made Head of the Civil Service, and Bracken, who had been ill, wanted a change from the M. of I.

Incidentally we thought Bracken who is good at the M. of I. would be deplorable at the W.O. ... This led me to suggest that Dick might be promoted to take [Sir William] Jowitt's[16] job as Minister without Portfolio in charge of reconstruction. Originally Jowitt was intended to do all reconstruction both home and foreign, but he proved such a failure that the foreign side lapsed back to Dick doing it entirely at the F.O. under A.E.

If Dick took this on, he could do both. He was extremely interested in it and the foreign and the home dovetailed into each other. A.E. liked this idea which had the additional advantage of avoiding a second cabinet post in the F.O. as such. Dick could do the F.O. side of reconstruction he was doing now, as M. of Reconstruction, and would of course work through our departments here.

But what about the M. of Information? If A.E. was to put this to the P.M., he must have a name ready as an alternative for M. of I. We thought of all the alternatives we could. It is a most difficult and thankless post. Duff had failed at it already. R.A. Butler couldn't be taken from his educational reforms. Finally, I said why shouldn't a newspaper proprietor do it? Bracken himself was a newspaper proprietor and the Ministry itself now was organised and only needed routine direction. Why not Camrose, who was respectable and respected among his fellows? A.E. was attracted by this and so was Alec and he agreed to put it to the P.M. in order to keep Dick for us as M. of Reconstruction ... (The P.M. has apparently got it into his head that Mrs Dick is a Communist!)

Eden saw Churchill again before dinner with these suggestions and that evening was also an Other Club night. Churchill told William of the intention to appoint Lyttelton Chancellor, to which William expressed astonishment. His objection was not, as Harvey opined, that Lyttelton 'the smart City man who would [not] go with the country', but the very opposite. When Lyttelton had been plucked from the City in 1940 to be President of the Board of Trade he had had to have his debts from pre-war gambling in tin paid by the industrialist, Sir Wyndham Portal.

[16] Lord Chancellor in the Attlee Government.

The appointment of a failed speculator as Chancellor might have left the country unmoved but would be ill-received in the City. Churchill must also have referred to the idea of making William Minister of Information, but he never mentioned it again.

Next day, Friday, Harvey continued his narrative:

This morning I tackled A.E. again. He had had a long night session with the P.M. after his dinner. It is now proposed that Lyttelton should not be Chancellor but should remain at M. of Production. Anderson is to be Chancellor. The appointment of Dick as M. of Reconstruction vice Jowitt is approved. Camrose as M. of Infn. is approved (my appointment!) A.E. sold these ideas to the P.M. who now is quite persuaded they were his own. But the P.M. is opposing Jim [Thomas][17] as U.S. here because he wants George Hall [Labour] to come from the Admiralty and to insert Duff Cooper as an Asst. Foreign Sec. P.M. does not like Jim for some reason (? his loyalty to Baldwin) and adores Duff.

A.E. told me this evening after a further talk with the P.M. that Labour were now demanding a larger share of seats and this had upset the plan again. Attlee had also vetoed Duff Cooper. As a result it had been decided not to move Jowitt or Simon, as we had hoped, but to make Dick Law Assistant Foreign Sec. In consequence of this, it was not possible to have 3 Tory Ministers in the F.O. and it was intended to put George Hall here (unless we could think of a better Labour man) and give him his place at the Admiralty ...

September 25
List of new appointments out today including the Beaver, Anderson as Ch. Excheq., Attlee as Ld. P. of C., Bobbety [Cranborne] at D.O. ... All the rest of the changes – Grigg, Bracken, Jowitt, Simon – are postponed or abandoned because of Labour difficulties.

Harvey was not, however, as well informed as he thought he was. Lord Cherwell, a long-standing friend, told William afterwards that it was not Attlee's general objection which had caused William's appointment to be revoked.

Beaverbrook had had a second meeting with Churchill and found that he was not to be Leader of the Lords (that job went to the 'aristocrat' Cranborne, later fifth Marquess of Salisbury). If he could not have that nor his own nominations, he was determined to put his jealous spoke in the wheel. William, he told Churchill, was still a sick man after his illness five years before and would inevitably break down.

[17] First Lord of the Admiralty in Churchill's 1951 Government.

It was a great disappointment, even though the Ministry of Information was hardly a plum. It would have been something and, without it, running a shrunken newspaper throughout the tumultuous war, when 'ignorant armies clashed by night' but no backseat driving was necessary, was a time of frustration. Like Trenchard, he yearned to 'serve'.

* * *

This is the last occasion when I refer in this narrative to the crossing of paths between William and Beaverbrook. I am aware that I may have seemed to be too much my father's 'champion' and that I may perhaps have gone out of my way to decry the virtues of Beaverbrook, an outstanding, remarkable man. I could do worse than to quote the appreciation of him by David Farrer, his Personal Secretary throughout the war from March 1940 onwards, who remains devoted to his memory:

Beaverbrook possessed an exceptional brain, great powers of concentration and of inspiring others, immense drive: he was adept at solving an immediate problem. But the long view too often escaped him and his vision was anyway too often clouded by prejudice. Personally he was capable of great generosity and kindness, but he lacked magnanimity: a slight or insult, real or unintentional, was not easily forgotten ... He had neither the balance of intellect and judgment nor the staying power to lead the country ...

After the affair of the Ministry of Information, William bore no long grudge, though his disappointment was acute. Characteristically he kept it deep within his immense personal reserve. Two years later, on 7 February 1945, he wrote to me:

Spent the weekend before last with Beaverbrook. Motored down in a snowstorm. [The last mile they had to stumble through a snowdrift with their mutual friend, Bracken.] Had quite an interesting time. He has bought quite a lot of land there [in Somerset] and in Lincolnshire. We are quite pals at the moment.

CHAPTER TWENTY-TWO

War III – General

NEWSPAPER SALES THRIVE in wartime. At first, there was plenty of newsprint to feed them. The finished product continued to arrive from Canada and Scandinavia under long-term contracts and there were large stocks of pulp to keep the home mills humming. The big London newspapers had learnt their lesson in the 1914–18 War and at first there was a self-denying ordinance to keep consumption down. All the penny newspapers agreed to keep their sizes down to twelve, ten and finally eight pages, while *The Times* was allowed two pages more on the grounds that it would publish service casualties in full (at first there were few casualties and, when there were more, they went unrecorded nationally).

It was a wise precaution. In France, where there were no home mills, consumption proceeded gaily at pre-war levels until the stocks ran out. As the winter of 1939/40 approached, the position became desperate. Many papers were reduced to single sheets and 'the failure of the newspapers to perform their national duty was one of the decisive factors in the downfall of France'.[1]

After the Norway débâcle the situation in Britain became worse. To Gomer, who suggested a winning idea to Beaverbrook, goes the credit. The idea was to form the non-profit-making Newsprint Supply Company,[2] which would take over all the contracts, guarantee the necessary £1 million finance and 'ensure that every newspaper in the country, from the smallest local weekly to the largest London consumer, should have a ration of newsprint', proportionate to previous consumption, at a common price.

The effect on the *Telegraph*, which before the war was the largest of all with an average of twenty-six pages, was more severe than on any other paper. *The Times*, as a twopenny, received the larger ration accorded to those at that price. As the ration screw turned – too many U-Boats and too few dollars – the daily page numbers quickly sank

---

[1] Article by William in *The Daily Telegraph*, 12 March 1942.

[2] Unlike any other Fleet Street body, before or since, the constitution provided that no 'alternate' directors were allowed. Each office was represented by its chairman and no decision could be deferred for 'in-house consideration'.

until four pages daily was the norm. This, William felt, would desecrate the character of the paper.

As J.B. Firth,[3] the paper's aging star writer, put it:

> When *The Daily Telegraph* conformed to the standard size of six pages, there were many forebodings of the hated knife which threatened to shear away so many attractive and pleasant features. It seemed as if the paper must shrivel into a lean shadow of its former self. So in bulk it did, but in bulk only. Most of the popular features, though in curtailed form, contrived to retain their pith and flavour ... But further contraction would spoil all and compel omissions disastrous to the individuality and personality of the paper ... Abbreviation easily degenerates into dullness ...
>
> The world never seemed to spin so fast. The international kaleidoscope never shook its pieces into patterns so bizarre and bewildering. Issues so vast never hung on threads so few ... The fibre of humanity was never so tough; the power of the common man to stand up and take the worst was never proved so gloriously night after night; the resolution to beat down the forces of tyranny, corruption and evil was never so invincible. A daily newspaper of six pages is all too inadequate to set forth the immortal hour in which we live, with a jealous selection from the myriad items which make up the common news incidents of the day ...

William therefore stretched his ration to provide six pages Tuesdays to Fridays[4] and took the cut in reduced circulation. What had been three-quarters of a million in August 1939, the last full month of peace, had grown to 900,000 in April 1940, and a million was within sight. Now 200,000 readers were chopped off overnight. Further cuts followed, but, with some relaxation, the *Telegraph* did not return to its pre-war figure until the month of VE Day in 1945. It had fared worse than most. By that day, by dint of a lighter-weight paper and reduced page margins, most rations had been used to increase sales and William doubted 'if there is any newspaper in the country – morning, evening or weekly – which is selling fewer papers than it did in 1939'.

Financially, too, the first effect was worrying. William had borrowed £200,000 from the National Provincial Bank for six months in 1937. At

---

[3] To compensate for the lack of non-war reporting in the paper, William put Firth on to edit *The Daily Telegraph* 'Miscellany', a pot-pourri of prose and poetry from the past. In the first, Firth inscribed in William's personal copy: 'To Lord Camrose, first journalist of his day. With sincere thanks for many kindnesses. The last not the least.' In all, five 'Miscellanies' were produced.

[4] To illustrate the absurdity of a four-page paper on Saturdays, the whole of the City section had to be compressed into a four-inch double column on the leader page.

the outbreak of war the debt was still outstanding and increasing. The chief general manager did not want it back, but he did want a higher rate of interest. It took three letters and two lunches to get him to 'see sense'.

At first, the drop in advertising and the rocketing price of newsprint caused serious losses, accentuated by guaranteed salaries to those called up for war service. Harold Nicolson, who wrote a weekly book review, recorded in his diary for 6 September, the third day of the war:

> I go round to the D.T. Camrose, Bishop [Literary Editor] tells me, has guaranteed full pay for six months to people who have been called up. This is typical of his generosity.

Thereafter, the tiny production staffs needed for the smaller papers, with less newsprint per copy and higher advertising rates for what spaces could be carried, produced quite large profits in most offices, though the *Telegraph*, because of its sacrifice of circulation, had to increase its cover price to a penny ha'penny.[5]

When William went to America in October 1942:

> The President [Roosevelt] asked me about the newspaper situation in England – was it true, as Beaverbrook had said, that the newspapers were making more money than ever, or was it one of Max's tales? When I told him it was true he seemed disappointed. He said, with some satisfaction, that the American papers were going to be cut in their paper supplies and didn't think they would like it.

(When William, on the same trip, lunched at the *New York Times*, he found that Arthur Sulzberger (the Publisher) 'expects paper to be rationed to 50% and is running unnecessarily large papers to qualify for as large a ration as possible'.[6])

If the responsibilities of the Chairman were worrying – though 'worry' was never in his vocabulary – the task of the Editor-in-Chief was frustrating. He continued the routine of intervention, described in Chapter 12, revised, after the first edition, leading articles he did not like, but complained he 'never could get anything in' – by which he meant it was of no use having ideas for news stories as there was never any room for anything extra. He recognised the great strain on the night editor, shoe-horning so much material into so small a space, and

---

[5] Costs had also been increased by printing the northern editions in Manchester from October 1940. The object was partly to provide later news in them and partly as an alternative printing source in case the London plant was bombed out.

[6] In Britain, at the most stringent period, newsprint use was down to 14 per cent of pre-war, at three times the price.

made himself a new rule never to comment on the first edition unless he had at least three alterations to suggest. He had always regarded himself as the supreme sub-editor. He now set about reducing the lineage of routine features – he was pleased with himself when he was able to cut six lines a column from the horse-racing programmes. As he wrote to Edward Iliffe when the latter bought the *Birmingham Post* in 1944: 'I had to go through space very religiously when the war came ...'

As Brian Roberts, wartime Night Editor, put it:[7] 'He would often point out that sloppy sub-editing was allowing too many paragraphs to spill over onto a new line ... He was critical but never unfair.'

He always backed the staff against outside interference, even from the highest level.[8] Churchill had the habit of telephoning the *Telegraph* and the *Express* at midnight every night to find out what was their lead story. One night Churchill discovered that the *Telegraph* was leading with the story of the sinking of a big British ship, claimed by German radio. He reacted violently and accused Roberts of 'creating despondency'. Roberts stuck to his guns but thought it prudent to protect his back and to ring William. William asked whether Roberts was sure he was right. When reassured he merely replied, 'Roberts, remember you, and not Mr Churchill, are Night Editor of *The Daily Telegraph*.'

*   *   *

In the Blitz of 1940 the windows of William's St James' Place[9] home were twice shattered and, the house being in any case too big for wartime, he moved to the Carlton Hotel, off Trafalgar Square. There, he found the traffic too noisy – which was fortunate as the hotel was soon bombed out. He moved instead into a suite at the Dorchester Hotel, overlooking Hyde Park, with a sitting room and dining room, where he could entertain on hotel rations.[10] The Dorchester, having been finished in the mid-1930s, was supposed to be exceptionally strongly built. My mother and he never used the air raid shelter, the old Turkish bath rest rooms, where so many notables came for the night – a night

[7] Roberts was later Managing Editor of *The Daily Telegraph* and, later still, the second Editor of the *Sunday Telegraph*.

[8] Gomer was different with the *Sunday Times*. H.V. Hodson, the last Editor before Lord Thomson bought Kemsley Newspapers, records that he once turned down an article by one of Gomer's friends. 'After this [Gomer] must see every article [submitted]. This lasted three weeks, during which he was buried with them.'

[9] The house was burnt to the ground in a fire bomb attack in 1941. Beaverbrook's Stornoway House was badly damaged at the same time.

[10] He usually managed to get his guests out by the time the first edition arrived about 11 pm. A tray of soft drinks was wheeled in, whereupon he would say cordially, 'Will you have something from the grog tray before you go?' No fire alarm could have been more efficient.

made the more hideous by the nearby heavy anti-aircraft gun site.[11]

I do not think William ever went to an air raid shelter during the whole war. A friend who came to lunch at the *Telegraph* wrote:

> The alarm was sounded just as I emerged from the lift. I said, 'Don't announce me yet – I will stay in the corridor until the alarm is over.' I asked the Sergeant [commissionaire] where Camrose went on such occasions and was told he always stayed at his desk.

In the country, Hackwood was requisitioned[12] in 1940 as a Canadian hospital but William was fortunate to be offered the rent of a nearby house, Audley's Wood, by Arthur Simonds, a member of the Reading brewing family, who was moving away. Thus he was able still to use the 3,000-acre park for shooting and walking when he was not venturing further afield. One of his neighbours was Brendan Bracken, who had been lent a cottage on the estate of Sir Wyndham Portal, who found it a convenient way of keeping in with the Prime Minister.[13] Bracken's cottage was some ten miles from Audley's Wood and they now cemented a friendship which had already formed before the war. Both had a compendious knowledge of newspapers and of personalities in the City. Bracken, too, could give many anecdotes about the lighter side of government. Both, too, were compulsive walkers and their meetings were usually accomplished on foot.

William always took his pedometer with him and kept a record. One weekend he reckoned he had done 'just over 100 miles' including one walk 'after dinner starting about 11 o'clock of just over $6\frac{1}{2}$ miles. It was a cold night but I enjoyed it very much. Strange form of amusement but very healthy.' For these achievements he did not always win acclaim. On one occasion, my mother's housemaid of a dozen years' standing, taking a walk herself, saw 'a shabby and disreputable looking man approaching her across the fields and hurriedly changed course to avoid him'. Afterwards William said to her, 'Why were you so anxious to avoid me?' She replied: 'Oh, I thought you were a tramp, my Lord.'

When his dressing table was ransacked by a petty thief he was much

---

[11] The site was commanded by Churchill's youngest daughter, Mary, now Lady Soames. It was said at the time, though she always denied it, that she occasionally burst a short-fused shell over the Dorchester to liven up her father's generation.

[12] He accepted no compensation.

[13] Portal was Minister for Works from 1942. When the outcome of the General Election of 1945 was announced, Portal went to Moyses Stevens, the florists, and instructed that his weekly order of flowers for Mrs Churchill be transferred to Mrs Attlee. He was a cold fish, too. When William had him to tea at Audley's Wood he found, on seeing him off, that he had been driven over by Lady Portal, who had been left sitting in the car.

less affected by the loss of his dress studs and a gold pocket knife than by the theft of his four pedometers.

Perhaps all this exercise was good training for a five-week trip he took in October/November 1942 to the United States and Canada. It would have been a gruelling schedule for the fittest man, but for a sixty-three-year old diabetic it was formidable, not least the return journey in a bomber:

Went to 15,000 feet right away and flew for $1\frac{1}{2}$ hours at 19,000. Bitterly cold and oxygen all the way. Seven a side upright on two benches with practically no room to move and conversation impossible owing to oxygen masks. Sleep equally impossible for same reason. A very rapid but unpleasant journey (8 hours 18 minutes), not easily forgotten ...

I happened to get leave the day he returned and found him sitting in a chair, green with exhaustion.

The journey must have been well prepared for almost every day of his four weeks on the American continent there was a lunch and dinner for him, at many of which he had to speak or answer questions in lieu. Reading his résumé of it, there seems to have been nobody of account on the East Coast, from the President and the Prime Minister of Canada downwards, whom he did not see.

His dry comments show that his observant reporter's eye had not dimmed. Of 'Cissie' Patterson, proprietor of the *Washington Times/Herald*, 'which she had bought to prevent Eugene Meyer [*Washington Post*] becoming too powerful in Washington':

It is said that the lady drinks rather freely and her appearance supports the idea.

Of Joseph E. Davies (late Ambassador to Moscow):

The house is full – too full – of works of art.

Of the Managing Editor of the Pittsburg Hearst paper:

... literally took possession of me ... Had the Manager of the hotel escort me to my room ... caused a bottle of whisky to appear immediately. Expressed great disappointment that I would not partake of it as he thought whisky was the great necessity for every

Englishman.[14] Brought a reporter in to interview me and sat talking until I literally had to ask him to go ...

Of a cocktail party:

A large attendance of Government people who, *en masse*, are a strange looking lot, many not unlike our English ideas of the old time gangsters. Halifax was there and I could not help being sorry for him in the boisterous way he was greeted and 'claimed' by them ...

Of Cordell Hull, the Secretary of State:

A great talker and not a very interesting one.

William had arrived at the right time. America had recovered her self-confidence after Pearl Harbor and had retaken the initiative in the Pacific. The President was feeling confident and William saw the immense new factories for tanks and aeroplanes at Ford's, General Motors, and Chrysler, and in Canada. The British star had not rearisen after the Battle of Britain, nor was the fighting in the desert yet acknowledged. It reinforced William's opinion formed at the Ministry of Information, as expressed by Harry Hopkins, the President's closest adviser, who came and talked for an hour and a half: 'Anti-British feeling had to be reckoned with and it kept on cropping up. Victories were the real antidote and propaganda on our part was of little value.'

*   *   *

As the tide of war began to turn and he was still without a war job,[15] his mind turned increasingly to the post-war disposition of his publishing empire. He decided to pass over the whole of the ordinary shares in the *Telegraph* to his two elder sons, who had both been in newspapers since they had left university. The instrument was a new trust, which, when

---

[14] It wasn't that William did not like a drink. Alex Faulkner, Chief New York Correspondent of the *Telegraph*, told Birkenhead that when William and my mother visited together 'there was always both tea and iced champagne waiting for them in the sitting room'.

[15] He made several speeches in the House of Lords during the war on several aspects of the Press, and on the BBC overseas services. On one occasion he refused to sign a BBC contract offering him '15 guineas including all expenses' ('only my sense of humour prevents me from expressing my reactions ...'). The only intervention I can trace that he wished to make on general affairs was in October 1944, a month after the fall of Paris, when the Allies had not yet released it from Eisenhower's overall military control. 'We have had one or two leaders on the subject [of recognising de Gaulle's Government] and I had given notice of my intention to move a motion about it. Cranborne asked me privately to hold it for a few days.' (The delay had been occasioned by Admiral Leahy, Roosevelt's chief of staff, who, as an ex-ambassador to Vichy, had a pathological opposition to de Gaulle.) 'I am of course both disappointed and relieved!' In addition he wrote Trenchard's speeches – Trenchard called William 'my English merchant' – for the House of Lords.

it was dissolved in 1946, then became free of his death duties. (He gave no news of it until the trust was dissolved, after which he announced at a staff Christmas lunch: 'I have the permission of the proprietors to wish you a happy Christmas.' To which the *Telegraph enfant terrible*, Malcolm Muggeridge, who had joined in June 1945, emitted a loud stage whisper: 'That is rather like Stalin being authorised by the OGPU[16] to smile.) He did not himself thereby give up control, though he drew no salary or dividend. He altered the Articles of Association so that he remained Chairman and Editor-in-Chief for as long as he wished, with power to appoint his successor.

He also simplified the investment in Condé Nast Inc., the publisher of *Vogue* and other up-market American magazines. Fifty-one per cent of Condé Nast had been bought in 1930 from its founder of the same name, not because of any faltering in its fortunes but because Nast had given power of attorney to his lawyer for speculating on margins on the New York Stock Exchange. William now had the Amalgamated Press (A.P.) purchase the stock, which was a logical financial step, since A.P. was all magazines. It was not, however, a laying-aside of responsibility, as A.P.'s magazines were chiefly down-market. Hence William, to the end of his life, dealt personally with the Condé Nast executives. (Nast and his successor bored him terribly with the endless provision of statistics – called by them 'Facts and Figures' (pronounced Fig-yours).)

The biggest problem was the *Financial Times*. Though the paper easily surpassed its only rival, the *Financial News*, in prestige, circulation and profitability, it was beginning to be a thorn in the flesh to the *Telegraph*. As the *Telegraph* had advanced so rapidly in the 1930s and could be expected to continue its rise after the war, it had begun to feel the competition for advertising with a paper under joint control. When I joined the *Financial Times* in 1937, immediately after the 'split' with Gomer, it was still being said to advertisement canvassers of one or other paper, 'We've done the Berrys.'

Until Brendan Bracken had become Minister of Information in 1941, he had been Chairman of the *Financial News*, and now remained in unofficial contact with its directors, in particular Garrett Moore (later eleventh Earl of Drogheda). In their country talks he and William wondered whether, in the to-be-presumed difficult post-war trading conditions, there was room for two financial papers, and whether a combined paper would not be a desirability. William, for his part, was assuming that, as after the First World War, newsprint rationing would

---

[16] Predecessor to the KGB.

soon be abolished, enabling the *Telegraph* greatly to expand its City section with the capacity to take all the City advertising on offer. He reminded himself that 40 per cent of *The Times'* pre-war advertising revenue had been financial.

By October 1944 Bracken had instructed Moore to make a formal approach. Moore was told the price of William's family 70 per cent holding plus the remainder held by the public would be 'upwards of the 30 shilling market price', or more than £750,000, which William thought 'more money than [the directors] can see, I imagine'. Bracken, now as cautious as he had been imprudent when forming the *Financial News* group in 1928–9, wished to hold back but the owners, the Crosthwaite-Eyre family, and the new Chairman, General Dawnay, founder of the merchant bank Dawnay Day, pressed on. So did the price. As the 1944 results and the prospects for 1945 came through, so William raised his sights. By December, he was asking 'nearer 35 shillings than 30'; in January 1945, '35 shillings or better', and in March, his firm price was two guineas.

At this point, William seems to have told Gomer what was going on. Gomer later maintained that, at the 'split', he had been given first refusal of the *Financial Times* if ever William wished to sell. There is no record, nor did I ever hear, that such a promise had been made. In addition, Lady Kemsley, who feared her husband was taking on too great a load of responsibility, had already vetoed Gomer's attempted purchase of the Iliffe Press (see Chapter 13). Moreover, the William/Gomer relationship was now much less cordial than it had been. William had been disturbed by Gomer's self-aggrandisement, both socially and in the *Sunday Times* and the *Daily Sketch*. He had felt, along with certain colleagues, that Gomer 'was inclined to indulge in certain schemes which would bring him personal kudos at too great a cost to the business'. He had been upset when the name of Allied Newspapers had been changed to Kemsley Newspapers with head-quarters in Kemsley House.

But he had been outraged when Gomer, a non-journalist, put 'A Kemsley Newspaper' below the title of the *Sunday Times*, virtually William's creation. (Nobody raised an eyebrow when Beaverbrook put 'Founded by Lord Beaverbrook' below the title of the *Sunday Express*, because that was literally true.) The assumption that the *Financial Times*, highly respected in the City, should also be labelled 'A Kemsley Newspaper' stuck in his gullet.

Fortunately Gomer did not rush to match the price of two guineas. He might be interested if the accountants, Price Waterhouse, thought it 'a reasonable price', but that meant authorising Price Waterhouse to go through the books. Thus, William froze him out and said that, to Gomer, the price would be 45/-, which seems to have ended the conversation. In May, William was further alienated. Gomer, a perennial Chamberlainite and publisher during the war of several anti-British American articles, wangled a step in the peerage, which William had secured for him, from Baron to Viscount from Churchill in the Dissolution Honours, on the promise that Kemsley Newspapers would support him in the General Election campaign. The first William heard of it was when he read the List.

Still there was dickering on the *Financial News* side, but it finally accepted the price on 15 May without argument. It was also provided that thirty of the *Financial Times* staff should have two- to three-year contracts and that any other member of at least five years' standing must be given a minimum of one year's notice before dismissal.

Completion of the deal proved technically difficult. As David Kynaston in his *Financial Times – a Centenary History* wrote:

> Moore was greatly helped by Camrose himself, who did everything he could to ease the F.N.'s path[17] ... A great man with a large, disinterested mind and deeply committed to the well-being of the press as a whole as well as his own particular ventures, he must have known that one combined paper would ensure the future of daily financial journalism, whereas the continuing existence of two might not.

As one result, William undertook to buy out all the outside shareholders and provided a 'bridging loan' before the *Financial News* could raise all the money.

William kept me, as an old *Financial Times* hand, abreast of all the negotiations. My reaction, bearing in mind the very patchy profits of 1931–9, and the price of 4/- on 1 July 1939, well before the war had started, may be taken as representative of contemporary reaction. Certainly David Kynaston bears me out: 'One day later and the FN might have had to pay rather less for what was still an exceedingly good bargain.'

The agreement was announced on the same day as the unexpected General Election results showing a Labour landslide and I wrote to William from Germany on 27 July 1945:

> What a smashing defeat! And all the more smashing for its

---

[17] The *Financial Times* held £300,000 worth of investments, mainly in Amalgamated Press shares and *Daily Telegraph* preference stock. These William offered to buy, providing the *Financial News* with extra money to complete the deal.

unexpectedness ... Taking a telescopically long-term view, I suppose the defeat might be interpreted as not such a bad thing. I remember Cranborne saying one night at dinner at the Dorchester that it might almost be good policy to lose this election for the likelihood of getting in for very much longer at the next. Yet I don't know that one could draw that conclusion from any of the big swings of this century. Losing an election and losing it by a clear margin of 150 seats are different ...

I always thought you were pretty hot stuff in a deal but the timing of the FT deal – though of course due to their dilly-dallying – seemed almost fictional. On the tape machine we have here, the announcement appeared directly above the first election result! Whether or not the price was full-valued on the long view, it will no doubt seem an excellent one for the next week or so ... I suppose this will mean that almost the whole of the 130,000 are bought out. So the result will be that, in all, you will be left with one quarter of the purchase price locked up for the time being.

To which letter William replied three weeks later, having had time to think it over:

The date of completion of the FT deal was indeed extraordinary but even allowing for what has happened in politics I still think the FN people have secured a very cheap purchase ... I also think, as I told you before, that I should not have stuck to the price I named in March before the year's business had developed so strongly. However the deal is done, and while at the moment I do not think it is a good one from our point of view, political events may later prove it to be better. In any case I am glad that I guaranteed to take up half the shares which may come in as the result of the offer made to outside shareholders ...[18]

Bad deal or not, it was broadly in line with William's philosophy. Reviewing all the purchases and sales recounted in earlier chapters, there are no examples of his getting anything on the cheap nor calling it a bargain. He always felt that in any deal there should be no big winners or losers and that neither side should be left with any sourness. At one time he saw much of William Graham, Sir John Ellerman's solicitor and his nominee as chairman of the *Financial Times*. He was always fascinated and slightly disgusted at Ellerman's habit of sitting

---

[18] These shares were still held by the family on William's death in 1954 and were retained long after the *Financial Times* control was bought by Lord Cowdray's S. Pearson conglomerate in 1957.

at lunch by his telephone and getting great satisfaction from haggling in sixty-fourths (the lowest unit of a stock bond).

So it was that Malcolm Muggeridge completely misunderstood him when he recounted in his diary for January 1951:

> lunched upstairs with Camrose, guest of honour being Portuguese Ambassador – an ex-professor (like Salazar) now big business. We spoke of Gulbenkian, Armenian oil magnate who lives in a Lisbon hotel. Camrose slightly annoyed when Ambassador said that Gulbenkian had £200–300 million. 'Is he happy?' Camrose asked eagerly and Ambassador (to my delight) replied, 'Yes, I think so.' I weighed in to say that I never could understand this business of the burden of wealth, being always myself in the position of wanting to shoulder some. This also didn't please Camrose but did his son, Michael, sitting beside me, immensely.[19]

*　　*　　*

This chapter is intended to bring my narrative up to the end of the war. Some subjects which had their beginnings during the war period have had to be followed to their conclusions post-war. I now return to strict chronology with the vivid account, which William wrote down in a memorandum, of the evening of VE day, when he dined *en famille* with Churchill (Mrs Churchill was in Moscow), his daughters Diana and Sarah, and Diana's husband Duncan Sandys, MP:

> Molly asked, but inclined to stay with the small family party at the Dorchester. At the end of dinner, Winston was informed by Commander Thompson and Desmond Morton that there was a tremendous crowd in Parliament Street and that they were calling for a speech. Winston said simply, 'I will go up in five minutes.' He was wearing his 'boiler' suit, and when asked by Morton if he would change he replied emphatically that he would go as he was.
>
> I accompanied him on the long walk from the Annexe through the various Government buildings, and the roar of enthusiasm which came up from the crowd at the sight of him and his grandson, Julian Sandys, was deafening. I went on to one of the adjoining balconies. Not only was the space immediately in front of the building packed, but there was a sea of faces stretching far up Whitehall and right down to Parliament Square.

---

[19] Gulbenkian ('Mr Five Per Cent') was understandably a sad figure. He spent his life wheeling and dealing. His wife was living apart from him and he was not on speaking terms with his son. He had an extraordinary picture collection but nowhere to enjoy it. I suppose the explanation for my seemingly bad manners must have been that I was laughing with Muggeridge, not at my father.

It was half past ten. As Churchill spoke, William noted, 'the crowd roared and roared again'.

'The roaring and cheering,' wrote Elizabeth Layton, who was on the adjoining balcony, 'exceeded by double anything I can remember at the Coronation.'

Churchill told the thousands assembled below him: 'My dear friends, this is your hour. This is not victory of a party or of any class. It's a victory of the great British nation as a whole. We were the first, in this ancient island, to draw the sword against tyranny. After a while we were left all alone against the most tremendous military power that has been seen. We were all alone for a whole year.

'There we stood, alone. Did anyone want to give in?'

'No,' shouted the crowd.

'Were we downhearted?'

'No!'

The crowd replied by singing 'Land of Hope and Glory' and 'For He's a Jolly Good Fellow'. Churchill then returned to the small study in the Annexe, where he spent the rest of the evening alone with William. William's account ends:

In the middle of our conversation he called in Rowan, one of his secretaries, to ask if there were any telegrams for his attention, whereupon Rowan brought in a pile of files 6 inches high ...

Then he called for the newspapers. Was very annoyed with a cartoon in the *Daily Mail*, praised the D.T. pictures and proceeded to read *Times* leader. This led him to recall D.T. leader in his favour in regard to the air programme in 1934 and to say that Baldwin lunching with him two years ago had admitted how great a mistake he had made on the question of air preparedness.

I left him at 1.15 with the pile of files before him, all of which he said would be dealt with before he went to bed. On the point of my leaving he had Rowan in again and said he had found some request in the files that he should visit the City today (Wednesday). Asked Rowan whether the Lord Mayor was very anxious for the visit. On the latter saying he thought so he replied, 'Very well, I shall go to Mansion House at 4 o'clock tomorrow to take a glass of wine with his lordship.' (He also had an idea of calling on the Russian Ambassador and perhaps the American. This is what he actually did, calling also on the French Ambassador.)

CHAPTER TWENTY-THREE

The Last Years

BY THE END of the war William was sixty-six. Though he still had to inject himself daily with insulin, he was otherwise pretty fit. He had had no recurrence of the blood poisoning, probably caused by his teeth – all had to be extracted – which had kept him away from the office for four months on end in the early 1930s. He had given up his very strong Markovitch Turkish cigarettes and now smoked American Lucky Strike, but none before lunch. For lunch he took a single dry Martini (instead of sherry) and perhaps half a bottle of hock. At dinner he and my mother always had extremely iced champagne and, in later days, he enjoyed a single villainous liqueur, a mixture of brandy and benedictine. He never drank between meals nor had a nightcap. In office hours it was tea all day and much Malvern water at all other times.

As to family affairs, he had, he reckoned, put his house in order. He had provided financially for all his eight children, four of whom were married, so that their combined net wealth in terms of investments greatly exceeded his own and my mother's.[1] He now started on his grandchildren,[2] giving them each covenants of £2,000 a year, and caused my mother to do the same. For all his dependents he provided what are now called Financial Services – management, tax and insurance – with a staff of two, then three,[3] which together with their various personal problems occupied him for an hour or so daily.

Marjorie Eden, assistant on the private office staff from 1933 and in charge from 1952, described to Birkenhead how he always kept private affairs strictly separate from his publishing interests. She thought him 'a financial wizard. He had excellent judgment, many contacts and very great patience.' (He had three criteria for investment – quality of management, timing and the 'long pocket' (the reserves necessary for patience).)

He had a gift for getting the best out of his employees. He did not

---

[1] He had divided his investments with her. Hackwood and its contents were held half and half.
[2] At the time of his death their number had grown to twenty-two.
[3] At first, they had been a 'scratch lot'. The original head of the office had been company secretary of *Health & Strength* when William took it over.

pay them particularly well, but they always tried hard. He never paid direct compliments – more likely, 'I can't find any mistakes in this', than 'a good piece of work here'... He liked people to be there when he wanted them and could get very annoyed when they were not.

In business he retained control of the Amalgamated Press but not in a hands-on sense. He lunched regularly with the managing director at the *Telegraph* office and with the head of its subsidiary, the Imperial Paper Mills. He also ran the Iliffe (trade magazines) subsidiary directly through its own managing director. The only editor he saw regularly was the editor of the *Farmer and Stockbreeder*, the market leader, with whom he liked to talk farming. He had, before the war, entertained all the directors of the joint enterprise for an annual weekend in northern France on his yacht, and was to do so again when he had got another one. But he purposely never went to their offices because he wished the managing directors to be masters in their own house, though, as one remarked, 'He could be tough as hell.' Claude Wallis, the Managing Director of Iliffe's, who hero-worshipped him, told Birkenhead a droll story:

During the war the south bank of the Thames opposite the *Telegraph* [on the north side] was badly bombed. [William] asked Wallis if they had escaped unscathed. 'Yes', he said, pointing out the view of the Cornwell Press from the window. 'Oh,' said [William], 'I had always wondered what that building was.' He had never been there. Cecil King [who bought the business in 1959, after William's death] went there all too often ...

With the *Telegraph*, of course, it was a very different story. He continued to read every line of it and most lines in other papers too. But, unlike other proprietor/journalists,[4] he had seen to it that his two sons, now thirty-six and thirty-four, had had experience in almost every department of newspaper journalism. He would still be in charge but his sons must now do the donkey work. As he wrote to me when the war seemed to be ending: 'I am looking forward to the day when you and Seymour are free again and can tackle some of the difficulties here. I suppose you'll want a holiday first and I won't grudge you that. But afterwards, oh boy!'

---

[4] C.P. Scott, of the *Manchester Guardian*, had ensured that one of his sons was trained as a journalist but shortly after his father's death he too died, drowned in a boating accident. His other son, Laurence, though very able, was purely a businessman.

William was intending to take things easier, but not to take it easy.[5] Now that the *Telegraph* was his only paper he had big plans for its development as soon as newsprint rationing was abolished. But rationing never was abolished in his lifetime so that no new papers were possible and only limited expansion could take place in *The Daily Telegraph* itself. Three times the *Telegraph* advanced through the 'magic milion' sale: the first was a statistical fluke for a single day when unlimited sales were first permitted; the second, in April 1947, was a genuine average (when William could claim, in a leader-page article, the first quality million sale in the world, the next nearest being the *New York Times* at 540,000), quickly cut back by the fuel crisis of that winter and the run-down of the American loan. The third and final passage through the million was not until April 1953, while *The Times* wallowed at 250,000. Before the war, when the *Telegraph* was increasing so rapidly, *The Times* had looked upon it as a 'semi-popular' paper and its increase 'a mechanism for weaning readers from the popular press and preparing them for *The Times*'. Robin Barrington-Ward, the Deputy Editor, expected 'to skim the cream of these new readers in due course'.

It was still an unsatisfying period. Rationing was by tonnage. Sales were theoretically infinite but pages limited. William had hoped that some of the prestige of *The Times* would be transferred to the *Telegraph*, first from *The Times*' 'Munichois' record and now from its seeming flirtation with mild Marxism under Robin Barrington-Ward (now its Editor), and his supposed guru, Professor E.H. Carr. But the *Telegraph* was limited to ten pages, whereas *The Times* had twelve. Small though it was, the latter was able to print very fully the 'documents of State'; the blue books and technical law reports, so that it was called 'the paper of record', a 'must' for mandarins. It was also pre-eminent in its Letters column and in its voluminous obituaries.

(Attlee, the new Prime Minister, told Barrington-Ward, 'I'm old-fashioned. I read *The Times* every morning at breakfast. I glance at the *Daily Herald* [the Labour paper]. Must I read the *Daily Mail?*' William, though he knew all the other Labour leaders who had been in the Coalition Cabinet, never met Attlee until the end of his period in office, when he asked William to Downing Street.) The *Telegraph* could not afford space for such narrow interests and concentrated, in news, on a

---

[5] By now he had become the most respected of all the Fleet Street proprietors, the model of what a newspaper proprietor ought to be. As with Lord Goodman, when he ceased to be Chairman of the Newspaper Publishers' Association in the 1970s, old-timers appealed to him as the last court of appeal. At his instigation Stanley Bell, Managing Director of Associated Newspapers, who had been pushed aside by Rothermere in favour of the latter's brother-in-law, was rewarded with a £68,000 (now £900,000) pay-off.

comprehensive, accurate coverage of all events, great or small, international, national or local, which appealed to the average educated reader. As Paul Johnson was later to write of this period: 'If you wanted to know what was going on, at home and abroad, in full accurate detail, you could not beat the *Telegraph*.'

Politically, though, William unwittingly limited the prestige of the *Telegraph* by his perhaps too invariable support for Churchill – though not necessarily for his colleagues – in or out of office. He felt that Churchill, now that he had shed the eccentricity and short-termism of his earlier years, was incomparably the greatest statesman of the age. He knew that Churchill, having been the great war leader, was setting out to be an equally great leader in peace. Churchill, however, particularly when in Opposition, was a politician again and, as a politician, revelled in controversy. During the war he told Barrington-Ward, who regarded himself as a 'Tory Radical', that, after all the other papers, he read *The Times* 'last but one', finishing up with the *Telegraph* 'because I know it will be all right'. After the war he told his son, Randolph, he would rather have one favourable comment in *The Times* than twenty in the *Telegraph*. It came to be said that the *Telegraph* was 'predictable', though it was never accused in any quarter, as were others, of distorting news or suppressing facts in opposition to its political views. (How long William's regular support of the Conservative Government would have survived Churchill's retirement (nine months after William's death) is debatable. Anthony Eden he regarded as solely a foreign affairs man, while Harold Macmillan he thought 'not a man of character', unlike Cranborne (Salisbury).)

Even so, William was disappointed that the *Telegraph*'s virtually unique unflappability during the worst moments of the war had not merited more public recognition. He had long felt that *The Times* no longer deserved its continued high reputation, dating from the nineteenth century. In a telling extract from Barrington-Ward's diary, I quote an entry of 22 March 1945, less than two months before the European war's end. He was seeing Brendan Bracken at the Ministry of Information, whose views, he shrewdly observed, 'may take some colour from his company'. 'Camrose has evidently been talking in a superior way about what *he* would do if he had it ... What a property to develop etc. All the same he is obsessed with jealousy of it.' However, there was nothing personal about it. William and he often met at Grillon's dining club, where he recorded 'some friendly chat with Camrose'.

Certainly, the battle for prestige over *The Times* was never won. The *Telegraph*, with its horror of socialism, came down too much into the arena. It became too shrill in its attempt to reverse, at the next election, the verdict of the people and could see no merit in the administration of the arrogant 'new masters'. *The Times*, on the other hand, though battered by friend and foe alike, retained its authority, not, as had been assumed in pre-war days, as 'the voice of the Foreign Office', but as the calm, disinterested observer. Robin Barrington-Ward put the position magisterially to his diary:

> While it is the duty of the Opposition to oppose, it is the duty of *The Times* to get the best it can out of the Government of the day. The King's Government has to be carried on.

Such an attitude infuriated Churchill. He said, it was reported to Barrington-Ward, that the paper is 'parlour socialism'. Conservative MPs thought it 'often ambiguous: it will not nail its colours to the mast on either side.' To which the diary rejoined: 'Why the devil should it? People like an independent Press but hate "an independent newspaper".'

Ernest Bevin, Labour's Foreign Secretary, was equally damning. He told Barrington-Ward to his face *The Times* was 'spineless'. 'I had a lot of pink intelligentsia down there. [*The Times*] was taken abroad as a national newspaper. He was going to tell the House of Commons that it was not – it was pro-Russian and not pro-British.' (This was a reference to the influence of E.H. Carr, described to the diary as 'bosh', though Carr was often 'in charge' at night.)

Only General Smuts, much respected internationally, was reassuring to him:

> You are still the greatest newspaper in the world and you deserve to be. You are the only exporter of opinion. Those others, *The Daily Telegraph* and so on, are all local. You can influence opinion abroad.

The verdict must be that William expected too much from the *Telegraph*'s fine pre-war and wartime record, and its greatly superior news coverage. In peace time, its views were too often 'party political' and, through the insistence on immediacy (unlike *The Times*, they were always 'on the news'), too little thought-through. Even in the news columns, the Labour Party was always called the Socialist Party (it certainly *was* socialist, but that was not its name). *The Times*, on the other hand, because of, rather than in spite of, its aberrations, was quite obviously 'independent'.[6]

*　　*　　*

[6] This was the view of the 'intelligentsia' who dribbled to the *Telegraph* over the years. They felt, in their superior way, they had taken a step down.

The prospects for development had to be dropped. The *Evening Tele-graph* (or *Post* as it was to be called) was the first to go, though not without a struggle. In the first, optimistic days of 1946 William recorded a memorandum of a meeting with Gomer:

K – 11th January, 1946
Repeated what he told me before that Beaverbrook had told him in definite terms that in no circumstances would he start an evening paper in Manchester in opposition 'to such an old friend'.

Asked me whether I was going to start an evening paper and, on my replying in the affirmative, said, 'but when?' To this I replied rather quickly, 'as soon as circumstances permit', and reminded him that we had already invested the best part of £200,000 in preparation for the venture.

He gave me the impression of being disappointed with my reply and made me feel quite certain that he is most anxious to start one himself.

However, the evening project, which meant printing half from the *Telegraph* building and half from a building in Stamford Street (south of the river), did not last long and neither my brother nor I remember it being mentioned again after the war. A couple of years later he had Bartholomew, now Chairman of the *Daily Mirror*, to lunch and sold him twelve units of machinery (representing £100,000) and the building in Stamford Street in which they were stored.[7]

A *Sunday Telegraph* was a more serious proposition. It could all be printed on the *Telegraph* presses, though that would mean aborting the *Sunday Times* printing contract. William saw Gomer in October 1952 and 'stated definitely we should start a Sunday paper as soon as circumstances permitted'. Gomer was perturbed by the £300,000 loss being made by the *Daily Graphic* (the name had been changed from *Daily Sketch*) and was thinking of selling it to the *News of the World* (actually, he sold it to the *Daily Mail*). His very large building in Gray's Inn Road (north of Holborn) would then be sold to Cecil King, who had ousted Bartholomew as Chairman of the *Daily Mirror*. (King was known to be seeking a new building.) The *Sunday Times* could be moved to the *News Chronicle* in Fleet Street, which had no Sunday work.

Gomer appears not to have taken this seriously. When the two brothers met in December, Gomer 'had come to the conclusion that I would never start a Sunday paper against the *Sunday Times*'.

William now tried a new tack and blamed his threat on his sons:

[7] The *Mirror* was to start its weekly magazine, *Reveille*, there.

I pointed out that the decision did not necessarily rest with me ... it would be impossible for the proprietors of the DT to tie their hands behind their backs for all time in what today was to my mind an inevitable development of such a paper as *The Daily Telegraph*. He clung to his idea that I could never do it – and we left it at that.

Gomer evidently confided his alarm to Brendan Bracken, who three weeks later wrote to Beaverbrook:

Kemsley was much irritated by Camrose telling him that the decision to publish a *Sunday Telegraph* was taken by his family who will be in charge of the paper in years to come, rather than by him. It is for this reason that he wants to start a Sunday Edition as soon as possible.

I do not remember hearing of these exchanges from William. Certainly no plans were made, nor was there any talk of giving the *Sunday Times* the necessary twelve months' notice to quit. All I do remember was William saying meditatively: 'If I were ten years younger I think I could do it', which suggests Gomer had some cause for irritation in that the new enterprise was blamed on the sons he had been generous to as adolescents now challenging his hard-won position, but the inspiration would come from the father – far from retired.

I do not know how serious his intention of starting a Sunday may have been, though he had mentioned it tentatively in wartime letters. It may be that his chief aim was to curb Gomer's self-importance – naming the *Sunday Times* 'A Kemsley Newspaper' still rankled – and to make him realise that he must be prepared to meet strong competition from which war had cocooned him. Certainly William made no attempt to build up a cash reserve with which to nourish a new enterprise. Sunday companion or no, he conceived *The Daily Telegraph* as an Institution – a paper constructed on its own peak of readership and readability that few educated people could be without. He had no feeling that family money should be made out of the *Telegraph*, in contradistinction to all his other pre-war enterprises. He merely said, briefly, summing up these unspoken feelings: 'To make less than £5,000 a week would be undignified.' I think, too, that he believed a new Sunday could be floated on the enormous goodwill of the Daily and that, like Beaverbrook's 1918 *Sunday Express*, it could be a seventh day edition of the Daily. I am inclined to give that explanation as I myself, who had 'sat at his feet' for so many years, came to believe in the seventh-day idea and acted upon it – disastrously – in 1961,[8] following Gomer's willing sale of the *Sunday Times* to Roy Thomson.

As William handed over the ordinary chores to his sons – like postmortems, news editing and scrutiny of the weekly accounts – so he changed his habits. He rarely came into the office on Mondays and left much earlier in the evening. He still kept a watchful eye and though he did not copy Northcliffe's habit of dictated written bulletins, they were none the less vivid, coming down the telephone. At first he kept to himself, but soon abandoned, the evening conference with the editor about the leading articles. He kept in touch with the top editorial staff by playing host to frequent lunches of six to ten seniors of the fifth floor, which before and during the war he had tended to keep for outsiders.

Post-war, William was by now a generation older than most of the editorial staff, with the exception of Watson, the Editor, who was soon to retire. He had a reputation with most of them as 'a very stern and unapproachable person', partly because he was a shy, non-back-slapping character and partly because he rarely ventured on to the editorial floor and so knew few except by telephone. In the latter connection, there was perhaps an apocryphal story of his once enquiring of a passing sub-editor where was the editor's office. The sub is said to have replied: 'Why don't you do the proper thing and ask at the Lodge in the front hall. They will enquire whether the editor can see you and, if so, will take you to him.'

A better picture of him at this time is provided by Desmond Flower, son of Sir Newman Flower, of Cassell's, who used often to call by request to discuss book publishing matters. When talking business Flower described him to me thus:

> He was a large man, resembling a cross between an elder statesman and Buddha, but there was a twinkle in his eyes. When he spoke, for he was a man of few words, a smile would wander across his stern features and be gone so quickly that one wondered if its existence had been a trick of memory. He sat behind a huge desk on which I never once saw a piece of paper ... Sitting alone with this dynamo which worked so silently I developed a love and respect which after so many years remain in affectionate memory.

Withal, as Muggeridge testified, 'he was peaceful and easy to be with. Compared to Beaverbrook and [C.P.] Scott [of the *Manchester Guardian*]

---

[8] The sale of the *Sunday Telegraph* quickly fell back to about half of the Daily. A reorientation took about nine months but much goodwill had been lost.

he was a very considerate man who didn't try to make monkeys out of his staff and bully them.' He disliked 'yes-men'. Roy Pawley, Foreign News Editor, remembered him saying to one executive: 'No, you're saying what you think I think. I can do that for myself.' He liked people to stand up for themselves. He was much amused with his exchange with an elderly reporter working on a financial story:

William: I don't think you know anything about money.

E.R.: If I did, I'd be at your end of the telephone.

He was less tolerant with a member of the New York staff. Alex Faulkner, long-time chief correspondent, told Birkenhead how the man:

> had got rather worked up about his need for a larger salary, decided (without telling me) to beard [William] at the St Regis Hotel, where he waited for him in the lobby and told him he wanted to talk to him. Lord Camrose invited him up to his sitting room, where [the man] spoke at length and with considerable emotion. 'What a thing to do!' I said to Lord Camrose when he told me about it. 'Oh, I didn't mind that,' he replied, 'but what really bothered me was his total lack of understanding of money. It's all right to ask for more, but not to be so confused about it.' He didn't get it.

He could also be whimsical. The number of his office telephone must have been close to that of the canteen. Once he intercepted a call from the news editor saying angrily: 'For God's sake, send down my coffee and sandwiches at once.' A little later the news editor got a call from William asking if they had come down all right.

He knew what it was like to be fired, and he rarely fired anyone with any length of service, though he once sacked a senior sub-editor out of hand for getting all the new salaries wrong in a page-one report of a Cabinet reshuffle (rejecting representations from a delegation from the National Union of Journalists). His usual reaction to some folly was 'Better replace him. What else can you offer him?' Or sometimes he would send him to the Amalgamated Press, where lack of immediacy could be tolerated. But with pretentious people, he was more abrupt. When Colin Coote was Editor after Watson, he brought up to a fifth-floor lunch an executive he had newly taken on. William had a few words with him alone as the lunch was breaking up and said to me afterwards: 'Pay him well but get rid of him.'

For the fifth-floor lunches William was much more relaxed. There, he was host rather than employer. One frequent luncher recalled, 'They were free and easy with a lot of bantering.' Muggeridge and Hugo Wortham, the Editor of 'Peterborough', the Court Jester, the only man in the building who was permitted to be slightly drunk after lunch, were given free rein. After lunch, however, 'normal relations would be restored. He would ring down and ask for something AT ONCE. He could be very frightening.'

At home, he was even more relaxed. He encouraged his children to bring their friends home: 'They were a pretty noisy family,' one said. 'There was constant chatter and argument.' Of course, there was a good deal of nonsense talked and impossible positions maintained. Like 'F.E.', but unlike Churchill, he showed interest in their opinions and never made 'put-downs'. He drew them out and 'talked to them in an equal, unpatronising way'. He was not above taking the mickey out of a petulant, newly-married 'Society beauty'. He kept up her husband late playing billiards and then advised him on a ploy allegedly learnt in his youth: 'Open the door quietly, throw one shoe in and see what sort of a reception it gets. If it comes back, sleep on the sofa.'

One of them, Murrough O'Brien, grandson of Lord Inchiquin, with a fund of Irish stories to which he was always being asked to add, he made an advertising representative on the *Financial Times* and finally Advertising Manager. O'Brien was witness to one of William's boyish escapades. The two of them were sitting after dinner at Hackwood with Brendan Bracken when the subject of a mutual *bête noir* came up – Edward Beddington-Behrens. Behrens had been a partner with Mossy Myers but, fancying himself as an amateur singer, had been sacked following his distribution of a record with himself singing 'Parlez-Moi d'Amour' to Myers' elderly clients as a Christmas present. William had got it into his head that Behrens had been at Eton and could not understand how an Etonian could commit such an appalling error of taste. Bracken said that he had not been there. When each stuck to his position, they bet each other 1,000 cigars, and then discovered from the *Telegraph* library that Bracken was the winner. As they saw Bracken off, William turned to O'Brien and said, with a charming smile, something O'Brien has never forgotten: 'Let that be a lesson to you all your life, my boy. Never make foolish bets about things you don't really know about.'

The sequel was more bizarre. William always smoked 'green' Corona cigars, only obtainable in New York, and took several weeks to assemble them. He then sent them to Bracken with a not very funny card – 'With the Compliments of Edward Beddington-Behrens'. Bracken had by now forgotten the bet and wondered whether it would be too rude to send them back to Behrens, by now a company promoter. Finally, Bracken thought he had solved his problem by going to a Bond Street dealer and buying Behrens an Impressionist picture.

* * *

Soon after the war, Labour members of parliament, on behalf of the National Union of Journalists, began campaigning for a Royal Commission on the Press. The contention was that the Press was increasingly controlled by monopolies, for the benefit of advertisers, and with consequent suppression of essential news and free speech. William had already addressed the issue in an article before the war, in the context of the appeasement of Hitler, when the question was whether the newspapers were largely controlled by Jews and unknown international financiers. He had always believed that the public was both ignorant of, and interested in, the ownership of the Press. He proved right in that when he enlarged the article into a pamphlet, *Newspapers and Their Controllers*,[9] it sold 40,000 copies. When the appointment of a Commission was delayed, he decided to update the pamphlet and this time included the provincial press and the opinion-forming weeklies. His researches took him some six months and he published the result in a book, *British Newspapers and Their Controllers*, which ran to several editions.

It was largely a work of reference, embellished by 'the narration of a certain amount of newspaper history of which I have become possessed in nearly fifty years of life in Fleet Street' – some fascinating examples of why good and bad newspapers had failed. The book pleased the public but not the intelligentsia. They wanted something on the lines of, but not necessarily in the sense of, Kingsley Martin's (Editor of the left-wing *New Statesman*) *The Press the Public Wants*, unkindly described as 'the Press Martin wanted the Public to want'. But that was, as I hope the whole of this book makes clear, not William's style. Not for him the paradoxes and ambiguities of the theoretician. 'I have not attempted to analyse the motives and policies by which these papers are directed.'

* * *

A great deal of time in the immediate post-war years was taken up, too, by the matter of Churchill's *War Memoirs*. It had taken Churchill some time to make up his mind. In 1943 William had recorded that Churchill was aware that he must earn something for his family and in January 1945 he wrote to his son, Seymour, that the *Telegraph* was promised *'first refusal*, though it's problematical that they will get written.'

Churchill lunched alone with William at the *Telegraph* office on 7 August 1945, ten days after his crushing defeat at the polls. After expressing his disgust at being excluded from peace-making he said that he might stand down as Leader of the Opposition. As to his war

---

[9] With photographs of all the principals but, typically, not his own.

memoirs, he was re-reading all his wartime minutes which he had had specially printed by the Government printers – 'Each month's printing is equal to, say, two volumes of a weekly review like the *Spectator*.' 'But at the moment he has decided that he will not publish his account ... in his lifetime.'

William does not explain this but I think the explanation must be that, with tax at 98 per cent, there would be virtually nothing left. If, on the other hand, he were to live seven years he might pass the manuscript to his children as a gift without tax. If he did not so live, death duties would at least be less punishing than income tax.

The problem was solved for him at the end of the year when his tax advisers came up with a scheme, which was adopted thereafter by many public figures with families and a story to tell. It was arranged that all the Churchill papers would be given by Churchill to a trust in favour of his children. The trust would then make a contract with a publisher who would, in turn, employ an author to write the history. As the history would sell all over the world it was obvious that the publisher should deal with world rights. It so came about that the *Telegraph*, which already had 'first refusal', became the publisher and a special company, Churchill & Telegraph Publications, was registered to deal with all the legal problems arising. When the contract came to be drawn up, Churchill said whimsically to William: 'Bill, I do hope you'll think of me.' (Actually it was provided that if Churchill was to be incapacitated, the work should be finished by Duff Cooper, though I do not know if he was ever consulted.)

And so it came about that William, without any publicity, set forth in the maiden voyage of the *Queen Elizabeth* (other than as a troop ship) to New York in November 1946. William had undertaken to sell the world rights without fee and clearly the American serial rights would be the most lucrative.

There were two competing syndicates, each of one national magazine and one newspaper, all of whose principals were known to William – *Time Life* and the *New York Times*, the *Saturday Evening Post* and the *New York Herald Tribune*. William felt that there would be more prestige with the first syndicate and soon found there was more money.[10]

All the sales, concluded by the end of 1946, came to the vast sum of £568,000[11] for five volumes, of which Churchill's share was £175,000

[10] Mrs Helen Reid, Publisher of the *Tribune*, disputed this. She pursued William to his departing liner, where he had to hide in his cabin.

[11] Contributors were *Life/N.Y.Times* £287,500 ($1,150,000), *Montreal Standard* £27,500 ($110,000), US and Canadian book rights £62,500 ($250,000), *Telegraph* £75,000, Cassell (British Book rights) £40,000, Keith Murdoch (Australia) £75,500.

(£35,000 per volume) and the trustees' £393,000 for the whole. At 1992 prices (a comparison calculated by the Bank of England based on the Retail Price Index – an unsatisfying comparison but the only one there is) the total would have been almost £100 million.

Thereafter a verbal agreement with these publications was the least of the worries. Two teams of executives and lawyers descended on the *Telegraph* building and split legal hairs with the single *Telegraph* lawyer for ten days, including a lunch at Hackwood. Before the lunch, Seymour questioned the rather frugal fare that had been ordered: 'Couldn't they at least finish with cheese?' 'No,' replied William, 'I don't want them to think we're too rich.'

It seemed that New York copyright law is largely German-inspired and the *New York Times* was especially wearing. The position was complicated by the method of publication – *Life* would publish in large weekly chunks whereas the *New York Times* and the *Telegraph* (the latter more slowly as it had less space) would print daily. Much of the argument turned on the prevention of 'newsworthy scoops', a concept clear to the New York lawyers but incomprehensible to any British journalist.

Life celebrated the deal by running a profile of William, asserting that if he had not been a British peer he would have made a perfect Tammany Hall 'boss'. He was 'very much amused' by this as he had read many books about the pre-First World War bosses and their ingenious ways. His real American 'heroes', however, were the big city gangsters, flowering in the Prohibition era. The film critic of the *Telegraph* was forever borrowing gangster films from the distributors to be shown in the basement cinema room at Hackwood.[12]

*   *   *

Before Churchill's tax experts had dreamed up the arrangements by which he could have his *War Memoirs* cake and eat it, he had explained his financial position to William. On 7 August 1945, at lunch at the *Telegraph*, he recounted a tale of woe to William. He had been so much in debt before the war that he had put his home, Chartwell Manor (near Westerham, Kent) on the market in 1938. His old friend, Sir Henry Strakosch, had heard of it, paid off his debts and had him cancel the sale. Now he explained that he was in a better position, with 'between £110,000 and £120,000 in the bank'. ('In the bank' seems unlikely as Churchill was an inveterate speculator. Once, when early for

---

[12] Beaverbrook preferred Westerns while Churchill, at Chequers, preferred sentimental action films about the Empire, repeated *ad nauseam*.

lunch at Chartwell, William surprised an embarrassed Churchill looking at the Stock Exchange prices on the tape machine in the hall).[13] 'He reckoned,' however, 'that he could not live on less than £12,000 a year' (presumably after tax). Therefore he felt that he should again think of selling Chartwell and add to his capital.

In 1938 he had expected £20,000 to £25,000 and he thought nowadays he might at least get the same figure. William was 'amazed that he should contemplate selling his beloved Chartwell' and seems to have faced the new situation with his usual lightning speed. There and then he asked Churchill whether he would sell the house for £50,000 'privately to friends', who would then let him stay in it for the rest of his life, after which it could be maintained as a memorial to him. Churchill replied 'Yes', adding with one of his characteristic chuckles, 'and throw in the corpse as well'. William continued a memorandum of the conversation.

> I told him he could consider the matter settled and that I would undertake to arrange the finance with myself and a limited number of other people. He was rather taken aback by my ready undertaking and thought it might be difficult to achieve. When I told him that the cheque would be forthcoming as soon as the formalities were concluded he seemed very affected. Later he became very enthusiastic and his mind started working as to how he could help to make the memorial an interesting and permanent one. Said he would leave a lot of papers and documents in the house and was sure Clemmie would co-operate most willingly.

William's confidence that he could raise the money quickly proved well founded. Characteristically, all of it was raised by telephone and there was no written correspondence at all. He chose sixteen names of his acquaintance, all of whom, he thought, could quite easily part with £5,000 (now about £75,000).

Only in two cases did 'a victim' fail to give an affirmative reply within three minutes of hearing of the scheme. In one of these, time was requested to 'talk to my wife' and the cheque arrived next morning. The second hesitator was Lord Nuffield, 'who was very worried and depressed about the doings of the Labour Government and declined to join the scheme'. But he spoke later to Lady Nuffield, 'who waxed very enthusiastic about Winston and in due course the cheque arrived'.

As to what body would maintain Chartwell, William must have been

---

[13] At the same lunch, William found himself served champagne. Shamefacedly, Churchill explained he had it for both lunch and dinner. 'It makes it so much easier for the butler.'

thinking of the National Trust. They, of course, knew nothing about it so that he could not mention the Trust by name. What he did have to calculate was what endowment they would need to keep up the house after Churchill's death. He somehow fixed upon £45,000. The National Trust seems to have been underwhelmed by the present of the British Mount Vernon. Negotiations took a year and a day before the deal could be announced. The endowment was reduced to £35,000 and Churchill's rent in his lifetime was fixed at £350. The rest of the fund was later released to the Trust for buying Churchilliana while, as Churchill lived till 1965, the value of the Endowment greatly increased before any of its income had to be spent.[14]

Another joint venture was in the racing field. Churchill, who had before shown no interest in the sport,[15] was enthused by his son-in-law, Christopher Soames, to buy several cheap and apparently indifferent horses. One of them, Colonist II,[16] though hardly in the stud book, proved an extraordinary success and won eight good races in a row. Of course he could not enjoy being an owner without betting on it and he inveigled William, who had no interest in horses,[17] to have bets put on by him. The result of the bets was usually recorded through secretaries but sometimes dictated and signed by Churchill himself on Downing Street or Chequers notepaper. Churchill, for his part, bet often in 'monkeys' (£500) but the largest he put on for William was £100 on Colonist at evens. All told, over four years, William was £169 net in credit after losses of £460.

The betting came to an end in 1953 when Churchill suffered a stroke while entertaining the Italian Prime Minister, de Gasperi, to dinner at Downing Street. At first his disability was only in walking but after two days he began to go downhill or, as his doctor, Lord Moran, put it: 'There was a spreading of the thrombosis.' After two days he was driven down to Chartwell, where he became steadily worse. Moran feared the thrombosis would spread to his throat, when he would surely choke to death.

---

[14] Contributors were William £15,000 and £5,000 each from Viscount Bearsted, Lord Bicester, Lord Catto, Sir Hugo Cunliffe-Owen, Bt., Sir James Caird, Bt., Lord Glendyne, Lord Kenilworth, Lord Leathers, Sir James Lithgow, Bt., Sir Edward Mountain, Bt., Viscount Nuffield, Sir Edward Peacock, Viscount Portal of Laverstoke, James de Rothschild, J. Arthur Rank, Sir Frederick Stewart. The total sum raised was £95,000 – £50,000 for Churchill, £35,000 for the Endowment, and the rest, after legal expenses, for memorabilia.

[15] Though his father, Lord Randolph, had been a member of the Jockey Club.

[16] It was said that Colonist, like its owner, was only at his best on right-hand courses. In one left-hand race, Gordon Richards, the champion jockey and a worshipper of Churchill, found his own horse falling back and gave Colonist a crack with his whip to direct him in the left-hand direction.

[17] My mother, on the other hand, as the daughter of a successful owner, always followed the form, though I doubt she ever bet herself.

His principal Private Secretary, John Colville, was in a quandary. Churchill was due to leave for a summit with President Eisenhower in Bermuda. This must obviously be cancelled but some statement must be made to justify the cancellation. He therefore hit on the idea of summoning 'three particular friends of Churchill': Beaverbrook, Bracken, and William, who happened also to be press chiefs. As Colville recalled: 'All three immediately came to Chartwell and paced the lawn in earnest conversation.' What they were discussing was the health bulletin which must quickly be issued.

William was the last to arrive and found that the other two were inclined to agree to a bulletin drafted by Moran and the specialist, Sir Russell Brain, reading:

> For a long time the Prime Minister has had no respite from his arduous duties and a disturbance of the cerebral circulation has developed, resulting in attacks of giddiness. We have therefore advised him to abandon his journey to Bermuda and to take at least a month's rest.

William was appalled. He pointed out that the phrase 'cerebral circulation' could mean only one thing to the public – a stroke. There would be an immediate call for Churchill to resign but whom could the Queen send for? That very same week, the natural heir, Anthony Eden, was having a serious gall bladder operation in Canada, and it would be unfair to him to have R.A. Butler succeed.

He therefore suggested a redraft which was immediately issued:

> The Prime Minister has had no respite for a long time from his arduous duties and is in need of a complete rest. We have therefore advised him to abandon his journey to Bermuda and to lighten his duties for a month.[18]

Colville seemed unaware of the importance of the revised wording and recorded that the three Press Lords 'achieved the all but incredible, and in peacetime possibly unique, success of gagging Fleet Street, something they would have done for nobody but Churchill. Not a word of the Prime Minister's stroke was published until he himself casually mentioned it in a speech in the House of Commons a year later.'[19]

This was nonsense. William might have gagged Gomer, Beaverbrook

---

[18] Moran, in his book published after Churchill's death, attributed the new draft to Butler. But Butler did not arrive at Chartwell until after the bulletin had been issued. My account came from William himself who, having appointed me Deputy Editor-in-Chief, thought I ought to know.

[19] Colville's memory was at fault. After Churchill's recovery, rumours of a stroke were published in American newspapers, repeated with blazing publicity by the *Daily Mirror*.

and Rothermere, but nobody could have gagged Cecil King[20] of the *Daily Mirror* and the *Sunday Pictorial*, nor the American Press. After all, the bulletin might infer, all prime ministers 'feel the heat' at the end of a summer session and Churchill was seventy-eight – still younger than Gladstone when he formed his last administration but, still, getting on.

By the autumn Churchill seemed to have made a splendid recovery, though his concentration was not quite as intense and, occasionally, so some said, he did not recognise ministers not specially familiar to him. He himself often spoke vaguely of retirement. Those who had supported him so loyally during his illness now began to become impatient.

William told me that Churchill had sought his opinion and asked me, rhetorically of course, whether I agreed with his negative answer. A little while later Cranborne (or Salisbury as he now was) called on William at the *Telegraph* to ask him to use his influence on Churchill to get him to go. William replied evenly that it was for Cranborne, a peer and so disinterested personally in the succession, to do the persuasion.

Similarly, William refused to intervene when a Palace official came to ask him to get Churchill to rescind Air Ministry permission for the Duke of Edinburgh to use Buckingham Palace lawn for a helicopter.

*   *   *

After the war, William did not quickly resume his old style of living. Hackwood, though, was no problem. Perhaps through his habit of asking the senior hospital officers to dinner at Audley's Wood, there had been little damage and the move back was achieved in the new year of 1946. St James's Place was, of course, a write-off and the claim for war damage compensation lingered on until long after his death.[21] He stayed on at the Dorchester until 1950, when he bought from Edward Iliffe the remaining nine years of a Crown lease on 24 Carlton Gardens (behind the Nash terraces of The Mall). It had proved too big for Iliffe and was really too big for William, his family having nearly all moved out. It had a fine garden but, as it was shared with the United Services Club, he could not use it for his outdoor workplace, as he had used the small garden of St James's Place.

His 500-ton yacht, *Sona*, had, as I have recorded, been sunk and paid

---

[20] King hardly knew William, thought Beaverbrook 'evil' and despised Bracken. In any case, King would not have been interested in 'gagging' for Churchill. It was the *Mirror* which had campaigned against him in the 1951 General Election with the punch line: 'Whose Finger on the Trigger'.

[21] Curiously, the penthouse floors of a new building erected on the site are now occupied by another newspaper proprietor, Rupert Murdoch, son of William's old friend Keith Murdoch.

for – £30,000 – under requisition. He now bought another one, the 750-ton *Virginia*, built in 1930, having served in the Red Sea in the war, upon which about £100,000 had to be spent for re-equipment. There is an apocryphal story that a lady had commiserated with him after the war: 'What a pity, Lord Camrose, you won't be able to have a big yacht again.' 'Nonsense,' he was said to have replied, nettled. 'I shall have a bigger one.'

He now took longer holidays. He was always in the Isle of Wight for Cowes week, where *Virginia* was the largest yacht apart from the royal *Britannia*.[22] He would then take the yacht to western Scotland, where he would motor to Gleneagles Hotel, Perthshire. He always took the same first-floor suite overlooking the putting green and paid for what members of the family could join. He had been there for its opening in 1924 and loved the walks and the scenery there. He no longer played serious golf except to taunt the experts. One of his favourite ploys was to partner a fellow 'duffer' against two short-handicap players in a foursome (i.e., each side plays alternate shots with the same ball). His terms and wager, worked out at an hilarious pre-match lunch, were always the same – thirty-six bisques and the right to tee up their ball wherever he or his partner found it. The match usually ended early in their favour when the experts fell out with each other. Thereafter he would take another week or so on the yacht in northern waters.

I have checked through his cuttings' books and find that, after the 1946 trip to the United States and Canada selling the Churchill *War Memoirs*, only in 1948 did he fail to take a winter holiday from one to two months. Usually it was to some part of the Mediterranean that he took his new yacht. On one occasion it was to the Caribbean, eleven days at sea from the Canary Islands, when finishing up in New York, he reckoned he had done 12,000 miles. Wherever he went he always looked up the local newspaper owner. Wherever his yacht docked he was met by a 'traveller' with a bundle of newspapers, which annoyed him as diverting the traveller from his normal duties. The Fleet Street office knew, however, that he would be much more annoyed if the *Telegraph* had not been available.

One frequent guest on these trips was Ted Hunter, now himself taking it easier. Hunter, with his constant assumed gloom (making him an easy butt) but droll humour, was always game for the three- or four-hours'

---

[22] As Vice-Commodore, he spent the mornings ashore at the Royal Yacht Squadron's 'Castle'. At about 12.30 pm the steward on the *Virginia* was accustomed to receive the signal, 'Five more for lunch'.

drive in a closed car to find a good restaurant, which William and my mother found normal.

In the early days, currency restrictions proved irksome. William solved it by sending out his car and chauffeur from England to the northern Mediterranean and stocking up the yacht in Gibraltar, in the sterling area. For ready money, he provided each member of the twenty-eight-strong crew with travellers' cheques and managed to live pretty comfortably. In the South of France they often ran across another big yacht owner, Sir Bernard Docker, the industrialist who had always been intelligent company when not in the presence of his exhibitionist wife. On one occasion, the two yachts were tied up alongside in Cannes harbour, so that Hunter was able to taunt them both, with one foot on each yacht: 'Extraordinary how you fellows manage to jog along on £50 a year.'

Hunter was also with him on the Caribbean trip when they lunched with Beaverbrook, who had a house in Jamaica: 'Two very pretty nurses,[23] a furious discussion in which his Canadian lordship, thoroughly needled, tried to prove that a rich man *could* somehow sidle, or squeeze, into the Kingdom of Heaven'.

*   *   *

As I have often remarked, William was the least sentimental of beings. Once something was done with that was the end of it. On revisiting places where important things had happened to him he never fell into reminiscence. There was one exception – he had an extraordinary feeling for old buildings and their history and the people who had inhabited them. My earliest example of this is an excerpt from Malcolm Muggeridge's diary. William, Muggeridge recorded, appeared unexpectedly at an editorial conference in December 1945:

> He had been walking about the City – strange, on a Sunday afternoon, this millionaire newspaper proprietor wandering about the ruined City. He was really a touching figure, asking about the American loan and whether the terms might have been easier, and then going off again.

Similarly, Alex Faulkner, long-time chief correspondent in New York, told Birkenhead: 'Driving round New York with him I was always struck by his intimate knowledge of who owned what building (and covered with shame when he asked me a question in that field that I could not answer).'

[23] Margaret, Lady Birkenhead, another yacht guest, called one of them 'the brown job'.

A final example came from his oldest friend's daughter, Eileen Hunter, who recounts how her father, packing before going on holiday was 'summoned' to dine with William at the beginning of June 1954. William seemed perfectly fit then and I am sure had no premonition but, with hindsight, the recounting has an element of the macabre:

Bags packed, and his housekeeper cooking dinner, [he] was writing last minute notes at his desk upstairs when William Camrose rang: 'Ted – you must come to dinner tonight. Change and come along.' This was most unusual, for though he often dined with the Camroses *en famille*, even these informal occasions were, without exception, arranged well beforehand. 'But, William, I can't, I'm off tomorrow, you know, and besides my housekeeper's just going to dish up dinner.' 'Ted – it can't be helped – just change and come along!' Such was the insistence in his voice that my father felt he had no option, much as he still had to do, much as he deplored 'upsetting' Ethel by such a late cancellation of the meal.

Ethel, summoned, quickly laid out his dinner jacket, rang Taylor the chauffeur, and thirty minutes later my father was on his way. 'Ethel', he called, as he stepped into his car. 'Sir?' – 'When Taylor comes to fetch me – 10.30 sharp – you come too, a breath of fresh air – just for the ride.' He often made this suggestion and this evening it might specially have occurred to him to make up for the wasted dinner.

At the Camroses he spent an evening like many others – with Molly Camrose, William and one or two members of their large family. No special reason emerged for the last-minute invitation. William looked very well, and teased and chaffed him as usual. At the time appointed my father's car arrived. The two old friends stood on the doorstep saying good-bye and William had just wished my father a happy holiday when, as the car was leaving, he called out – 'Stop, Ted, I'm coming with you, let's drive round the city and look up some of our old haunts.'

He got into the car, and chatting together of the past, they made for Fleet Street where, according to Ethel, they directed Taylor to drive more slowly while they drew each other's attention to this building or that, all deserted at this time of night, but for them peopled with memories . . .

'We dropped his Lordship back at his house, he looked very handsome with his usual white carnation', she told me.

A week later, while my father was still abroad, William Camrose entered hospital – nothing grave – he was making a good

recovery – there was no cause for alarm. A few days later he was
dead.

The afternoon before his death, my mother and Seymour, on return
from the hospital, had been sitting on the terrace at Hackwood. It was
a perfectly still day when a huge branch of an ancient cedar ('my
favourite tree', William used to say) fell with a crash. My mother was
much distressed by the 'omen'.

Appropriately, the leading Danish newspaper, the *Berlingske Tidende*,
began its obituary with the words: 'One of the great trees of the World
Press has fallen'.

*   *   *

A few days after that evening with Ted Hunter, William had had an
upset stomach and could not eat anything. He was quite cheerful and
did not seem otherwise to be unwell. But he had always been a bit of
an amateur doctor. Without telling my mother he cut out his insulin
altogether, he later confessed, on the assumption that the insulin would
have no sugar content to balance. It seems that exactly the opposite is
true – when a diabetic is not eating he needs a greater supply of insulin.
The lack of it made him feel groggy. He motored down to Hackwood
and, when in bed, fell into a coma, which was the first time a doctor
was summoned. Ambulance men rolled him roughly on to a stretcher
('a good thing for them he was not conscious', said my mother grimly)
and he was taken to the Royal Southampton Hospital an hour away.

There he seemed quickly to recover, though he was placed on a drip.
He still read the papers and could chat easily. One morning, however,
he was called by the nurse at 7 am, on 15 June, eight days short of his
seventy-fifth birthday, made a joke to her and fell back dead.

The certified cause of death was:

Acute myocardial failure, due to Atheroma of the Coronary Arteries.
Contributory cause of death: Diabetes mellitus.

Just as the absence of insulin had weakened his system so, I think,
had exceptional physical exertion weakened his heart. When he returned
to Hackwood he found that laurels had multiplied horribly in wartime.
His favourite recreation then was to hack at them with a machete. I
joined him once and, though still in my thirties, found it exhausting.
After an hour I was soaked with sweat.

I did not know of it until I began to write this book, but he had kept
a file of his doctors' recommendations. He did indeed have a 'damaged

heart muscle' and he was recommended in 1951 to increase his insulin intake to combat 'your vast activities with hedges and ditches'. The file ends in November 1951.

*   *   *

Harold Nicolson recorded in his diary for 15 June:

> I see the flags at half-mast in Fleet Street and on the posters the news that Camrose has died. He was a staunch friend and wise counsellor. He showed that one could be a Press Lord and a gentleman. He was an example to the newspaper world, and I am wretched at his death.

Churchill who, though five years older, outlived him by nine, wrote a letter to my mother in his own hand the following day:

> My dear Lady Camrose,
> I know how you and Bill were devoted to one another, and depended upon each other in all the joys and griefs of human existence. His life and career do him honour achieved by few. His work remains as a living monument which will long endure for the good of our hard-pressed country ... Please accept my fervent sympathy. I know your courage.
> Yours affectionately,
> Winston S. Churchill.

My mother replied:

> You could have had no more devoted admirer than Bill. He would, I know, have laid down his life gladly for you.

And in May 1956 he paid a similar tribute when unveiling a memorial to William in St Paul's Cathedral:

> In dark and uncertain times no man could be more steady and persevering. During the war his unfaltering confidence helped to sustain all who knew him. [To his friends] and to the causes in which he believed he was steadfastly loyal.

Acknowledgments and Bibliography

My particular thanks are to Lord Iliffe, who has allowed me to see and quote at length from his father's (the first Lord Iliffe's) unpublished autobiography and diaries 1931–3. For a long period in their joint lives my father and Edward Iliffe were fast friends and business partners. These documents have been a great help to me in describing my father's 'middle period'.

Of books and papers not normally available for public inspection, I am grateful to Harper Collins for permission to quote from sections of Sir Harold Nicolson's diary (not included in the published diaries, edited by Nigel Nicolson) in Balliol College Library.

Other unpublished documents I have been allowed to use are: the diaries of Robin Barrington-Ward (Editor of *The Times* 1941–8) in the possession of his son, Mark Barrington-Ward. Mr Barrington-Ward took great trouble sorting his father's papers and indicating those passages relevant to my narrative; the autobiography of Sydney Carroll, in the possession of his daughter, Mrs Nina Steane; the booklet 'The Berry Brothers' prepared from family albums by my cousin, Robert Smyly, grandson of Lord Buckland, my father's elder brother, and for the sight of further papers; and *The War of the Newspaper Giants* by the late William Redpath, Editor-in-Chief of my father's Newcastle papers during the great battle of the early thirties.

Also most valuable to me has been permission to quote the vivid pen-pictures of my father and his friends, from Eileen Hunter's *Profound Attachment*. Her father, Edward Hunter, was almost the first of my father's friends when he came to London at the turn of the century, a friendship broken only by death.

Other specific permissions to quote sizeable extracts from published sources were from Sir Robert Rhodes James, *Churchill – A Study in Failure,* and *The Davidson Papers;* Andrew Roberts, *The Holy Fox: A Biography of Lord Halifax;* David Kynaston, *Centenary History of The Financial Times;* Mrs John Harvey for her father-in-law's, Lord Harvey's, *Diplomatic Diaries 1937–1940;* Ian McLaine, *The Ministry of Morale.*

My thanks are due, too, to the librarians and staff of: House of Lords

Record Office; House of Lords Library; Public Record Office, Kew; Colindale Newspaper Library; *The Daily Telegraph;* London Library; Dr C.A. Fox, Keeper, Printing, Prints and Drawings, Museum of London; Mr D. Doughan, Fawcett library; Mr J.M. Hamill, Library and Museum of The United Grand Lodge of England (Freemasons); Mr K. Beard, *Daily Express;* Miss T. Morris, Secretary, All England Women's Hockey Association; Miss Ianthe H. Hoskins, Theosophical Society; Mr Alan Tadiello, Assistant Librarian, Balliol College; Administrator, University of Cambridge Library (Templewood Papers); Mr Michael Bott, Reading university Library (Lord Astor Papers); Dr B.S. Benedikz, Birmingham University (Neville Chamberlain Papers).

I am grateful to the following for providing information: Jim Joel; John Price (PA to chief executive and town clerk, Merthyr Tydfil); Ray Gibson; William Wightman; Mrs Sydney Carroll; United Grand (Masonic) Lodge of England; H.E. Scrope, Archivist of Vickers Limited; R. Kitchen, lately manager, National Westminster Bank, Temple Bar; the late Sir Denis Hamilton; Desmond Flower, MC, Murrough O'Brien; Kenneth Rose; W.J. Carpenter; D.G.H. Linton; Ray Boston; Richard Benfield, Richards Butler, researcher; Dr Edgar Jones, GKN Group Historian; John Holmes, Director, Audit Bureau of Circulations; Eileen Hunter; Kenneth R. Jones.

Particular thanks are due to David Cole, lately Managing Director of Thomson Regional Newspapers, for showing me round old Merthyr where my father was born and started in journalism, and Camrose, the Pembrokeshire hamlet from which he took his title and whence the family originated. Mr Cole had a fund of reminiscence concerning his own father and mine, who were 'cub reporters' together in their earliest days.

As explained in the Preface, research for this book was undertaken by the late Robin Birkenhead 1976–7 before he abandoned the writing of the book himself. Among those who gave interviews to him were: eleventh Earl of Drogheda, Hon. Richard Lyttelton, Douglas Woodruff, H.V. Hodson, Michael Verey, Claude Wallis, William Redpath, Sir Colin Coote, H.J.C. Stevens, Malcolm Muggeridge, Alex Faulkner, Brian Roberts, S.R. Pawley, Marjorie Eden, Miss E. McIlherene, Douglas Rees.

I am much in the debt of members of my family, in particular my sister, Mary McNair Scott; her husband Major Ronald McNair Scott; my elder brother, the present Lord Camrose; my sons, Adrian and Nicholas Berry; and my daughter Harriet Cullen, for reading the various drafts, correcting mistakes and making major constructive suggestions. I am also in debt to Harriet Cullen for re-photographing framed photographs and to my daughter-in-law, Marina Berry, for suggesting the use on the front of the dust jacket the painting of Fleet Street in the 1890s by Atkinson Grimshaw.

Finally I have to thank my long-time secretary, Eileen Fuller, who, during the five years this book has been in preparation, has taught herself to be a 'grandmaster' of the word-processor and unerringly to decipher my sick spider handwriting.

* * *

Apart from those for which special permissions have been obtained, I have consulted the following books:

Addis, John, *The Crawshay Dynasty: A Study in Industrial Organisation and Development 1765–1867* (University of Wales Press, Cardiff, 1957)

Andrews, Linton and Taylor, H.A., *Lords and Labourers of the Press* (Southern Illinois University Press, 1970)

Arnold, Matthew, *Friendship's Garland: Being the Conversations, Letters and Opinions of the Late Arminius, Baron von Thunder-Ten-Tronckh* (Smith, Elder and Co., London, 1871)

Ayerst, David, *Garvin of the Observer* (Croom Helm, London, 1985)

Barnes, John and Nicolson, David, *The Empire at Bay: The Leo Amery Diaries* (Hutchinson, London, 1988)

Beecham, Thomas, *A Mingled Chime: Leaves from an Autobiography* (Hutchinson, London, 1979)

Bentley, E.C., *Those Days* (Constable, London, 1940)

Bettinson, Arthur and Bennison, Ben, *The Home of Boxing* (Odhams Press, London, 1922)

Birkenhead, Earl of, *Halifax: The Life of Lord Halifax* (Hamish Hamilton, London, 1965)

Blumenfeld, Ralph, *The Press in My Time* (Rich and Cowan, London, 1933)

Boyle, Andrew, *Trenchard* (Collins, London, 1962)

Brendon, Piers, *The Life and Death of the Press Barons* (Secker & Warburg, London, 1982)

Bright-Holmes, John (ed.), *Like It Was: the Diaries of Malcolm Muggeridge* (Collins, London, 1981)

Bullock, Alan, *The Life and Times of Ernest Bevin* (Vol. I, 1960; Vol. II, 1967; Vol. III, 1983; Heinemann, London)

Burnham, Lord, *Peterborough Court: the Story of the Daily Telegraph* (Cassell, London, 1955)

Campbell, Doon (ed.), *The British Press: a Look Ahead* (Commonwealth Press Union, 1978)

Camrose, Viscount, *British Newspapers and Their Controllers* (Cassell, London, 1947)

Christiansen, Arthur, *Headlines All My life* (Heinemann, London, 1961)

Cockett, Richard (ed.), *Twilight of Truth: Chamberlain, Appeasement and the Manipulation of the Press* (Weidenfeld & Nicolson, London, 1989)

————, *My Dear Max: The Letters of Brendan Bracken to Lord Beaverbrook 1925–1958* (Historians' Press, London, 1990)

Colville, John, *The Fringes of Power: Downing Street Diaries 1939–1955* (Hodder & Stoughton, London, 1985)

Colvin, Ian, *Vansittart in Office* (Gollancz, London, 1965)

Coote, Colin R., *Editorial: The Memoirs of Colin R. Coote* (Eyre & Spottiswoode, London, 1965)

Cross, J.A., *Sir Samuel Hoare: A Political Biography* (Jonathan Cape, London, 1977)

Dalton, Edward, *The Fateful Years: Memoirs 1931–1945* (Frederick Muller, London, 1957)

Dilks, David, *The Diaries of Sir Alexander Cadogan 1938–1945* (Cassell, London, 1971)

Donaldson, Frances, *Edward VIII* (Weidenfeld & Nicolson, London, 1972)

Driberg, Tom, *Beaverbrook: A Study in Power and Frustration* (Weidenfeld & Nicolson, London, 1956)

Falk, Bernard, *He Laughed in Fleet Street* (Hutchinson, London, 1933)

———, *Five Years Dead* (Hutchinson, London, 1937)

Farrer, David, *G – For God Almighty: A Personal Memoir of Lord Beaverbrook* (Weidenfeld & Nicolson, London, 1969)

Feiling, Keith, *The Life of Neville Chamberlain* (Macmillan, London, 1946)

Field, Eric, *Advertising: The Forgotten Years* (Ernest Benn, London, 1959)

Flower, Ernest Newman, *Just As It Happened* (Cassell, London, 1950)

Fyfe, Henry Hamilton, *Press Parade: Behind the Scenes of the Newspaper Racket and the Millionaires' Attempt at Dictatorship* (Watts & Co., London, 1936)

Gilbert, Martin, *Winston S. Churchill, Volume V. 1922–39. Companion 1929–35: The Wilderness Years* (Heinemann, London, 1981)

———, *Finest Hour: Volume VI. Winston S. Churchill 1939–41* (Heinemann, London, 1983)

———, *Never Despair: Volume VIII. Winston S. Churchill 1945–65* (Heinemann, London, 1988)

Gross, Joseph, *A Brief History of Merthyr Tydfil* (Starling Press, Newport, 1980)

Hamilton, Denis, *Editor-in-Chief: The Fleet Street Memoirs of Sir Denis Hamilton* (Hamish Hamilton, London, 1989)

Hammerton, John, *With Northcliffe in Fleet Street* (Hutchinson, London, 1932)

———, *Books and Myself: Memoirs of an Editor* (Macdonald, London, 1944)

Hart-Davis, Duff, *The House the Berrys Built: Inside the Telegraph 1928–1986* (Hodder & Stoughton, London, 1990)

Harvey, John, *The War Diaries of Oliver Harvey 1941–5* (Collins, London, 1978)

Hobson, Harold, Knightley, Phillip and Russell, Leonard, *The Pearl of Days* (Hamish Hamilton, London, 1960)

Howard, Philip, *We Thundered Out: 200 Years of The Times* (Times Books, London, 1985)

Jenkins, Simon, *The Market for Glory* (Faber, London, 1986)

Jones, Dr Edgar K., *A History of GKN,* volume 1 (Macmillan Press, London, 1987)

Jones, Roderick, *A Life in Reuters* (Hodder & Stoughton, London, 1951)

Jones, Thomas, *A Diary with Letters 1931–1950* (Oxford University Press, 1954)

Kersaudy, François, *Norway 1940* (Collins, London, 1990)

King, Cecil, *Strictly Personal* (Weidenfeld & Nicolson, London, 1969)

Koss, Stephen, *The Rise and Fall of the Political Press in Britain* (Hamish Hamilton, London, 1984)

Lane, Margaret, *Edgar Wallace* (Heinemann, London, 1938)

MacLeod, Iain, *Neville Chamberlain* (Frederick Muller, London, 1961)

Mansfield, Frederick, *The Complete Journalist* (Sir I. Pitman and Sons, London, 1936)

Middlemass, Robert and Barnes, Anthony, *Baldwin: A Biography* (Weidenfeld & Nicolson, London, 1969)

Minchinton, Walter (ed.), *Industrial South Wales 1750–1914: Essays in Welsh Economic History* (Frank Cass, London, 1969)

Minney, R. J. (ed.), *The Private Papers of Hore-Belisha* (Collins, London, 1960)

Moran, Lord, *Winston Churchill: The Struggle for Survival* (Constable, London, 1961)

Morgan, Dewi, *The Phoenix of Fleet Street: 2000 Years of St Brides'* (C. Knight, London, 1973)

Namier, Lewis Bernstein, 'Anthony Bacon, MP, An Eighteenth-Century Merchant', in *Journal of Economic and Business History,* Vol. II, No. 1, pp. 20–70, 1929

Nicolson, Nigel, *Lord of the Isles: Lord Leverhulme in the Hebrides* (Weidenfeld & Nicolson, London, 1960)

—— (ed.), *Harold Nicolson: Diaries and Letters 1930–1939* (Collins, London, 1967)

Northcliffe, Viscount, *Newspapers and Their Millionaires* (Associated Newspapers, London, 1922)

Nowell-Smith, Simon, *The House of Cassell 1848–1958* (Cassell, London, 1958)

Pakenham, Valerie, *In the Noonday Sun: Edwardians in the Tropics* (Methuen, London, 1985)

Pemberton, Max, *Lord Northcliffe: A Memoir* (Hodder & Stoughton, London, 1922)

Pound, Reginald and Harmsworth, Geoffrey, *Northcliffe* (Cassell, London, 1959)

Reader, W.J., *Bowater: A History* (Cambridge University Press, Cambridge, 1981)

Rhodes James, Robert, *Chips: The Diaries of Sir Henry Channon* (Weidenfeld & Nicolson, London, 1967)

Rhondda, Viscountess, *This Was My World* (London, 1933)

Richards, Gordon, *My Story* (Hodder & Stoughton, London, 1955)

Robbins, Alan, *Newspapers Today* (Oxford University Press, Oxford, 1956)

Roberts, Andrew, *The Holy Fox: A Biography of Lord Halifax* (Weidenfeld & Nicolson, London, 1991)

Simonis, H., *The Street of Ink: An Intimate History of Journalism* (Cassel, London, 1917)

Smith, Anthony, *The British Press Since the War* (David and Charles, Newton Abbot, 1974)

Smith, Wareham, *Spilt Ink* (Ernest Benn, London, 1932)

Symon, James D., *The Press and Its Story* (Seeley Service, London, 1914)

Taylor, A.J.P., *Beaverbrook* (Hamish Hamilton, London, 1972)

Templewood, Lord, *Nine Troubled Years* (Collins, 1954)

Thomson, George M., *Vote of Censure* (Secker & Warburg, London, 1968)

Tuohy, Ferdinand, *Twelve Lances for Liberty* (Nicholson & Watson, London, 1930)

Tunstall, Jeremy, *The Media in Britain* (Constable, London, 1983)

Vansittart, Lord, *The Mist Procession* (Hutchinson,London, 1958)

Vaughan, Herbert M., *The South Wales Squires* (Golden Grove Book Co., Dyfed, 1988)

Vines, C.M., *A Little Nut-Brown Man: My Three Years with Lord Beaverbrook* (Leslie Frewin, London, 1968)

Wheeler-Bennett, J.R., *Munich: A Prologue to Tragedy* (Macmillan, London, 1966)

Williams, Francis, *Dangerous Estate: the Anatomy of Newspapers* (Longman, London, 1957)

Winterton, Lord, *Orders of the Day* (Cassell, London, 1953)

Wintour, Charles, *The Pressures of the Press* (André Deutsch, London, 1972)

——, *The Rise and Fall of Fleet Street* (Hutchinson, London, 1989)

Woods, Oliver and James Bishop, *The Story of The Times* (Michael Joseph, London, 1983)

Wrench, Evelyn, *Geoffrey Dawson and Our Times* (Hutchinson, London, 1955)

Wyatt, Woodrow, *Distinguished For Talent: Some Men of Influence and Enterprise* (Hutchinson, London, 1958)

Young, George, *Stanley Baldwin* (Rupert Hart-Davis, London, 1952)

Among other titles consulted: *Dictionary of Business Biography* by T.A.B. Corley; *One Hundred Years of Fleet Street* by A. Ewart and V. Leonard; *Advertising in Victorian England* by Diana and George Hindley; *Birth of a Nation 1880–1981* by Leland, *Industrial Revolution in South Wales* by Edward Ness; *Notes on My Way* by Lady Rhondda; *Ace of Diamonds* by Joel Stanhope; *A History of Merthyr Tydfil* by W.E. Wilkins; *The British Press 1898–1948* (Newspaper World).

Index